THE RIVERSIDE PUBLISHING COMPANY
PO BOX 1970
IOWA CITY, IOWA 52244

D0206121

Applied Psychometrics

Robert L. Thorndike

TEACHERS COLLEGE, COLUMBIA UNIVERSITY

Houghton Mifflin Company   Boston

DALLAS   GENEVA, ILLINOIS   HOPEWELL, NEW JERSEY   PALO ALTO   LONDON

Cover lettering and design by Martina Mikulka

Printed in the U.S.A.

Library of Congress Catalog Card Number: 81-81699

ISBN: 0-395-30077-0

Contents

Preface *ix*

Chapter 1
Introduction *1*

The Domain Mastery Approach to Testing *1*
The Latent Trait Approach to Testing *4*
  Attributes *4*
  Test Scores *5*
  Test Items *6*
The Preparation of Test Items *9*
Plan of the Book *10*

Chapter 2
Planning the Development of a Test *11*

Definition of the Latent Attribute or Test Domain *12*
Purposes to Be Served by the Test *13*
Constraints on the Test *15*
Content Specifications or Blueprint *16*
Format Specifications *21*
Plan for Item Tryout and Selection *23*
Plans for Analyzing and Using the Tryout Data *25*
Plans for Gathering Normative Data *26*
Test Manual and Supporting Materials *28*
Schedule *29*

Chapter 3
The Development of Test Exercises *32*

Test Directions *32*
Constructing Exercises for Ability Tests *36*
  Item Formats for Ability Tests *38*
  Generating Misleads *42*

Constructing Exercises for Achievement Tests   *44*
Issues in Performance Measurement   *47*
Issues in the Development of Interest, Attitude and Temperament
   Measures   *49*

Chapter 4
Item Selection   *53*

Procedures for Getting Information about Test Items   *53*
   Tryout Procedures   *54*
   Conventional Item Statistics   *58*
Estimating Test Parameters from Item Statistics   *76*
Using Item Statistics in Selecting the Items for a Test   *79*
Controlling Test Parameters when No Tryout Is Possible   *87*
Analysis of a Heterogeneous Item Pool   *90*
The Role of Item Analysis in Domain Mastery or
   Criterion-Referenced Tests   *93*
Scaling Items and Scores Using the Rasch Model   *96*

Chapter 5
Scales, Norms, and Equating   *105*

Procedures for Score Conversion   *107*
   Age and Grade Units   *108*
   Linear Score Conversions   *113*
   Area Conversions   *115*
   Scaling Scores with the Rasch Model   *121*
Establishing Test Norms   *123*
   Multistage Sampling   *125*
   Constraints and Compromises   *128*
   Preparing Norms Tables   *130*
Equating   *133*
   Model I   *135*
   Model II   *137*
   Model III   *140*

Chapter 6
Reliability   *143*

Some Useful Relationships Stemming from the Classical Reliability
   Model   *144*
   Basic Assumptions and Resulting Relationships   *144*

Effects of Increasing or Decreasing Test Length   148
Problems in Defining True Score and Error   154
Reliability Estimates and Variance Components   156
The General Multifacet Model   161
Nonrandom Questions and Readers   166
Confounding   167
Reliability with Conventional Data-Collection Strategies   171
Reliability Estimated from Equivalent Forms   173
Reliability Estimated from Retesting   175
Reliability Estimated from Internal Consistency   175
Internal-Consistency Estimates for Speeded Tests   178
Reliability in the Context of Domain Mastery or
Criterion-Referenced Tests   181

Chapter 7
Validity   *184*

Content Validity   184
Construct Validity   186
Comparison of Test Tasks with Conception of Attribute   186
Correlational Evidence of Construct Validity   187
Group Differences as Evidence of Construct Validity   190
Treatment Effects as Evidence of Construct Validity   191
The Role of Counterhypothesis   192
Predictive Validity   193
Shortcomings of Criterion Indicators   194
Types of Criterion Indicators   198
Practical Problems in Empirical Validation   201
Statistics of Validity   203
Dichotomous Criterion Variables   204
Correlations Estimated from Tails of a Distribution   206
Curtailment   208
Nonlinear Relationships   215
Partial Criterion Measures   218
Group Membership as a Criterion Variable   220
Reliability and the Interpretation of Validity Coefficients   222
Validity and Practical Utility   223

Chapter 8
The Issue of Bias in Testing   *228*

Bias at the Item Level   230
Discrimination Indices   231
Difficulty Indices   232

Bias in a Complete Test   *235*
   Group Differences in Mean Score   *236*
   Group Differences in Reliability   *237*
   Group Differences in Relationship to a "Criterion" Variable   *238*

Chapter 9
Using Multiple Measures *246*

Multiple Measures in Prediction   *246*
Shrinkage, Cross-Validation, and Population Weights   *253*
   Nonlinear Expressions   *256*
   Loss from Approximate Weights   *257*
   Selection of Items to Maximize Validity   *258*
   Effects of Curtailment on Multiple Measures   *259*
Alternatives to Multiple Regression   *263*
   Multiple Cutoffs   *263*
   Unique Patterns   *266*
   Clinical versus Actuarial Combination of Data   *268*
   Moderator Variables   *269*
Multiple Measures in Differentiation   *270*
Multiple Measures in Description   *277*
Issues to Be Dealt with in Factor Analyses   *286*

Chapter 10
Bayesian Approaches and Testing *288*

Bayes' Theorem   *289*
Some Measurement Applications   *294*
   Estimating "True Score"   *294*
   Combining Information from Earlier Testing with
   Present Test Results   *295*
   Using Collateral Information from Other Measures   *297*
   Using Information from Other Individuals or Groups   *298*
Tailor-Made Testing   *299*
The Bayesian Model   *302*
Alternative Testing Procedures   *307*
   Multilevel Test Format   *307*
   Two-Stage Test Administration   *311*
   Self-Selected Testing   *315*
   Alternation Testing   *316*
   The Pyramidal Test   *317*

The Stradaptive Test   *326*
Summary Statement   *333*

Chapter 11
Selection, Placement, Classification, and
Guidance   *334*

The Utility Matrix   *336*
Selection   *338*
Multiple Selection   *340*
Placement   *345*
Classification   *348*
Guidance   *362*
Concluding Statement   *366*

Bibliography   *369*

Appendix A   Table of Flanagan r's   *373*

Appendix B   Table for Estimating Tetrachoric Correlation   *379*

Appendix C   Iterative Procedure for Estimating Regression Weights   *381*

Index   *387*

Preface

For the past 30 years I have taught, at Teachers College, Columbia University, a course titled "Test Construction and Theory of Measurement." The objective of the course has not been to create theoreticians, but rather to develop soundly grounded practitioners of the test-making art. The course grew and changed as the years went by, and this book corresponds to the course in its final form. Draft versions of the manuscript have been used in the course for the past three years and modified on the basis of that use.

I have tried to combine the tried-and-true notions of classic measurement theory with materials from the recent developments of latent trait theory, generalizability theory, and criterion-referenced testing. Concepts of adaptive testing, sample-free scaling, and assessment of mastery are introduced, as well as conventional discussions of true-score and error. The practical difficulties encountered in empirical studies of validity are considered in some detail. In total, I have tried to produce a current, soundly based, and useful introduction to the profession of test making and test analysis.

As in the course, my goal in this volume is to develop better practical test makers. With this end in view, for economy of space and ease of reading by the nonspecialist, most formulas are presented without their mathematical derivation or proof. Persons interested in such material may refer to standard statistics texts or to more technical treatments of measurement theory, as in Gulliksen (1950), Lord and Novick (1968), or Lord (1980).

The book does assume a familiarity with basic statistical concepts such as might be achieved through a sound one-year sequence in statistics. Materials presented here will require that familiarity as a foundation on which to build if the book is to be read with profit.

The author and the publisher are grateful for the assistance of those who made professional reviews of the manuscript. These reviewers, to whom we give thanks were Kurt Geisinger (Fordham University), Arvo Juolo (Michigan State University), David Kleinke (Syracuse University), and James Wardrop (University of Illinois).

R. L. T.

Chapter 1

Introduction

Although it is still relatively young in comparison to other areas of disciplined inquiry, the field of psychometrics has a history of growth and development extending over some 75 years since the early work of Binet in France and Spearman in England. The work of these two men serves to illustrate two distinct facets of test-making. Binet's work focused primarily on the practical aspect of invention and assembly of a useful set of test exercises. Spearman undertook to provide a conceptual model into which one might fit such a set of test exercises and the statistical theory to analyze and evaluate the resulting test data. These two aspects of test-making continue to this day. On the one hand, test makers must be concerned with item formats and the practical skills of writing effective test exercises. On the other, they must direct their attention toward providing more realistic means of indicating what the actual test represents and more powerful and appropriate statistical procedures for analyzing test data. *Applied Psychometrics* is devoted largely to this second aspect, though with a definitely practical orientation. Consideration of the art of preparing test exercises is dealt with primarily in one chapter (Chapter 3).

As we turn our attention to conceptual models of human attributes, we find two conceptions of these attributes prevalent in current psychometric literature. These models may be identified by the labels *domain mastery* and *latent trait theory*. Let us see what each of these considers to be the role of a test and what implications this has for the selection and assembly of test exercises. These matters will be further elaborated in the following chapters.

THE DOMAIN MASTERY APPROACH TO TESTING

The approach that focuses on degree of mastery of some defined domain of knowledge or skill corresponds to what has, in recent years, come to be called *criterion-referenced* testing. Basic to this approach is the existence of some clearly definable and delimitable domain of knowledge or skill. "Correct use of capital letters in writing" might be such a domain, and tests of capitalization have been a part of achievement test batteries for at least 50 years. However, a domain defined as it is above might be considered too broad and inclusive to be useful in guiding instructional decisions in the classroom or the evaluation of an instructional program at a given level. So the domain might be subdivided, and one part might become "correct use of capital letters at the beginning of a sentence." A test assessing mastery of this more limited domain of grammatical knowledge (or skill) might be expected to show more clearly the effects of specific teaching and, if it showed lack of mastery, to be more specifically diagnostic of what should be taught.

The fruitfulness of the orientation in terms of domain mastery depends on the possibility of defining a domain clearly and incisively, so that the range of performances that lie within the domain can be fully specified and agreed on. It should then be possible to sample tasks from that domain in such a way that the complete domain is adequately represented and inferences about completeness of mastery of the domain are a reasonable possibility. The approach really applies only to aspects of school achievement. This is about the only setting in which the boundaries of a domain can be set forth with any definiteness. Imagine trying to set out the boundaries that would delimit "reasoning ability," including all performances that are instances of such an ability and excluding all that are not! And even many aspects of school achievement include so much and have boundaries that are so vaguely defined that obtaining agreement about what constitutes a representative sample from that domain would be close to impossible. One might assess a student's mastery of the names of Napoleon's marshals, but what would constitute mastery of the history of the Napoleonic era?

When one has specified a domain of knowledge or skill with definite boundaries and limits, measurement becomes a matter of sampling from the tasks that make up that domain, testing the individual on those tasks, and inferring what proportion of all the tasks in the domain the examinee can do. The desired inference can be expressed as "how many" rather than "how much," which is the desired inference in the case of a latent attribute.

Design of a domain-sampling test calls for (1) defining the boundaries of the domain, (2) deciding in what form stimuli are to be presented to the examinee, (3) deciding in what form the examinee shall be asked to respond, (4) deciding what type and size of sample shall be drawn from the domain, and (5) specifying what percentage of the domain the individual must appear to have learned in order to be credited with "mastery" of that domain. By way of illustration, the domain might be defined as the 100 basic multiplication combinations. It might be specified that a sample of these would be presented in written form as "$5 \times 8 = $," and that the examinee would write the numerals representing the correct response. The examinee would be given as much time as needed to complete the task. It might be decided that the difficulty of each of the 100 combinations would be estimated in a preliminary study, the items divided into fourths on the basis of their difficulty, and a 20-item test prepared by drawing at random 5 combinations from each fourth in difficulty. Finally, it might be specified that the 20-item test would be administered at a single sitting and that 18 correct out of the 20 would be accepted as constituting satisfactory mastery.

Note that there have been a number of fairly arbitrary decisions in the procedures we have set forth. Such arbitrary decisions will always be required. They define operationally what "mastery" has meant to the teacher, evaluator, or research worker.

As one leaves the field of academic achievement and moves into the assessment of aptitudes, attitudes, interest, or temperament (and at times even within the field of achievement), it is more usual, and usually more productive, to think of a trait or attribute of a person. By contrast to a defined domain, which may perhaps be completely mastered and which has definite boundaries or limits, a trait is thought of as a characteristic that exists in different degrees in different persons, without any limit at either the upper or the lower end. Although we might possibly say that a person has mastered 80% of the basic multiplication combinations, in the sense that we have already defined the domain, it would never make sense to say that a person had 80% mastery of reasoning, was 80% favorable to disarmament, or was 80% sociable. In these latter cases, we recognize an attribute with respect to which people differ widely, but we can set no clear limits to the specifics that fall within the attribute dimension, and we have no ready-made scale in which to express those differences. We hope to identify those differences by testing and to develop some reasonable way to quantify them using latent trait theory.

One way to clarify the difference in emphasis between the domain mastery and latent trait concepts of testing is to think of a horizontal and a vertical dimension. The horizontal can be visualized as range or scope and the vertical as difficulty or level. Domain mastery approaches tend to play down the vertical dimension, giving minimal attention to variations in the difficulty level of specific tasks. Focus is on the number (or proportion) of the tasks, spreading out horizontally to form the defined domain, that are passed by the examinee. By contrast, latent trait models focus very sharply on the vertical dimension, which represents the level of performance. While they acknowledge the need for some breadth or scope in order to produce items that are not too redundant and a trait that is not so narrowly defined as to be trivial, makers of latent trait tests set as their primary goal estimation of the level at which a given individual falls on the specified latent trait.

In practice, the distinction between these two orientations may become blurred. Thus the typical standardized achievement test is designed so that it samples rather widely from a domain of educational content. At the same time, tasks may be arranged in a hierarchy of difficulty, and test interpretations may be expressed in terms of grade equivalents or other scores implying level of performance. Recognizing the genuine difference between the two models, the test maker as well as the test user must be prepared to encounter a certain amount of ambiguity in practice.

The balance of this chapter is devoted primarily to mapping the general outlines of the latent trait approach to test-making and test analysis. Where a domain mastery approach would lead to different procedures or interpretations, these will be set forth from time to time in later chapters.

THE LATENT TRAIT APPROACH TO TESTING

In most of psychometrics we are concerned with attributes of people, with tests that are intended to measure those attributes, and with the single exercises or items that in combination make up such tests. We are concerned with understanding what relationships hold between the properties of the component items and the test that they make up and with what relationships will be found between score on the test and standing on the underlying attribute. Beyond that, we are interested in how attributes relate to one another in the hierarchy that represents human ability or human personality. In this chapter we shall explore in general terms attributes, tests, test items, and the relationships among them. The issues that we identify here will be dealt with in some depth in subsequent chapters.

ATTRIBUTES

We use thousands of different terms—nouns, adjectives, and adverbs—to describe the characteristics of people. We speak of a person as having mechanical ability, showing a high level of reading comprehension, or being aggressive in relationships with others. Whenever we use terms such as these we imply some quality in the person's behavior that shows up with at least some degree of consistency over time and over a range of specific situations. We do not observe the attribute. It is not observable; it is, rather, a notion that we construct to account for consistencies that we observe in what the individual is able to do or elects to do as that person meets the circumstances of life. The consistency is not perfect because circumstances change, people change, and people are to a degree unpredictable and erratic. But only to the extent that there is a core of consistency does it make any sense at all to develop a test of an attribute and to report a score for an individual.

Attributes differ in both their nature and their scope. At times we may be interested in attributes that refer to abilities—what the person is able to do. We may wish to divide these into aptitudes and achievements: attributes that refer to potential for learning and attributes that refer to past learnings. At times we may be interested in temperamental characteristics or the dispositions that represent interests and attitudes.

For many attributes in the fields of aptitude and temperament, it may seem natural to think of the attribute as a trait that somehow resides within the person—her verbal ability or his sociability. This seems less suitable when we are concerned with educational outcomes, where attributes seem to be defined more by the branches and objectives of the school curriculum. But in this case, as in the other, we must believe that there is a certain cohesiveness of the domain if "reading ability" or "knowledge of chemistry" is to have any meaning.

As stated earlier, we cannot observe an attribute. It is a construct that we have formulated to organize our experience of consistency of behavior within an in-

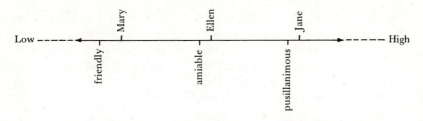

Figure 1.1   Illustration of a latent attribute of verbal ability.

dividual, together with differences among persons. Since an attribute is not observable as such, we sometimes speak of a *latent attribute,* meaning the hypothesized but unobserved characteristic that accounts for a particular set of consistencies within and differences among persons.

We typically think of this latent attribute as having the property of amount or degree—in the sense that one person can have more of it than another or that a person can have more of it at one time than at another. Thus, if we think of an attribute such as "verbal ability," we think of it as having a linear form, as shown in Figure 1.1. We think of persons being located at different points along this dimension: Mary would be characterized as having low verbal ability, Ellen as having moderate ability, and Jane as having high ability. By the same token, we classify test tasks or items with respect to the level of demand that the task imposes. Identifying a meaning of the word *friendly* would call for only a low level of verbal ability, whereas recognizing the meaning for the word *pusillanimous* would call for a much higher level. Much of our concern in psychometrics can be summarized by the query: How can we construct or select test exercises and combine them in a test so that the resulting score will identify with considerable precision where each person falls on the scale of a latent attribute of interest to us?

TEST SCORES

With the latent trait orientation, we value a test score as a representation, however imperfect, of some latent attribute. The relation between test score and attribute is thought to be monotonic (though not necessarily linear), so that with increasing levels of the attribute we get a steady increase in the expected test score and so that, as the test score goes up, the best estimate of the person's standing on the attribute also goes up. The relation is not linear, at least at the extremes, because the test has a "floor" at a zero or chance score and a "ceiling" represented by getting all items right. The attribute, on the other hand, is considered to extend without definable limits both up and down.

The test score is always an imperfect representation of the attribute. This is so because success on the separate test exercises that go to make up the test score depends on factors other than the individual's standing on the attribute. A test exercise may call, in varying degrees, for general attributes other than the one that it is intended to assess. Or success may depend on specific past experiences of the individual that are related to the content of that item. For items in which the respondent merely selects from given alternatives, success may depend on sheer luck in picking the keyed response. Thus persons who fall at a given level on the attribute display a distribution of scores on the test with some considerable dispersion. Conversely, persons receiving some one score on the test represent a distribution of values on the attribute.

It must be recognized that the latent attribute assessed by a test may be psychologically complex. Thus a test of verbal analogies, composed of items such as

house : room :: book : cover   <u>chapter</u>   print   paper

transparent : opaque :: unique : unusual   priceless   <u>banal</u>
                                                                         recherché

may involve a composite of word knowledge, flexibility of mental set, ability to educe relationships, and perhaps other cognitive skills and tempermental traits. Psychology sets as a goal the definition of conceptually simpler and more incisive attributes and the development of corresponding measures, but the psychometrics of test construction does not require that each item in a set be psychologically pure. It *does*, in general, require that each item in the set approach uniformity in the common attribute—simple or complex—that the several items measure.

TEST ITEMS

The typical test is composed of a set of test exercises or items. A scoring procedure is established for each item; ordinarily the test score is the sum of the item scores. It may pay to give some attention to other ways of pooling the information from the component items, but in the overwhelming majority of cases a simple summing of item scores has been used and will be used in the future.

A test item is designed to depend for its successful solution on the latent attribute of concern to the test maker. However, even more than success on the test as a whole, success on a single item depends on a variety of systematic and chance factors other than and in addition to the examinee's standing on the latent attribute. For an item to be acceptable, the *probability* of an examinee succeeding on the item must increase steadily as the examinee's standing on the latent attribute increases, but the increase will be gradual rather than abrupt, owing to the host of other factors that influence success on the item. Thus we can think of a function that expresses probability of success on the item as a function of standing on the latent attribute. Such a function is displayed in Figure 1.2 for several different test items. The base line in the figure represents level on the scale of the latent attribute, and the ordinate represents probability of getting the right answer for the item. The line that displays probability of succeeding on

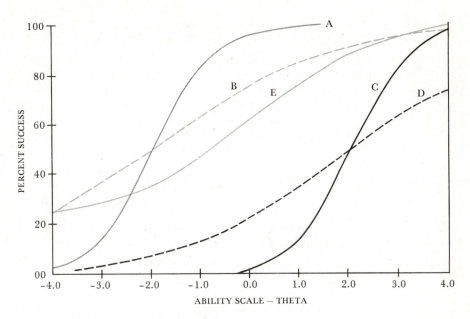

Figure 1.2   Selected item characteristic curves.

the item as a function of level on the latent attribute is called the *item character-istic curve*. In general, these curves can be described by three parameters:

1. A parameter that indicates the "steepness" of the curve—the rate of change in probability of success as one goes up the scale of the latent attribute.

2. A parameter that indicates where on the scale of the latent attribute the curve falls—that is, that represents the difficulty of the item.

3. A parameter that indicates the base level for the curve at very low levels on the latent attribute—the "chance" level of success for true-false or multiple-choice items.

Curves A and B in Figure 1.2 represent easy items, for which there is a substantial probability of success even for persons at a low level on the latent attribute. Curve A is a "steep" curve, in which probability of success increases rapidly as level on the latent attribute increases. This is an item that depends almost solely on the latent attribute, and very little on anything else, so that a person with the requisite amount of the latent attribute is almost sure of success and a person with less than the requisite amount is almost sure of failure. By contrast, curve B is a relatively flat curve, and the probability of success increases only slowly as level on the latent attribute is increased. This is a task in which success depends largely on factors other than the latent attribute with which we are concerned, and in which degree of possession of this latent attribute is only a minor determinant of success.

Curves C and D are parallel in shape to curves A and B, respectively, but they are moved up the scale of the latent attribute. These are difficult items in that success is likely only for those standing high on the scale of the latent attribute. Curve C shows an item that discriminates sharply between those with more and those with less of the latent attribute. Curve D discriminates weakly. Curves A through D are all asymptotic to the base line of 0% and exhibit items in which the person very low on the latent attribute has essentially *no* chance of getting the item right. Curve E illustrates an item of moderate difficulty in which there is 1 chance in 4 of getting the item right by blind guessing. The asymptote for the item is 0.25, with parameter 3 for this item being 0.25 rather than zero.

For a given item g, we will label the three item parameters as follows:

1. a_g is the steepness parameter. In Chapter 4 we use the biserial correlation of the item with a measure of the latent attribute as an index of the item's ability to differentiate persons with different levels of the latent attribute. When a trait is normally distributed the parameter a_g displays the relationship

$$a_g = \frac{r_{\text{bis}_g}}{\sqrt{1 - r_{\text{bis}_g}^2}} \tag{1.1}$$

2. b_g is the difficulty parameter. When b_g is exactly equal to θ, a specified level on the latent attribute, then exactly 50% of examinees at that level know the answer to the question or are able to work out the solution to it.

3. c_g is the level of "chance success." This is the level that the item characteristic curve approaches as an asymptote when θ, the level of ability, becomes extremely low.

For much of the theoretical work on the properties of test items and of tests that result from the combination of those items, one or the other of two mathematical models is used. (The two produce very similar results. The choice depends in large part on the tractability of the mathematics that arises from using one or the other.) The first is the normal ojive—the cumulative form of the normal curve. This takes the form

$$P_g(\theta) = \int_{a_g}^{\infty} (b_g - \theta)\, \phi\,(t)\, dt \tag{1.2}$$

when $c_g = 0$. The value of this integral depends on the lower limit of the range over which integration is carried out, and hence on the expression $a_g(b_g - \theta)$. The multiplier a_g (the steepness parameter) determines the rate at which this expression changes with change in θ, and the value of b_g (the difficulty parameter) determines the value of θ for which $b_g - \theta$ will equal zero and hence P_g will equal 0.50.

The second model is a function called the *logistic* function. This takes the form

$$P_g(\theta) = \frac{1}{1 + e^{-Da_g(\theta - b_g)}} \tag{1.3}$$

Like the normal ojive, this function has a range from 0 when θ is very much less than b_g (that is, when the ability level of the examinee is much lower than the difficulty level of the item) to 1 when θ is very much greater than b_g. It has a value of 0.50 when $\theta = b_g$—when ability level and task difficulty just match.

The logistic function is readily modified to accommodate the case in which there is a nonzero probability of getting a correct answer even by persons at an extremely low value of θ. The formula then becomes

$$P_g(\theta) = c_g + \frac{1 - c_g}{1 + e^{-Da_g(\theta - b_g)}} \tag{1.4}$$

In equations 1.3 and 1.4, the factor D is a constant of scale, usually 1.7, that depends on the units in which θ is expressed and serves to make the scale units of the logistic comparable to those of the normal ojive.

These expressions for the relationship between P_g, the probability of success on the item, and θ, the individual's standing on the latent trait, will become important to us in Chapter 4, when we try to understand the relationship between item parameters and the effectiveness of a test.

In general, the size and nature of the curvilinear correlation between test score and latent attribute is determined by the item characteristic curves of the component items. The nature of this relationship will be developed more fully in later chapters. It is a complex function of the steepness of the curves for single items and of the dispersion of item difficulties. In the fabrication of a test we shall be concerned to assemble a set of items all of which, to a satisfactory degree, depend for success on the latent attribute we are trying to measure and which collectively reflect different levels of possession of this latent attribute.

THE PREPARATION OF TEST ITEMS

The construction of effective test items is a rather demanding exercise in creative writing. It calls for a precision and clarity of expression that are rarely demanded in more discursive forms of composition. Over the years, agencies concerned with test preparation have assembled an assortment of guidelines to help item writers, especially novice item writers, avoid some of the more common forms of ambiguity and of test-item cueing. When the novice starts to write true–false items, for example, it is likely that the false items will be shorter than the true items and will often contain such universals as "always" and "never."

The novice can be warned against this tendency. A problem that often arises in writing multiple-choice items is that the stem* does not clearly formulate and state a problem to which there is, then, a specific answer. An item is believed to be clearer and more effective if the stem rather fully formulates a problem that could be presented in question form, rather than merely constitutes a fragment of a sentence that might conceivably be completed in many ways. Guides for writing test exercises are developed somewhat further in Chapter 3. By and large, the guidelines for item writing are distillations of professional experience, and even of personal taste, rather than principles based on a firm research foundation. And even when all the guidelines are scrupulously observed, much of the excellence of a set of items depends on the insight, originality, and clarity of expression of the author.

PLAN OF THE BOOK

In the next chapter we indicate the range of issues that a test maker faces as he or she starts to plan a test. These are decisions that must be dealt with at some point and are best confronted before actual work on the test starts. In Chapter 3, attention is given to some of the distinctive problems of preparing test exercises for different sorts of tests — aptitude, achievement, temperament, and so forth — but detailed guides for item construction are not given. Chapter 4 is devoted to the tryout of test exercises, analysis of the data from that tryout, and selection of the exercises to compose the final test. Chapter 5 considers issues related to score conversions, in which a raw score of number correct (or a formula score corrected for guessing) is transformed into a score that either (1) better matches the scale of the latent attribute or (2) seems easier to interpret to the user of test results — or, ideally, both of these. Chapter 6 concerns the *internal* characteristics of the test that result from administering a set of items — topics generally of reliability and error of measurement. Chapter 7 is devoted to test validity, including on the one hand the question of how faithfully the test corresponds to the latent attribute it was designed to measure and, on the other, how useful the test is in predicting specific practical events in the outside world. Chapter 8 considers problems of item and test bias. Chapter 9 is concerned with optimal procedures for combining information from two or more tests or from tests and other types of information. Chapter 10 develops some ideas on the application of Bayesian statistics to testing problem and discusses ways of adapting testing procedures to each individual examinee. Finally, Chapter 11 considers several models for use of test data, models that can be identified as selection, placement, classification, and guidance.

---

* The statement that formulates the question, by contrast to the "options" that represent the answer choices.

Chapter 2

Planning the Development of a Test

The development of a test, inventory, or other measurement instrument that is to be published and used beyond a specific local setting is a complex undertaking that involves a host of decisions and proceeds through a number of stages. It is desirable, so far as possible, to view in advance the complete sequence of operations when work on the instrument is started, so that the work at each stage can be most effectively oriented toward the final goal. It is also desirable to plan a schedule of work that will realistically produce the desired instrument at the specified time. Devising a rather formal plan and schedule for test development offers two main advantages. (1) It requires test makers to clarify their own thinking on just what they plan to do and how they plan to do it. Fuzzy thinking becomes more obvious when test makers attempt to be explicit about each step in the process of development. (2) It facilitates communication among all the persons involved in a test-making enterprise. Because development of an instrument often involves a number of different individuals — item writers, editors, field examiners, statisticians, sales personnel — a clear, written plan for the development of the test or testing program helps to guarantee that all will work together effectively toward a common end, rather than at cross purposes.

Here are some of the components of a test plan. Each will be elaborated further in the following sections of this chapter.

1. An initial definition of the domain or the latent attribute that the instrument is designed to assess.

2. A statement of the uses planned for the instrument, indicating the clientele to be served and the types of decisions to be based on it.

3. An indication of the constraints within which the instrument must operate — constraints of time, media, and testing conditions.

4. A set of content specifications, indicating topics to be covered, skills to be tapped, or subabilities to be tested — sometimes called a test *blueprint*.

5. Specification of the format of test items, indicating the nature of stimulus materials, the type of response to be made by the examinee, and the procedure for scoring.

6. A plan for the tryout of proposed test exercises, for analyzing the tryout data and for selecting the items to be included in the final instrument.

7. Specification of the statistical parameters that are desired in the finished test, in order that it may achieve the required difficulty level and reliability.

8. A formulation of the procedures to be used for standardization testing and for carrying out statistical analyses of that testing in order to prepare test norms.

9. An outline of other data-collection and analysis activities that should be carried out to evaluate validity, bias, and the like.

10. A plan for the organization of the test manual and any other needed auxiliary materials.

DEFINITION OF THE LATENT ATTRIBUTE OR TEST DOMAIN

It is probably trivial to say that, before one starts to develop a test or other instrument, one should know what it is that one wants to test. Perhaps it is not quite so trivial to say that one should express that intention as clearly and explicitly as possible. The intention is expressed in a general way by the label that we attach to the attribute or domain—"verbal ability," "skill in arithmetic computation," "mastery of capitalization of proper names," "proficiency in typing," "mechanical interest," or "impulsivity." However, labels may mean rather different things to different people. Even something as specific and tangible as "skill in arithmetical computation" might mean speed and accuracy of simple computations with whole numbers to one person, while to another person it might mean ability to carry through to completion lengthy and complex calculations involving fractions, decimals, and parentheses. The two could constitute noticeably different attributes, and a person who was outstanding on one might be no more than average on the other. For this reason, some further specification and delimitation is generally to be desired.

The detailed and operational specification of the attribute comes about at the stage of preparing the test blueprint. At that point, one attempts to lay out in detail the particulars of content and mental process to be tapped by the test exercises. However, some narrowing and clarification of the meaning of the attribute can well be undertaken as a very first step in thinking about a test-development project. Some illustrations of expanded definitions follow.

Verbal ability evidenced by knowledge of meanings of a large number of words and choice of the best word to fit a given context.

Skill in arithmetical computation shown by speed and accuracy in carrying out simple numerical operations.

Mastery of capitalization of proper names When given a paragraph of prose in which no capitalization is shown, recognizes with 90% accuracy the proper names that require capitalization. (Note that in this instance a rather specific domain is defined, together with the acceptable level of mastery—a typical criterion-referenced interpretation.)

Proficiency in typing evidenced by rapid and accurate preparation of typed copy with proper form and spacing from rough hand-written copy.

Mechanical interest indicated by a liking for activities involving the construction, maintenance, repair, or operation of mechanical devices and a preference for such activities over those relating to words, numbers, or interpersonal contacts.

Impulsivity shown by a tendency to subscribe to self-descriptive statements implying quick decisions and readiness for unplanned, spur-of-the-moment activity and to reject self-descriptive statements implying deliberateness, tendency toward careful planning, and restraint.

These expanded definitions of attributes or domains do two things. On the one hand, they elaborate somewhat further what is intended by the attribute's designation. On the other, they begin to suggest the testing operations by which the attribute will be assessed. In the test-making process, one moves back and forth in continuous interaction: clarifying the definition of an attribute as one undertakes to develop assessment procedures and modifying assessment procedures as one's conception of the attribute is clarified. Of course, the conception of an attribute emerges not simply from a single test maker's thinking but rather from the whole history of research dealing with the construct in question. Thus, for such a trait as impulsivity, there is an accumulated research literature in which various self-descriptive and behavioral indices have been related to one another in an attempt to get a clearer picture of the nature and generality of the construct.

PURPOSES TO BE SERVED BY THE TEST

A testing instrument is — or should be — planned with a particular clientele and particular sorts of decisions in view. An arithmetical computation test may be intended for use with fifth-graders to identify individuals with deficiencies and to diagnose the nature of those deficiencies, or it may be intended for use as part of a selection program for employing bank tellers. A typing test may be intended as part of a course examination for a high school typing class or as an employment test for secretarial job applicants. In planning a test, it is important to have clearly in mind the clientele for whom the test is intended and the types of decisions that are to be based on the test results. The specifications for test content, for difficulty level, for test length, for scores to be obtained, and for the manner in which they will be reported all depend on what groups are to be tested and what decisions are to be made about them.

It will help in the balance of planning to be as clear as possible about the groups to be tested. What age or grade levels will be represented? Will persons displaying the complete range of the attribute be represented? Or will the group be selected in some way? (Selected groups might consist of persons of outstanding ability, persons who are candidates for scholarships or fellowships, or, by contrast, persons of marginal ability who are being considered for remedial instruction or special classes.) Will the examinees bring special backgrounds of language or culture? With what motivation will they take the test?

It is also important to know how the test results are to be used. Is the test designed merely to be a research tool — to place all examinees as accurately as possible on the scale of the latent attribute so that this attribute can be studied in relation to other characteristics of the persons or in relation to treatments that are applied to them? Or are the results to be used for one or another type of applied decision? If the latter, what type of applied decision? We can identify a number of types of applied decisions that call for rather different design of the testing instrument. It will be clear as further issues are discussed that the composition of a test and the level of difficulty of its exercises may be influenced considerably by the types of decisions for which the results are to be used. We need to consider the following types of decisions:

1. *Instructional decisions* Here the issue is typically whether an individual (or a group) has mastery of certain entry skills so that it will be worthwhile to present a new topic or whether a person (or group) has achieved enough mastery of a domain of knowledge or skill that has just been taught to warrant moving ahead into some new unit of instruction.

2. *Diagnostic decisions* The objective in this case is to identify particular deficiencies or errors in a person's learning or performance in order to initiate remedial actions. For both instructional and diagnostic decisions, testing typically focuses on degree of mastery of one or more quite precisely defined domains.

3. *Selection decisions* These are decisions to admit or exclude, to employ or reject. Ordinarily they are, to a degree at least, competitive and relative decisions in that the number of vacancies is limited and the testing is carried out in order to admit the most promising candidates.

4. *Placement decisions* This term usually refers to a hierarchy of training programs or positions. The issue is to determine where in the hierarchy each person can most advantageously be placed. At what level should a transfer student enter a school's program? From what type and level of English or math program will an entering college freshman profit most? How complex are the tasks to which a new clerical or trades employee should be assigned?

5. *Classification decisions* These differ from placement decisions in that the decision is one of kind rather than level. To what training school should a new recruit in the Armed Forces be assigned? Will this person be more readily trainable as a clerk or as a mechanic, as a cook or as a truck driver?

In selection, placement, and classification decisions we are usually interested in measures of attributes that seem likely to be good predictors of general level of later performance in some type of training program or job.

6. *Guidance decisions* This category covers a wide variety of decisions that a person makes, perhaps with professional help, about his or her own future. To go to a four-year college or to a junior college. To take a liberal arts program or a job-oriented trade or technical program. To consider a person-oriented job or a thing-oriented job.

CONSTRAINTS ON THE TEST

Any testing must be carried out within limits set by certain practical constraints. It is important that the test maker be aware of these constraints and make realistic adjustments to them.

The most obvious constraint is that of time. Time for testing is often grudgingly given. In schools, teachers tend to consider testing time as time stolen from their instructional program, and administrators often view a testing program as a nuisance that disrupts the smooth flow of the school day. In employment offices, candidates can be expected to devote only a limited time to the process of applying for employment. The pressure for brevity in testing is very real. But the pressure for precision in test appraisals is equally real, and the test maker is in a perennial conflict between producing a test that is brief enough to be acceptable to users and creating one that provides accurate enough information to permit useful decisions. In planning a test, the test maker must recognize the reality of practical time constraints, so that specifications for test length will produce an instrument that will fit within those limits and hence will be used.

A second constraint that often operates is that the test must be administered on a group basis rather than an individual basis. A common, though not an absolutely necessary, corollary of group administration is that testing is limited to material printed in a test booklet. If this constraint does hold, it should be acknowledged and included in the plan for the test.

Even when a test is to be individually administered, it is necessary to be realistic about what a typical examiner with a typical level of training and skill can handle. Will the test materials be unwieldy to manipulate? Will the examiner have to make quick decisions about what task is to be presented next? Must judgments about the correctness of responses be made "on the wing" as the test is being given? How complex is the recording that the examiner must do?

It may be desirable to impose other constraints on the test design. Thus one might wish to specify, in a reading test, that the content favor neither males nor females and that the content be appropriate for minority and low socioeconomic groups. Or, for a science achievement test to be used in junior high school, one might wish to specify that the reading difficulty of the material not be above sixth-grade level, so that the test would not function primarily as a reading test. One might want to specify that the words used in a verbal-reasoning test be drawn from the commonest 5000 in a count of word occurrences, so that difficulty would lie in the relationships expressed rather than in lack of familiarity with the words themselves.

Those constraints within which a test must operate, whether external and practical or internal and substantive, should be recognized and made explicit. Only by doing so can we judge whether a test can be made that will be both psychometrically sound and practical for use under the circumstances under which it is designed to be used.

CONTENT SPECIFICATIONS OR BLUEPRINT

Specification in some detail of what topics and processes are to be included in a test is the core of planning a test, and it is sometimes all that people have in mind when they speak of a plan for a test. The blueprint tends to become most explicit and most fully elaborated in the case of a survey test of achievement in some academic field. A test of this type is usually viewed as having two dimensions—a dimension of content expressing what has been taught and a dimension of process indicating what the examinee is expected to do with that content. It is common to prepare a two-dimensional grid showing in one dimension the topics to be included and, in the other, the types of operations to apply to that content. Table 2.1 is an example of such a grid.

The content categories of a blueprint are, of course, specific to the particular subject area and have nothing in common from one field to another. There have, however, been some attempts to generate uniform taxonomies to express the various levels of process to be tested. The most widely publicized, which was prepared by a committee of the American Educational Research Association chaired by Benjamin Bloom (1954), lists the following hierarchy of objectives for education:

Knowledge
Comprehension
Application
Analysis
Synthesis
Evaluation

This hierarchy provides one framework to guide the preparation of test exercises and focuses the attention of the test maker on the need to develop items that require the examinee to do more than merely recall facts or recognize names, dates, definitions, and the like. Because it is often far from easy to judge at just what level of the hierarchy a given item fits, some test makers have found it easier to work with somewhat simpler and more descriptive categories such as those given in Table 2.1.

The content outline for an achievement test is expected to mirror what has been taught, or what should have been taught, in a given segment of the school curriculum. If the test is for a single instructor's course, that instructor should be able to specify what was covered, what was emphasized, and what students were expected to learn and retain. For a test that is to be used more broadly the test maker must rely on widely used texts, courses of study, and the critique and suggestions of people who teach the subject matter. In the last analysis, the content outline represents a pooling of judgments about what should have been taught and learned.

When the test being developed is to be used as a mastery test, or criterion-referenced test, leading to judgments about mastery of a specific domain, the key feature of the blueprint should be very clear specification of the domain to be covered. This specification should indicate (1) the form of stimulus to be presented to the examinees, (2) the form of response to be given, and (3) the standard (inevitably somewhat arbitrary) that will be considered to represent satisfactory mastery.

For example, we might specify: "When presented a sample of 20 multiplication problems in the format $a \times b = ?$, writes the correct answer to at least 18." Or again: "Given 4 paragraphs without punctuation, each composed of 5 simple sentences, and being instructed to put in any needed punctuation, puts periods at the end of 16 or more of the sentences."

The plan should indicate how the sampling from the domain is to be set up as well as any further boundaries and delimitation of the domain. In the multiplication illustration, for example, it might be specified that each of the 10 digits appear the same number of times. Or, in the second illustration, it might be specified that sentence length not exceed 10 words, and that vocabulary be limited to the 2000 commonest words in the English language. The purpose of such further specification is (1) to make the difficulty level of the sample closely match that of the total domain and (2) to specify the domain so clearly that the user (and others) will know just what has been mastered.

The blueprint for a job proficiency test is in many ways like that for an academic achievement test. However, the focus is on a job. One asks: What must a person know and do on this job? What knowledge and skills are critical for adequate job performance? Sources for needed information about job performance are quite different from those that are useful in specifying the content of an academic achievement test. The job analysis that tells what knowledge and skills are necessary for satisfactory job performance relies heavily on inputs from skilled workers and from supervisors. The plan for a proficiency test tends to emphasize functional competency—being able to do critical job tasks—rather than the abstract knowledge that underlies practical competence.

Content specifications for a test of aptitude also have a somewhat different

Table **2.1**   Sample Test Blueprint for Biology Unit Test.

CONTENT AREAS

Process Objectives	A. Nutrition, 40%
1. Recognizes Terms and Vocabulary	Nutrients · · · Incomplete Protein Vitamins · · · Complete Protein Enzymes · · · Amino Acids Metabolism · · · Glycogen Oxidation · · · Carbohydrate
20%	4 or 5 items
2. Identifies Specific Facts	Nutrients Essential to Health Good Sources of Food Nutrients Parts of Digestive System Process of Digestion of Each Nutrient Sources of Information About Foods and Nutrition
30%	7 or 8 items
3. Identifies Principles, Concepts, and Generalizations	Bases of Well-Balanced Diet Enzyme Reactions Transfer of Materials Between Cells Cell Metabolism Functions of Nutrients in Body
30%	7 or 8 items
4. Evaluates Health Information and Advertisements	Analyzes Food and Diet Advertisements Interprets Labels on Foods Identifies Good Sources of Information About Foods and Diets
10%	2 or 3 items

* From R. L. Thorndike and E. P. Hagen, *Measurement and Evaluation in Psychology and Education*, 4th ed. New York: Wiley, 1977. Used by permission.

CONTENT AREAS

B. Communicable Diseases, 40%		C. Noncommunicable Diseases, 20%	Number of Items
Immunity	Epidemic	Goiter	
Virus	Pathogenic	Deficiency Diseases	
Carrier	Endemic	Diabetes	
Antibodies	Protozoa	Cardiovascular Diseases	
Incubation Period		Caries	
4 or 5 items		2 or 3 items	12
Common Communicable Diseases		Specific Diseases Caused by Lack of Vitamins	
Incidence of Various Diseases		Specific Disorders Resulting from Imbalance in Hormones	
Methods of Spreading Disease		Incidence of Noncommunicable Diseases	
Types of Immunization			
Symptoms of Common Communicable Diseases		Common Noncommunicable Diseases of Adolescents and Young Adults	
7 or 8 items		3 or 4 items	18
Basic Principles Underlying Control of Disease		Pressure Within Cardiovascular System	
Actions of Antibiotics		Control of Diabetes	
Body Defenses Against Disease		Inheritance of Abnormal Conditions	
Immune Reactions in Body		Abnormal Growth of Cells	
7 or 8 items		3 or 4 items	18
Distinguishes Between Adequate and Inadequate Evidence for Medicines		Identifies Errors or Misleading Information in Health Material	
Identifies Misleading Advertisements for Medications		Identifies Appropriate Source of Information for Health Problems	
2 or 3 items		1 or 2 items	6

Table **2.1**   Sample Test Blueprint for Biology Unit Test. (*cont.*)

	CONTENT AREAS
Process Objectives	A. Nutrition, 40%
5. Applies Principles and Generalizations to Novel Situations	Identifies Well-Balanced Diet Computes Calories Needed for Weight-Gaining or Weight-Losing Diet Predicts Consequences of Changes in Enzymes on Digestive System Identifies Services and Protection Provided by the Federal Food and Drug Act
10%	2 or 3 items
Number of items	24

Total time for test — 90 minutes

flavor and usually tend to be somewhat less full than specifications for an achievement or proficiency test. Because such a test is designed to measure some fairly general and persisting characteristic of the person, not the outcome of any specific program of instruction, there is no well-defined body of content to which to refer. Often several subtests or item types can be specified. For example, one could specify that a verbal ability test is to be composed of synonym–antonym, verbal analogy, and sentence-completion items. One could then indicate whether these were to appear as separate subtests or be mixed together. One could also indicate certain general aspects of content balance. For example, if reading comprehension were part of a test, one might specify that reading passages be drawn in approximately equal proportions from the fields of natural science, social science, and literature. A mechanical reasoning test might specify how many items were to be based on the lever, how many on the wheel, how many on the screw, how many on the pulley, and so forth.

Content specifications for tests of interest, temperament, and attitude are likely to be fairly sketchy. When the latent trait is defined, an elaborated definition often tends to indicate some of the aspects of content. Thus the definition of impulsivity on page 13 suggests, as content, statements dealing with the following:

B. Communicable Diseases, 40%	C. Noncommunicable Diseases, 20%	Number of Items
Recognizes Conditions that Are Likely to Result in Increase of Communicable Disease Identifies Appropriate Methods for Sterilizing Objects Gives Appropriate Reasons for Regulations, Processes, or Treatments	Predicts Consequences of Changes in Secretion of Certain Hormones Predicts Probability of Inheriting Abnormal Conditions	
2 or 3 items	1 or 2 items	6
24	12	60

Total number of items — 60

Quickness of decision
Liking for unplanned activities
Freedom from restraint or inhibition
Dislike of careful planning

Further study of and meditation on the research on impulsivity would almost certainly suggest other aspects of the attribute that should be added to the list. The test constructor makes an initial judgment on how much emphasis (how many items) should be given to each aspect.

FORMAT SPECIFICATIONS

At a fairly early stage in planning, the test maker must make it clear what format the test exercises are to take. In an ability test, the first and foremost decision is whether the examinee will construct the answer to items or select the correct or best answer from a given set of alternatives. During the past 50 years practical considerations have generally tipped the balance in the direction of selective rather than constructed response items. With selected response items many more questions can be handled by the examinee in a given time period, and responses can be scored much more rapidly and more objectively. In most cases these considerations are likely to continue to prevail. However, developments in optical scanners and document readers appear to open up some options for item formats and patterns of responding that have not been practical in the past. A document reader can read numerals written in a specified location in a standard block format, and this makes possible the mechanized scoring of a constructed response to an arithmetic problem that can take any numerical value. Again, a document reader can read underlining of any word in a passage, so that a passage could be presented devoid of capitalization and the examinee instructed to underline each word that should be capitalized.

During the past 30 or 40 years, the multiple-choice item format has been by all odds the most popular. This is due to (1) the readiness with which this format lends itself to mechanized scoring and (2) the flexibility of the format for testing a wide range of contents and processes. Except for tests used by young children, the number of response options has typically been four or five. There is nothing sacred about these numbers, but they seem to be a reasonable compromise between the desire to reduce the probability of getting a correct answer by blind guessing and the difficulty of preparing a number of answer choices that are sufficiently plausible to attract examinees who don't know the right answer. However, the test maker should not automatically gravitate to multiple-choice items but should consider whether matching, two-choice (Yes–No or True–False), or some other format is better adapted to measure the attribute or the domain of knowledge being tested. Especially for personality measures, a useful format has been items in which the response alternatives are Yes–No, Agree–Disagree, or Like Me–Not Like Me or in which a scale of Strongly Agree–Agree–Doubtful–Disagree–Strongly Disagree is presented.

Format specifications often need to cover the auxiliary stimulus materials on which test exercises are to be based. These include such things as reading passages, charts and maps, diagrams, and tables. If such materials will be needed, the plan should specify this and should describe any properties that they are to have. For example, the length, difficulty level, and type of content of reading passages might be spelled out. Or the number and type of maps and charts might be indicated. The number of test exercises to be based on each passage, map, or chart might be stated as a guide to the number that will need to be prepared and tried out.

At some point, a decision must be made about formats for recording answers and procedures for scoring. The most critical decision is whether a separate answer sheet is to be used or answers are to be marked directly in the test booklet. Because of the greater ease of scoring and the economy resulting from reusing test booklets, separate answer sheets have become nearly universal above the primary grades for anything other than limited local testing. However, the separate answer sheet tends to limit item formats—typically to multiple-choice items — and does increase slightly the possibility of clerical error by the examinee in recording responses. When these limitations appear to be undesirable, answers may be marked or written in the test booklet, which will either be hand-scored or fed whole through an optical scanner.

Another key decision is whether to use a score that is simply the number of right answers or one that exacts a penalty for errors. The issues involved in this decision, and the arguments in favor of each alternative, will be considered in some detail as a part of the discussion of item analysis in Chapter 4.

PLAN FOR ITEM TRYOUT AND SELECTION

Items designed to measure a latent trait must be tried out in order to determine their level of difficulty and their ability to differentiate those falling higher from those falling lower on the latent attribute. At a fairly early stage in the development of the test it is necessary to answer the following questions:

1. At what age or grade levels are the materials to be tried out?

2. What size tryout sample is desired at each level?

3. What special subgroups (sex, socioeconomic, ethnic, or other) are to be isolated for special analysis?

4. How lengthy are the tryout forms to be?

5. How much time is to be allowed for the tryout forms?

6. What test score is to be used as the criterion against which each item is evaluated?

Once these decisions have been made, the next stage of preparation involves making the necessary arrangements with schools, employers, or other sources of a sample. This is hardly a research task, but it is a necessary and often demanding one.

With respect to age or grade level, the general guiding principle is that one would like the tryout groups to be as similar as possible to those with which the test is eventually to be used. Thus one tries to draw samples from that population, covering the range of ages or grades, and replicating so far as possible the level of ability (or other attribute) that characterizes those with whom the test will be used. As we will see in later chapters, it is possible to adjust item statistics to take account of differences between the tryout sample and the population that will eventually be tested, but it is more satisfactory if such adjustments are minor and certainly simpler if they do not have to be made at all.

Ideally, the tryout group should be drawn from a number of schools and/or locations, so that item statistics are not distorted by the peculiarities of a single location. Thus a specific item — say an item on prime numbers — might be especially easy in one school if the topic had been thoroughly taught the previous week. Using a multitude of locations tends to minimize any such local effects. When, as in some national testing programs, a section of research material can be incorporated in an operational test that is widely used, a broadly representative sampling may be possible. In the usual case, however, the test maker must be satisfied with a "lumpy" sample that comes from perhaps half a dozen schools or companies. Where this is so, it is most desirable that the group be diverse, representing the same geographic, ability, or specialization range that will be encountered when the test is used.

It is not easy to specify minimum numbers. Clearly the larger the tryout samples, the more stable the resulting estimates of difficulty and discrimination parameters. For a test that is intended to be widely used, two or three hundred in each age or grade group is ordinarily the minimum that should be considered adequate for providing useful item parameters.

Due to recent interest in "fairness" of test exercises for culturally different or economically deprived groups, it is sometimes maintained that test materials should be tried out on special groups representing ethnic minorities or the economically deprived. The purpose of such tryout is presumably to identify certain specific items that either are particularly difficult for the special group or fail to differentiate the more from the less capable examinees in that group. One would hope that most of the items involving terms and content inappropriate for the special group would have been identified by editorial review—particularly review by members of the group in question. However, tryout may serve to supplement, or in some cases to replace, such a review. If the tryout data from special groups are to be useful, the samples from these groups must be large enough for us to feel confident that the apparently unfavorable properties of certain items in the special groups do not represent simply chance fluctuations. In general, it would seem that the minimum size for special groups should not be lower than the minimum for the general tryout sample. As a practical matter, adequate samples from those groups are often difficult to obtain.

The issues of length of tryout booklets (in terms of number of items) and time limits for a tryout are closely interrelated. The principle that determines both is that one wants, insofar as possible, to have every examinee attempt every item. If the time limit is so short, in relation to the length of the test, that a number of examinees do not have time to attempt the later items, the item statistics for those items are distorted. Sometimes no provision is made to differentiate between items that were read but then not answered and items that were not reached. Clearly these are not equivalent, and it is not desirable that they be treated as equivalent. But even when provisions are made to identify and exclude the "not reached" cases, it is still true that the sample responding to the later items differs—typically being more capable—from the total sample that responded to the early items. Thus every effort should be made to provide time limits long enough (or test forms short enough) for nearly everyone to read and attempt every item. Because groups for tryout administration may be available for no more than a 40- or 45-minute class period, it is a good idea to prepare tryout materials in a number of parallel short forms, so that the material presented to a single examinee is no more than he or she can handle in a single period. It often proves easier to multiply the number of examinees by 2, 3, or 4 than to multiply the testing time by the same factor.

One early decision is the choice of a score to be used as the criterion against which to judge each item's ability to differentiate those with more from those with less of the latent attribute. In those cases in which new items are tried out as an adjunct to a regular testing program, in order to develop new test forms for that program, the natural and the most satisfactory procedure is to use score on the existing test, or some specific section of it, as the criterion against which the new items are to be judged. However, because score on such a pre-existing test is rarely available to the test maker, it is usually necessary to use total score on the pool of items in the tryout form as the criterion. Though there may be a few weak items that water down the precision of the tryout booklet as a measure of the latent attribute, this effect is usually minor and total score provides quite a serviceable criterion indicator.

PLANS FOR ANALYZING AND USING THE TRYOUT DATA

Once decisions have been reached on the tryout samples to be tested, a plan must be formulated for the analysis and use of the results from the tryout. What statistical analyses shall be carried out? What use shall be made of the statistical results? What weight shall be given to them in relation to considerations of content and representative coverage of the domain to be assessed by the test?

The statistics that will usually be of interest are (as discussed in detail in Chapter 4) the difficulty of the item and its ability to differentiate those higher from those lower on the latent attribute, as defined by the criterion score used to represent that attribute. It may also be of interest in certain ability tests to find how many examinees select each of the wrong answers and to what extent each error alternative is chosen by the less capable examinees. This last information is useful primarily if the test maker proposes to revise the item in order to improve its effectiveness. Opinions differ about how profitable it is to try to salvage a defective item. Some test makers feel that the energy is better expended on writing new items, rather than on trying to bolster up weak ones. But if such a rescue operation *is* undertaken, information about the functioning of each of the error choices (assuming a multiple-choice item) will prove invaluable.

Items that fail to differentiate the more from the less able, especially those that show a reverse discrimination, should ordinarily be eliminated from further consideration. Some attention may be paid to selecting items that discriminate as sharply as possible, but the chief use of discrimination indices is usually to exclude defective items. A minimum level of correlation with the criterion score may be set, below which items will be rejected. This minimum tends to be lower for homogeneous groups expected to have little variation on the latent attribute and for heterogeneous items in which a single common factor plays a less dominant role. Conversely, it will be higher when the population is quite diverse and/or the items are highly redundant in representing a single basic trait. For example, items for a simple vocabulary test applied to a random sampling of 10-year-olds might be expected to show relatively high discrimination indices, and one might specify a minimum biserial correlation of .40 or even .50. By contrast, a set of items (1) covering a broad, varied range of application of medical knowledge and (2) applied to the select group represented by medical school graduates would probably tend to yield considerably lower indices of ability to differentiate the more from the less able, and one might be willing to set the minimum biserial correlation with the criterion score as low as .30 or even .20.

For items that surpass the established minimum, one's plan might specify that preference would be given to those items with higher discrimination indices if they satisfied the needs for content representation and appropriate levels of item difficulty.

In formulating specifications for item difficulty, it is important to consider how the test results will be used. What decisions will be based on them? If there is some one point on the scale of the latent attribute that is a critical decision point, items should be chosen to make the test differentiate as sharply as possible those falling below from those falling above that critical point. To the extent possible, all items will then be chosen so that their item characteristic curve is steepest, that is, the percent of passers is increasing most rapidly, at this critical point. In the model presented in Chapter 1, the parameter b_g should be at or very close to the level at which the critical decision falls. This might be the case for an exam to be used to award a limited number of scholarships when there are a large number of applicants or, at the other end of the scale, to identify a limited number of deficient students who should receive some type of special remedial instruction. Frequently, however, a test is desired that gives information of approximately equal precision over a fairly wide range of the latent attribute, and then the plan for the item difficulties should be such as to achieve this. The problem will be considered in greater detail in Chapter 4.

PLANS FOR GATHERING NORMATIVE DATA

When the function of a test is to locate each individual on some latent attribute, it is usually desirable to be able to place that person in relation to others. We rarely, if ever, have any absolute or pre-established scale for such attributes as reading comprehension, spatial visualizing, understanding of mechanical principles, and so forth. The domain of admissible tasks has no clear boundaries, and the possible range of the latent attribute has no clear 0 point and no definable upper limit. When this is so, the performance of groups of persons of different ages, levels of education, or types of background or experience provides the basis of reference for expressing the performance of some given individual.

This is not always the case. With domain sampling tests, the domain is limited and rather precisely bounded, and a person's status can be described in absolute terms with reference to his or her level of mastery of the defined domain. Thus we may say: "Given a passage with 20 proper names in it that require capitalization, the examinee identifies at least 18 correctly." This may appear to us an acceptable criterion of mastery, and we say that, on this criterion-referenced test at this time of testing, the examinee displays mastery of capitalization of proper names. Such a narrowly specified achievement may be useful in guiding instructional decisions about what has been learned and what now needs to be taught. However, for tests of more general and comprehensive abilities, normative data for appropriate reference groups are typically needed.

We must first decide what the appropriate reference groups are. Then we must develop plans for gathering data on those groups.

The appropriate reference group is the group with which the individual, or the local group, can most meaningfully and appropriately be compared. For some purposes this might be the group of all candidates for a particular type of job or a particular type of training. Thus the College Entrance Examination Board develops percentile norms for all applicants for college admission who are taking their Scholastic Aptitude Test in a given year, and the individual may compare himself or herself to or be compared with that group. Sometimes the normative group may represent a particular region or a particular type of school or community, as when a test publisher develops "big city norms." Often it is hoped that the normative group is a nationally representative sample that reproduces accurately the properties of the whole country. The ways in which the test results are to be used dictate which type of population constitutes the most meaningful comparison group.

When a decision has been reached about the population with which comparisons can best be made, one must then (1) design a sampling procedure that will reproduce the properties of the population efficiently and without bias and (2) carry out the design with as little "slippage" as possible. Issues of sample design will be discussed more fully in Chapter 5. However, the most elegantly designed sample is of little use unless the groups called for in the sample can actually be tested. Arranging to give tests to the individuals or groups called for in the designed sample becomes a major task of administrative organization and skill. Planning involves eliciting the cooperation of local persons who will supervise and carry out the testing, following specified procedures, meeting the established schedules, and getting results back to the central data-processing installation on time. A smoothly operating normative testing program must be planned in meticulous detail.

At the time when normative testing is planned, one must try to envisage all the analyses that will be carried out on the data. A program for these analyses should be spelled out in detail to assure that all needed data will be gathered. Otherwise one may find, for example, that one now wishes to make separate analyses for black, Hispanic, and Oriental children but that no information was gathered on the ethnicity of each child. If one is establishing norms for a new form of a test, one's plans may need to provide a design for testing that will permit the equating of that form to already existing forms. Several possible models for equating are discussed in Chapter 5. If correlational analyses of part scores are required, plans must be made to score the parts separately.

The planning must, of course, include decisions about the types of converted scores that will be required — percentiles, standard scores, scores on a basic scale of the latent attribute. Once these decisions have been made, planning must set forth, step by step, the statistical analyses of the test data that will be required to produce those converted scores.

TEST MANUAL AND SUPPORTING MATERIALS

If a test is being prepared for use by others, the test maker will have to prepare one or more manuals for the test user. Planning should include specification of what is to appear in such a manual (or manuals). This planning helps guarantee that the manual will be complete and that the data needed to produce it will be available as needed. Among the elements that should appear in the manual are the following:

1. A statement of the uses for which the test is designed.

2. Full directions for administering the test.

3. Norms tables by which raw test scores are translated into interpretable converted scores.

4. Evidence on the test's reliability and precision in measuring.

5. Evidence on the validity of the test for the purposes for which it was designed. (This might include evidence on predictive validity in the form of correlations with specific criterion variables. It is even more likely to include a wide variety of evidence on the construct validity of the test as a measure of the latent attribute that it is designed to assess, including correlations with other tests, factorial structure, and evidence on group differences or on the effect of experimental interventions.)

6. Possibly, guides and suggestions for use of the test results.

Various people will need the supporting materials: those who will be administering the test, those who will be making immediate practical use of the test results, and those who will be evaluating the test for possible use or who will be carrying out research based on it. This may dictate that several separate types of supporting documents be prepared, such as an examiner's manual, a counselor's or administrator's manual, and a technical manual.

SCHEDULE

A great many tests are constructed with the requirement that they be available for administration on a particular date. This is true of examinations that are part of a recurring examination service, such as the College Boards or various forms of licensing examinations. It is true also of course examinations or comprehensive examinations in school or college. And any commercially published examination has a target date by which it is due to be offered to the public. In much of test-making, then, deadlines are of the essence. If these deadlines are to be met, a realistic production schedule must be set up, and that schedule must be followed.

The natural way to generate a schedule is to work backwards from the target date, when the test is to be ready for use, establishing the date of D-day minus so many days, weeks, or months by which each preliminary step must be completed. The sequence of steps will vary somewhat with the type of test involved. Thus the step of preparing national norms, which would loom large in most tests meant for commercial distribution, might not be involved at all in a local civil service or licensure examination. Though a schedule must be primarily linear, with one step following another in sequence, there will always be some overlapping of steps and some activities that can proceed concurrently.

In any schedule, there are certain critical times that are determined by the sequence of events outside the control of the test maker. Suppose norms are to be established for grade groups at the beginning of the school year. Such groups become available only once a year, so the rest of the schedule must be tailored to make all materials ready for normative testing in September (or, perhaps better, October) of a given year. Again, if item tryout is to be carried out through an experimental section included as part of some scheduled administration of a recurring test, then all items to be tried out must have been written, edited, and reproduced in test booklets by that pre-established date.

The sequence from initial planning to finished test ready for operational use is quite complex. Only as the full sequence is set forth will the novice test maker get a realistic sense of the lead time that must be provided if a well-wrought test is to be ready by the date it must be put into use. Table 2.2 is a sample schedule for the development of a commercially distributed test of scholastic aptitude, or general cognitive abilities. The particular time intervals would not be directly transferable to other circumstances, in which the type of test material and the way in which the test was to be used were different, but the example should provide a sense of what a schedule should comprise and what constitutes a realistic

Table 2.2   Illustrative Development Schedule

D-day	(1) Test Available for Commercial Distribution. Test Booklets and All Auxiliary Materials, Including Manuals and Norms Tables, Complete and Printed.
D − 60	(2) Final Copy for Manuals and Norms Tables to Printer.
D − 90	(3) Statistical Analyses for Manuals Completed and to Authors of Manuals, for Use in Preparing Copy for Manuals and Norms Tables.
D − 120 D − 270	(4) Normative Testing Completed and All Answer Sheets in Hands of Test-Scoring and Analysis Agency. (The dual time interval provides for school testing in both autumn and spring.)
D − 360	(5) Final Form of Tests and of Instructions for Administration and Data Collection in Hands of Field Agencies (Schools) Carrying Out Normative Testing.
D − 420	(6) Final Form of Tests and Auxiliary Materials to Printer.
D − 450	(7) Items Selected, and Choice of Items and Copy for Auxiliary Materials to Publisher's Copy Editor.
D − 480	(8) All Statistical Analyses of Tryout Data in Hands of Test Author(s), to Be Used for Item Selection.
D − 510	(9) Tryout Testing Completed and in Hands of Scoring and Statistical Analysis Agency.
D − 570	(10) Tryout Forms and Directions to Field Agencies for Tryout.
D − 600	(11) Tryout Booklets to Printer.
D − 630	(12) Items, Edited for Form and Substance, to Copy Editor for Assembly into Tryout Booklets.
D − 660	(13) Draft Items to Reviewers, for Critique of Item Wording and Content.
D − 720	(14) Item-Writing Assignments Sent to Item Writers.
D − 750	(15) Design and Specifications for Test Completed.
D − 780	(16) Planning for Test Initiated.

time frame. As Table 2.2 shows, the time interval from the beginning of planning to the publication of a finished test, ready for commercial distribution, is more than two years. This may seem like a long time, but experience indicates that it is none too much. Of course, when a test is being developed for strictly local use, some of the steps can be abbreviated and the developmental time substantially reduced. The important thing, in each case, is to anticipate the complete sequence of steps that must be carried out — one after the other — to arrive at the final product, and to make a realistic time allowance for each step.

Chapter 3

The Development of Test Exercises

This chapter undertakes to provide a certain amount of guidance for the person who must prepare a set of test exercises. The guidance is necessarily limited; item writing remains largely an art in spite of some attempts to mechanize and computerize it. Shrewdness in selecting the concepts to be tested, ingenuity in embedding the concept in a specific problem, incisiveness in phrasing the problem so that it is clearly stated, and perceptiveness in designing distractors that will appeal to the incompetent or uninformed can only to a limited extent be inculcated by a text. They must be developed through direct experience on a foundation of talent for this particular form of literary expression.

The demands that different types of tests impose on the test maker are rather distinct, so we shall consider in separate sections tests of (1) general abilities or aptitudes, (2) achievement of knowledge or understanding in specific content areas, (3) performance or skill, and (4) attitude, interest, or personality. Though certain issues recur, we shall tend to concentrate on the ones that are central to tests of a given type.

TEST DIRECTIONS

One element that is characteristic of any type of test is a set of directions to guide the examinee. With rare exceptions, the test maker wants each examinee to understand clearly what is to be done and to be motivated to do it well. The test directions should be designed to achieve these ends.

In the matter of motivation, the goal of the test maker is to evoke serious effort without arousing a debilitating level of anxiety. This is a delicate balance to maintain, for individuals differ markedly in their reactions to tests. The balance also depends very markedly on the context in which the test is given. If the context is one of qualifying for college admissions or for a job, there is not likely to be any difficulty in evoking serious effort, but anxiety may well become a problem. Wording of test directions should thus be planned with a view to easing the tensions. However, in tests given as a part of routine school activities, it may be desirable to emphasize how important the test results can be in helping teachers and/or counselors to plan for and work with the student—that is, to try to convey the real value that test results can have for the examinee.

When identifying to the examinee what a test is designed to measure, it is usually desirable to avoid loaded and threatening labels — *not* "This test will tell how intelligent you are," but "This test gives you a chance to show how well you can do on some problems with words and numbers." Especially as one begins to measure aspects of personality, a degree of ambiguity is often appropriate both in test titles and in the statement of what the test is designed to assess. Thus we would describe an inventory as one concerned with "your usual reactions to other people" rather than with "social ascendance and withdrawal."

Directions for an ability test (except possibly for domain mastery tests) should usually make it clear that the test exercises cover a considerable range of difficulty and that there will be some items that any examinee will find quite difficult. Being warned that some items are designed to be very difficult and that they are not expected to be able to do all the exercises may reduce the examinees' anxiety when they encounter items that they cannot do.

The directions should, of course, provide one or more illustrative items, telling how each is to be solved and giving the correct answer and the rationale for its correctness. In addition, there should be an adequate number of practice items, to be completed by the examinee and later explained by the examiner. What constitutes "adequate" practice depends on how familiar the type of exercise is and how experienced the examinees can be expected to be with that type of test exercise. For example, by the end of elementary school, most pupils in the United States have had a number of experiences with multiple-choice items measuring academic aptitude and achievement, and little or no practice is needed for items in a conventional format. (By contrast, pupils in some developing countries may never have encountered such an item, in which case a full-scale practice test may be desirable to familiarize examinees with all aspects of the testing process.)

If there is any question about the test-wiseness of the examinee group, using a practice test as a teaching device may be a very sound procedure. It can help to reduce anxieties and to assure that low scores do not appear solely as a result of an examinee's failure to understand how to attack the types of items on the test.

Young or naive test takers may need practice in the skill of marking a separate answer sheet. When a separate answer sheet is used to facilitate scoring, a brief practice test using that answer sheet format may be well worth the additional testing time and cost, especially if the format is likely to be unfamiliar to the examinees.

Two elements of test-taking strategy that the directions should deal with are how to allocate one's time and what to do about guessing. Practical considerations dictate that almost all tests be given with a time limit. A few tests are definitely speeded, and in them speed of work is of the essence. More often, the time limit is planned so that most examinees will have time to attempt nearly all the items, or at least all those for which they know the answers. If the test *is* speeded, examinees should be made aware of this fact and should be urged to work rapidly. Even if time limits are fairly liberal, it is usually wise to instruct examinees not to waste time on single items but to move on through the test, returning later, if time permits, to the items that gave them difficulty.

The test maker must decide whether the score for the test is to be simply the number of correct answers or whether a penalty is to be exacted for errors (in other words, for "guessing"). If score is to be simply the number of correct answers, the examinee should be told this fact and should be strongly urged to answer all the questions. It should be made very clear that the examinee can only lose by omitting items.

When a correction formula is used, providing instructions that will be optimal for the examinee is somewhat more tricky. However, experience indicates that most examinees tend to lower their score by omitting too many items. In general, instructions should encourage examinees to guess whenever they can rule out one or more of the answer choices as clearly wrong. A strategy that might be suggested is: (1) try to find a single answer choice that you believe is correct and mark it, but (2) if no correct answer can be identified, try to identify one or more that are clearly wrong, rule them out, and mark one of the others.

One does not want certain examinees to have an advantage simply because they have better test-taking strategies. The test directions should therefore aim at giving all examinees guidance that will lead them to the optimum strategy.

This chapter focuses primarily on test exercises in which the examinee is called on to choose one (or possibly more than one) answer from a set of given response options. Most widely used tests exhibit this format, primarily because this type of exercise can be quickly and objectively scored. Much current test scoring uses an optical scanner to determine what responses have been chosen and a computer to process the information from the scanner and report a score. One might ask whether significant advantages are sacrificed in order to gain this objectivity and efficiency. The question is really a dual one:

1. Is there a loss in going from a brief *constructed*-response format to a *selected*-reponse format?

2. Is there a loss in going from an extended essay to a brief response?

The first issue can be illustrated by a pair of items.

   I. What do we mean by the word *grief* ?

   II. *grief* A. cry B. fried C. pain D. sickness E. sorrow*

The first format appears in the Stanford–Binet; the second occurs in the Cognitive Ability Test, Verbal Form 3. The percentages of examinees getting credit for an acceptable answer are roughly as follows*:

---

* From R. L. Thorndike and E. P. Hagen, *Cognitive Ability Tests*. Iowa City, Iowa: Riverside Publishing Co. Used by permission.

	I	II
10-year-old	15	50
11-year-old	27	65
12-year-old	42	75

Both formats correlated substantially with total score on the corresponding test. Thus it appears that the selected-response format is easier and that this would be so even if a correction were made for guessing. In this illustration, as in any other that we could choose, the success of the item in multiple-choice format is critically dependent on the material that is chosen for the misleads, or wrong alternatives. In this instance the proportions choosing each alternative were as follows:

	AGE GROUP		
	10	11	12
cry	0.08	0.07	0.07
fried	0.06	0.05	0.04
pain	0.12	0.12	0.09
sickness	0.05	0.04	0.04
(omit)	0.17	0.06	0.02

All options were chosen by some pupils, though errors were made less frequently in the older groups, and (this is not shown here) all wrong options tended to be chosen by pupils scoring lower on the test as a whole. Thus we can speculate that the proportion correct would not be likely to be reduced by better error choices. In this illustration, at least, producing the correct answer is clearly more difficult than merely recognizing it. However, this does not necessarily mean that the produced answer is a more valid indicator of verbal ability.

The second issue can be illustrated by the following contrasting questions:

I. Identify the chief factors that would be likely to influence the reliability coefficient of a test, and indicate what the effect of each could be expected to be.

II. A 15-word spelling test had a reliability coefficent of 0.50. What reliability could one expect if 15 comparable words were added to the test?
A. 0.55   B. 0.67   C. 0.75   D. 0.85

Table **3.1**   Ability Factors Proposed by French from Analysis of Factor-Analytic Studies.

Ai	Aiming	P	Perceptual speed
At	Attention	PC	Psychomotor coordination
FD	Finger dexterity	Pl	Planning
FE	Fluency of expression	S	Space
GF	Gestalt flexibility	SA	Speed of association
GP	Gestalt perception	SJ	Speed of judgment
I	Induction	Sm	Span of memory
IF	Ideational fluency	SO	Spatial orientation
In	Integration	Sp	Speed
J	Judgment	V	Verbal comprehension
M	Associative memory	Vi	Visualization
MD	Manual dexterity	VM	Verbal memory
ME	Mechanical experience	W	Word fluency
N	Number		

(From John W. French, The Description of Aptitude and Achievement Tests in Terms of Rotated Factors. Psychometric Monographs No. 5. Chicago: University of Chicago Press, 1951. Used by permission of the Psychometric Society.)

The set of *several* such multiple-choice items could be expected to take up no more testing time than would be required to formulate and write out a full response to the one question in essay format, and one should compare the reliability and validity of one essay question with that of the set. No clear comparison of difficulty is possible here, because so much would depend on the grading standards of the essay reader.

Essay questions have their place in the appraisal of certain aspects of educational achievement, notably the assembly and organization of materials to present some topic or support some position. However, these complex responses and their subjective evaluation are difficult to fit into any coherent psychometric theory, and we shall have relatively little to say about them in this volume.

CONSTRUCTING EXERCISES FOR ABILITY TESTS

In this section we consider the construction of what have often been called aptitude tests. These tests are designed to assess some general attribute of ability, without reference to where or how the ability was developed. They may be contrasted with achievement tests, which are designed to appraise what has been learned from some specific program of instruction and in which the test exercises

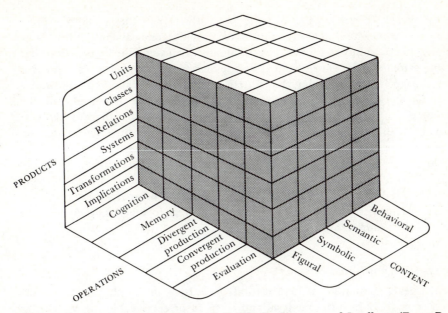

Figure 3.1   Pictorial representation of Guilford's Structure of Intellect. (From R. L. Thorndike and E. P. Hagen, *Measurement and Evaluation in Psychology and Education,* 4th ed. New York: Wiley, 1977. Used by permission.)

need to be related explicitly to the objectives of the instructional program. We prefer to avoid the term *aptitude* because in some quarters it has come to imply "innate and genetically determined." Because we never know to what extent score on an ability test depends on genetic factors and to what extent on the complex interaction of life experiences, we prefer to use the neutral term *ability test,* which carries no implications about how the abilities were developed.

When one embarks on the construction of exercises for an ability test, the first requirement is to be as clear and precise as possible about the nature of the ability that is being measured. Over the past 70 years, the interplay among armchair theorists about human abilities, inventors of formats for test tasks, and statistical analysts of test results has led to an extensive catalogue of proposed, and to some degree measured, human abilities. In a summary of factor-analytic studies up to that time, French (1951) included the ability factors displayed in Table 3.1. The most formal and elegant, though not fully documented, guide to possible abilities is found in Guilford's (1967) "structure of intellect," a three-dimensional structure diagrammed in Figure 3.1. If one takes any combination of content, operations, and products, this structure can be thought to define one ability dimension for which test exercises can then be developed. Conversely, any existing test can be thought to fit in one or several of the 120 pigeonholes of this structure.

With guidance from the past, as codified in such summaries as French's or such organized structures as Guilford's, and with such further wisdom as one's own observation of human abilities and skills provides, one conceptualizes a trait or dimension of ability that one wants to measure. Have defined a function that one wishes to measure, one must next decide on a type (or types) of test item that seems appropriate for assessing that function. In practice, there is a continuous interaction between our conception of the attribute to be measured and our development of formats for test exercises. Thus, if we feel that there is evidence for an ability that we designate "reasoning with verbal concepts," we may decide to prepare sets of items in the form of (1) verbal analogies, (2) verbal classification, and (3) sentence completion. Analysis of the correlations among these and a battery of other sorts of items will help to determine whether the three verbal item types do appear to define a common ability. The analysis can reinforce or raise questions about our choice of these three item formats as procedures for assessing one common ability.

ITEM FORMATS FOR ABILITY TESTS

Over the years, a number of item formats have been invented. They have appeared repeatedly in different tests and seem to be serviceable for measuring significant ability functions. The person embarking on a test-making project should review these familiar formats before searching for something new and different. We provide a brief catalogue of item types below to suggest some of the possibilities.

Synonym
Find the word that means most nearly the same as the given word.
loquacious   A. juicy   B. talkative   C. friendly   D. frequent   E. rational

Antonym
Find the word that means most nearly the opposite of the given word.
loquacious   A. dry   B. taciturn   C. hostile   D. rare   E. absurd

Analogy
loquacious is to *taciturn* as *friendly* is to
A. lively   B. hostile   C. busy   D. talkative   E. silent

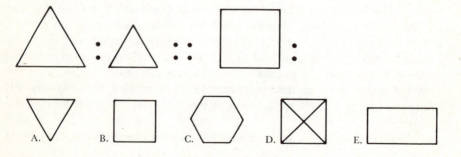

Classification
Which one goes with the first three?
orange   grapefruit   lime
A. peach   B. pear   C. tomato   D. lemon   E. apple

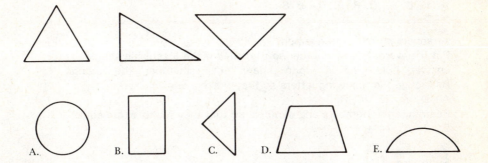

A.   B.   C.   D.   E.

Series
Which one comes next in the series?
3   6   9   12   A. 13   B. 14   C. 15   D. 16   E. 17
a   c   e   g   A. h   B. i   C. j   D. k   E. l
cool   chilly   cold   A. frigid   B. warm   C. temperate   D. hot
                           E. comfortable

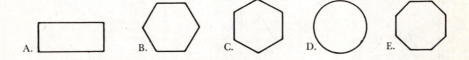

A.   B.   C.   D.   E.

"Multimental" (called in England "odd man out")
Which one of the following does *not* belong with the rest of the set?
A. poodle   B. dachshund   C. beagle   D. tabby   E. setter
A. 4   B. 10   C. 7   D. 6   E. 12

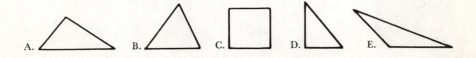

A.   B.   C.   D.   E.

Completion
What goes into the blank space to make a sensible completion of the
sentence? (series)
The girl _____ her bicycle up to the village.
A. chased   B. rode   C. threw   D. gone   E. left
1   3   5   ___   9   11
A. 4   B. 5   C. 6   D. 7   E. 8

Arrangement or Rearrangement
Put the words below in order so that they make a sensible sentence.
answer could he it John knew not remember the though
Rearrange the following letters so they make a sensible word.
A   D   N   O   P   R
Rearrange the numbers and symbols so that they make a true equation.
2   2   3   4   ( )   +   ÷   =

Synthesis
Use the three words given below so as to produce a sensible sentence.
Public   Relate   Purpose
Using the set of blocks that you have been given, make this design.
5.

Matrices
Which one belongs in the vacant spot?
6.

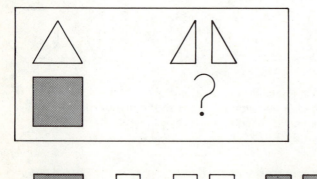

```
2    4    6
3    6    9
4    8    ?
```

A. 10   B. 12   C. 15   D. 16   E. 18

```
cold    hot
wet     ?
```

A. dry   B. weather   C. summer   D. wetter   E. rain

Verbally Stated Problem
    John walked from his house in to the store going 3 miles per hour and walked back at 2 miles per hour. If the trip took just an hour, how far is John's house from the store?
A. 0.8 miles   B. 1.0 miles   C. 1.2 miles   D. 1.5 miles   E. 1.8 miles

    John walks due north, turns right, turns right again, and then turns left. What direction is he now facing?

    "I walked up hill all the way to town and up hill all the way back." What is silly about that?

Most of the problem formats that we have illustrated with multiple answer choices can also be presented without the answers, the examinee's task being to supply an appropriate one. The task then becomes one of producing rather than recognizing the correct answer. There are then likely to be a number of variations in the answer that is offered, so the objectivity and convenience of mechanical scoring are sacrificed. A variant procedure that appears to require that examinees generate for themselves the answer that the test maker has chosen as correct is one that provides only partial cues to the answer—for example, giving only the first or the first and last letter of the word that constitutes the answer. Thus our "synonym" example might become

loquacious   A. f   B. j   C. r   D. t   E. w
    or   A. f—y   B. j—y   C. r—l   D. t—e   E. w—l

Note that this item now requires not merely that the examinee generate a synonym for *loquacious*, but that it be the particular synonym that the test maker has selected. A new and additional source of difficulty has been introduced.

GENERATING MISLEADS

Multiple-choice questions have two main components: the stem, which presents the problem, and the answer choices. With many formats of ability tests, the stem is relatively simple and straightforward. By contrast to achievement tests, where clear and incisive formulation of a problem in the stem is a critical aspect of good item-writing, phrasing the stem for ability test items is often simple and relatively mechanical. The main outlet for editorial skill lies in the choice of answer options, especially the incorrect answers. In some informal explorations of item writing, we have found that a group of novice item writers tends to scatter widely in choice of misleads (wrong answers). Of course, many different wrong answers may function equally well, but when an ability test item fails to differentiate the more from the less capable (as represented by some total test score), the difficulty often lies in one or more of the misleads for the item.

How does one go about generating misleads? It is sometimes proposed that one should try the item out initially in open-ended form and find out what the common errors are for each item. These common errors would then be offered as options when the item is cast in multiple-choice form. But this is a laborious procedure, requiring a whole additional cycle of item tryout. Furthermore, very large tryout samples are required if they are to provide dependable evidence about which are the most common misconceptions. So this empirical approach to the selection of misleads is rarely used. The usual procedure is the "If I were a horse, where would I go?" approach, which relies on the ability of the item writer to play the role of examinee and identify likely confusions on the part of examinees.

Misleads may fail because they are too remote and implausible, because they are too appealing, or because they appeal to the wrong individuals. Furthermore, misleads that function well with examinees who are at one level of sophistication may function poorly with examinees at another level. This is illustrated by the tryout results for the following analogies item*:

sheep : lamb :: lion :
A. lioness B. puppy C. den D. cub E. tiger

To get the correct answer on this item, the examinee must recognize that the meaning of lamb is "baby sheep," and must know that a young lion is called a cub. The misleads were picked as either bearing some other relationship to lion or (as in "puppy") some relationship to animal young. Below are shown, for grades 4, 6, and 8, the percentage choosing each option and the correlation of that choice with total score.* The analysis is based on over 2500 cases at each grade level, so the statistics are quite dependable.

* From R. L. Thorndike and E. P. Hagen, *Cognitive Ability Tests*. Iowa City, Iowa: Riverside Publishing Co. Used by permission.

		A	B	C	D	E	OMIT
Grade 4	%	12	4	4	26	39	14
	r	.04	−.42	−.27	.50	−.02	−.45
Grade 6	%	13	4	4	46	33	1
	r	−.01	−.57	−.43	.58	−.38	−.52
Grade 8	%	14	1	2	52	31	0.1
	r	−.08	−.47	−.34	.56	−.50	−.14

Many aspects of these statistics are instructive. In the first place, the correct answer (D) showed a substantial positive correlation with total test score at all levels, so the item did function acceptably in the test. However, the persons who chose *lioness* (choice A) were, at all grades, about as able as the persons who did *not* make this choice. (The correlation of choosing versus not choosing this option is approximately 0.) This option appears to attract persons of all levels of ability about equally. Consequently, it adds little or nothing to the item's ability to differentiate levels of ability and could well be replaced. Even more interesting are the results for choice E (tiger). This was a very seductive option. The family relationship of lion to tiger attracted a large fraction of the respondents at each grade level, perhaps those who did not know that an infant lion is called a cub. But these respondents were of average ability among fourth-graders, whereas they were clearly the less able sixth- and eighth-graders. The lion–tiger association was too strong and too appealing for all ability levels among fourth graders, but it was effective in pulling in the less able eighth-graders. The option functioned in different ways at different levels of maturity and sophistication. Note finally that the four misleads differ quite markedly in their popularity. The model proposing that the person who does not know the answer guesses at random is a gross distortion of typical test-taking behavior.

When a test of any sort is being prepared, it is desirable that the items prepared by a given item writer be reviewed by one or more critics to try to identify in advance and correct any deficiencies in the item. Questions that a reviewer might have in mind in relation to each ability test item are suggested below.

1. Is the item keyable? Is there one and only one clearly correct or best answer? Ideally, the reviewer should answer the item without knowledge of the author's key and should verify that author and reviewer are in agreement.

2. Does each wrong option have a degree of plausibility, so that a person who does not know the answer might reasonably choose it? If not, perhaps a more attractive option can be suggested.

3. Does the item appear to favor or to handicap any special groups of examinees? Does it seem "fair" to both sexes? To people from different regions? To those with different socioeconomic or cultural backgrounds?

4. Does the difficulty seem reasonable for the level or type of group for which the test is intended? Verification of appropriateness will come from item tryouts, but we would like to waste as few items as possible through putting into tryout forms items that turn out to be too difficult or too easy to be useful.

CONSTRUCTING EXERCISES FOR ACHIEVEMENT TESTS

The preparation of items for an achievement test is primarily controlled by the test blueprint. This blueprint should provide specifications in some detail of the content and processes that are to be appraised in the test. Exercises will be written to fit certain cells of that blueprint, and assignments to item writers will usually specify how many items a given author is to prepare for certain cells. Periodic checks must be made to verify that the quotas for the different topics and types of manipulation of that content are being met.

When multiple-choice items are being prepared for an achievement test, the focus of concern tends to shift from the options to the stem of the item. The stem of an achievement test item tends to become an extended statement, and it is important that this statement be clear and explicit. Achievement test items can be quite varied in the problems that they pose, so the problem must be clearly formulated for the examinee. One way of being sure that the stem formulates the problem fully is to use a format in which the stem is actually a complete question.

> If a test the reliability of which has been found to be .80 is made twice as long, without otherwise changing its nature, what reliability should one expect for the lengthened test?

This form is perfectly adequate, but it sometimes seems more efficient and compact to phrase the item as an incomplete statement.

> If a test the reliability of which has been found to be .80 is made twice as long, without otherwise changing its nature, the reliability of the lengthened test could be expected to be about . . .

The important point is that a specific problem has been fully stated in each case. We are not faced with an item such as:

> Test reliability
>   A. is increased as a test is lengthened.
>   B. decreases as the group becomes more varied.

    C. depends on the correlation of the test with an external criterion.
    D. cannot be greater than test validity.

Here the stem formulates no explicit problem, and each of the options involves a different issue related to test reliability.

A good way to check on the adequacy of the stem when it is phrased as an incomplete statement is to ask whether the statement could be converted to a question by a minor rearrangement. If it could not, one may question whether the statement presents a problem clearly. It may be insufficiently specified or a hodgepodge of several quite unrelated ideas and be correspondingly unclear.

As a matter of general style, as much of the item as possible should be included in the stem, and the response options should be as short as possible. Thus any wording that would otherwise have to be repeated in each option should be incorporated into the stem, where it will need to be read only once. At the same time, the stem should include no unnecessary material (except in the rare instance in which the examiner is trying to determine the examinee's ability to sort out the relevant from the irrelevant information). The stem should present the problem clearly and as concisely as is consistent with completeness.

The stem should ordinarily be expressed in a positive form. Negative statements tend to present somewhat greater reading difficulty, and double negatives are particularly troublesome.

The issues that arise in creating response options for achievement tests are much the same as those that we discussed for ability tests in the previous section. The keyed answer must be clearly right, whereas the other options must have a degree of plausibility but not be so close to correct as to confuse the informed examinee. Experience has suggested a number of points to watch for in the formulation of response options.

1. The keyed answer should be about the same length as other options, so that length does not become a cue.

2. "All" or "none" should be used sparingly in the wrong options, because these modifiers tend to serve as cues that the choice is indeed wrong.

3. All options should be grammatically correct and, insofar as possible, they should be parallel in form.

4. One should avoid repeating in the correct answer a key word from the stem that might serve as a cue that the answer is the correct one.

5. "None of the above" should be used as an option *only* for items for which there is an unequivocally correct (as distinct from a best) answer. These tend to be primarily items from mathematics. If this option is used, it should be the correct answer in a reasonable proportion of the cases.

6. "All of the above" is a rather unfortunate response option because, when it is used, it tends to be the correct answer in a high proportion of cases. Test writers tend to resort to this option when a phenomenon has multiple causes, multiple symptoms, or multiple outcomes. Such situations do not fit well into the standard multiple-choice format. They *can* be accommodated by using a slightly involved format, as illustrated below.

Which of the following is likely to increase the reliability of a test?
I. Making the test longer.
II. Making the test more homogeneous in content.
III. Making the group tested more homogeneous in ability.
A. I only   B. I and II   C. I and III   D. II and III   E. I, II, and III

There are, of course, item types other than multiple-choice that can be used effectively in achievement tests. We tend to give little consideration to simple true-false items because of the limited range of significant learning outcomes that can be cast in statements that are unequivocally true or unequivocally false. However, variants of the format are frequently usable. One variant consists of presenting a situation and then a series of conclusions that do or do not follow from the information given.

Test A has been found to have a reliability of .90, a mean of 45, and a standard deviation of 10 in a group chosen carefully to be representative of fifth-graders. Scores have a normal distribution. Which of the following statements are true?
1. Mary, with a score of 50, falls half a standard deviation above the group mean.
2. A raw score of 35 corresponds to the 25th percentile.
(and on for four or five more statements)

The "master list" format is also efficient and frequently useful.

Look at the underlined word in each of the following sentences. Indicate whether it is
A. a noun
B. an adjective
C. a verb
D. an adverb
1. The boy walked <u>slowly</u> down the road.
2. We must <u>decide</u> whom we want for president.
(and on for four or five more sentences)

It is often appropriate to base a set of items on a common graph, table, clinical case, or other set of data. The items referring to the material may be cast in multiple-choice format, or in one of the other patterns illustrated here.

The role of the item reviewer changes somewhat as we go from an ability to an achievement test. Because of the achievement test's emphasis on the content of a specific area, a major focus of the critic's concern should be the importance of the content tested by an item and the clarity, technical accuracy, and authenticity of the stem together with the keyed answer. Attention should focus on the wording of the stem to be sure that it is clear, complete, and accurate. Beyond that, the critic should be concerned with the correctness of the keyed answer as well as the plausibility of the misleads.

ISSUES IN PERFORMANCE MEASUREMENT

Though much testing in education and some in the world of work can be adequately handled by paper-and-pencil measures, there are some educational and many work skills for which a performance measure seems indicated. We need only mention such examples as typing, shop work, art, music, and laboratory skills to provide examples from a school setting. And most of what one might like to assess in work settings consists of performance skills. The reliable and objective appraisal of performance skills presents many problems of both a practical and a psychometric nature. We shall consider a few of the major issues here.

First, of course, one must decide what aspects of skill it is important to measure. This decision will follow from an analysis of a job and its component skills or of an educational program and its formulated objectives. Once the skills have been identified, the next issue is usually whether the performance is to be evaluated as it occurs as a "process" or whether one is to focus on a tangible end result, a "product."

Process evaluation is almost necessarily the choice for performances that yield no tangible product. The actions of a nurse in administering a hypodermic or some other nursing procedure, the acts of a teacher in conducting a lesson, and the steps carried out by a biology student in setting up a microscope are all instances in which the process may be observed in terms of some standard of correctness but in which no tangible product is produced.

For those performances in which the payoff lies in the product that is the end result of the performance, it is worthwhile to focus testing efforts on getting and evaluating that product. A job applicant's typing skills can appropriately be evaluated in terms of the copy that is produced—how quickly, how accurately, and how esthetically. A student's woodworking or metalworking skills can be appraised by measuring the precision with which a blueprint is turned into a well-wrought birdhouse, bracket, or other artifact.

In those instances in which a tangible product is the natural end result of a skill, there are real advantages in basing evaluation of the student or job applicant on that product. The product constitutes a permanent record that can be unhurriedly examined and analyzed in as much detail as desired. By contrast, a process is fleeting and must usually be hurriedly observed as it occurs. With a product, a uniform scoring procedure specified by a scoring guide can be applied to products from different students or job applicants, and a relatively high standard of objectivity and reliability of scoring can be expected. The key issues are (1) just what performance will best represent the skill one wants to appraise and (2) just what aspects of the product should be evaluated and how they should be weighted in the total evaluation.

Using a typing test as an illustration, we would need to decide whether the skill we were interested in was simply copying rapidly and accurately a perfectly typed and spaced original, or whether we were also concerned with ability to work from rough copy, rearranging phrases as indicated, and placing the message neatly on the page. We might even be interested in ability to transcribe from a dictated tape, with no visual model for a guide and with a somewhat unclear and mixed up message. The standard stimulus for the typing test would differ depending on which of these alternatives seemed closer to the on-the-job skills that were important for job effectiveness.

Several facets of the product can usually be evaluated. One is the speed with which it is produced. Another is the level of perfection of the product. Consider a typing test. In addition to time to complete, there could be a count of mis-hit keys and perhaps a rating of page placement, correctness of form, or other aspects of format. These could be assessed as separate facets of performance or weighted in a single score to reflect the relative importance they are judged to have. In a shop test, time to complete could be recorded, any wastage of material noted, certain key dimensions of the product measured as a check on their accuracy, and aspects of neatness of finish rated. A fairly detailed scoring guide would be needed, in order to be sure that the same standards were applied to all examinees. This should specify the elements to be considered and the scoring standards for each. Weighting of errors and discrepancies usually has to be based on some pooling of judgments about their importance, though data from a sample of examinees, yielding information on the range or frequency of error, can provide some basis for guiding this judgment.

A process evaluation is ordinarily made while the behavior of interest is actually occurring. However, one must seriously consider the possibility of tape recording performances in such areas as music or public speaking and photographing or videotaping tests in which the critical aspects of the performance are visual rather than (or as well as) auditory. Such a recording permits replay of the action as often as necessary, allows scorers to observe it in detail, and makes the behavior sample available to multiple scorers or evaluators if this is necessary in order to get evidence on reliability or to increase it.

Evaluation of process necessarily depends on the judgments of observers. These judgments tend to vary much more than one would like, even when observers all see the same performance. Different observers are likely to attend to different aspects of the performance, and different observers establish different standards of severity in using any rating scheme. The effectiveness of any procedure to reduce this subjectivity is limited, but several alternatives may be suggested.

1. The procedure may be analyzable into more elementary acts, and these can be organized into a check list. The observer can then be called on simply to note whether each of the approved steps in the procedure was carried out in its proper

sequence. Score can be a simple count of omissions or errors—or a weighted count if some elements are more critical than others.

2. Any ratings used can be on specific aspects of performance that have been identified in advance. Thus an oral presentation might be divided at least into evaluation of speaking voice, of carriage and gesture, and of content.

3. Observers may be trained through all observing one or more cases (live or recorded), then comparing their observations or ratings, and discussing differences in an attempt to arrive at more uniform standards.

4. Especially if the performance is recorded, it may be possible to pool the judgments of two or more observers and thus get improved reliability.

Often one of the most difficult aspects of performance evaluation is providing a uniform, standard task for all examinees, while at the same time making the task reproduce the essential properties of a realistic life task. If equipment is to be used (typewriter, lathe, or the like), it should be in good working order for all examinees and uniform from one examinee to the next. The surrounding conditions of lighting, comfort, and freedom from noise and distraction should be kept as uniform as possible. The stimulus material and product to be produced should be kept uniform for all examinees.

It is in the evaluation of process that uniformity is most difficult to achieve. If observation is of a nurse on the nursing floor or of a teacher in the classroom, the situations that may arise are almost infinitely variable, and a standard task that can be performed by each in turn and that represents a significant aspect of the job is hard to find. At this point, simulated tasks are sometimes used: providing a rubber dummy to which the treatment can be given, for instance, or a mini-class that can be taught a standard lesson. Achieving a realistic and yet an adequately standard situation through such simulations is an extremely demanding undertaking. We shall not consider it further here.

Performance evaluation tends to be subjective and unreliable at best. The problems that arise vary widely from one testing situation to another. Each case requires thoughtful analysis to determine what task provides a good approximation to the skills that one wants to appraise, what precautions are called for if one is to provide a uniform task for all examinees, what facets of performance should enter into a score, and what procedures will make the evaluation as objective and reliable as possible.

ISSUES IN THE DEVELOPMENT OF INTEREST, ATTITUDE, AND TEMPERAMENT MEASURES

This section addresses questionnaire and inventory procedures for assessing interest, attitude, and temperament. Though a moderate amount of effort has been directed toward devising performance measures of one sort or another to serve as indicators of personality characteristics, we will not consider them here. The prototype of the item that we will be concerned with reads somewhat as follows:

Yes No   You sometimes feel you have to get away from other people.
True ? False   You feel you would enjoy the job of forest ranger.
Strongly Agree Undecided Disagree Strongly Women should get the
agree   disagree same pay as men for
                                                 the same job.

Typically, one starts with one or more constructs that one aspires to measure — constructs such as "sociability," "ascendance," "emotional maturity," "mechanical interest," or "attitude toward abortion." The construct or constructs may arise from one's general exposure to psychology and human behavior or, more formally, from correlational or factor-analytic studies that have suggested personality dimensions for more refined study. The statements that become items grow from one's reading about the construct and from one's analysis of the elements and behaviors that might serve to indicate or represent it. The types of statistical analyses to be considered in Chapter 4 can serve to refine and select from the array of items originally proposed.

The usual goal in preparing personality test items is that they be clear and unambiguous in the message that they convey to the reader. One does not want syntactic complexity or semantic obscurity to blur the communication. So a few standard practices should help to promote clarity.

1. Limit each statement to a single idea. Avoid complex or double-barreled statements. *Example* (of a poor item): "Human life is sacred, but no woman should have to bear an unwanted child." (as a statement of attitude on abortion)

2. Use the simplest language that will accurately express the desired idea.

3. Avoid negative statements, where possible, especially when the statement and response could combine to form a double negative. *Example* (of a poor item): "I do not like to talk to strangers. Yes *No*"

4. Be sure each statement represents a statement of feeling, attitude, or belief, not a statement of fact. *Example* (of a poor item): "More and more women are entering professional careers." (as a statement of attitude on equality for women)

5. Be sparing in the use of vague modifiers representing degree or amount. "Often," "occasionally," "somewhat," "strongly," and the like can be interpreted differently by different readers. "About once a week," "every day," and "less than once a month" are more uniform in significance and preferable if they are appropriate.

There are two key differences between ability measures and personality measures. In the first place, though ability is typically thought of as extending in a single direction from "little or none of" to "much of" the ability, most personality dimensions are conceived of as *bipolar*. Thus we think of an opposite to "sociable," which we may label "solitary." We conceive not simply of an absence of liking for "working with numbers" but of an active dislike for computation. Attitudes on abortion range from the most affirmative feeling that abortion should be available to *any* pregnant woman who wishes it to the most negative view that abortion is *never* acceptable under any circumstances. The point of neutrality lies somewhere in the middle. Hence items to be used to appraise likes, attitudes, and personal attributes must provide for the negative limb of the bipolar dimension as well as the positive, and scoring must provide for a score range falling below the neutral or indifference point.

This leads to the possibility that items may fail to show a monotonically increasing relationship to standing on the bipolar trait. For example, to the intermediate statement "Once or twice a week I have trouble getting to sleep," we may get a "No" response both from the person who almost never has trouble going to sleep and from the person who has chronic and frequent difficulty. To the item "Abortion should be permitted only if the health of the mother is endangered" we may get a "No" response both from those who believe abortion is *never* permissible and from those who think that the stated limitation is much too severe. Items should be selected and edited to try to minimize this ambiguity in the meaning of a response, but it is probably not possible to eliminate it completely.

The second main difference between ability and personality measures is in the response set that is desired in the respondent. On an ability test we want the examinee to give the *best* response of which he or she is capable. On a personality test we want a frank and *truthful* response, indicating what is *typical* of the respondent's feeling or behavior. We may not get such a response because the respondent (1) does not choose to give it, (2) does not have enough self-insight to give it, or (3) does not comprehend the question that is being asked.

We have already given some suggestions for reducing the third source of deficient response. Turning to the first, we must try to make respondents understand that it is in their best interest to respond accurately (or, at least, that it will not be contrary to their best interest). This requirement suggests that there are quite severe limitations on the contexts in which self-report personality instruments are useful. In particular, they are *not* likely to be useful or acceptable in admissions testing or in other contexts in which "whatever you say may be used in evidence against you." The conditions should be such that accurate and truthful responding will be to the examinee's advantage, and the instructions must convince the examinee that this is the case.

There is not a great deal that can be done about an examinee's lack of self-insight. However, some procedures for generating a scoring key do not imply self-insight by the examinee. This is when the key is developed purely on an empirical basis, with no requirement that the response be accurately self-descriptive or even truthful. Empirical keying takes place when scoring a response depends on the effectiveness of that response in identifying some criterion group. The procedure has been most commonly used in establishing the scoring keys for interest inventories. Here the usual procedure has been to select some criterion group (perhaps life insurance salespersons who have persisted in the occupation for at least five years) and to compare it to some suitable reference group (perhaps a representative sample of persons in white-collar occupations). If the life insurance agents give a positive response significantly more often than the reference group to the statement "I enjoy classical music," this response gets a positive weight in the key for life insurance salespersons—whether the responses are accurate representations of the truth or not. In this case we may feel that it is unnecessary to worry too much about the insightfulness or even the truthfulness of Mary Dee's response to this item. If she endorses it, for whatever reason, she is behaving like an insurance salesperson.

The point is that there are two different perspectives on the responses to an inventory item. One is to think of the responses as generally truthful and accurate expressions of the examinee's feelings, to be accepted at face value. Then truthfulness and insight become quite important, and everything possible should be done to achieve them. The other is to think of the response as a bit of behavior the significance of which must be determined empirically from its correlates. It then becomes important that the testing conditions that elicit that behavior be uniform from one examinee to another. But it is not so crucial that the response be an accurate description of the examinee—only that it be a useful sign.

The discussion of item-writing techniques in this chapter has been quite condensed. For a more detailed exposition of specific considerations in writing achievement test items, interested readers may refer to Wesman (1971) or to Thorndike and Hagen (1977). A more extended discussion of preparing performance tests is provided by Fitzpatrick and Morrison (1971).

Chapter 4

Item Selection

The building blocks for a test are the single items of which it is composed. In this chapter we shall consider the procedures used to get information about test items, the bases on which a set of items may be selected so as to compose the most suitable test for a given purpose, and the relationship of item parameters to the resulting test parameters. Most of the presentation is oriented toward tests intended to estimate the examinee's position on a latent attribute. The role of tryout and item statistics in a domain sampling test is considered on pages 93–96.

PROCEDURES FOR GETTING INFORMATION ABOUT TEST ITEMS

For this presentation, we assume that a pool of items has already been assembled for tryout. Construction of the items in the pool will have been guided by the test plan, the designing of which was considered in Chapter 2. A surplus of items will have been prepared so that a choice may be made of the better items.

There is no universal prescription for the percentage of surplus items to be prepared for a test-construction project. The surplus required depends on too many variables. A plausible minimum might be 50%. Conditions that would call for a larger surplus include the following:

1. The type of item is difficult to prepare, and past experience has shown that a good many items tend to be ambiguous or nondiscriminating.

2. The items are in subsets (such as a set of items on a reading passage) and, accordingly, enough satisfactory items are required in *each* set if the set is to be usable.

3. The test must match a detailed content outline, so satisfactory items are needed for each of the content areas.

4. The test maker wishes to maintain precise control of item difficulty, to match the difficulty of an existing test, or to control the information provided at specified levels on the scale of the latent attribute.

TRYOUT PROCEDURES

We assume now that an adequate pool of items has been prepared and that we are ready to try them out. We shall consider two levels of tryout. The first, which we might call a pre-tryout, is needed primarily when one is developing novel test materials of a sort with which one has had no background of experience. With such materials, it is often a good idea to run an informal tryout on a small scale. This helps to assure that the test instructions are clear to examinees and provides feedback on any difficulties they may be experiencing. It also provides a rough estimate of rate of work and helps the test maker set preliminary time limits. For tryout at this stage, numbers can be quite modest—20 or 30 examinees, ideally tested individually or in quite small groups so that they can be observed closely and so that the examiner has a chance to interact with them. It is important to make sure that some of the examinees are of the age or ability level at which difficulty in taking the test is *most* likely (the youngest and least capable who will be called on to take the test) so that any general problems they encounter in taking the test will be exposed.

The main tryout is for the purpose of estimating item parameters. Ideally, groups for the main tryout should (1) constitute a representative sample of those with whom the test will subsequently be used and (2) be large enough to yield stable estimates of the item parameters.

An illustration of very nearly ideal item-tryout procedures is found in those procedures that have been used by the Educational Testing Service in trying out new items for use in later forms of the Scholastic Aptitude Test of the College Entrance Examination Board. In each administration of the SAT, one separately timed section, not identified as such to the examinees, has been used for various developmental aspects of the examination. There have been a number of different forms of this experimental section, so that different examinees in a given testing location take different sets of items. At the same time, each set will have been tried out with a nationwide representative sample—usually several thousand of the SAT population. Because examinees do not know which is the research section, their motivation remains the same as for the operational test. Finally, score on the operational test is available, and the experimental materials can be evaluated against it.

Most test makers cannot achieve such ideal try-out conditions, but the illustration defines the objectives for which they should strive: (1) large and representative samples, (2) tested under realistic conditions of motivation, (3) with an appropriate and accurate measure of the attribute being measured, against which the new items can be evaluated.

Sample Size and Test Item Parameters

The usual test developer does not have access to populations of the size of those that take the SATs and may not have "captive" populations of any size. It is usually necessary to depend on the good will of colleagues, school ad-

Table 4.1   Amount by Which Sample Percents Correct Will Deviate from Population Percent Correct Half of the Time

	PERCENT CORRECT AND INCORRECT		
Sample Size	50–50	75–25	90–10
25	6.7	5.9	4.0
100	3.4	3.0	2.0
200	2.4	2.1	1.4
400	1.7	1.4	1.0
1000	1.1	0.9	0.6

ministrators, personnel officers, or others who have access to the desired types of examinees in order to get groups to test. This being so, what size group should be considered adequate for the main tryout of a set of items? Alas, there is really no answer except that, the larger the sample, other things being equal, the better. We can, however, look at the precision that will result from samples of different sizes and relate this to the types of decisions about the items that we will be called on to make.

The test maker needs to estimate two parameters of each test item, a parameter expressing the item's difficulty level and one expressing its ability to differentiate levels of the attribute in question.* In the past, the conventional estimator of difficulty has been the percentage of the group getting the item right. Precision of an estimate of difficulty can then be expressed by the standard error of a percentage, for which the standard formula is

$$\text{S.E.}_\% = \sqrt{\frac{p \cdot q}{N}}$$

A small table applying this formula will give an impression of the precision that results from representative samples of different sizes. Table 4.1 shows the size deviation of sample values from the population value that can be expected to occur 50% of the time (50% of the area of a normal curve lies within ±.6745 times the standard error). A difference 3 times as large as those shown could be expected about 5% of the time.

For routine test-making, one is ordinarily satisfied if the sample values for the difficulty of single items fall within 5 to 10 percentage points of their value in the population. This suggests that a representative sample of 200, or possibly even 100, will be large enough so far as estimation of difficulty is concerned.

---

* A third parameter, the asymptote percent of success at very low ability levels, is also sometimes estimated.

Table **4.2**   Fifty Percent Confidence Interval for Selected Values of Sample Size and Sample Biserial Correlation

Sample Size	BISERIAL CORRELATIONS FROM SAMPLE			
	.00	.40	.60	.80
25	− .17 to .17	.25 to .54	.47 to .71	.71 to .87
100	− .08 to .08	.32 to .47	.54 to .66	.76 to .84
200	− .06 to .06	.35 to .45	.56 to .64	.77 to .83
400	− .04 to .04	.36 to .44	.57 to .63	.78 to .82
1000	− .03 to .03	.38 to .42	.58 to .62	.79 to .81

Based on H. M. Walker and J. Lev, *Statistical Inference* (New York: Holt, Rinehart and Winston, 1953), pp. 269–270. Used by permission.

A similar analysis can be applied to item discrimination indices. The index of item discrimination that has been most commonly used is the correlation between success on the item and total score on some measure that is accepted as representing the attribute. (The alternative correlation indices will be discussed later in this chapter.) For purposes of the present discussion, let us assume that we are using the biserial correlation coefficient. This treats the item as though it, like the total score with which it is being correlated, arranged people in order on a continuous variable. All who fall above a critical level are recorded as "pass" and all who fall below that level are recorded as "fail." The biserial can be thought of as an estimator of the product-moment correlation between two continuous variables, each having a normal distribution.

There is no simple formula that is appropriate for the standard error of a biserial correlation, but the range of variation under specified conditions can be estimated.* Table 4.2 shows the 50% confidence interval (i.e., the range within which there is a 50-50 chance that the population value lies) for selected sample sizes and values of the sample correlation coefficient. Again, the range that would represent the 95% confidence interval is roughly 3 times as great as that shown in the table. A practical interpretation of this table must consider (1) the range of discrimination indices that is typically encountered in practice and (2) the size difference that represents the difference between an item that would be considered marginal (just barely acceptable) and one that would be considered

---

* See H. M. Walker and J. Lev, *Statistical Inference* (New York: Holt, Rinehart and Winston, 1953), pp. 269–270 for the estimation procedure, but note an error in Step 5 on p. 270. The multiplier should be 1.118, not .8944. This procedure is, strictly speaking, appropriate only when close to 50% pass the item.

Table 4.3   Biserial Correlations Obtained within Grade Groups from Tryout of Three Kinds of Test Items

| | NUMBER OF ITEMS | | |
Biserial Correlation	Vocabulary Test	Quantitative Relations Test	Figure Analogies Test
.90 +	6		16
.80-.89	5	6	10
.70-.79	5	14	20
.60-.69	20	22	24
.50-.59	23	27	24
.40-.49	34	14	13
.30-.39	28	10	12
.20-.29	20	6	3
.10-.19	12	5	
.00-.09	4	1	1
Negative	2	1	
p_{75}	.56	.67	.76
Median	.44	.55	.64
p_{25}	.30	.43	.50
Number of items	159	106	123

thoroughly satisfactory. There can be no pair of values that would be universally applicable here, because the values that are typically obtained depend on both the type of test exercise and the type of group. However, two or three illustrations can be given. The three frequency distributions shown in Table 4.3 illustrate the range of correlation values that were obtained from items of the indicated types tried out in grade groups from grades 4 through 12. The correlations are in most instances based on samples of 200 to 250.

Comparing Table 4.2 with Table 4.3, one might conclude that even a fairly modest sample (say 100 to 200) would be large enough to identify dependably most of the really weak items. If one had decided to include in each final test only those items with biserials at or above the median value for the set, samples of this size would only occasionally lead one to accept an item that really belonged in the bottom quarter. However, sizable differences between sample and population value would still occur occasionally with samples as large as 200. If one were seriously concerned with maximizing the precision of a test, substantially larger samples would certainly be desirable.

Nonrepresentative Samples

All our discussion up to this point has been concerned with random sampling variations, based on the assumption that the cases in the sample *are* randomly drawn from the population they are intended to represent. A much more serious, and unfortunately rather common, problem is that the sample may be nonrepresentative and biased. When, as is often the case, the test maker must make do with "chunks" of cases tested in a few locations where cooperation can be obtained, it is highly likely that the "chunks" may not be truly representative of the total population for which the test is designed and with which it will be used. What can be done to permit the test maker first to identify and then to adjust for such nonrepresentativeness?

The best procedure would seem to be to administer to the tryout sample an existing test, or items from an existing test, for which data have previously been obtained from a group known to be representative of the population. The test scores or item statistics for the already calibrated test or items can be used to guide adjustments to the statistics for the new items, as discussed on pp. 66–70. Due to their greater precision, a set of test scores is to be preferred as anchoring information, but such a set of scores may not be available for the tryout sample, and time may not permit giving an existing test when the new items are tried out. However, it is often practical to include a few items with known parameters among the new items that are being tried out and to use them as the basis for an adjustment of the item parameter estimates for the new items. The anchor items for such a project should be items with satisfactory discrimination indices and should cover a wide range of difficulty, so that adjustments can be made to the item parameters of new items throughout the difficulty range.

There has been a good deal of discussion in recent years of so-called sample-free item statistics. The procedures that have been developed are really procedures for calibrating item difficulty by using a reference set of items that serves to anchor any new items to an established scale of the latent attribute. The simplest of these procedures is the Rasch model, which assumes that the items in a set differ only in difficulty (represented in Chapter 1 as the b parameter). The item characteristic curves for all items are assumed to have the same steepness (the a parameter), and to approach an asymptote of 0% correct at very low levels of the latent attribute. Procedures for applying this model to scaling items and to attaching them to an existing scale for the latent attribute are considered on pages 96–105.

CONVENTIONAL ITEM STATISTICS

Ideally, we would like to determine for each test item the parameters that relate its item characteristic curve (that is, the curve showing the probability of success on a pass–fail item or the mean score on a test exercise with a scale of scores) to the scale of the underlying latent attribute. Unfortunately, we never have a direct measure of the latent attribute that permits us to determine each examinee's true position on that latent attribute at the time she or he responds to a set of test items. At best we have some type of test score that is a fallible measure and has a relationship to the latent attribute that is imperfect and usually nonlinear. Thus the observable statistics for an item are only approximations to the ideal. We need to be concerned, in the case of each item, chiefly with two parameters:

A "steepness" parameter, which we have designated a_g, that indicates how rapidly the probability of success rises as one moves up the scale of the latent attribute.

A position parameter, b_g, that locates the difficulty of the item in relation to the scale of the latent attribute.

Recent developments in test theory attempt to estimate these parameters in such a way that the estimates will be sample-free and will not depend on the characteristics of the group within which the estimate was made. We shall examine these procedures presently. However, the original data on items *are* obtained on a specific sample of cases and the basic statistics from which more elegant estimates of parameters may be made, given the assumptions of the model on which the estimation procedures are based, come from that specific sample. For a good deal of practical work in test construction, direct use of the sample statistics may prove quite serviceable. Therefore, we shall first consider the more venerable and conventional item statistics. More recent developments will be considered later in the chapter. Attention will be directed first to estimates of item difficulty and then to estimates of the item's effectiveness in differentiating between more and less capable individuals.*

Estimates of Item Difficulty

Difficulty (or the reverse, facility, as it is somewhat more logically designated in England) has usually been represented by the percentage of examinees getting the item right. The raw percentage suffices for rough and ready work, but it is a somewhat crude and unsatisfactory estimator for several reasons, partly psychological and partly statistical.

1. The mere fact of failure tells us nothing about the reason for failure, so we do not know whether an item that is frequently answered wrong is conceptually difficult or merely unfamiliar. Relatively few people could define the word *wom-*

---

* The language of *difficulty* and *discrimination* that is used here is specifically applicable to ability tests. The type of analysis, however, is more broadly applicable. Applying such analysis to measures of interest, temperament, or attitude requires a simple translation. The p-value that has been an index of *difficulty* of a task now becomes an index of the *popularity* of a response option — that is, the proportion who chose it. The discrimination index does not separate the more from the less *capable*, but rather the higher from the lower on a specific trait of interest, temperament, or attitude.

bat, but the definition is no more difficult than that for *kangaroo* — another Australian mammal. By contrast, the word *reciprocal* is relatively familiar, but framing a precise definition remains difficult.

2. Raw percent correct takes no account of guessing. With selective response items, it may be anticipated that some fraction of the correct answers occurred as the result of a lucky guess. The problem is to estimate what percent.

3. The scale based on percent correct can hardly be thought of as a scale of equal units of difficulty. The item characteristic function, to which we were introduced in Chapter 1, is typically much steeper in its middle range, so that here a considerable change in the percent passing moves one only a small distance up or down on the scale of the basic attribute. By contrast, as the percentage comes close to 100 or to a chance level, the same percentage change represents a very substantial shift on the scale of that basic attribute. For many uses of item data, a unit to express difficulty level is needed that corresponds to equal amounts on the basic dimension that the items in the pool were designed to measure.

The first problem, that of judging the *source of difficulty* in an item, is essentially just that — an exercise in judgment. With some types of materials (for example, arithmetical problems), it may be possible to refine judgment by systematically varying one and then another aspect of the problem and seeing what this does to difficulty. More often, however, preparing items in which difficulty arises from the desired aspect of the task is an art — one major component of item-writing skill. Some of the guidelines for item writing are directed specifically at avoiding unwanted sources of difficulty arising from unfamiliar vocabulary or complex wording of the problem.

How to deal with *guessing* has been a problem ever since selected response item formats began to be used in the first quarter of this century. The problem arises in relation to directions to the examinee. To what extent should the instructions encourage guessing when the examinee does not know or is not sure of the answer? The problem is next encountered in choosing a scoring formula. Should an examinee's score be simply the number right, or should it incorporate some penalty for items presumed to have been gotten right by guessing? The problem finally rears up again as one plans for an index of item difficulty. Should one use a corrected *P*-value and, if so, what correction should be applied?

If one could assume that each person knew (or worked out) the answer to a question, left it blank, or guessed entirely at random, the problem would not be too messy. Unfortunately this is not a realistic view of test-taking behavior. Examinees may have partial information that enables them to exclude one or more options, they may have misinformation or use mistaken procedures that lead them to a wrong answer with complete conviction that it is correct, or they may have a feeling falling far short of certainty that a particular answer is probably correct. Thus no simple mathematical model really reproduces people's test-taking behavior, and any attempt to deal with guessing at the level of either test scoring or item analysis is at best an approximation.

As indicated above, we must address the issue of guessing at three levels, which are to some extent interdependent. These are (1) the instructions given the examinee, (2) the formula used for scoring the test, and (3) the formula used to estimate P, the percentage of examinees knowing the answer to the question. Let us focus on each in turn.

The appropriate and honest instruction to give the examinees depends on what scoring procedure is being used. If the score being used is simply the number of correct answers, examinees should be told that this is the case and that they will penalize themselves if they fail to answer *every* question. They should be encouraged to guess even if it is a completely blind guess. With this scoring procedure, any examinee who omits items incurs an automatic penalty. Examinees differ substantially in their willingness to guess, so instructions should attempt to overcome any such reluctance.

Unfortunately, blind guessing introduces error variance and reduces test reliability. Furthermore, a fair number of educators consider the encouragement of sheer guessing on examinations to be educationally (and perhaps even morally) unsound. These reasons offer good justification for trying to develop a scoring procedure, and a corresponding set of instructions, that will eliminate any gain from blind guessing and will put examinees with different propensities for guessing on an equal footing. The usual scoring procedure has been to use a formula score that distinguishes between wrong answers and omissions and takes the form

$$\text{Score} = \text{rights} - \frac{\text{wrongs}}{n - 1} \qquad (4.1)$$

where n is the number of choices in each item. (As applied to a single item, the formula becomes $P_{\text{corrected}} = P_{\text{right}} - P_{\text{wrong}}/(n - 1)$.)

This formula makes the very simple assumption that each person either knows the answer to a question or guesses entirely at random. If a person guesses on G items, each of which presents n choices, that person will on the average get G/n right and $(n - 1)G/n$ wrong. The ratio of rights to wrongs is $1/(n - 1)$. On that basis, with W wrongs it is estimated that $W/(n - 1)$ were gotten right by guessing, and this amount is subtracted from the score as a correction. Assuming blind guessing among *all* of the options, this formula will, on average, provide that there will be no advantage either to the person who guesses frequently or to the person who guesses sparingly or not at all. Of course, if a person has partial information that permits elimination of one or more of the wrong options, the probability of picking the correct answer is increased, and the person who systematically answers all such items will, in general, get an increase in score.

It may be of interest to see how this increase would operate. Consider a 100-item test made up of 5-choice items and assume that, uniformly over all items, one group of examinees can exclude no options, another group can exclude one option, another two options, and so on. The average scores that would result for the several groups are shown below.

WRONG OPTIONS EXCLUDED	AVERAGE NUMBER RIGHT	AVERAGE NUMBER WRONG	AVERAGE SCORE, $R - \dfrac{W}{n-1}$
0	20	80	0
1	25	75	$6\frac{1}{4}$
2	$33\frac{1}{3}$	$66\frac{2}{3}$	$16\frac{2}{3}$
3	50	50	$37\frac{1}{2}$
4	100	0	100

It is easy to see that the successive eliminations of options are not of equal value so far as score is concerned. Each additional choice that is eliminated becomes progressively more valuable, and being able to make the final crucial choice and focus on the *one* right answer is by far the most highly weighted. Such an operational valuing of degrees of knowledge is quite arbitrary, but it has a certain plausibility.

The foregoing table demonstrates that, with the standard correction formula, it *is* to the examinee's advantage to guess whenever it seems possible to rule out one or more of the answer choices, and the instructions to examinees should make this clear. Studies have shown that, with the correction formula, examinees tend to omit items more than is to their best advantage, so instructions should encourage them to mark an answer whenever they can confidently exclude even one of the answer choices.

The model that we have just been considering assumes that all of the answer choices are equally plausible and equally likely to be chosen by a person who does not *know* the correct answer. This is rarely the case. For example, an analysis of one set of verbal analogy items from a published test showed that the most popular mislead was, on the average, chosen by 19.8% of the examinees, the second in popularity by 11.5%, the third by 7.2%, and the least popular by 3.6%. On the average, the most popular was chosen more than 5 times as often as the least popular. In short, those examinees who got an item wrong were *not* guessing at random. Certain misleads were clearly less attractive, or easier to rule out, than others. What are the implications of this for test scoring and for estimating the percentage of examinees who *know* the answer to an item?

For scoring, this hierarchy of popularity provides a kind of rationale for the accelerated increase in expected score (as shown in the table above) as the examinee eliminates more and more possibilities. One could argue that it is proper that a person get a bigger bonus for eliminating some of the more seductive choices than for eliminating the less generally appealing. However, this assumes that options are eliminated in order of their popularity—that only the least able examinees are tripped up by the unpopular options—and that it is the somewhat more capable who rule out these least appealing choices but fall victim to the more attractive options. There is little evidence that this is generally the case. Scrutiny of the total scores of those who mark the least popular error options and of those who mark the most popular indicates that the two groups differ little, if at all.* Thus there is little support for the notion that error choices can be arranged in a hierarchy, with some one option being consistently ruled out first and some other being the last to be excluded, as was suggested by Horst (1933) in an alternative model for estimating the percentage of examinees who *know* the answer to an item. Thus, for all its limitations, the conventional model as set out in formula 3.1 seems to be the most reasonable one to work with. However, it is important to realize that its assumptions are *not* fully met and that it provides at best a fairly rough adjustment in our attempt to estimate the percentage of examinees who really know the answer to a given test item.

In spite of the good case that can be made for using a formula score—both in fairness to examinees with differing propensities to guess and in improved reliability due to reduction of error variance introduced by relatively random guessing—there are a number of published tests in which a simple number-correct score is used. The reasons for this are primarily practical rather than theoretical. In the first place, when scoring is done manually by clerks, formula scoring *is* more complex and clerical errors *are* more likely to occur. This consideration can assume some importance when teachers do the scoring and calculating on test papers or when this task is turned over to clerical personnel. However, this argument loses weight when scoring is done on a scoring machine or with an optical scanner and computer.

There is also the contention that it is difficult to explain to examinees why a "penalty" is applied to their score and they are given a score lower than the number that they got right. This might be of some importance when raw scores are reported to examinees. It ceases to have significance when, as is typical with standardized tests, all discussions with examinees or their families are based on converted scores of the types to be discussed in Chapter 5.

In general, except when practical concerns are quite compelling, it would seem best to use the score based on formula 4.1.

If a correction for guessing is used in scoring the test, the correction formula should also be used in estimating the percentage of examinees who "know" the

---

*In one item type, the median biserial correlations for the most and least frequently chosen misleads were −.30 and −.34, respectively, and for another item type −.40 and −.46.

answer to the question. Four categories of behavior with respect to an item need to be differentiated:

R = items attempted and gotten right
W = items attempted but gotten wrong
O = items the examinee considered but elected not to answer
NR = items not reached because of limited time

Item tryouts should be designed in such a way as to hold this fourth category to a minimum. When any substantial fraction of the examinees does not have time to attempt an item, data on that item become meager and also biased by elimination of the slower workers. It is usually assumed that any unanswered items occurring earlier in the test than the last item attempted are omits and that any subsequent to the last item attempted were not reached.

On the basis of these four categories, the formula for estimating the percent "knowing" the answer to the item is

$$P_c = \frac{R - W/(n - 1)}{R + W + O}$$

It must be admitted that using such corrected values is statistically messy and occasionally gets one into anomalous situations. This occurs especially when some mislead is especially attractive and draws a high proportion of examinee choices. Then the proportion of correct answers may fall below the theoretical chance level, and by literal interpretation yields the absurdity that the proportion "knowing the answer" is less than 0. Much of the statistical analysis of test items that we shall consider in the following pages is based on the simple dichotomy of "right" and "wrong" responses, without any attempt to differentiate between "true right answers" and "lucky guesses."

If percent knowing the answer to an item as a function of position on the scale of the latent attribute that the item is designed to measure follows the usual item characteristic function (see page 7), then item difficulty is *not a linear function* of that percent. Small percentage differences near 50 correspond to only small differences in level on the latent attribute, because the item characteristic function is ascending relatively steeply in this range. The same percentage difference near 0 or 100 corresponds to a much greater shift on the underlying scale. Therefore, if one wishes to express difficulty on an equal-unit scale, it is necessary to transform the obtained *P*-values.

A case can be made for each of two different transformations that have quite distinct meanings. On the one hand, we can ask: How difficult is this item, for whatever reasons? On the other, we can ask: Where shall we locate this item on the scale of the specified latent attribute; that is, what is its *b* parameter? The most plausible procedure for answering the first question is simply to use tables of the normal curve and convert the percent correct into a normal deviate. By way of illustration,

PERCENT CORRECT	NORMAL DEVIATE	T-SCORE
95	$+1.64$	66
38	-0.31	47
17	-0.95	40

If a correction for guessing is being used, the percent correct should be the value adjusted by formula 4.1.

Suppose, however, that we wish to estimate for each item the parameter, b_g, that expresses its difficulty *as a measure of the latent attribute* that the set of items is presumed to measure. Then we need to attend not only to the percent getting the item right but also to the steepness of the item characteristic curve—that is, to the parameter a_g. As stated in Chapter 1, for normally distributed traits this steepness parameter is related to the biserial correlation of the item with a score that serves as an indicator of the attribute by the formula

$$a_g = \frac{r_{\text{bis}_g}}{\sqrt{1 - r_{\text{bis}_g}^2}}$$

Unfortunately, there is no formula that provides a simple and appropriate procedure for estimating the difficulty parameter, b_g, from just the proportion correct and the biserial correlation. However, if we are willing to assume that r_{bis} represents the correlation of the item with the underlying latent attribute and that the attribute has a normal distribution in the population with which we are dealing, it is possible to develop one or more tables that estimate b_g from P, the proportion of correct responses, and r, the biserial correlation.* One such table for 5-choice multiple-choice items is shown as Table 4.4.

Table 4.4 seems almost paradoxical, in that more extreme positions on the scale of the latent attribute tend to be assigned to items with low correlations with that attribute. But remember that we are trying to estimate the location of the point of inflection of the item characteristic function. Where r_{bis} is low, the function is relatively flat, and it will take a longer distance on the scale of the latent attribute to move from, for example, 80% correct responses to 50%.

It is also true that, with a flat item characteristic curve, the point at which that curve crosses any specific percentage of correct responses is determined with

---

* The tables are prepared by taking selected values of $(b_g - \theta)$ and r_{bis}; calculating at a number of discrete scale points the product of P, the proportion correct at that value of $(b_g - \theta)$, times the proportion of cases in a slice of the normal curve at that point; and summing over the complete score range. This gives the overall proportion correct corresponding to different values of $(b_g - \theta)$ and r_{bis}. With these entries, we can reverse the process and interpolate a set of values of $(b_g - \theta)$, working from P_g and r_{bis_g}.

Table 4.4   Estimates of Difficulty Parameter, b_g, Assuming Normal Distribution of the Attribute (5-choice items)

RAW PERCENT CORRECT	BISERIAL CORRELATION					
	.35	.40	.45	.50	.55	.60
98	−5.60	−4.85	−4.51	−4.10	−3.73	−3.42
95	−4.40	−3.79	−3.51	−3.16	−2.87	−2.64
90	−3.40	−2.85	−2.60	−2.34	−2.12	−1.94
85	−2.56	−2.15	−1.98	−1.79	−1.61	−1.48
80	−1.91	−1.66	−1.50	−1.35	−1.22	−1.12
75	−1.37	−1.23	−1.08	−0.97	−0.88	−0.80
70	−0.89	−0.78	−0.70	−0.63	−0.58	−0.53
65	−0.44	−0.39	−0.34	−0.31	−0.29	−0.26
60	00	00	00	00	00	00
55	0.44	0.39	0.34	0.31	0.29	0.26
50	0.89	0.78	0.70	0.63	0.58	0.53
45	1.37	1.23	1.08	0.97	0.88	0.80
40	1.91	1.66	1.50	1.35	1.22	1.12
35	2.56	2.15	1.98	1.79	1.61	1.48
30	3.40	2.85	2.60	2.34	2.12	1.94
25	4.40	3.79	3.51	3.16	2.87	2.64
22	5.60	4.85	4.51	4.10	3.73	3.42

relatively low precision. As a practical guide, perhaps the important message in Table 4.4 is to reinforce the practice of excluding from a final test those items with low biserials. They are not only poor measures of the latent attribute, but are also items whose difficulty *so far as that attribute is concerned* is known only to a rough approximation.

Estimating Item Difficulty in a Different Group

If a common set of test exercises has been administered to two different groups, the sets of scale values for the two groups can be used to estimate the difference between the two groups in average ability level on the latent attribute and in dispersion of ability. That difference can then be used to adjust difficulty estimates based on group A and to express them on the scale of group B. This can be done for those items that have been administered only to group A, and in this way new items tried out on new groups can all be expressed on a common scale. All that is necessary is a core of "bridging" items that have been given to both the reference group and the new group. The procedures are illustrated below, using as a bridge 14 items all of which had biserial correlations of 0.40 or

		BISERIAL CORRELATION				PERCENT CORRECT BY FORMULA
.65	.70	.75	.80	.85	.90	
−3.17	−2.93	−2.72	−2.54	−2.38	−2.26	.975
−2.42	−2.25	−2.10	−2.00	−1.87	−1.76	.9375
−1.80	−1.67	−1.56	−1.48	−1.40	−1.32	.875
−1.38	−1.28	−1.19	−1.13	−1.08	−1.02	.8125
−1.04	−0.97	−0.91	−0.86	−0.81	−0.76	.75
−0.75	−0.71	−0.66	−0.62	−0.59	−0.56	.6875
−0.49	−0.46	−0.43	−0.40	−0.38	−0.36	.625
−0.24	−0.23	−0.21	−0.20	−0.19	−0.18	.5625
00	00	00	00	00	00	.50
0.24	0.23	0.21	0.20	0.19	0.18	.4375
0.49	0.46	0.43	0.40	0.38	0.36	.375
0.75	0.71	0.66	0.62	0.59	0.56	.3125
1.04	0.97	0.91	0.86	0.81	0.76	.25
1.38	1.28	1.19	1.13	1.08	1.02	.1875
1.80	1.67	1.56	1.48	1.40	1.32	.125
2.42	2.25	2.10	2.00	1.87	1.76	.0625
3.17	2.93	2.72	2.54	2.38	2.26	.025

above in both groups. The test in question was a test of verbal analogies, and the two groups were, respectively, groups of sixth- and eighth-grade pupils.

The first column on the left in Table 4.5 gives identifying item numbers. The second and third columns give the percentage of examinees choosing the keyed correct answer for the sixth- and eighth-grade groups, respectively. The fourth and fifth columns give the biserial correlations of this correct response with total score on the set of 55 tryout items. The biserial correlation provides an estimate of the correlation of the item with the underlying latent attribute. The sixth and seventh columns show scale values obtained by interpolation in Table 4.4.

The mean of the scale values for grade 6 is +0.099, indicating that the difficulty of the average item falls slightly higher on the scale than the ability level of the average sixth-grade pupil. For grade 8 the mean is −0.406, indicating that the average item falls about two-fifths of a scale unit below the ability level of the average eighth-grade pupil in that tryout sample. The standard deviation of item scale values is 0.668 in grade 6 and 0.596 in grade 8. The lesser dispersion of item-difficulty scale values in relation to the eighth-grade group implies a correspondingly *greater* dispersion of pupil ability in that eighth-grade group.

Table 4.5   Scale Values of a Common Set of Items in Two Grade Groups

ITEM NUMBER	P_g		r_{bis}		SCALE VALUE		GR. 8 CONVERTED TO GR. 6
	Gr. 6	Gr. 8	Gr. 6	Gr. 8	Gr. 6	Gr. 8	
3	66	77	.67	.65	$-.29$	$-.87$	$-.42$
8	70	76	.40	.43	$-.78$	-1.22	$-.81$
14	81	83	.59	.43	-1.21	-1.86	-1.53
19	59	63	.56	.55	.06	$-.17$	.36
20	50	58	.50	.47	.63	.14	.71
21	66	72	.56	.40	$-.34$	$-.96$	$-.52$
32	63	79	.84	.75	$-.11$	$-.86$	$-.41$
33	53	57	.65	.72	.34	.14	.71
39	49	49	.62	.64	.50	.51	1.13
44	28	39	.56	.56	2.38	1.28	1.99
49	64	73	.62	.70	$-.20$	$-.61$	$-.13$
50	49	58	.51	.53	.69	.12	.69
51	57	68	.51	.53	.18	$-.48$	.02
55	70	74	.68	.54	$-.47$	$-.84$	$-.39$
					Mean 0.099	-0.406	
					S.D. 0.668	0.596	

The correlation between the two sets of scale values is found to be .948, indicating an encouragingly high degree of consistency between the relative difficulties of the 14 items in the two samples. However, as we shall see, this still permits appreciable error in estimating the difficulty in one sample from the difficulty obtained in the other.

Given the scale values of the 14 items expressed as deviations from the mean ability level of each group separately, we can calculate the means and standard deviations of the scale values for each of the groups, as shown at the bottom of Table 4.5. Then, because the difficulty parameter of any one test item in relation to the scale of the latent attribute is assumed to be invariant over groups (it is, after all, the same item), the average difficulty parameter for the set of items will also be invariant. Only the arbitrary scale changes as we go from one group to the other. The scales for different groups can differ both in the point designated as the zero point (equal to the mean ability level in the group) and in the size of the scale unit (proportional to the variability of the group). We have, for any pair of groups,

$$\frac{(\bar{b}_A - \bar{\theta}_A)}{S.D._{b_A}} = \frac{(\bar{b}_B - \bar{\theta}_B)}{S.D._{b_B}}$$

where $\quad \bar{\theta}_A$ and $\bar{\theta}_B$ = average ability level in groups A and B

$\qquad \bar{b}_A$ and $\bar{b}_B$ = average scale value of the set of anchor items in groups A and B

$\qquad S.D._{b_A}$ and $S.D._{b_B}$ = standard deviation of item scale values in groups A and B, respectively

Solving for $\bar{\theta}_B$, we get

$$\bar{\theta}_B = \frac{S.D._{b_B}}{S.D._{b_A}} (\bar{\theta}_A - \bar{b}_A) + \bar{b}_B \qquad (4.2)$$

Equation 4.2 gives the distance of the group-B average ability level from the group-A average, expressed in units that reflect the dispersion of ability in group A. We can use essentially the same relationship to convert the scale value of any single item from a scale value determined in group B to the value for that item when the group-A mean ability level defines the zero point of the scale and the group-A dispersion determines the size of the scale units. The equation becomes

$$b_g(A) = \frac{S.D._{b_A}}{S.D._{b_B}} (b_g(B) - \bar{b}_B) + \bar{b}_A \qquad (4.3)$$

In this way, a core of common items can be used to provide a transformation through which any new items, tried out on a new group, can be expressed on the uniform scale based on a selected reference group that has been chosen to provide the universal yardstick.

An estimate of the precision of the equating can be obtained by calculating the scale value based on the application of the equating formula, 4.3, to each of the items in turn. This has been done for each of the 14 items in the illustrative example, and the resulting values are shown in the last column of Table 4.5. The discrepancy between the observed scale value in grade 6 and the estimated grade-6 equivalent based on the scale values obtained in grade 8 can be determined for each item, and the standard deviation of these discrepancy values can be computed. (Except for rounding, the mean discrepancy must be zero.) In this instance, the standard deviation of the 14 discrepancy values is 0.275 scale units and, by the usual formula, the standard error of the mean is $S.D./\sqrt{n-1}$ or $0.275/\sqrt{13} = 0.076$ scale units. The precision in estimating the scale difference between groups can be expected to increase approximately as the square root of the number of items used to establish the equating. It will also increase as the size of the samples of persons used in obtaining the item statistics is increased.

The precision of the *sample* values of b_g and a_g as estimates of *population* values depends, of course, on the accuracy of the sample as a representation of the population. The precision of the sample depends on its size, because the standard error of P_g is equal to $\sqrt{(P_g Q_g)/N}$. However, a more critical issue is the sample's representativeness. The design and execution of sampling procedures in such a way as to minimize bias will be considered in some detail in Chapter 5.

To illustrate the transformation from percent right in one group to expected percent in the other, consider the following item, which was tried out in grade 8 but not in grade 6.

afraid : brave : : confused : A. confident B. stupid
C. cheerful D. honest E. forgetful

In grade 8 the percentage of correct answers was 80 and the biserial correlation with total score was .84. From Table 4.4 we estimate a grade-8 scale value for this item of -0.82. Entering the appropriate values in equation 4.3, we have

$$b_6 = \frac{.668}{.596}(-.82 + .406) + .099 = -.365$$

Once one has reasonably good estimates of (1) the mean and dispersion of any age or grade group (or other specialized group) on the scale of the latent attribute and (2) the difficulty and discrimination parameters of an item, expressed in relation to the same scale, one can estimate with reasonable precision the proportion of persons in any of the groups who will get the particular item right. Assuming that the same biserial was obtained in grade 6 as in Grade 8 (.84), we can enter Table 4.4 with that value and a scale value of $-.365$. We find by interpolation an approximate percentage of correct answers for the group in which no data are available. For this item in grade 6, the result is 69%.

Discrimination Indices

The conventional index of item discrimination has been the correlation, either biserial or point biserial, between success or failure on the item* and score on a measure that is considered to represent the latent attribute. The measure may be an already existing test of the latent attribute, as is used in the development of the College Board SATs. More frequently, it is score on a pool of items that are thought collectively to provide a reasonable approximation to that attribute. It *may* even be an independent external criterion of educational or job performance, such as a grade point average or a job proficiency rating. We will consider later in Chapter 7 the circumstances under which such an external criterion measure might be appropriate. Here, we will first present the general rationale and computing formula for biserial and point biserial correlation and then discuss further the considerations that might lead a test maker to prefer one or the other statistic.

---

* Actually, choosing or not choosing a specific response to the item. It is possible to calculate a correlation for each of the wrong answers, but interest usually centers on the correlation for the one that is considered correct.

The *point biserial correlation* is a special case of the general Pearson product-moment correlation. The product-moment correlation can be expressed in this form when one of the variables being correlated is a continuous variable but the other can take only one or the other of two discrete values. Thus, if one assigns the numerals 1 and 0 to pass and fail, respectively, the correlation formula can be expressed in the form

$$r_{\text{pbis}} = \frac{\overline{X}_{pi} - \overline{X}_{fi}}{S_t} \cdot \sqrt{p_i q_i} \qquad (4.4)$$

where r_{pbis} = point biserial correlation

$\overline{X}_{pi}$ and $\overline{X}_{fi}$ = the mean scores on the continuous variable of the passers and failers, respectively, on item i

p_i and q_i = percents of passers and failers on item i

S_t = standard deviation of the total score with which item i is being correlated

The *biserial correlation* is based on the assumption that we are dealing with *two* basically continuous variables, one of which has been divided at some point into a higher and a lower group. The dividing point may be quite arbitrary, but the essential consideration is that each variable is conceived of as basically continuous. When a test item divides a group into passers and failers, the passers are thought to differ from the failers only in having more of whatever the item measures — that is, as having enough to get over the threshold and get the item right. Furthermore, both the dichotomized and the continuous variable are considered to have a normal Gaussian distribution.

When these assumptions are met, the biserial correlation can be expressed in the form

$$r_{\text{bis}} = \frac{\overline{X}_{pi} - \overline{X}_{fi}}{S_t} \cdot \frac{p_i q_i}{y_i} \qquad (4.5)$$

where y_i is the ordinate of the normal curve corresponding to p_i, and the rest of the notation remains the same as for the point biserial.

It is worth noting that there is a systematic relationship between the two coefficients. It is given by the formula

$$r_{\text{bis}} = r_{\text{pbis}} \cdot \frac{\sqrt{p_i q_i}}{y_i} \qquad (4.6)$$

It is always a simple matter to convert from one coefficient to the other. Let us turn now to the theoretical and the practical considerations that argue for one versus the other of these two correlation indices.

Conceptually, the point biserial correlation is clearly appropriate when the dichotomized variable is composed of two groups that are categorically and perhaps qualitatively distinct. Sex used to be such a variable, though modern medical science seems to be making it less clearly so. Nationality and ethnicity have a categorical quality, as does marital status. Being or not being an only child would seem to be an appropriately discrete variable. So would a response stating that one did or did not plan to continue education after high school, or that one did or did not currently have a checking account.

Thinking of passing or not passing a test item as two distinct categories is more debatable. The passers would seem to differ from the failers in *degree* rather than in *kind*. Furthermore, passers could represent all degrees of ability above the critical threshold and failers all degrees below it. Thus it is easy to think of a continuum of the ability i represented by that item, with passers falling above a critical level and failers falling below it. With this view of the matter, a biserial correlation would seem the more appropriate index. However, there are also certain practical issues to consider.

One very real advantage of the point biserial is that it fits directly into the algebra of multivariate analysis. We shall have occasion presently to develop procedures for estimating test parameters — mean, standard deviation, and reliability coefficient — from item parameters, and in all of these estimation formulas it will be necessary to use the point biserial. Thus, for some uses of item statistics, it is the point biserial that is required.

However, this advantage is countered by another characteristic of the point biserial that some test makers consider a serious disadvantage. This is that, when the distribution of scores in the total group is continuous, the range of possible values of the point biserial does not extend from $+1$ to -1, as the product-moment correlation does, but has a curtailed range. If the distribution in the total group is normal, the point biserial can never go beyond ± 0.8. Furthermore, the range of possible values depends on the percents of passers and failers, becoming less as the split becomes more uneven. The limiting values of r_{pbis} for certain values of p (or q) when the total distribution is normal are as follows:

p	MAXIMUM r
.01	.27
.05	.48
.10	.58
.25	.73
.50	.80

The location of the p–q split affects not only the maximum possible value but also, proportionately, all values less than the maximum. This is demonstrated by the relationship between the biserial and the point biserial set out in formula 4.6. Thus, if the correlation in the underlying bivariate normal population is

.50, and hence the corresponding biserial correlation is also .50, the value obtained for the point biserial will be as follows, depending on the point at which the population is split into an upper and a lower group.

p	r_{pbis}
.01	.13
.05	.24
.10	.29
.25	.36
.50	.40

Thus, as an indicator of an item's ability to discriminate levels of the latent attribute, the point biserial is confounded by the factor of item difficulty. In one sense, the lower correlation is a true statement of the item's contribution to the functioning of the test, because a very easy or very difficult item makes relatively few differentiations between more and less capable examinees. However, in evaluating items for a test, it seems more incisive to give separate consideration to the two factors of difficulty and discrimination than to muddy them up in a single index. Remember that, in the equation for estimating the steepness parameter of an item's item characteristic curve, it is the *biserial* correlation that is required. (See Chapter 1, page 8.)

The biserial correlation is not free from problems. As previously noted, it cannot be used in the various formulas that estimate test parameters from item statistics. Furthermore, within a sample of data, the biserial is not limited to the range from -1 to $+1$ but can take values of any size. When the distribution of scores deviates from normal, especially when it is bimodal or badly skewed, it is quite possible to obtain biserials greater than 1.00. This is a disconcerting experience for the test maker whose whole experience with correlational statistics is that such values are impossible. Fortunately, the occurrence of such values *is* limited to rather extreme circumstances, and the biserial correlation is usually quite serviceable as a descriptive statistic. However, these anomalies and the fact that no really good estimate of precision is available for this statistic make it less satisfactory for *analytic work*.

Correcting Estimates for Spuriousness

When a pool of items has been tried out and item statistics are calculated, the item for which statistics are being computed may have been included in the pool that yielded the total score with which the item is being correlated. When this is the case, the obtained correlation is spuriously high. It is easy to see why. In the total score, those who pass item X receive a point of credit for that item, raising their total score by one point, whereas those who fail the item receive zero credit. Thus the difference $\overline{X}_p - \overline{X}_f$ is inflated by one full point over what the difference would have been on the remaining items. (At the same time, the standard deviation of the total score is increased by a fraction of a point.) To obtain an estimate of what the correlation of the item would have been with the measure of the attribute provided by the balance of the pool, excluding item X itself, it is necessary to adjust for this inflation.

One approach, which is no longer impossibly laborious given present computer capability, would be to rescore the test booklets for each item, getting in each case the score based on the remaining items, excluding item X, and to compute the correlation—biserial or point biserial as the case may be—with this residual set. However, this represents a fairly substantial computational burden, and in a good many instances it is more efficient to introduce a correction to the correlations based on the complete item pool. This correction undertakes to adjust the difference in means and the test score standard deviation, removing the influence of item X from each. It estimates the correlation of each item with the common factor (the latent attribute) measured by the whole set of items, freeing it of any specific variance of the item in question. The formulas* are

$$_c r_{\text{bis}} = \sqrt{\frac{n}{n-1}} \cdot \frac{r_{\text{bis}} S_t - \dfrac{p_i q_i}{y_i}}{\sqrt{S_t^2 - \sum_{i=1}^{n} p_i q_i}} \tag{4.7}$$

and

$$_c r_{\text{pbis}} = \sqrt{\frac{n}{n-1}} \cdot \frac{r_{\text{pbis}} S_t - \sqrt{p_i q_i}}{\sqrt{S_t^2 - \sum_{i=1}^{n} p_i q_i}} \tag{4.8}$$

where $_c r_{\text{bis}}$ and $_c r_{\text{pbis}}$ = the corrected correlations
n = number of items

and the other symbols are as defined previously.

The amount of correction for spuriousness is in inverse proportion to n, the number of items entering into the total score with which each item is correlated. When n is large—say 40 or 50—the correction is too small to be of any practical significance. Furthermore, the correction will rarely alter noticeably the *relative* size of the correlations for different items. Thus decisions about which items to

---

* From Sten Henrysson, "Correction of Item-Total Correlations in Item Analysis." *Psychometrika*, 1963, 28, 211–218. Used by permission.

include in the final form of a test are not often likely to be changed as a result of applying the correction. For analytic work using item statistics, however, the corrected values are ordinarily preferable.

Item Statistics Without a Computer

At this stage in technology, most test makers are likely to have access to a computer, and the computation of a long series of biserial or point biserial correlations presents no problems. It wasn't always thus. In the earlier days of test-making, most item analyses had to be done by hand tallying, or at best with the assistance of a graphic item counter on a test-scoring machine. Such an undertaking becomes somewhat laborious, but it is not overpowering. The analysis is very much facilitated by a table originally prepared by Flanagan (1939), which is reproduced in Appendix A.

The sequence of steps for obtaining a set of "Flanagan r's" for a set of test items is as follows:

1. Score each examinee's paper for the total pool of items, and enter the score on the answer sheet.

2. Arrange the answer sheets in order of total scores, from high to low, and count the total number of sheets.

3. Calculate how many answer sheets would represent 27% of the total. Count off this number from the top of the pile and from the bottom of the pile. These will be designated the upper (U) and lower (L) groups.

4. Tally the responses for these two groups. It would be possible to tally only the correct responses, but one is usually interested in numbers choosing each wrong alternative, so one usually tallies all responses.

5. For a given item, calculate the percentage of examinees choosing the correct response for the upper and for the lower group.

6. Enter the table in the column corresponding to P_U and the row corresponding to P_L, and read the value of the correlation. If P_U or P_L is odd, it will be necessary to interpolate between table entries.

7. The average of P_U and P_L, $(P_U + P_L)/2$, provides a good working estimate of P for the total group.

The Flanagan r is based on the same underlying assumption as the biserial correlation. That is, a bivariate normal distribution is assumed for test score and item. The value obtained for a Flanagan r approximates that obtained by computing a biserial and can be treated in the same way. It happens that a more accurate approximation can be obtained from use of 27% at the tails of the distribution, leaving out the middle 46%, than from just two groups of any other size, and the precision of a Flanagan r is approximately the same as that of a biserial.

ESTIMATING TEST PARAMETERS
FROM ITEM STATISTICS

If the usual item statistics for item difficulty and discrimination are available for each item (to wit, the percent passing and the point biserial correlation with a measure of the attribute), very serviceable estimates can be made of the mean, standard deviation, and reliability of a test assembled from those items. For the estimates to be free from systematic bias, the estimates of the item parameters must be based on a sample that has the same characteristics as the population with which the final test will be used. Otherwise, the estimates must be adjusted to refer to such a population by the procedures set forth on pages 66–70. In what follows, it is assumed that the sample was appropriate or that any necessary adjustments have been made.

The relationship between item difficulties and mean test score is very simple. It is given by the expression

$$\overline{X}_{\text{test}} = \sum_{i=1}^{n} P_i \tag{4.9}$$

That is, one simply sums the P-values of the n items composing the test to yield an estimate of the mean score. If the test is to be scored with a correction for guessing, we must get corrected P-values, using the same formula that is used to get a corrected score on the test, $R - W/(n - 1)$. This relationship between item difficulties and test score is easy to see if one looks at the matrix of item-by-person responses, where the matrix has an entry of 1 for a correct answer and 0 for a wrong answer. Such a matrix is illustrated below:

				ITEMS				Sum over items
Persons	1	2	3	· · ·	i	· · ·	n	
1	1	1	0	· · ·	1	· · ·	0	t_1
2	1	0	0	· · ·	0	· · ·	1	t_2
3	0	1	1	· · ·	1	· · ·	1	t_3
⋮	⋮							⋮
j	1	0	1	· · ·	0	· · ·	1	t_j
⋮	⋮							⋮
N	1	1	1	· · ·	0	· · ·	0	t_N
Sum over persons	P_1	P_2	P_3	· · ·	P_i	· · ·	P_n	$\sum_{i=1}^{n} P_i = \sum_{j=1}^{N} t_j$

Each row total, t_1 to t_N, represents the number of correct answers for a person, whereas each column total, P_1 to P_n, represent the number of correct answers for an item. Both Σ_t and Σ_p equal the total number of correct responses for all persons over all items, so they are equal to each other and

$$\overline{X} = \frac{\Sigma t}{N} = \frac{\Sigma P}{N} = \sum p$$

For each item, then, $P/N = p$, the proportion of right answers, and the sum of these proportions equals the total score.

Some straightforward algebra (see Gulliksen, 1950, pp. 375–377) establishes that the standard deviation of the test is given by the expression

$$S.D._{\text{test}} = \sum_{i=1}^{n} \sqrt{p_i q_i} \ \ r_{it} \tag{4.10}$$

in which r_{it} is the point biserial correlation of each item with the total test. Of course, the statistic that is actually available for each item is its correlation with some score composite available at the time of item tryout. This statistic is only an approximation to the value that will be obtained for correlation with the final test. There are several factors that tend to give it a systematic bias; some tend to cause it to be an overestimate and some an underestimate. The following points should be considered.

1. In item selection, one will tend to have selected items post hoc in part, because they showed high discrimination indices in the tryout sample. Simply because of statistical regression, such selected items tend to have lower indices in a new sample.

2. If in the tryout we used total score on the pool of tryout items as the criterion score against which the individual items were correlated, the correlations often tend to have been slightly attenuated by the presence of a certain number of defective items in the item pool — items that would not get into the final test. So far as this attenuation had occurred, the selected items could be expected to show higher correlations with the refined final test.

3. If an external measure (such as an already existing parallel form of the test) was used as the criterion measure, it would not have included the item for which the discrimination index was being computed, whereas the test now under construction would include it. For that reason we would expect the discrimination indices available for entry into the formula to be an underestimate of item correlations with the present test.

The first influence referred to above works in opposition to the second or the third, and it is hard to judge what the net effect will be. One guide would be to look at some sets of data, as we have done below. The analysis was carried out for 4 sets of verbal ability items that had been selected from a pool roughly 3 times as large for inclusion in the Cognitive Abilities Test, Verbal. The table shows

25th, 50th, and 75th percentiles of the biserial correlations for each of the sets of items, both for the tryout administration and for a random sample of cases drawn from the final standardization of the completed test.

	VOCABULARY		SENTENCE COMPLETION		VERBAL CLASSIFICATION		VERBAL ANALOGIES	
	Try-out	Standard-ization	Try-out	Standard-ization	Try-out	Standard-ization	Try-out	Standard-ization
75th %tile	0.73	0.71	0.74	0.75	0.66	0.69	0.68	0.66
Median	0.60	0.62	0.65	0.66	0.60	0.59	0.62	0.58
25th %tile	0.52	0.52	0.55	0.57	0.51	0.52	0.53	0.51
Number of Items	60		58		47		60	

In general, the results from the tryout of an item in a preliminary item pool and those from administration as an item in the final subtest are very similar. The differences are small, favoring sometimes one and sometimes the other administration. Thus, as far as these results can be trusted to be representative, item discrimination indices from tryout in a sizable preliminary pool of items, where the pool is composed of reviewed and edited items, provide a relatively unbiased estimate of the correlation of the item with the final test of which it becomes a member. The evidence suggests that estimates of the test's standard deviation based on formula 4.10 are sufficiently accurate for all practical purposes.

If one has an appropriate estimate of the standard deviation of the test that will result from the assembly of a given set of items, one already has at hand the elements one needs to estimate the reliability of the test in the sense of internal consistency. (See the discussion of internal consistency estimates of reliability in Chapter 6, pages 175–178.) Reliability by Kuder-Richardson Formula 20 is given by

$$r_{11} = \frac{n}{n-1} \left(1 - \frac{\sum_{j=1}^{n} p_i q_i}{S.D._t^2} \right) \tag{4.11}$$

The proportion of correct answers, p_i, is known for each item. Hence, as soon as one has an estimate of the test standard deviation, one can solve the equation for r_{11}, the Kuder-Richardson reliability.

Whenever one can estimate in advance what the average difficulty of a set of items will be and the average point biserial correlation between the items and test score, one can make very serviceable estimates of the parameters of a test composed of such items. In situations in which a test maker has had a fair amount of experience in constructing items of a given type and with the characteristics of the population with which the items will be used, estimates of this sort can be fairly accurate and quite useful for predicting the mean and standard deviation of test scores or for planning how long a test must be in order to achieve a desired level of precision.

The estimated mean score on the test is, of course, $n\bar{p}$, where $\bar{p}$ is the average percent correct on an item. The estimated standard deviation is given by

$$ n\sqrt{\bar{p}\,\bar{q}\,\bar{r}_{it}} \qquad n\sqrt{\bar{p}\bar{q}}\;\,r_{it} \tag{4.12}$$

where, again, each of the symbols with a bar represents an average value. Because $n\sqrt{\bar{p}\,\bar{q}}$ is always greater than $\Sigma\sqrt{pq}$, the foregoing expression tends to overestimate slightly the standard deviation that will result. The estimated average values and estimated standard deviation may be substituted in formula 4.11 to provide an internal consistency estimate of reliability. We get

$$ r_{11} = \frac{n}{n-1}\left(1 - \frac{n\,\bar{p}\,\bar{q}}{n^2\,\bar{p}\,\bar{q}\,\bar{r}_{it}^2}\right) $$

This simplifies to

$$ r_{11} = \frac{n}{n-1}\left(1 - \frac{1}{n\,\bar{r}_{it}^2}\right) \tag{4.13}$$

A concrete illustration will show how the estimation procedure works out. Suppose that a test maker plans to prepare a test composed of a set of items for which the average percent of correct answers will be 65, and that past experience indicates that the average r_{pbis} for items of this type retained in the test can be expected to be about .40. A test of 80 items is to be prepared. We then estimate as follows:

$$\begin{aligned}
\overline{X} &\cong 80\,(.65) = 52 \\
S.D. &\cong 80\,[(.65)\,(.35)]^{\frac{1}{2}}\,(.40) \cong 15.3 \\
r_{11} &\cong \frac{80}{79}\left(1 - \frac{1}{80(.16)}\right) \cong .95
\end{aligned}$$

USING ITEM STATISTICS IN SELECTING
THE ITEMS FOR A TEST

Selection of the items to make up a test is based on two types of considerations: item content and item statistics. A word first about item content. Whenever a test blueprint specifies a set of topics to be covered with specified weights in terms of proportions of items on each topic, those specifications constitute one requirement that must be met in the selection of the items that are to go into the test. The blueprint may also set out certain specifications on type of item format or on mental process to be called for. All these are nonstatistical considerations and in tests of academic achievement or job proficiency they may be quite compelling. In a test that is to be thought of as a sample from a domain of knowledge, the statistical properties of the test items are only supplementary considerations, which function to generate the most effective test possible while still maintaining the representation of the content domain that is specified in the test outline. In other tests, especially those designed to measure "traits" of ability or temperament, the content outline tends to be less fully spelled out, and then the statistical properties of items may play a more primary role.

We have said that one uses item statistics to generate the most effective test possible. However, we still have not defined what we mean by "effective." Effective for what? And by what criterion is effectiveness to be judged?

We return at this point to the basic premise that we get test scores in order to permit us to make decisions. These may be practical decisions leading to action or theoretical judgments leading to knowledge. The effectiveness of a test is defined by the degree to which it enables us to make sound decisions. But decisions are many and varied, and the reading test that would help us most to decide which college seniors to admit to law school would be of limited value in guiding decisions on which freshmen to assign to a course in remedial English.

In this connection, it will help to introduce and to explore somewhat the notion of the *information function* of a test item and the related notion of the information function of a test. We have spoken of the *item characteristic curve*, which describes the probability of succeeding on the item at each possible value, θ, of the latent attribute. At each possible value of the latent attribute, this function has two parameters of current interest to us. One is the *slope*, or steepness of the curve at that point. We can illustrate the slope on Figure 4.1 by considering a small interval extending on either side of some value, θ, of the latent attribute. We have shown an interval extending from $\theta - k$ to $\theta + k$ and having a width of $2k$. Over this interval, the curve rises by an amount that is designated m on the diagram. The ratio $m/2k$ approximates the slope at ability level θ and, as k becomes smaller and smaller, the ratio $m/2k$ approaches the slope at θ as a limit. If the item characteristic curve can be considered a normal ogive, the rate of increase is equal to the steepness parameter a_g times the derivative of the cumulative normal frequency curve. The derivative is exactly the ordinate of the normal curve at the point $a_g(b_g - \theta)$, and this ordinate can be read from tables of the normal curve.

The other parameter of interest is the variance of item scores for a set of persons all of whom fall at level θ on the latent attribute. If p represents the proportion of successes on the item by persons falling at level θ, then $p_\theta q_\theta$, where $q = 1 - p$, equals the variance on the item for persons at that level.

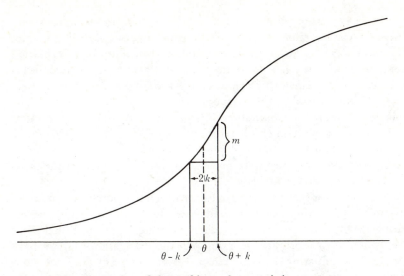

Figure 4.1   Illustration of slope of item characteristic curve.

The information function of an item at any given level θ can be defined as the ratio of the square of the slope to the variance:

$$\text{Information at } \theta \; = \; \frac{(\text{slope at } \theta)^2}{p_\theta q_\theta} \qquad (4.14)$$

That is, the more rapidly the probability of success on the item is changing relative to the variability of that percent, the more information the item is providing about an individual's status on the latent attribute. Both slope and variance depend on the item parameters a_g, b_g, and c_g, which were defined in Chapter 1.

Limiting our consideration for the moment to items where $c_g = 0$ and hence the asymptote at very low values of θ is zero, the size of the maximum slope is proportional to a_g and the location of the point of maximum slope is specified by the equation $b_g - \theta = 0$. That is, it occurs where the difficulty of the item exactly matches the ability level of the examinees, so that each examinee has a 50-50 probability of getting the correct answer.

If the item characteristic curve approximates a normal ogive, the slope at any value of θ is equal to a_g times the ordinate of a normal curve in which the table is entered with a normal deviate value equal to $a_g(b_g - \theta)$. Thus, if $a_g = 0.8$ and $(b_g - \theta) = 1.5$, the slope equals 0.8 times the ordinate at $(0.8 \times 1.5) = 1.20$ or $0.8(.1942) = 0.155$. The percent correct is 0.115 times the abscissa at (0.8×1.5), so the information is

$$(0.155)^2/(0.115)(0.885) \; = \; 0.236$$

The value of this expression drops off slowly at first, then more rapidly, and finally slowly again as the value of $(b_g - \theta)$ increases from zero to a large value.

Using the foregoing relationships, it is possible to calculate the information function for an item with any given parameters, a_g and b_g. Table 4.6 gives the information functions for items for which a_g is equal to 0.50 and to 1.00 and for which b_g is -3.00, 0.00, and $+3.00$, respectively.

This table deserves careful examination. First, it shows that, at the maximum, those items with the steeper item characteristic curve ($a_g = 1.00$) provide *much* more information on which to base a decision than those with the flatter curve. In fact, when the ratio of the two parameters a_g is 2 to 1, the ratio of the maximum information provided is 4 to 1.

Second, the table shows that the range of θ over which the more discriminating items function is less than (in this case actually half) the range over which the less discriminating items function. The more discriminating items are much more informative—but over a more limited range. In the illustration that we have given, the more discriminating items are effective over a range of $(b_g - \theta)$ from about $+2.0$ to -2.0 in standardized units. Beyond those limits, the less sharply discriminating items are more informative. Finally, the table provides some indication of the rate at which the amount of information drops off as we move away from the optimal level—that is, where the difficulty of the item just matches the ability level of the examinees.

If we make one assumption, which usually seems reasonable for most types of test items, it is possible to synthesize the information function for a test from the information functions for the component items. This is the assumption of *local independence*. The assumption states that, *for persons located at any given level θ on the latent attribute, the probability of a person passing any one item X_A is independent of whether that person is known to have passed (or failed) another item X_B.* Suppose, for example, that we have a group of tenth-graders who are somehow known all to fall at the same point on a dimension of "quantitative reasoning" and that half of them have passed and half have failed on the item "How many quarters of a quarter is half of a half?" Local independence would assert that the passers and failers would be equally likely to succeed with the item "By what must you multiply 24 to make the product equal to half of the square of 12?"

When local independence holds, at least to a close approximation, the information function for a test is equal to the sum of the information functions for the items composing that test. This being so, it is possible to formulate hypothetical tests, with different mixes of item difficulty and discrimination, and to see how the resulting test information function turns out. Examination of a set of such functions should help us decide what parameters are desirable in a test for a defined purpose.

Once items have been screened in terms of their ability to differentiate degrees of the underlying latent attribute (which weeds out the ambiguous items and those that are related to some other trait than the one that most of the items are

Table **4.6**   Information Function for Items with Different Values of a_g and b_g

Value of θ	$a_g = 0.50$			$a_g = 1.00$		
	$b_g = -3.0$	$b_g = 0.0$	$b_g = +3.0$	$b_g = -3.0$	$b_g = 0.0$	$b_g = +3.0$
+3.0	.003	.067	.159		.015	.636
2.5	.007	.088	.156		.050	.581
2.0	.012	.110	.145		.130	.439
1.5	.021	.130	.130		.270	.270
1.0	.033	.145	.110		.439	.130
0.5	.048	.156	.088	.003	.581	.050
0.0	.067	.159	.067	.015	.636	.015
−0.5	.088	.156	.048	.050	.581	.003
−1.0	.110	.145	.033	.130	.439	
−1.5	.130	.130	.021	.270	.270	
−2.0	.145	.110	.012	.439	.130	
−2.5	.156	.088	.007	.581	.050	
−3.0	.159	.067	.003	.636	.015	

assessing), it is perhaps reasonable to assume a common average value for the parameter a_g, the ability of each item to differentiate degrees of possession of the attribute. (In part, the observed differences among items in sharpness of differentiation may be attributable to sampling fluctuations.) In the illustrations that follow, we have assumed such a common value in order to simplify the presentation.* However, data comparing pairs of large samples suggest that values of a_g do differ consistently from one item to another.

Table 4.7 and Figure 4.2 show the information functions for 9-item tests with 2 levels of item discrimination a_g and with 3 patterns of item difficulties. The levels of discrimination are $a_g = 0.50$, which is equivalent to $r_{\text{bis}} = 0.44$ or a fairly low level of item discrimination (characteristic of items from a rather heterogeneous domain), and $a_g = 1.00$, which is equivalent to $r_{\text{bis}} = 0.70$ or a level of discrimination somewhat above that usually found in measures of ability. The patterns of item difficulty are (1) all items of middle difficulty for which $b_g - \bar{\theta} = 0$; (2) 3 very easy ($b_g - \bar{\theta} = -3.0$), 3 of middle difficulty ($b_g - \bar{\theta} = 0.0$), and 3 very hard ($b_g - \bar{\theta} = +3.0$); and (3) a uniform spread of items by half-S.D. units from $b_g - \bar{\theta} = -2.0$ to $b_g - \bar{\theta} = +2.0$.

The information functions for the 6 tests shown in the table and figure

---

* The assumption of uniform a_g is basic to the Rasch model of test development considered on page 96.

Table 4.7 Information Functions for Selected 9-Item Tests

	$a_g = 0.50$			$a_g = 1.00$		
θ	All items $b_g - \theta = 0$	3 items easy, 3 middle, 3 hard	Uniform spread of difficulty	All items $b_g - \theta = 0$	3 items easy, 3 middle, 3 hard	Uniform spread of difficulty
+3.0	0.58	0.69	0.65	0.14	1.95	0.91
2.5	0.82	0.75	0.80	0.45	1.89	1.49
2.0	1.09	0.80	0.94	1.17	1.77	2.13
1.5	1.36	0.84	1.06	2.43	1.62	2.71
1.0	1.58	0.86	1.16	3.95	1.77	3.15
0.5	1.74	0.87	1.22	5.23	1.89	3.32
0.0	1.79	0.88	1.24	5.72	1.95	3.45
−0.5	1.74	0.87	1.22	5.23	1.89	3.32
−1.0	1.58	0.86	1.16	3.95	1.77	3.15
−1.5	1.36	0.84	1.06	2.43	1.62	2.71
−2.0	1.09	0.80	0.94	1.17	1.77	2.13
−2.5	0.82	0.75	0.80	0.45	1.89	1.49
−3.0	0.58	0.69	0.65	0.14	1.95	0.91

demonstrate the generally greater amount of information provided by the test with the more discriminating items. The only reversal occurs at extreme values of θ, when the test of discriminating items is composed solely of items having a difficulty well removed from the extreme in question. It is also clear that a test composed entirely of items of middle difficulty, in relation to the group being studied, is the most appropriate design when individual item discrimination is relatively low. In our illustration, such a test provides the most information up to and including ± 2.5 standard units on the scale of θ. By contrast, with high discrimination, the equal-difficulty test is optimal only through ± 1.0 standard unit.

The tests with a spread of item difficulties provide a more uniform amount of information throughout the range covered in the table and figure. This is especially so in the case of the set of more discriminating items. But the *total* area under the curves of these tests, within the ± 3.0 standard units range, is less than for a test with all items grouped at the center of this range. This is due, in a manner of speaking, to the fact that difficult and easy items "waste" part of their information in making differentiations outside the range in which we were interested on this table and graph.

Clearly, when all interest focuses on making decisions within a fairly narrow range on the latent attribute — say a total range of 2 standard units — the most information for such a decision is in all cases provided by a test in which all the

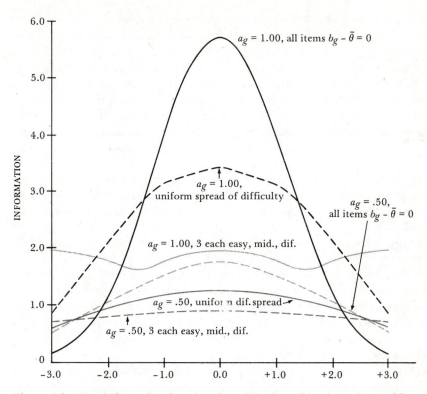

Figure 4.2   Test information functions for selected combinations of a_g and b_g.

items are of the same difficulty and the value of b_g, the difficulty parameter, is centered in the range within which decisions must be made. Thus, if a test were being used to place about 5% of an entering college freshman class in a remedial English course, and we wished to identify the poorest 5% in skills of English usage, a test in which $(b_g - \bar{\theta})$ was -1.64 for all the items would, other things being equal, be optimal. That is, the test would be composed of items for which the item characteristic curve was rising most steeply at the fifth percentile (-1.64 S.D.) of the entering group. Equally clearly, however, with the level of item-trait correlation that we often encounter, an exact prescription of item difficulty is not very critical. Under these conditions the information curve is then fairly flat, and any reasonable mix of item difficulties is about as acceptable as any other in the information that it provides.

When one intends to use the test to make decisions involving examinees who score over a wide range on the latent attribute, as when one wishes to use the same test to place some students in a remedial and some in an honors section, it becomes important that item difficulty cover a considerable range. And this becomes more important as the range increases and as the homogeneity of the items (their saturation with the common latent attribute) increases.

Whenever a test maker has available a set of items for which estimates of the item parameters a_g, b_g, and c_g are available, it is a straightforward but somewhat laborious undertaking to calculate the amount of information provided by that set of items at selected values of $(b_g - \theta)$. Using the selected points, one can sketch in the information function of the test for the complete range of values and judge how effectively the test is providing information in the ability ranges in which one is especially interested. Working in the opposite direction, one can formulate one's objectives in terms of the value that one sets on information in certain ability ranges and then try out different combinations of test item parameters to see which of them maximizes the amount of information, weighting different levels on the attribute according to their judged importance. Unfortunately, this is a cut-and-fit rather than an analytic procedure, but at the present time there does not appear to be any analytic solution that is generally applicable.

Up to this point the information function has been discussed in terms of the normal ogive. The logistic function (see Chapter 1, page 9) can be used instead and yields slightly different values. The logistic is more convenient for computational purposes, especially for selected response items on which the correct answer can be selected on the basis of a fortunate guess. With such items the information function becomes asymmetrical, because guessing is more prevalent for low-ability examinees, and will attenuate the information provided by the item at the low end of the ability scale.

Lord* offers the following convenient formula for calculating the information provided by an item:

$$\text{Information at } \theta = \frac{2.89a_g^2 (1 - c_g)}{(c_g + e^{1.7L_g}) (1 + e^{-1.7L_g})^2}$$

where $L_g = a_g(\theta - b_g)$, and a_g, b_g, and c_g refer to the steepness parameter, the difficulty parameter, and the lower asymptote parameter of the item characteristic curve, respectively.

Table 4.8 shows the values of the information function in the case in which $a_g = 1.00$ and with values of c_g taken as 0.0, 0.2, and 0.5, respectively. For purposes of comparison, one column from Table 4.6 (based on the normal ogive) is shown on the far right. The influence of the c_g parameter appears quite dramatically, especially at the lower end of the ability range. This occurs because the item characteristic curve becomes quite flat at those levels, while the item variance $p_g q_g$, remains substantial.

Unfortunately, it is impossible to get good estimates of c_g for individual items unless tryout samples are much larger than those commonly available. One may

---

* From F. M. Lord, *Applications of Item Response Theory to Practical Testing Problems*. Hillsdale, N.J.: Lawrence Erlbaum Associates, 1980, p. 73. Used by permission.

Table **4.8** Comparison of Item Information Functions Assuming Different Values of c_g

$\theta - b_g$	BASED ON LOGISTIC FUNCTION			BASED ON NORMAL OGIVE
	$c_g = 0.0$	$c_g = 0.2$	$c_g = 0.5$	$c_g = 0.0$
3.00	.0174	.0139	.0087	.015
2.00	.0903	.0718	.0444	.130
1.00	.3774	.2913	.1727	.439
0.00	.7225	.4817	.2408	.636
−1.00	.3774	.1441	.0505	.439
−2.00	.0903	.0103	.0028	.130
−3.00	.0174	.0004	.0001	.015

have to be content with the assumption that $c_g = 1/k$ for each item, where k is the number of response options for the item. Making such an assumption is likely to overcorrect for the attenuating effect of guessing. However, it almost certainly gives a better basis for estimating the information provided by an item at different ability levels than assuming that c_g equals zero. And consequently, summing item information functions that assume that c_g equals $1/k$ provide a more conservative, and probably a more accurate, basis for evaluating the effectiveness of a test at different ability levels.

CONTROLLING TEST PARAMETERS WHEN NO TRYOUT IS POSSIBLE

Situations sometimes arise, especially in civil service testing, where a new form of a test must be used operationally in the absence of advance tryout of the test items. When security is a matter of high concern, and when the test questions and the answer key must by law be published after a test is given, a new test form must be prepared each time the test is used. Security considerations and/or the difficulty of locating an appropriate sample may make it impossible to try out the items in advance. Law or regulations may specify the use of a raw score of number right and may set in advance a passing mark as a certain percentage of the items on the test. Then, uniform difficulty of the test from one testing to another is required as a matter of equity to examinees who are job candidates at different testings. At the same time, the employer wishes to maintain a test that will qualify an adequate flow of candidates without unduly lowering standards.

When items cannot be administered to a sample of examinees, often they can still be presented to a panel of judges. The judges can be asked to estimate the difficulty level of each item. But how well can judges make these judgments? In some early research on this problem, Lorge and Kruglov (1952, 1953) found that judges showed fair agreement, and fair agreement with empirical tryout data, in appraising the *relative* difficulty of items. The correlation between difficulty estimates for pairs of judges was fairly substantial. However, judges varied widely in the *absolute* difficulty that they assigned to the items. Each judge had his or her own constant error in the judgments of difficulty, and it appeared that one could not count on judgments to control absolute item difficulty—and through this the mean score on a test.

The finding that judges do show fair agreement on relative difficulty suggests that an effective procedure for using judges would be to include, in the set of items to be rated, some previously tried items for which empirical data on difficulty are available from a group like that on which the test currently under construction is to be used. The anchor items should cover a wide range of difficulty, so that reference points will be provided covering most of the range represented in the new items to be rated. The set of items, new ones and anchor ones mixed together, should be rated by a panel of judges—preferably people who are somewhat familiar with the content of the test. High reliability in the judging of single items is not necessary so long as the errors are random rather than systematic. Even with appreciable errors for single items, the average difficulty of a set of 50 or 100 items, relative to the anchor items, should be determined with satisfactory precision. But several judges should be used in order to neutralize any idiosyncrasy of single judges.

Judgments could be called for in any convenient form. For example, a 9-point scale could be used, with 9 defined as "extremely difficult," 5 as "average in difficulty," and 1 as "extremely easy." Judgments would be averaged for the panel of judges. Scale values would be assigned to the *anchor* items, based on the percentage of examinees getting the item right when it was used in an operational test, following the procedures on p. 64ff. Ordinarily one would need to assume some reasonable value for the discrimination or "steepness" parameter a_g, choosing a value that matches the average discrimination of items in previous forms of the test. Then scale values would be interpolated for the new items, based on their average rating, and from the scale values one would estimate the percentage expected to get each item right, using Table 4.4.*

The miniature example shown in Table 4.9 involves 5 anchor items and 6 new, untried items. For this example, a value of 0.50 has been assumed for a_g, corresponding to a biserial correlation of approximately 0.45 and a point biserial (for items with a fairly even pass–fail split) of 0.36. In the table, the first

---

* The relationship between the rated difficulty and the empirically determined scale values of the anchor items will not be perfect. If the relationship is very low, the ratings of the anchor items will not provide a useful basis for scaling the new items. If the relationship is substantial but not perfect, it may be best to plot a line of relationship of rating to scale value and to read the scale values for the new items from this line.

Table 4.9   Calculations for Estimating Percent Success on Untried Items (r_{bis} assumed to be 0.45)

1 ITEM*	2 AVERAGE RATING	3 OBSERVED PERCENT CORRECT	4 SCALE VALUE	5 ESTIMATED SCALE VALUE	6 ESTIMATED PERCENT CORRECT
A1	7.6	32	2.35		
2	7.3			2.05	34
3	6.4			1.06	45
A4	6.2	48	0.85		
5	5.3			0.48	53
A6	4.8	56	0.27		
7	4.5			0.16	58
8	3.7			−0.25	64
A9	3.2	67	−0.48		
10	2.8			−1.42	79
A11	2.6	84	−1.88		

Estimated average score on 6 item test = 3.34 = 55.7%

*Items with the prefix A are anchor items.

column identifies the item and the second gives the average rating on a 9-point scale. The third column gives the percentages of right answers obtained in a previous use of the anchor items, while the fourth column gives difficulty scale values, b_g, for these items. These were estimated from Table 4.4. Scale values for the new items, given in the fifth column, are estimated by linear interpolation. Finally, the sixth column translates these scale values back into percentages of correct answers, again by using Table 4.4.

Given the difficulty estimates and some sense of the average level of discrimination of the items, one can estimate mean, standard deviation, and reliability coefficent from equations 4.9, 4.12, and 4.13. Thus the total score on these 6 items would be estimated to be 3.34, or 55.7% of the possible score. If a total 100-item test had been assembled from items of average difficulty equal to these 6, and with point biserial correlations averaging 0.36, we would get an estimate for the mean of 55.7 and an estimate for the standard deviation of $100 \sqrt{(0.557)(0.443)} (0.36) = 17.9$. If it is also given that the passing score is set by law as 70%, we find that the passing score is $14.3/17.9 = 0.80$ standard deviation units above the mean. If the score distribution is approximately normal, the percentage of candidates passing the test will be about 21. If the needs of the employing agency are well served by a pass rate of 1 in 5, we can accept the set of items as they stand. However, if policy indicated that more nearly one-third of the candidates should achieve the passing score, this would imply a normal deviation value of 0.43, and we could work back to a mean percentage of $70 - (0.43)(17.9) = 62.3$ and then replace some of the more difficult items by easier items until the average predicted score is raised to 62.3.

From equation 4.13 we estimate that the internal consistency reliability of our 100-item test will be approximately 0.93.

ANALYSIS OF A HETEROGENEOUS ITEM POOL

Usually when we accumulate a pool of items, all are designed to be measures of a single, defined latent attribute. Sometimes, however, we have only a vague notion of what dimensions are to be found in some territory that we wish to explore. For example, we might wish to determine what dimensions will be found in the general field labeled "job satisfaction" and might wish to develop a measure of each. Or we might have a pool of items all relating to aspects of "masculinity" and might wish to develop more analytic scores to cover that territory. We might have prepared a pool of questionnaire items that we felt covered a large number of facets of the territory in which we were interested and might wish to (1) define the dimensions that are represented in the item pool and (2) prepare effective instruments to assess some or all of the dimensions that we had identified. How should we proceed?*

Given today's computer capability, a natural first step is to carry out a factor analysis of all, or at least a large sample, of the items in our item pool. Factor analyses of sets of 100 or 200 variables are no longer beyond the bounds of feasibility. However, there are two problems associated with such an approach. One of these problems is relatively easy to overcome, but the other is more troublesome.

The first problem arises because test items are typically scored as dichotomies: pass–fail or agree–disagree. The analogue of the product-moment correlation in the case of a dichotomy is a phi-coefficient, and these coefficients are greatly influenced by the proportions in each of the categories for a pair of items. When used in a factor analysis, they tend to produce unwanted "difficulty" or "popularity" factors that have nothing to do with the content of the items. It is therefore appropriate to use tetrachoric correlations for the between-item correlations. These make the assumption that each item represents some continuous (and approximately normally distributed) underlying variable. This assumption may not be fully justified, and can rarely if ever be tested, but it does provide a workable basis for proceeding.

The second problem is that single items typically have a large amount of unique variance, representing the specific content of the item as well as "chance"

---

* The procedures presented here assume familiarity with some concepts presented in later chapters. Some readers may wish to return to this section after Chapters 6 and 9 have been read.

in an individual's response at a specific moment in time. This means that all the correlations in the set of interitem correlations tend to be attenuated down to relatively small values. The correlations among several *items* that measure a given attribute are much smaller than the correlations among several *tests* of that attribute. Very roughly, the correlations among items may be expected to be about the square of the correlation among tests.

Because of the attenuation, not only the single correlations but also the differences among them will be reduced in size. But correlations are subject to sampling fluctuations, which, for a correlation of .00, can be represented by

$$S.E._r = \frac{1}{\sqrt{N - 3}}$$

Thus, if all the correlations were to be reduced by half, and we wished to maintain the same precision in our estimates of the relative size of different correlations, it would be necessary to increase our sample by a factor of 4. We must conclude that meaningful factor analyses of the correlations among items require *much* larger samples than factor-analytic studies of tests. Samples of 500 or 1000 would seem none too large.

Let us assume that we have obtained data from a sample of adequate size, have prepared a matrix of tetrachoric interitem correlations, and have applied our favorite method of factor analysis to the table. (Your author is disposed to use communality estimates as diagonal elements in the correlation matrix, but in a large matrix the diagonal elements have relatively little impact.) We have then applied our favorite factor-rotational procedure in order to define distinct clusters of items that will serve to represent the separate factors. How shall we now proceed to select the items that are to be included in the score that represents a specific factor?

It would seem reasonable to start with those items that show the largest loadings on the factor for which we are trying to develop a scale and to add additional items until we have the "best" measure of the factor. But by what criterion shall we define "best"?

One plausible, simple, and objective definition would say that the best set of items is that set with the highest internal consistency, as represented by coefficient alpha (or Kuder–Richardson Formula 20). If we accept this definition, we can proceed as follows:

1. Prepare a matrix of item covariances. (The covariance equals $p_{ij} - p_i p_j$).

2. Pick out the set of 3 or 4 items with the largest loadings on the factor of current interest. If any item has a significant *negative* factor loading, it should be scored with a negative weight, and the signs of all its covariances should be reversed.

3. Sum the covariances C_{ij} of each item in the set of 3 or 4 with every other item.

4. Sum the variances V_i of the items in the set.

5. Determine coefficient alpha of the initial set of items by the equation

$$\text{Alpha} = \frac{n}{n-1}\left(\frac{\Sigma\Sigma C_{ij}}{\Sigma\Sigma C_{ij} + \Sigma V_i}\right) \tag{4.15}.$$

6. Find the item k with the next highest loading on the factor under study.

7. Sum the covariances of the new item k with all the items already in the cluster, and add this sum, ΣC_{ik}, to the previous sum of item covariances, $\Sigma\Sigma C_{ij}$.

8. Add the variance of the new item, V_k, to ΣV_i, the previous sum of item variances.

9. Using the new $\Sigma\Sigma C_{ij}$ and ΣV_i and the augmented n, repeat step 5.

10. Continue adding items until alpha shows no increase with the addition of a further item. The final value of alpha shows the internal consistency of the item set — that is, an estimate of the correlation of that set of items with an equivalent set drawn from the total pool of items representing the attribute.

After choosing the best set of items from the original pool, one might well examine the set in order to formulate a description that best characterizes the attribute represented by the set of items. With this conception of the attribute in mind, one could generate an additional group of items designed to assess that attribute. New data could be obtained for the items included in the original set and the newly prepared items. Working from the covariance matrix of these items, one could look for the best new item to add to the existing set. The most promising new item would be the one for which $\Sigma C_{ik}/V_k$ is the greatest. As each new item is added, coefficient alpha must be recomputed, and once again the addition of new items ceases when coefficient alpha stops increasing.

Once a first cluster of items defining a first factor has been completed, those items should probably be withdrawn from the item pool. It would generally not seem desirable to use the same item to define more than one attribute. The procedure we have just described can then be repeated for a second factor and the remaining pool of items. After the items for that factor have been selected and removed from the pool of items, the process can be repeated for further factors, continuing as long as a factor remains for which there are several items with significant factor loadings. As suggested above, examination of the items defining each factor can serve as a guide to the preparation and tryout of additional items written to enrich and strengthen the definition of the factor.

It may not always be practical to start with a complete factor analysis. A somewhat crude substitute procedure (Loevinger, Gleser, and DuBois, 1953) is to start by inspecting the item covariance matrix, identifying clusters of items with high covariances. Starting with the set of 3 or 4 items with the highest covariances, the sequence of steps that we have listed can be applied. In this case, it will help initially to compute, for each item in the pool, the sum of its covariances with the items in the core cluster. Inspection will usually identify a large number of items for which ΣC_{ik}, the sum of the covariances of item k with the initial core items, is close to zero. These items can safely be removed from further consideration; they obviously do not belong in the cluster defined by the core items. For the remaining items, one proceeds by adding to the core, at each stage, the item for which $\Sigma C_{ik}/V_k$ is the greatest. The cluster is complete when addition of the item next in line produces no increase in coefficient alpha.

After the first cluster has been removed, the remaining pool of items may be scanned for another nucleus of items with high covariances. Starting with these, the process is repeated. The process may be continued until no nucleus of substantially covarying items remains.

There are times when one's concern may focus not on isolating trait dimensions from a pool of heterogeneous items but rather on selecting a subset of items that will give the maximum prediction of some external criterion. Thus items of biographical information have been used to predict such varied outcomes as success in beginning flight training, employee persistence in routine clerical jobs, and probability of completing payments on an installment purchase. The goal of item selection in such a case is to generate a score that has maximum validity as a predictor of the external criterion measure, with no concern about the internal structure of the item set. This problem is one specific instance of combining predictor elements into an effective composite prediction procedure, and it will be considered in that context in Chapter 9.

THE ROLE OF ITEM ANALYSIS IN DOMAIN MASTERY OR CRITERION-REFERENCED TESTS

In our discussion of the collection and use of item statistics up to this point, a latent trait model has been assumed. An item has been described in terms of parameters of difficulty (b_g), discrimination (a_g), and in some instances a lower asymptote (c_g) representing the performance of persons very low on the attribute that the item was designed to represent. All of the items that were combined to yield a single score were thought to be estimators of the same latent attribute. But suppose our test is intended to be a measure of mastery of some sharply limited and precisely defined domain. What role is there now for analysis of single test items, and what form should this analysis take?

The view can perhaps be defended that, if we have defined the domain clearly and sampled from it in a representative fashion, the resulting set of test items is by definition appropriate to test degree of mastery, and no empirical data on the items are needed. There may be situations in which this is true. They would seem to be situations having the following properties.

1. The boundaries of the domain are clearly and sharply defined, so that there

is little or no question about whether a given test exercise falls within the domain.

2. Difficulty of the tasks falling within the domain is relatively uniform, or the relative difficulty of different tasks is already known, so that it is possible to assemble a sample of tasks that is representative of the difficulty of all tasks within the domain without gathering evidence on difficulty from actual tryout.

3. There is little possibility of ambiguity in the task arising from the form in which it is presented or of difficulty arising from factors in the task other than those constituting the domain that is being tested.

A fairly clearly defined domain might be that of capitalizing the names of persons. Within fairly broad limits, it would not be expected to matter whether the name was Mary or Helen, John or Henry, Mrs. Jones or Mr. Cohen. However, condition 3 might be violated if the name were Patience or Marmaduke, Senora Casablanca or Herr Kupfermann. To a child, these might not be readily identifiable as names of persons, and the child might fail to capitalize them for that reason. Item statistics might be of some value in defining the boundaries of the domain. Does success with such names as these correlate adequately with success on familiar names?

Often the specific tasks falling within a domain vary substantially in difficulty, and evidence on item difficulty is important to assure that the domain has been sampled appropriately in this respect. Thus the numerals 57 and 60 are not equivalent in testing for mastery of the concept of prime number. (Neither is prime, but 57 is much more likely to be considered to be.)

Given a range of difficulty for the tasks within a domain, it may be reasonable to think of the domain as corresponding to a latent attribute with finite limits. Thus the representation might be as shown in Figure 4.3, where the lower boundary would be set by a person who would perform at no better than a chance level on even the easiest tasks in the domain, and the upper boundary would be represented by a person who could succeed with substantially 100% of the most difficult of the domain's tasks. Within the range for person ability, a narrower band represents the range of task difficulty. If one wanted to know what percentage of *all* tasks in the domain a person had mastered, and if one were equally interested in estimating all levels of success, one would want a flat information function over the whole range. This would call for a sample of tasks that represented all difficulty levels about equally.

However, if one were interested only in determining whether the individual could do some high percentage (say 80% or 90%) of all the tasks, one would want an information function that peaked in the upper fraction of the range represented by the domain — at the tasks that represented the 80th or 90th percentile of the tasks in difficulty. Working in a narrowly defined domain, it seems likely that the item characteristic functions would be quite steep and that, as a consequence, success on the easier items within the domain would provide relatively little information on whether the mastery level had been achieved—

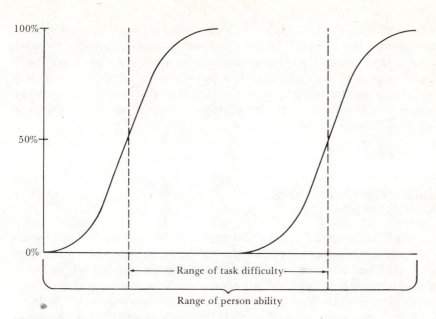

Figure 4.3   Representation of domain as trait with limited range.

though failure on these items would be a very persuasive indication that it had *not* been. If item characteristic functions are quite steep and there is a substantial spread of task difficulty, the most precise evidence, for a given test length, about whether success would be achieved with some high percentage of all the tasks in the domain would be provided through evidence that the person showed better than a 50-50 record of successes (after any necessary correction for guessing) on a sample of tasks the difficulty of which fell at that specified high percentile among the tasks in the domain.

When a domain corresponds to a unit of instruction, one useful type of evidence on the difficulty of tasks and on their relevance to the unit of instruction can be drawn from a comparison of success on the tasks before and after instruction. Granting some degree of effectiveness to the instruction, a comparison of percent correct before and percent correct after instruction can reveal, operationally, how closely the task corresponds to what has been taught. On the one hand, tasks that are nearly universally performed correctly before instruction can provide no evidence on the effectiveness of instruction or on progress toward mastery. On the other hand, tasks on which examinees show no gain after instruction are suspect as measures of the domain that has been the focus of teaching. They would appear either to lie outside the domain as it was defined in the operations of teaching or to be flawed in some other respect.

With the latent trait model, test items that are passed by 100% of a group are viewed as useless in locating members of that group along the scale of the latent trait. Within the domain mastery model, items with 100% success are somewhat more favorably perceived. They do indicate a degree of progress toward mastery of the domain. This is especially true if the 100% success represents the state after instruction, when the preinstruction state was much less. However, it is still important to know where a particular item lies within the hierarchy of difficulty that represents the domain. As indicated earlier, the value of an item as evidence of *mastery* of a domain depends very heavily on where it falls on the domain's often-bounded range of task difficulties.

SCALING ITEMS AND SCORES
USING THE RASCH MODEL

Rasch (1960) has proposed a simplified model of the properties of test items, which, if reasonably sustained, permits the scaling of test items and test scores on a scale of the latent attribute that does not depend on the population from which the scaling data are obtained. The procedures have been developed in detail and applications set forth by Wright and his associates (Wright and Stone, 1979). In terms of the item parameters a_g, b_g, and c_g that we have described in Chapter 1 and in this chapter, the Rasch model specifies that the slope parameter a_g can be considered uniform for all the test items that are being used to appraise a specific latent attribute, and that the asymptote parameter c_g can be considered to be 0. Thus the one respect in which the test exercises are considered to differ is in the difficulty parameter b_g. These assumptions are most plausible under the following conditions.

1. All items are quite homogeneous in form and content, so that they appear to deal equally with a common latent attribute.

2. Items have been screened through a preliminary tryout so that ambiguous items and others that are for some reason nondiscriminating have been removed.

3. Items are ones in which the examinee must generate the response (rather than selecting it from given options) so that the asymptotic percent correct for persons very low on the attribute can be expected to approach zero.

4. Items reflect general growth in some attribute rather than specific instruction. In measures of academic achievement, focused instruction could be expected to shift radically the relative difficulty of items involving a topic that had just been taught.

The Rasch model uses the logistic function to relate probability of success on the item to its position on the scale of the latent attribute. As we have stated, the shape of the logistic function is almost undistinguishable from that of the normal ojive, but its mathematical properties make it in some ways more manageable. In each case, we need to consider the difficulty level of the item in relation to the ability level of an examinee or group of examinees. The model says that, when the difficulty of an item and the ability level of a group of examinees just match, the odds are even that a member of that group will get that item right (that is, the odds are 1 to 1), and 50% will get the item right and 50% get it wrong. As we shift to an easier item or to a more capable group, the odds of success become better than even. As we shift to a more difficult item or a less capable group, the odds become less than even. The odds of "winning" can be expressed as

$$\frac{P_{ij}}{n_j - P_{ij}}$$

where $\quad P_{ij}$ = number of persons in category j getting item i right
$\quad\quad\quad n_j$ = total number of persons in category j.

The logistic function is based on the natural logarithm of the foregoing ratio and states that

$$b_j - d_i = \log\left(\frac{P_{ij}}{n_j - P_{ij}}\right) \tag{4.16}$$

where $\quad b_j$ = ability or competence level of group j and
$\quad\quad\quad d_i$ = difficulty parameter of item i*

When $b_j = d_i$, the value of the natural logarithm is equal to zero, so the value of the ratio is equal to 1.00. That is, the probability of success is equal to the probability of failure: $p_i = q_i = 0.50$. The following table shows the proportion of successes corresponding to selected values of $b_j - d_i$.

$b_j - d_i$	Proportion of successes
+3.00	95
2.00	88
1.00	73
.00	50
−1.00	27
−2.00	12
−3.00	5

The properties of the logistic function for an item, in relation to the basic scale of the latent attribute, are assumed to remain invariant with changes in the mean and variability of the population of examinees. The scale units in log

---

* The notation for the difficulty parameter has been changed from b to d to correspond to Wright's notation.

Table **4.10** Number of Failures on Vocabulary Items by Score Level

ITEM	SCORE										TOTAL
	1	2	3	4	5	6	7	8	9	10	
justice	10	10	10	7	7	4	2	1			51
parcel	10	14	14	12	17	12	5	1			83
envy	10	14	11	11	7	6	3				62
envelope	1	1		1							3
scorch	10	8	9	6	6	3	1	1			44
prophecy	10	14	14	15	21	21	12	6	2	1	116
molten	10	14	11	13	19	22	8	5		1	103
lease	10	14	8	8	12	7	1		1		61
famished	10	14	14	14	20	18	11	4		1	106
diversion	10	14	14	14	19	20	9	9	1	2	112
frustration	9	10	4	4	5	2					34
FREQUENCY	10	14	14	15	22	23	13	9	2	5	127

units, as given by equation 4.16, are determined by the average value of a_g, the steepness parameter, for test items of the sort that are included in tests of the latent attribute being measured. Initially, the zero point for the scale of the latent attribute is entirely arbitrary. But once a zero point has been selected, the difficulty levels of all items, even new groups of items tried out on other groups, can be referred to this pre-established reference point. This procedure is analogous to the adjustment of item difficulty estimates discussed on pages 66–70. By the same token, the ability level of any group can be referred to this same established zero point. Groups *may* be defined in any way (age, grade, occupation, etc.) but, so far as scaling test scores is concerned, the defined group is ordinarily all persons receiving a specific total score or falling within a specified range of total scores on the set of items that makes up a test.

The procedures for scaling item difficulties and score levels will become clearer after we review an actual example. This will also permit some review of problems that may arise in developing this type of scale. The data given in Table 4.10 were obtained from the tryout of a set of 11 vocabulary words in free-response format with a group of 127 pupils in grades 3 and 4. The table shows the number of pupils *failing* on each word at total score levels from 1 to 10. (Scores of 0 and 11 cannot be used in the scaling because pupils at these score levels are unmeasured, and it is not known how low and high, respectively, pupils receiving these scores fall.)

The column on the extreme right of the table shows the total number failing each item. The row at the very bottom shows the total number of cases falling at each score level. From the marginal frequencies of numbers failing on an item,

Table 4.11 Computations for Assigning Scale Values to Items and Score Groups

	Log odds	Log − $\overline{\text{Log}}$	(Log − $\overline{\text{Log}}$)^2	PROX Scale
		ITEMS		
justice	−0.40	−0.61	0.37	−0.87
parcel	0.70	0.49	0.24	0.70
envy	−0.05	−0.26	0.07	−0.37
envelope	−3.72	−3.93	15.44	−5.62
scorch	−0.63	−0.84	0.71	−1.20
prophecy	2.36	2.15	4.62	3.08
molten	1.46	1.25	1.62	1.79
lease	−0.08	−0.25	0.06	−0.41
famished	1.62	1.41	1.99	2.02
diversion	2.01	1.80	3.24	2.58
frustration	−1.01	−1.22	1.49	−1.75
Mean	0.21	Variance	2.709	

SCORE GROUPS

Score	Frequency	Log odds	f(log odds)	f(log odds)^2	PROX Scale
1	10	−2.30	−23.00	52.90	−3.93
2	14	−1.50	−21.00	31.50	−2.56
3	14	−0.98	−13.72	13.45	−1.71
4	15	−0.56	−8.40	4.70	−0.94
5	22	−0.18	−3.96	0.71	−0.31
6	23	0.18	4.14	0.75	0.31
7	13	0.56	7.28	4.08	0.94
8	9	0.98	8.82	8.64	1.71
9	2	1.50	3.00	4.50	2.56
10	5	2.30	11.50	26.45	3.93
		Mean	−0.28	Variance 1.038	

log odds of failing can be obtained. Thus, for *justice*, 51 failed and 127 − 51 = 76 passed. The ratio of failers to passers is 51/76 = 0.67 and the natural log is −0.40. For the score values, the log odds stem from the number failed and the total number of items. Thus, for a score of 2, we have 2 items passed and hence 11 − 2 = 9 items failed. The ratio of passes to failures is 2/9 = 0.22, and the log odds value is −1.50. Approximate scale values (called PROX values) are estimated by the procedures set forth by Wright and Stone (1979, p. 34 ff). The computations are shown in Table 4.11, and the steps involved are outlined below.

1. For each item and each score group, calculate the ratio of wrongs to rights — that is, the odds of getting the item wrong.

2. Using tables of natural logarithms or a calculator with a natural log function, determine the natural logarithms of the ratios W/R. (A convenient table is given by Wright and Stone on page 36).

3. Sum the log values over all items and calculate the average log value. Subtract the average from the value of each item to get its deviation log value.

4. Square the deviation log value for each item and sum over items. Calculate the variance of the log values. Similarly, calculate the variance of the log values for score groups.

5. Calculate an "expansion factor" to compensate for the fact that the log-odds values, as calculated, are averages for all persons or all items and do not take into account the variability in person ability or in item difficulty. The expansion factor for items is

$$Y = \left(\frac{1 + V/2.89}{1 - UV/8.35}\right)^{\frac{1}{2}}$$

where V = variance of log values of scores
              U = variance of log values of items

The expansion factor for score groups is

$$X = \left(\frac{1 + U/2.89}{1 - UV/8.35}\right)^{\frac{1}{2}}$$

6. Multiply the deviation log value of each item by the expansion factor Y to get the estimated scale value of the item's difficulty. This provides scale values centered around the difficulty of the average item as a zero point.

7. For each score group, multiply the log value for the group by the expansion factor X to get the scale value corresponding to that score.

At this point we have an initial set of estimates for the *easiness* of the items and the ability level of the score groups. However, these estimates suffer somewhat from the simultaneous estimation of parameters for both scores and items. Wright (1977) recommends carrying out an iterative maximum-likelihood solution that progressively adjusts both item and score estimates until they stabilize at a set of values that gives the best fit, in the maximum-likelihood sense, to the original table of log-odds values. Calculations for the successive iterations are quite laborious if carried out on a hand calculator* but quite manageable for a computer.

---

* The steps for carrying out the iterative maximum-likelihood adjustment to the initial scale estimates are as follows.

1. Prepare from the PROX values the matrix of $(b_j - d_i)$, where b_j is the ability level for score j and d_i is the difficulty level of item i. Each entry is the estimated log odds of getting the item right. (Score values are represented by columns, items by rows.)

2. For each cell, calculate the *probability* of getting the item right by the formula

$$P = \frac{e^{(b_j - d_i)}}{1 + e^{(b_j - d_i)}}$$

3. Calculate the weighted sum across each row of the matrix, weighting each entry by the number of cases in the score group. That is,

$$\sum n_j \frac{e^{(b_j - d_i)}}{1 + e^{(b_j - d_i)}}$$

For each item, this is the estimate from the model of the total number of persons who should get the item right.

4. Subtract each value obtained in step 3 from the actual number getting the item right. This is the discrepancy between the observed value and the theoretical value from the Rasch model.

5. For each cell, calculate the quantity

$$\frac{e^{(b_j - d_i)}}{\left(1 + e^{(b_j - d_i)}\right)^2}$$

This is the derivative of the cell entry. It tells how fast the value of P, the probability of a right response, will change as d_i is changed.

6. Sum the values you obtained in step 5, weighted for number of cases, across the row. That is,

$$\sum n_j \frac{e^{(b_j - d_i)}}{\left(1 + e^{(b_j - d_i)}\right)^2}$$

7. Divide each discrepancy value you obtained in step 4 by the corresponding rate-of-change value you obtained in step 6. The result is the adjustment to be applied to the values of d_i. Call it adj_i. That is,

$$d_i' = d_i - adj_i$$

8. Using b_j and d_i', prepare a new matrix of $(b_j - d_i')$.

9. Repeat steps 2 through 7 for each *column* to get the adjustment to be applied to the *score* values. Note that each item has a unit weight, so the weighting factor used in steps 3 and 6 disappears. The adjusted score values become

$$b_j' = b_j + adj_j$$

Note that the sign of the adjustment in this case is positive rather than negative.

10. Prepare a new matrix using values b_j' and d_i'. Repeat the cycle of calculations (steps 2 through 9) until the adjustments in the next cycle are small enough to be ignored. If a criterion is set of no correction greater than 0.01, convergence is likely to be achieved in 3 or 4 cycles.

11. It is not usually necessary to repeat steps 5 and 6 in cycles after the first, because the resulting values change only slightly. The original values obtained in these steps can serve in further cycles to determine the adjustment in step 7, unless the adjustment in the previous cycle has been substantial.

12. Calculations are *greatly* expedited by use of a programmable calculator with an inverse log function. Steps 2 and 3 and steps 5 and 6 can be programmed so that it is only necessary to enter the successive values of the matrix cell entries and n.

Table **4.12**   Comparison of PROX and MAXLIKE Scale Values

	Prox	Maxlike
	ITEMS	
justice	− 0.87	− 1.02
parcel	0.70	0.54
envy	− 0.37	− 0.48
envelope	− 5.62	− 5.79
scorch	− 1.20	− 1.39
prophecy	3.08	2.94
molten	1.79	1.72
lease	− 0.41	− 0.53
famished	2.02	1.94
diversion	2.58	2.48
frustration	− 1.75	− 1.98
	SCORES	
1	− 3.93	− 4.41
2	− 2.56	− 2.59
3	− 1.71	− 1.65
4	− 0.94	− 0.93
5	− 0.31	− 0.27
6	0.31	0.39
7	0.94	1.07
8	1.71	1.78
9	2.56	2.56
10	3.93	3.58

A computer program designed to start with the original item responses of examinees and to carry the computations through to the final estimates of item and score parameters is provided by Wright and Panchapakesan (1969).

Some sense of the size of the adjustments to the initial PROX estimates that result from three cycles of adjustment toward a maximum-likelihood fit can be seen in Table 4.12. The discrepancies between the two sets of scale values are mostly rather small. Most of them fall between 0.1 and 0.2 scale units, and items maintain their order of difficulty substantially unchanged. If the sample on which the scaling was based is fairly small, differences of this size are probably less than the sampling error in the scaling. However, one or two discrepancies for scores are substantially larger. For the adjustment of these values, if for nothing else, the adjustments are probably justified. With larger sample sizes and a concern for maximum precision, one would surely want to apply the maximum-likelihood procedure.

Table 4.13 Analysis of Discrepancies for the Word "Justice"

SCORE GROUP	LOG ODDS RIGHT	LOG ODDS WRONG	ODDS RIGHT	ODDS WRONG	NO. RIGHT	NO. WRONG	NO. RIGHT TIMES ODDS WRONG	NO. WRONG TIMES ODDS RIGHT	SUM
1	−3.06	3.06	.047	21.33	0	10	0	.47	.47
2	−1.69	1.69	.185	5.42	4	10	21.68	1.85	23.53
3	−0.84	0.84	.432	2.32	4	10	9.28	4.32	13.60
4	−0.07	0.07	.932	1.07	8	7	8.56	6.52	15.08
5	0.56	−0.56	1.75	.571	15	7	8.56	12.25	20.81
6	1.18	−1.18	3.25	.307	19	4	5.83	13.00	18.83
7	1.81	−1.81	6.11	.164	11	2	1.80	12.22	14.02
8	2.58	−2.58	13.20	.076	8	1	0.61	13.20	13.81
9	3.43	−3.43	30.88	.032	2	0	0.06	0	.06
10	4.80	−4.80	121.51	.008	5	0	0.04	0	.04

$$\chi^2 = 120.25$$

$$0.40 < P < 0.50$$

Once a set of estimates has been obtained for the difficulty parameters of each of the test items and the ability values corresponding to each score level, we may ask how well the original data can be reproduced from these scale values. How well does the model fit the data?

From the scale values, the log odds and the odds ratio can be calculated for each cell, and the odds can be compared with the actual frequency of successes and failures in the cell. A discrepancy value can be obtained for each cell by multiplying the odds of success times the frequency of failure and the odds of failure times the frequency of success. The expected value for the sum of these two products equals the number of observations in the cell. The discrepancy values can be summed across score values for an item, and across items for the whole table, to provide a test of goodness of fit item by item and for the test as a whole. In Table 4.13 the procedures are indicated step by step and illustrated for the PROX value of the first item.

1. From the item-difficulty scale value d_i and the score-level-ability scale value b_j, calculate the log odds of getting the item right, $(b_j - d_i)$, and of getting the item wrong, $(d_i - b_j)$.

2. From each log-odds value, determine the predicted odds of getting the item right—the antilog of $(b_j - d_i)$—and of getting the item wrong—the antilog of $(d_i - b_j)$.

3. Multiply the odds of occurrence of a success by the actual number of failures, multiply the odds of a failure by the actual number of successes, and sum the two products for that cell (item by score level).

4. Sum the values you obtained in step 3 across all score groups for a given item. The item sum can be tested for significance by a chi-square test with $N - n$ degrees of freedom, where N = number of examinees and n = number of score groups.

5. The overall goodness of fit can be tested by summing the sums obtained in step 4 across all items and applying chi-square with $Nk - k - n$ degrees of freedom, where k = number of items and n = number of score groups.

If the analysis of the items is being carried out as part of the process of test construction, it may seem desirable to eliminate items with a significantly large chi-square. These are items that appear not to conform to the model. At least, the items should be examined to see why they are yielding large discrepancies. It may be found that these items differentiate levels of ability less well than the other items do. That is, they have a low biserial or a_g parameter, which would raise a question about whether the items should be retained. It is also *possible* that the item is especially effective in differentiating levels and should be highly valued. Another possibility is that differentiation may be limited to a fraction of the score range, in which case excessive chi-square values would appear in cells at one or the other end of the range of score values. This would seem likely for difficult multiple-choice items if there were a substantial ability range over which large amounts of guessing occurred.

Chapter 5

Scales, Norms, and Equating

Once the items to make up a test have been selected and organized into a testing instrument, an early next step is to develop a meaningful scale of scores for the resulting instrument. One starts out with a raw score, which is usually simply the number of correct answers or that number adjusted by some penalty for errors. However, a raw score of 28, for example, conveys no real meaning standing by itself. Meaning attaches to a raw score only when we know (1) how many score points *could* be obtained and (2) what the difficulty would be of obtaining each possible score.

In so-called criterion-referenced tests, it is assumed that the test exercises in some narrowly defined domain are relatively interchangeable, so far as function measured and item difficulty are concerned, and that degree of "mastery" of the domain can be expressed adequately by the simple percent of items gotten correct. Interest is often focused on some specific level of performance, and a dichotomy is set up at 80%, for instance, to separate those who have from those who have not achieved "mastery." Thus we might present 10 tasks of the type

$$305$$
$$-123$$

and agree to accept 8 correct as defining mastery of "subtraction involving a zero in the minuend."

More often, however, we assume that we are dealing with a latent attribute that can be possessed in varying degrees and that there is no clear limit to, nor any uniquely meaningful level on, that attribute. We are interested in the score as implying some level or degree of that attribute, and we want to establish procedures for moving from the raw score to an estimate of status on the latent attribute. Because we ordinarily include in a test only test exercises that show a satisfactorily high, and usually fairly similar, correlation with some measure that stands as a surrogate for the latent attribute, it is reasonable to assume that the person who gets more of the test items right stands higher on the latent attribute than the person who gets fewer items right. That is, test scores may be accepted as constituting, to some degree of precision, an *ordinal* scale. However, it is not at all evident that each additional unit of raw score represents an equal increment on the scale of the latent attribute.

Suppose, for example, that we have a test composed of 5 very easy items and 5 very difficult items. The easy items will be defined as those for which the item difficulty parameter b_g is -3.0 and the difficult ones as those for which the dif-

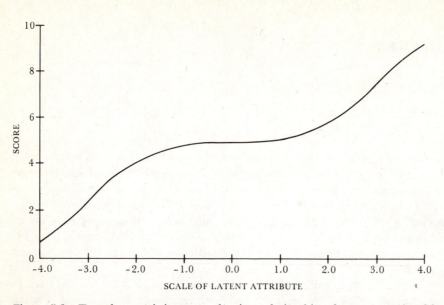

Figure 5.1 Test characteristic curve, showing relationship of score to scale of latent attribute.

ficulty parameter is $+3.0$. For all items, the steepness parameter a_g is assumed to be 1.00. The expected score on the easy items, the hard items, and the total test for persons falling at different points on the scale, θ, of the latent attribute is shown in Table 5.1 and Figure 5.1. The expected value of θ corresponding to different scores is shown in Table 5.2.* Clearly, equal raw-score increments do not correspond to equal increments in θ at all points in the raw-score scale.

The illustration that we have chosen is intentionally extreme. It produces dramatic inequalities in the raw-score-to-attribute conversion at different points along the score scale. Thus the difference between raw scores of 2 and 4 corresponds to 1.0 unit of the latent attribute, whereas the difference between raw scores of 4 and 6 corresponds to 4.4 units! In practice, inequalities as great as this are unlikely to occur. However, there can be no guarantee that a unit increment

---

* We find the expected number of correct answers at a given value of θ by first getting the probability of success on each item separately from the item characteristic function,

$$P_g(\theta) = \frac{1}{1 + e^{-Da_g(\theta - b_g)}}$$

and then summing the P-values over items to give the expected score. That is,

$$\text{Expected score} = \sum P_g(\theta) = \sum \frac{1}{1 + e^{-Da_g(\theta - b_g)}}$$

As many points can be determined as needed to plot a smooth score characteristic curve. The values in Table 5.2 can then be read from the curve.

Table 5.1   Raw Score Corresponding to Selected Values of Latent Attribute,
Five Very Easy and Five Very Difficult Items

VALUE OF θ	EASY ITEMS	DIFFICULT ITEMS	TOTAL SCORE
-3.0	2.5	0.0	2.5
-2.0	4.2	0.0	4.2
-1.0	4.9	0.0	4.9
0.0	5.0	0.0	5.0
$+1.0$	5.0	0.1	5.1
$+2.0$	5.0	0.8	5.8
$+3.0$	5.0	2.5	7.5

Table 5.2   Latent Attribute Values Corresponding to Selected Raw Scores, Five Very
Easy and Five Very Difficult Items

SCORE	VALUE OF θ
1	-3.6
2	-3.2
3	-2.7
4	-2.2
5	0.0
6	2.2
7	2.7
8	3.2
9	3.6

in raw score corresponds to the same increment in the latent attribute throughout the score scale. We need some rational way to verify the equality of raw-score
units or to adjust them if they are unequal.

PROCEDURES FOR SCORE CONVERSION

We shall consider four general types of procedures for trying to produce
converted-score values that represent an interval scale on the latent attribute — a

scale in which a unit of converted score represents the same increment in the latent attribute no matter where on the score scale it appears.

Age and grade units, which assume that a year of growth represents an equal unit.

Linear score conversions, which assume that the original raw units are in fact equal.

Area score conversions, which assume some standard shape in the distribution of the latent attribute in a population.

The Rasch model, which assumes uniform item steepness parameters and a reciprocal relationship between person ability and item difficulty.

AGE AND GRADE UNITS

One type of converted score is based on the assumption that a year of growth represents an equal amount at whatever age or grade it occurs. Thus, for age units, the difference between 6-year-old performance and 7-year-old performance is asserted to be equal to the difference between performance at 7 and at 8 or between performance at 10 and at 11. For grade units, the difference between third- and fourth-grade performance is asserted to be equal to the difference between fourth- and fifth-grade performance or between sixth- and seventh-grade performance. Note that we say *is asserted to be* equal; no evidence is typically offered to demonstrate that the increments are equal in any fundamental sense.

Age and grade units have a certain easy plausibility to the psychometrically naive. And they provide a reference frame that appears to carry a kind of down-to-earth meaning. "She is as tall as a 10-year-old." "He reads at the fifth-grade level." "He has a mental age of 8 years, 6 months." But quite obviously, this type of scale fails us completely when we go beyond the years of childhood—and perhaps early youth—when growth is fairly rapid and at least fairly uniform. "She is as tall as a 30-year-old" makes no sense. And neither does "She reads as well as a Ph.D." or "He has a mental age of 66."

Even in the childhood years, age and grade units present serious problems. Equality of successive steps on the scale is at best approximate. Even more troublesome, equal scores by individuals of different ages may represent *qualitatively* different performances. This can be seen most clearly in a subject such as arithmetic, where what can be done depends to a large extent on what has been taught. Thus, for example, a very capable fourth-grader might get the same score as an average sixth-grader. But she or he might do so by performing very well on material that has been taught up to the fourth grade, without knowing topics taught in grades 5 and 6, whereas the average sixth-grader might lose points by making a variety of mistakes even on topics taught at the earlier grade levels.

The procedure for developing a scale of age or grade equivalents is conceptually simple, but a number of practical problems arise. We will outline the basic steps and then comment on the practical problems.

1. Obtain access to a representative sample of persons at each age or grade level at which the instrument might be used. The theoretical and practical issues involved in obtaining a representative sample to test are discussed in some detail in the section on norms starting on page 123.

2. Administer the test or tests over the appropriate range of grades or ages. The time of year for testing presents certain problems, which will be discussed further on pages 112–113.

3. Assemble the data by grade or age groupings. Grade level is more or less self-defining, but the definition of age groupings must be decided on. When *individual* testing is done, it represents a desirable refinement to test each individual as close as possible to a birthday, or a half-birthday if finer grouping is desired. In the case of group testing, it is ordinarily necessary to lump together all cases falling within 6 months of a given birthday, or within 3 months of a half-birthday if half-year groupings are used.

4. Determine the average raw score for each age or grade grouping. This raw score is then the one assigned to that age or grade value.

5. Interpolate between successive age levels to determine an age equivalent for each possible raw score.

6. Extrapolate some distance beyond the lowest and highest grade or age actually tested in order to assign equivalents for scores at the high and low ends of the raw-score scale.

7. Prepare a table showing the age or grade equivalent for each raw-score value.

An illustration of the procedure for preparing a table of age equivalents is provided in Table 5.3 and Figure 5.2. (It does not seem necessary to display the steps in computing a mean from the distribution of raw scores for each age grouping.) In this illustration, data have been grouped by full-year units, and each individual has been assigned to the group corresponding to his or her *nearest* birthday. Two procedures are shown for estimating age equivalents for each raw-score value. In the numerical estimation procedure, values lying between 7-0 and 13-0 are calculated by use of the following proportion:

$$\frac{\text{Fraction of score difference needed}}{\text{Total difference of adjacent ages}} = \frac{\text{months needed}}{\text{twelve months}}$$

The extrapolated values are obtained by continuing the interpolated values of the last full-year interval, adding or subtracting the same number of months (eventually rounded to full months) for each additional score point.

It is also possible, and in some ways more reasonable, to estimate age or grade equivalents graphically, as is shown in Figure 5.2. In this figure the raw scores

Table 5.3   Illustration of Preparation of Table of Age Equivalents

AGE GROUPING	RANGE INCLUDED	MEAN SCORE	INTERPOLATED OR EXTRAPOLATED AGE EQUIVALENTS		
			Raw Score	Numerical Interpolation	Graphic Interpolation
7-0	6-6 to 7-6	15.3	10	6-2	5-0
			11	6-4	5-7
8-0	7-6 to 8-6	21.7	12	6-6	6-2
			13	6-8	6-6
9-0	8-6 to 9-6	32.2	14	6-10	6-9
			15	6-11	7-0
10-0	9-6 to 10-6	41.9	16	7-1	7-2
			17	7-3	7-4
11-0	10-6 to 11-6	50.7	18	7-5	7-6
			19	7-7	7-7
12-0	11-6 to 12-6	56.2	20	7-9	7-8
			21	7-11	7-10
13-0	12-6 to 13-6	59.9	22	8-1	8-0
			$\vdots$	$\vdots$	$\vdots$
Number of items = 65			55	11-10	11-9
			56	12-0	11-11
			57	12-3	12-2
			58	12-6	12-5
			59	12-9	12-9
			60	13-0	13-0
			61	13-4	13-3
			62	13-7	13-7
			63	13-10	14-1
			64	14-1	14-6
			65	14-5	14-10

for successive ages are plotted, and then a smooth curve is drawn that fits the points closely but smooths out what appear to be chance irregularities in the sequence of points. The curve is extended beyond the observed points, continuing so far as possible the shape that has been established within the range of observed values. Drawing such a curve is admittedly a somewhat subjective process, especially in the extensions at the extremes, but the smooth curve may yield results closer to the true values than purely arithmetical operations on a set of sample points. Note that the two methods agree closely within the range of observed scores but deviate quite markedly in the extrapolated sections. The

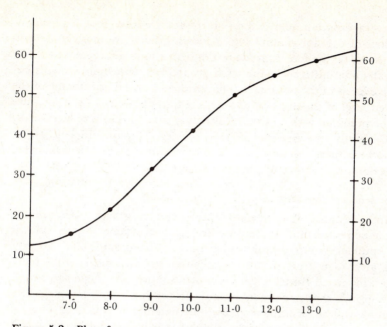

Figure 5.2   Plot of raw score versus age level.

deviations become greater the further one extrapolates. This fact illustrates the fallibility of, and limited faith to be placed in, extrapolated score conversions.

Several problems arise in connection with the preparation of a table of age or grade equivalents of the type illustrated in Table 5.3. In part, these problems are common to all procedures that attempt to develop a set of scales with normative reference, but they appear most clearly in relation to age and grade equivalents. We will discuss them here, but they should be kept in mind in the course of *any* scale development.

Different Levels of a Test

Whenever an attribute (for example, reading comprehension) is to be tested over a considerable range of ages or grades, efficient testing demands that there be several levels of the test. Thus a reading test that was appropriate for third- and fourth-graders would provide no useful information about high school students, and vice versa. The difficulty of the test tasks must be adjusted to match the ability range of those tested. So, if we want to develop a series of tests of the attribute that will permit us to express a wide range of competence on a single score scale, we must devise some procedure for tying the successive levels of the test together. It is necessary to know what score on Level A, designed for grades 3 and 4, corresponds to what score on Level B, designed for grades 5 and 6, and so on. In standardization of the test, children in each grade will presumably be given the test level that is designed for them, so there will be no *direct* evidence on what the average sixth-grader will do on the fourth-grade test. To assign a grade equivalent of 6-4, for example, to a fourth grader, we must be able to translate each score on the fourth-grade test into an equivalent score on the test that was actually administered in the sixth grade. We must build bridges between successive levels in the test series. This requires that either (1) some of the items in a given level of the test also appear in adjacent levels or (2) a separate bridging test be prepared with a range of difficulty that permits it to be given at both levels. Generally, the first procedure provides the most efficient use of testing time and the most precise equating. These issues will be discussed more fully in the section on equating beginning on page 133.

Obtaining Representative Age Samples

Whatever normative data are obtained to represent an age group, it is important that the sample be representative. Because practical constraints usually make it necessary to conduct group testing with intact grade groups, and because children of a given age are typically spread over several grades, it becomes necessary to test in several grades to get full representation of a single age group. For those age groups that are predominantly in the highest or lowest grades tested, the sample will be incomplete and will be systematically biased. Thus, if a test series is administered in grades 3 through 9, the retarded 8-year-olds will be excluded from the sample, as will the accelerated 14-year-olds. Testing over a span of 6 grades will yield reasonably complete representation of at most 5 age groups, and extensions beyond the range (for our example) of 9 to 13 will have to involve extrapolation and adjustment.

This problem arises to a degree for any normative interpretation, but it becomes particularly acute for age equivalents, which already require extrapolation at the extremes to provide equivalents for very low scores of younger children and high scores of older children.

Time of Year for Testing

An issue that becomes especially important for measures that are closely related to school instruction, but that is of some concern for all measures that have a normative reference, is that of when tests should be given in relation to the school year. The procedure of interpolating in age and grade norms (and in fact any procedure that interprets performance in relation to an undifferentiated grade or age group) assumes continuous and relatively uniform growth in performance throughout the 12 months from one year to the next. This is at best a rough approximation, and it deviates seriously from the facts for subjects such as arithmetic, where the nonschool summer months are often characterized by loss rather than gain. Thus growth over the years shows something of a saw-tooth profile rather than a smooth, steady gain.

Some achievement test publishers have dealt with this problem via the costly and administratively demanding but straightforward procedure of carrying out normative testing at several times of the year—typically autumn and spring or autumn, winter, and spring. A partial adjustment is often achieved by assuming a 10-month year and reporting grade equivalents as years and tenths of years, with the assumption that no increment occurs during the two vacation months. For functions that are less clearly related to in-school experience, such as most scholastic aptitude measures, the issue has frequently just been ignored.

LINEAR SCORE CONVERSIONS

Sometimes the issue of equality of test score units is dealt with by simply denying that the problem exists. That is, the raw-score units are implicitly assumed or explicitly declared to be equal without further ado. Raw scores are still often converted to some more attractive score scale, usually in an effort to express results in a set of numbers that have roughly comparable meaning from one test to another and, via equating, from one form to another. Thus various types of standard-score conversions are offered in which the mean and standard deviation are specified in advance. Typical standard-score reference frames are as follows:

	MEAN	STANDARD DEVIATION
T-scores	50	10
Army classification tests	100	20
College Board scores	500	100
Deviation IQs	100	15 or 16

The linear conversion formula becomes

$$X_{st} = \sigma_{st}\left(\frac{X_{obt} - \overline{X}_{obt}}{S_{obt}}\right) + \overline{X}_{st} \tag{5.1}$$

where   obt refers to values on the original raw-score scale
         st refers to values on the final standard-score scale.

As an illustration of linear conversion, suppose that we have prepared a 45-item reading test for sixth-grade pupils and have found, for a sample of sixth-graders, that the mean score is 25.0 and the standard deviation is 6.7. We have decided that we want to use a standard-score scale for which the mean is 50 and the standard deviation is 10. Entering these values in formula 5.1, we get

$$X_{st} = 10\left(\frac{X_{obt} - 25}{6.67}\right) + 50$$

which reduces to

$$X_{st} = 1.5X_{obt} + 12.5$$

We could prepare a table showing the converted score corresponding to each possible obtained score. The first part of the table would look like this:

OBTAINED SCORE	CONVERTED SCORE
45	80
44	78.5
43	77
and so on	

It would certainly be possible to assemble a test in which each additional unit of raw score would correspond to very nearly the same increment on the scale of the latent attribute over a considerable part of the raw-score range. If the items were approximately equally discriminating (had equal values of the a_g parameter) and were spaced uniformly over the scale of the latent attribute (had uniformly spaced b_g parameters), the successive raw scores would correspond to equal increments of θ, the latent attribute, for a considerable range. Thus, if 13 items with $a_g = 1.0$ were spaced out at equal intervals of 0.5 from -3.0 to $+3.0$ on the scale of θ, the raw score to θ equivalents would be as follows:

RAW SCORE	θ
1	-3.05
2	-2.35
3	-1.75
4	-1.25
5	-0.75
6	-0.25
7	0.25
8	0.75
9	1.25
10	1.75
11	2.35
12	3.05

From raw scores of 3 to 10, the increments in θ are equal, amounting to 0.5 for each raw-score point. At the extremes, the increments become somewhat larger.

However, the relationship between raw score and position on the latent attribute can be quite far from linear, as was shown in Figure 5.1. In particular, if items are chosen so that most of them cluster in some narrow range of difficulty, raw-score units in that region will represent smaller increments in θ, the scale of the latent attribute, than in other parts of the raw-score range. Thus some tests are made with most of the items of moderate difficulty in order to discriminate most accurately at the middle levels of ability where most of the examinees are found. For such a test, a point of raw score in the middle of the raw-score range represents a smaller increment than a point at either extreme. As a result the raw-score units are systematically unequal. Then the rational basis for a simple linear transformation from raw scores to scale scores becomes very weak. Rarely, if ever, is the raw-score scale for a multi-item test an interval scale throughout its full range.

AREA CONVERSIONS

An alternative type of assumption involves the shape of the distribution of the latent attribute in samples appropriately drawn from age or grade cohorts. The most familiar assumption is that the latent attribute has a normal distribution in the population from which the sample is drawn. It seems unlikely that any conclusive *proof* of the appropriateness of this assumption can be presented. Some of the lines of evidence that bear on its plausibility are as follows:

1. The mathematical derivation of the normal curve demonstrates that such a form is to be expected for an outcome that results from many independent causes, each of which contributes a small amount to the variance of that outcome. Where it seems reasonable to think of level on some attribute as the product of many small, independent or nearly independent causes, one could expect a normal distribution of that attribute. To the extent that any hereditary effect is the result of many genes, and to the extent that pre- and postnatal influences are multiple, diverse, and not closely related to one another, a normal distribution is a likely outcome.

2. To the extent that causal influences are themselves normally distributed and their impact on the outcome is approximately linear, the resulting attribute could be expected to be normally distributed.

3. If physical attributes for which a fundamental measurement is possible in units of known equality (for example, height or weight) are found to approximate a normal distribution, this lends some plausibility to the notion that other attributes for which equality of units *cannot* be directly demonstrated also have a normal distribution.

4. Perhaps most relevant would be the demonstration that, when raw scores for different groups are converted to a scale such that a normal distribution results, scaling for different age or grade groups produces consistent results in that scale distances that are equal at one age or grade are also equal at any other.

Table 5.4   Illustration of the Calculation of Normalized Standard Scores

SCORE INTERVAL	FREQUENCY	CUMULATIVE FREQUENCY	CUMULATIVE PERCENTAGE	NORMAL DEVIATE (z)	$100z + 500$
80–84	10	1425	100.00		
75–79	28	1415	99.30	2.46	746
70–74	54	1387	97.33	1.93	693
65–69	108	1333	93.54	1.52	652
60–64	126	1225	85.96	1.08	608
55–59	153	1099	77.12	.74	574
50–54	177	946	66.39	.42	542
45–49	158	769	53.96	.10	510
40–44	159	611	42.88	$-.18$	482
35–39	123	452	31.72	$-.48$	452
30–34	106	329	23.02	$-.74$	426
25–29	96	223	15.65	-1.01	399
20–24	71	127	8.91	-1.35	365
15–19	31	56	3.93	-1.76	324
10–14	20	25	1.75	-2.11	289
5–9	4	5	.35	-2.70	230
0–4	1	1	.07		

Computational Steps in Converting
Raw to Normalized Standard Scores

The data with which one starts consist of a distribution of raw scores, as shown in the first two columns of Table 5.4. It is ordinarily desirable to work with a grouped frequency distribution, in order to lend a greater degree of stability to the data. From the frequency distribution a column of cumulative frequencies is prepared, and from this a column of cumulative percentages. At this point one turns to a set of tables of the normal curve and determines the normal deviate (the abscissa value on the base line of the normal curve) corresponding to each percentage. These are the scale values presumed to represent equal increments in the underlying latent attribute. Because the size of the unit in which to express amounts of the attribute is arbitrary and a matter of convenience (note inches, feet, and centimeters) and because we do not know the location of a "true" zero point, any convenient linear transformation can be applied to the standard-score scale. In Table 5.4 we have applied the transformation

$$X = 100z + 500$$

which produces a set of scores with the mean set at 500 and the standard deviation set at 100. Any other convenient transformation could be used. Two aspects

Table 5.5 Portion of Table Converting Raw Score to Normalized Standard Score

RAW SCORE	STANDARD SCORE
79	741
78	730
77	720
76	709
75	699
74	689
73	681
72	672
71	664
70	656
⋮	⋮
50	513
49	507
48	502
47	496
46	490
45	485
⋮	⋮

of convenience are a score scale that (1) has no negative numbers and (2) needs to use no decimal points.

Given the standard-score equivalents of selected raw-score values, one can produce a complete table of standard-score equivalents by interpolation. When this is done, remember that (1) the cumulative percentage is the percentage to the upper limit of the corresponding interval and (2) by general convention, the limit lies midway between adjacent scores—that is, the limit of the interval 50–54 is 54.5. Table 5.5 shows a section of the conversion of the data in Table 5.4 from raw score to standard score.

The procedure just illustrated provides a standard-score scale in which the units may be presumed to be equal, given that the latent attribute is normally distributed in the population sampled (age or grade group) and that the sample was properly drawn. It is often desirable to extend that equal-unit scale over a range of several years or several grades, again assuming that a normal distribution holds for each of the ages or grades in question. In some cases, all ages or grades will have taken the same test, but the distributions of raw scores will cover different parts of the score range. More frequently, the tests taken at different age or grade levels differ in level, and the two groups will have been tested on a common *bridging test*. The bridging test may be a set of items that are included in and make up a part of the regular tests, or it may be a completely separate set of items chosen to represent the same latent attribute. An example of the former procedure is found in the tests of the multilevel series of the Lorge-Thorndike and the Cognitive Ability Tests, and we will illustrate the procedure with data drawn from that source.

The Verbal Ability Test of this series is composed of 100 items at each level. As one goes from one level to the next higher level, easier items are dropped off at the beginning of each subtest and harder items are added at the end. From one level to the next, 80 items are common and 20 are different. Within each level, normal deviates are computed for the common test of 80 items, following the procedures illustrated in Table 5.4. These are shown for two adjacent levels, D and E, in Table 5.6. The normal deviates are for adjacent grade groups. Our problem is to express the normal deviates for the two groups in a common unit of measure and in relation to a common mean. In the illustration, we will use the mean and the standard deviation of level D as our reference frame.

Because at the extremes a small percentage change will result in a sizable shift in the normal deviate, and because their values are consequently unstable, we will ignore the tails of the distributions in our equating. As a rule of thumb, we will not consider any score levels at which the normal deviate in either group surpasses ± 2.00. Thus the equating will be based on score intervals from 10-14 to 50-54.

Working within this set of intervals, we calculate

1. The sum of the normal deviates.
2. The sum of the squared normal deviates.
3. The mean of the normal deviates; that is, $\sum z/k$ where k is the number of class intervals.
4. The mean of the squared normal deviates.
5. The variance of the normal deviates.
6. The standard deviation of the normal deviates.

The calculations are indicated at the bottom of the table.

From the standard deviation of the normal deviates, we can calculate the relative sizes of the standard deviations of the two groups on the attribute measured by our test. This is given by the ratio

$$\frac{\sigma_E}{\sigma_D} = \frac{S_{z_D}}{S_{z_E}} \tag{5.2}$$

That is, the standard deviations of the groups are related as the reciprocal of the variabilities of the sets of normal deviates. A given range of ability will represent a *smaller* number of standard deviation units in the *more* variable group. For our set of data, we have

Table 5.6   Scaling by Use of the Normal Curve*

	Level D				Level E			
SCORE INTERVAL	FREQ.	CUM. FREQ.	CUM. %	NORMAL DEVIATE	FREQ.	CUM. FREQ.	CUM. %	NORMAL DEVIATE
65–69					20	1469		
60–64	13	1426			47	1449	98.63	2.21
55–59	38	1413	99.15	2.38	116	1402	95.43	1.69
50–54	73	1375	96.49	1.81	168	1286	87.54	1.15
45–49	134	1302	91.36	1.36	183	1118	76.10	0.71
40–44	169	1168	81.96	0.92	199	935	63.65	0.35
35–39	210	999	70.10	0.53	196	736	50.10	0.00
30–34	206	789	55.37	0.13	179	540	36.76	−0.34
25–29	193	583	40.91	−0.23	137	361	24.57	−0.69
20–24	162	390	27.37	−0.60	120	224	15.25	−1.03
15–19	143	228	16.00	−0.99	63	104	7.08	−1.47
10–14	57	85	5.96	−1.56	35	41	2.79	−1.91
5–9	21	28	1.96	−2.06	5	6	0.41	−2.67
0–4	7	7	0.49	−2.57	1	1	0.07	

Sum of normal deviates	1.37	−3.23
Sum of squared normal deviates	10.10	9.41
Mean of standard scores	.152	−0.359
Variance of normal deviates	1.099	0.917
S.D. of normal deviates	1.048	0.957

* From R. L. Thorndike and E. P. Hagen, *Cognitive Ability Tests.* Iowa City, Iowa: Riverside Publishing Co. Used by permission.

$$\frac{\sigma_E}{\sigma_D} = \frac{1.048}{0.957} \quad \text{or} \quad \sigma_E = 1.095\,\sigma_D$$

From the mean of the normal deviates and the standard deviation of the normal deviates, we can calculate how much the mean of group E is displaced from the mean of group D in group D standard-score units. This is given by the equation

$$\text{Mean of group E} = \text{mean of group D} + (\bar{z}_D - \bar{z}_E\sigma_E) \qquad (5.3)$$

In our example the mean of group D is serving as the zero point on our scale, so this becomes

$$\begin{aligned}
\text{Mean}_E &= 0.152 - (-0.359)(1.095) \\
&= 0.152 + 0.393 \\
&= 0.545
\end{aligned}$$

That is, the mean of group E falls 0.545 units above the mean of group D, where the unit is the standard deviation of group D.

If a still higher level of the test, say level F, is to be incorporated into the common-score scale, this can be done by equating level F to level E and then, by the already determined equations, to level D. Suppose that we have carried through computations parallel to those shown in Table 5.6 for levels E and F and have come out with the equations

$$\sigma_F = 1.068\sigma_E \quad \text{and} \quad \overline{X}_F = \overline{X}_E + 0.387\sigma_E$$

We can then substitute in these equations the values we obtained before for σ_E and $\overline{X}_E$:

$$\sigma_F = 1.068\,(1.095\sigma_D) = 1.169\sigma_D$$

and

$$\begin{aligned}
\overline{X}_F &= 0.545 + (0.387)(1.095) \\
&= 0.545 + 0.424 \\
&= 0.969
\end{aligned}$$

It is sometimes convenient to assign some value other than 0 to the mean of our reference group and some value other than unity to that group's standard deviation. Thus we might choose to set the mean of the reference group at 300 and the standard deviation of that group at 50. If we call the additive factor A and the multiplying factor M, for the standard deviation of any group we must multiply the previously computed value by M, and for the mean of the group we must add A to M times the previously computed value. Thus we would have

GROUP	MEAN	S.D.
D	300	50.0
E	327	54.8
F	348	58.4

Once the mean and standard deviation of each group have been established on the *bridging* test (referred to the common standard-score scale), those values may be assigned to that group on the *total* test that was designed for it. We assume that both bridging test and total test are measures of the same latent attribute, so that any group can be expected to show the same mean and variability of basic-scale scores on both tests. Thus, in Table 5.7, we show selected

Table 5.7   Conversion of Raw-Score to Standard-Score Scale for Level E of Test Series

SCORE INTERVAL	CUMULATIVE PERCENT	STANDARD SCORES			
		Level E Units	Level D Units	Level D Mean	Mean = 300 S.D. = 50
70–74	99.5	2.58	2.83	3.37	468
65–69	97.1	1.90	2.08	2.62	431
60–64	93.3	1.50	1.64	2.18	409
55–59	86.4	1.10	1.20	1.74	387
50–54	75.4	0.69	0.76	1.30	365
45–49	65.3	0.39	0.43	0.97	348
40–44	53.3	0.08	0.09	0.63	332
35–39	41.8	−0.21	−0.23	0.31	316
30–34	29.7	−0.53	−0.58	−0.04	298
25–29	18.9	−0.88	−0.96	−0.42	279
20–24	10.4	−1.26	−1.38	−0.84	258
15–19	5.0	−1.64	−1.80	−1.26	237
10–14	1.7	−2.12	−2.32	−1.78	211

(From R. L. Thorndike and E. P. Hagen, *Cognitive Ability Tests*. Iowa City, Iowa: Riverside Publishing Co. Used by permission.)

raw scores on the total test at level E, a test composed of the 80 bridging items plus 20 items generally more difficult than those in level D.*

SCALING SCORES WITH THE RASCH MODEL

Where using the Rasch model seems justified, it can be used to scale not only the difficulty level of a single test item but also the ability level represented by a test score. This was shown in the example worked through in Chapter 4 on page 98 ff. A set of scale values for each score is provided by the PROX solution that assumes a symmetrical distribution of item difficulties. This set can be refined by the maximum-likelihood iterations to give values that will be more appropriate if the distribution of item difficulties is noticeably skewed or deviates markedly from a normal distribution.

If different test forms have been administered to different groups of examinees, the score values for all forms can be expressed on a common scale, so long as different forms share a common set of items through which the several

---

* If the bridging test is appreciably less reliable than the full-length test, the appropriate procedures become somewhat more complex and should be based on estimated true scores rather than observed scores.

TABLE 5.8   Scale Values of Items by the Rasch Procedure

	FORM 68	FORM 88	DIFFERENCE
justice	−0.87		
parcel	0.70		
envy	−0.37		
envelope	−5.62		
scorch	−1.20		
prophecy	3.08	1.09	1.99
molten	1.79	0.65	1.14
lease	−0.41	−1.55	1.14
famished	2.02	0.30	1.72
diversion	2.58	0.39	2.19
frustration	−1.75	−3.74	1.99
mosaic		1.04	
puddle		−4.81	
leer		2.58	
divest		5.84	
terminal		.00	
priceless		−1.91	

forms can be calibrated. This is possible even if the forms have been given to groups of quite different ability levels, so long as the assumption is justified that relative item difficulty remains invariant across groups. We shall illustrate the procedure using adjacent levels of the vocabulary test, one level of which served as the illustration of Rasch scaling in Chapter 4.

The data consist of responses to Form 68 of the vocabulary test given to 127 children in grades 5 and 6 and responses to Form 88 of the test given to 141 children in grades 7 and 8. Table 5.8 shows the difficulty scale values of the words in each of the tests, as estimated in relation to the average difficulty of all the words in their own set. The final column shows the difference in scale value for each of the common items. The average of these differences is 1.70 log units. This is the amount that needs to be added to each Form 88 difficulty value to put it on the Form 68 scale. It is also the amount that must be added to each Form 88 score value to express it as an ability index on the Form 68 scale. Table 5.9 shows the ability scale values corresponding to each number of acceptable answers on Form 68 and on Form 88 and, in the final column, the Form 88 scores expressed in terms of the Form 68 scale.

The conversion is somewhat approximate, because the Form-68-to-Form-88 difference varies noticeably from one word to another. Equal relative difficulty is not perfectly maintained. The longer the set of shared anchor items, the more dependable the conversion to a common scale can be expected to be. Further-

Table 5.9 Scale Values of Scores Obtained by the Rasch Procedure

SCORE	FORM 68	FORM 88	FORM 88 CONVERTED TO FORM 68 SCALE
11		4.49	6.19
10	3.93	3.01	4.71
9	2.56	2.06	3.76
8	1.71	1.29	2.99
7	0.94	0.64	2.34
6	0.31	0.00	1.70
5	−0.31	−0.64	1.06
4	−0.94	−1.29	0.41
3	−1.71	−2.06	−0.36
2	−2.56	−3.01	−1.31
1	−3.93	−4.49	−2.79

more, vertical scaling such as this is critically dependent on the assumption that the location of an item's difficulty scale value is invariant from one level to the other. For material that is directly taught in school at certain grade levels, this assumption is certainly suspect.

ESTABLISHING TEST NORMS

Related to the problem of scaling scores, but still different, is the problem of establishing test norms. In scaling, we are attempting to express raw scores in terms of some invariant and equal-unit scale. In establishing norms, we are trying to relate a raw score (or else that scaled score, and through it the raw score) to the performance of one or more reference groups.

There are many possible reference groups with which the score of an individual might be compared. There are national groups, regional groups, and local groups; there are age groups and grade groups; there are job applicant groups and college applicant groups. The type of interpretation to be made in any given case determines the groups with which an individual, or perhaps a class or a school, can most appropriately be compared. When the judgment that is to be based (at least in part) on test results refers to a local situation, it may seem more appropriate to use local norms. Thus a clerical job applicant in a particular company might perhaps be most meaningfully appraised in relation to the total cohort of applicants for clerical jobs in that company. When the judgment refers to a more general situation, it may seem more appropriate to use national norms. Thus, in helping an eighth-grade student begin thinking about long-range educational plans, it might be more meaningful to compare that pupil's performance on a scholastic aptitude test to that of a national sample of eighth-graders or of 14-year-olds than to those in his or her own school.

Local norms are most likely to be of interest to a local test user. A test maker is ordinarily concerned with more general norms. The test manual will be used by persons in many different local settings, so the norms that are provided must have general reference. The reference group may be delimited in certain ways for special audiences, such as when a test maker provides norms for big cities, for parochial school students, or for a particular region of the country. But these more special norm groups are likely to be in addition to, rather than in place of, a national norm group.

Once one has defined the reference population, the next task is to administer the test to a sample from that population. Ideally, the sample should be one that will (1) provide an unbiased representation of the population, (2) provide an efficient representation of the population, and (3) permit an estimate of the precision with which the sample does, in fact, represent the population.

In the early days of test-making, norms were often based on what has been called a "sample of convenience." The test maker found a few cooperative individuals who would give the test in their school or company and send the results in. The author then pooled the results from these various sources, coming up with a composite-score distribution from which the norms were computed. However, it is hardly appropriate to call such a miscellany of data a sample, and the term "chunk" has been somewhat contemptuously applied. There is no guarantee that such an accumulation of data is unbiased. In fact, it is very likely that the results will have been reported primarily from the more enterprising and advantaged communities, school systems, or employers. The sample is likely to be "lumpy," consisting of large groups from a relatively small number of sources, and not efficient in approximating the characteristics of the specified population. Furthermore, no meaningful estimate of precision is possible.

In recent years, test makers have tried to apply more sophisticated sampling theory to the design of the sample to be tested and to carry out the design in a systematic way. In a population of limited size, it may be possible to make a complete list of all the specimens that make up that population. Thus one might prepare a list of all sixth-grade pupils in a school system. One could then design a procedure that would draw a completely random sample from that population. If pupils' names were arranged in alphabetical order and identification numbers assigned in series to each pupil, one could mix slips with the numbers on them thoroughly in a bowl and draw slips until a sample of the desired size had been assembled. A procedure that would be about equally random, but much less work, would be to pick a starting number at random and then take every kth number after that to produce a sample of N/k cases. That is, if one wanted a 10% sample, one would draw a number between 1 and 10 and take every 10th case from that starting point—for example, the 7th, 17th, 27th, and so on, to the end of the list.

This sampling procedure, which produces a simple random sample, would be unbiased but it would not be particularly efficient. Suppose the test to be normed was a reading test. Just by chance, we might get an excess of good readers, an excess of poor readers, or an excess of mediocre readers. How can we get a sample that will, for a given sample size, more accurately represent the population?

Let us assume that it is possible to get the classroom teachers to divide their pupils into good readers, average readers, and poor readers. Even though the teachers' judgments are subjective and may be somewhat fallible, they are certainly related — probably quite substantially related — to reading performance as measured by a reading test. We will now draw a random sample as before but will sample separately *within* each of the three strata defined by the teachers' judgments. This will guarantee us the proper proportion of "good," "average," and "poor" readers and will substantially reduce the possibility of our drawing a freakish sort of sample. The degree to which the precision of the sampling is increased depends on the size of the correlation between the stratifying variable and the test variable. The higher the correlation, the greater the precision.

MULTISTAGE SAMPLING

When the population is limited to the pupils in a single school or school system, it may be possible to prepare a complete listing of all the specimens in the population. In most cases, however, this is impossible. For the maker of an academic achievement test who aspires to provide national norms, the population consists of all the pupils in the country in a particular grade or a particular range of grades. Nobody could list them completely. How is one to give each pupil an equal and a specifiable chance of appearing in the tested sample?

The most practical and satisfactory solution is usually *multistage sampling*. Sampling must start at a level at which we can produce a complete (or nearly complete) listing of all the units that make up the population at that level. Thus it *might* be possible to develop a list of all the public school systems in the United States. A random sample of school systems could then be drawn, perhaps stratified by size, geographic region, or some index of socioeconomic level — or by two or three such variables. Within each school system, a second and possibly a third level of sampling would have to take place. Thus, in small school systems, it might be possible to list all pupils in a given grade or of a given age. A random sample could then be drawn from that list. (Day of the month on which a person is born provides one fairly simple and plausible basis for drawing a random sample.) In large systems it might be necessary to list the schools and draw a sample of schools first and then to draw a sample of pupils within each school in this sample.

Multistage sampling can become quite complex. There are, for example, only a small number of very large school systems, but each accounts for a great many pupils. Conversely, there are a great many small systems, each of which contains only a few pupils. To avoid lumpy sampling, it might be desirable to include most or even all of the very large systems, but only a few pupils from each. Practical considerations would probably make it necessary to include only a small fraction of the many small systems but, in order to have that category of pupils proportionately represented in the sample, it would then be necessary to include a much larger fraction from each system. The objective is that, in the final design, every pupil have an equal chance of being chosen in the sample no matter what size system (or other stratum) that pupil comes from.

We will give an hypothetical example of what is intended. Assume that there are 4,000,000 pupils in each school grade in the United States and that, as a test publisher, we can afford to test a sample of 20,000 in each grade in order to prepare national test norms. Assume that school systems are distributed as follows:

SIZE OF SYSTEM NUMBER OF PUPILS	NUMBER OF SYSTEMS	PUPILS PER GRADE	
		Total Number	Average Number
Over 100,000	40	800,000	20,000
10,000–100,000	500	1,500,000	3,000
1,000–9,999	2,500	1,200,000	480
Under 1,000	10,000	500,000	50

Our sample of 20,000 is 1/200 of the total population. We feel that about 200 systems is the maximum number in which we can afford to make arrangements and test. We decide to test in systems as shown below and to use the indicated sampling fractions for each category of school system.

SIZE OF SYSTEM	NUMBER IN SAMPLE	SAMPLING FRACTION	NUMBER OF PUPILS TESTED
Over 100,000	10	1/50	4,000
10,000 to 100,000	25	1/10	7,500
1,000 to 9,999	62	1/5	6,000
Under 1,000	100	1/2	2,500

By combining a progressively smaller fraction of the school systems with a progressively larger fraction of pupils, we arrive at a design in which a pupil has 1 chance in 200 of being chosen, regardless of the size of the system in which that pupil is enrolled.

In theory, at least, one can estimate the precision of alternative sampling plans if one knows or can make sound estimates of (1) the total variance of examinees in the population, (2) the variance among sampling units if multistage sampling is used, and (3) the correlation between stratifying variables and test score if a stratified sampling is carried out.

For simple random sampling, in which individuals are drawn at random from a complete listing of the population, the formula for estimating the standard error of the mean, $\overline{X}$, for a sample of size N is

$$S.E._{\overline{X}} = \frac{S_X}{\sqrt{N}} \qquad (5.4)$$

If all members of the sample have been arranged in order (with ties where a given value occurs more than once) with respect to some variable that correlates with the test, the standard error of the sample mean as an estimate of the population mean is given by

$$S.E._{\overline{X}} = S_X \sqrt{\frac{1 - r_{XY}^2}{N}} \qquad (5.5)$$

where Y is the variable with respect to which the specimens are ordered. This equation shows how, by using a correlated background variable, one can increase precision—or can get the same precision with a sample of substantially smaller size. If cases can be arranged in order on a background variable that correlates .70 with our test, we can get the same precision as for a simple random sample with a sample of half the size.

When a multi-stage sampling procedure is used, estimates of precision can become quite complex. This is because the precision is reduced in part by the variability of individuals within a sampling unit and in part by the variability from one sampling unit to another in the average performance of individuals within that unit. The appropriate formula for estimating precision depends on exactly how the sampling units were drawn at each stage in the sampling procedure and on how individuals were drawn from the unit at the last stage. When (1) the probability that a school (or other sampling unit) will be drawn is proportional to the number of individuals in the unit and (2) the same number of individuals are drawn from each unit, the precision of the estimated mean is given by

$$S.E._{\overline{X}} = \sqrt{\frac{1}{nk}\left(1 - \frac{n}{N}\right)\bar{S}_X^2 + \frac{1}{k}S_{\overline{X}}^2} \qquad (5.6)$$

where k = number of sampling units
N = number of individuals in each unit
n = number tested in each unit

$\overline{S}_X$ = average standard deviation of scores of individuals within a unit

$S_{\overline{x}}$ = standard deviation of means of units

If one has reasonable estimates of N, $\overline{S}_X$, and $S_{\overline{x}}$, it is possible to make an estimate of the relative precision of samples with varying numbers of sampling units and of persons tested per unit. Let us assume that $N = 100$, $\overline{S}_X = 10$, and $S_{\overline{x}} = 4$.

The following table gives the values that result for $S.E._{\cdot \overline{x}}$ for various combinations of n and k.

k	n			
	10	20	50	100
10	1.51	1.14	1.30	1.27
20	1.12	1.00	0.94	0.92
50	0.71	0.63	0.58	0.56
100	0.50	0.45	0.42	0.40

In this table, going across a row shows how much the precision is increased by increasing the number tested in each unit. Going down a column shows the gain derived from increasing the number of units while keeping the number tested in each unit constant. Going along a diagonal from lower left to upper right shows the efficiency derived from testing the *same number of pupils* in different combinations of n and k. In the illustration (which is believed to be fairly realistic), it is clear that, for a constant number tested, one gains precision by spreading them over many units. In the final analysis, of course, this gain would have to be weighed against the greater cost per examinee in money and time that would be required in order to achieve the highly dispersed sample. For a further discussion of estimates of precision in more complex sampling designs, refer to Angoff (1971).

CONSTRAINTS AND COMPROMISES

So far, we have talked about the design of a sampling plan from a purely theoretical point of view. Our discussion has made no mention of costs and has assumed that circumstances are such that the individuals designated by the sampling plan can in fact be tested. These two types of considerations are often quite compelling. Any norming of a test operates within a more or less fixed budget. That budget not only limits the size of the sample, but it also influences the design of the sample within the overall size limits. There are certain costs that relate primarily to the individual examinee—manufacture of a test booklet, scoring of the test booklet, statistical analysis of the resulting scores. Other costs relate primarily to the school or school system as a unit—making initial contacts and getting cooperation, manufacturing manuals and guides for administrators and supervisors, packing and shipping materials, preparing reports of results and interpretive materials. Within a finite budget, there is always a trade-off. We can spend a given amount of money to test a larger total number of individuals in a smaller number of units (fewer and larger clusters in our sample) or to reach a larger number of units at the cost of testing a smaller total number of individuals. With estimates of (1) the total budget available for norming, (2) the unit costs to acquire and process a school, school system, or similar entity in our sample, and (3) the per-person costs of testing within a sampling unit, we can try various combinations of number of units and number of examinees in an equation such as equation 5.6 and see what compromise appears to yield the highest precision.

This still assumes that we will be able to carry out the sampling procedure as designed without any serious "slippage." Alas, there is many a slip between the sample as designed and the testing as executed. In the first place, the civilian test maker is always in the position of requesting cooperation—never in the position of directing that the tests be given. Local cooperation must be won, and the winning is often difficult. Especially in the United States, control of education is highly decentralized, and authorization for testing in the schools must be sought at the local level. Even with the reward of free test materials and reports of results for pupils tested, success in obtaining cooperation falls far short of 100%. And after cooperation has been promised, testing can be disrupted by "acts of God" of one sort or another: floods, epidemics, teacher strikes—the list is endless. The problems of carrying through the designed sampling are very real, and consequently the theoretical precision estimates may apply only quite roughly in practice.

What can be done about this? Within limits, the discrepancies between designed sample and obtained sample can be compensated for by weighting. Thus, if the sampling design called for 8 sampling units in a particular cell (such as communities of a particular size and economic level) and if testing was actually carried out in only 6 of them, each pupil in the tested communities could be counted as 8/6 of a pupil, so that the group of pupils from that stratum would receive their proper weight in the total sample.

One procedure is to anticipate a considerable number of rejections of the testing by units that were chosen to be in the sample and to draw in advance replacement units from each stratum, to be used only if one or more of the original units from that stratum cannot be obtained. Such a procedure has become necessary quite generally in recent years, as the cooperation of school systems has become harder to obtain. To the sampling purist, this is not an acceptable procedure, because the randomness of the original sample is destroyed. Cooperating and noncooperating communities are not necessarily equivalent, and one must admit a possibility that systematic bias has been introduced into the sample actually tested when this type of selection and rejection has occurred. Unfortunately, there seems to be no way to avoid such biases. One can only hope that they are not serious.

In part because of the difficulties that arise in the design and execution of a probability sample, test makers have sometimes fallen back on what is commonly spoken of as a "quota sample." (In the rigorous use of the term, this is not a sample at all, but rather a stratified chunk.) Such procedures have most commonly been used with tests that must be individually administered by a trained examiner. With these tests, the norming sample is necessarily relatively small, due to the much higher cost (perhaps $20.00) of testing a single individual.

The procedure requires that one first select several bases of stratification. The bases might be age, sex, ethnic grouping, parental occupation, and region of the country. Bases are chosen that seem likely to be related to test score and that consequently increase the efficiency of the sample and reduce the chance of systematic bias. One then attempts to determine, from census reports or other sources, the proportion of the total population falling within each stratum — and preferably within each cell formed by the intersection of the strata. Thus, if one proposed to test a sample of 200 10-year-olds, one would want to test approximately 100 boys of whom perhaps 85 were white. A further breakdown might lead to the specification that in the northeastern states (as specifically defined), one wished to test three white 10-year-old boys whose fathers were employed in skilled trades. This assignment would be included in the allocation of cases to a testing center in the northeast, and it would become the responsibility of that center to locate and test individual children who met the specification.

It is hard to judge to what extent bias may enter into the final choice of cases under this type of procedure. Convenience certainly figures in the final selection of cases. They may be located in a convenient and cooperating school system. They may be identified through personal acquaintance or through friends. Cases procured in this way *may* be quite representative of all the cases in the cell from which they were drawn, but there is no guarantee that they are, no way of verifying that they are, and no basis for estimating either the precision or the bias in the resulting sample.

All in all, assembling normative data for a test is a complex mixture of sampling theory, compromises with practical reality, and the unpredictable hazards of data collection. One makes as sound a plan as one knows how within the realities of budget constraints and probable availability of examinees, carries it out as conscientiously as possible, and hopes for the best.

PREPARING NORMS TABLES

After the normative testing has been carried out, one faces the problem of analyzing the data and preparing those sorts of norms tables that will be most useful to the ultimate consumer of the test. Though age or grade equivalents may be reported (see pages 108–113), in their final form, norms are likely to be focused primarily on expressing an individual's standing within an appropriate reference group. An interval scale—often one that extends over a range that would cover a number of ages or grades—may be very useful as an intermediate step. However, the final interpretative information ordinarily relates the examinee to some specific group with which that examinee can meaningfully be compared.

The comparison is likely to take the form of a percentile or of a standard score. That is, the performance of the examinee is given meaning either by indicating what percentage of the reference group he or she surpassed or by reporting how far above or below the mean of the group he or she falls in standard score units. Both percentiles and standard scores should be familiar from introductory measurement and statistics courses and will not be explicated here. Percentiles have the advantage of directness and immediacy of meaning but the disadvantage that the unit does not signify the same increment on the latent attribute throughout the percentile scale, percentiles being crowded together near the median and more widely spaced at the extremes. Standard scores do approximate equal units if raw scores have been appropriately transformed to give an equal-unit scale (see pages 117–121), but a given standard-score scale acquires meaning only after a user has worked with it for a period of time. Unfortunately, a number of different standard-score scales have been in use, each requiring its own mental adjustment on the part of the user. Some have a certain rationale, and some have primarily an historical basis. Some common scales are listed below, in order of the size of the standard deviation.

	MEAN	STANDARD DEVIATION	RANGE REPORTED
stanine	5	2 (approx)	1–9
T-score, Navy	50	10	20–80 (approx)
Wechsler	100	15	45–155
Binet, some group tests	100	16	30–170
College Board	500	100	200–800

The 9-point stanine scale has received some support in discussions of reporting formats. It is considered to reduce the tendency to try to interpret small score differences. At the other extreme, even 5- or 10-point differences on the College Board scale are trivial and well within the measurement error of the test. However, in a very coarse scale such as the stanine scale, some information is certainly lost. A child who gets a stanine of 5 in reading and 7 in mathematics *may* differ in the two subjects by as little as 0.6 or by as much as 1.4 standard deviations. It seems generally desirable to provide a scale that is fine enough to represent most of the meaningful differences, but not so fine as to suggest meaning for differences that are in fact trivial. The choice of such a unit is not an easy one.

In general, the formula for converting a score on any obtained scale to one with a specified mean and standard deviation is

$$\text{Standard score} = A + \left(\frac{X - \overline{X}}{S.D._X} \right) B$$

where
A = desired mean
B = desired standard deviation
X = obtained score
$\overline{X}$ = obstained mean
$S.D._X$ = obtained standard deviation

When initially preparing a table of norms for groups at successive ages or grades, one often finds some irregularities and inconsistencies in the table. This tends especially to be the case if the norming sample is small, as it often is for individually administered tests. Thus, as originally calculated, a small section of a norms table might look like this:

RAW SCORE	STANDARD SCORE BY AGE			
	9	10	11	12
75	150	135	119	112
70	128	120	109	100
65	122	114	100	95
60	111	100	91	83

When the difference between each standard score and the ones both above and below it and to the right and left are examined, certain anomalies appear in the table. Thus the 128 for score 70 and age 9 is only 6 above score 65 and is 22 below score 75. It also shows a relatively small increment from age 10. Again, score 65 for age 12 appears too close to score 70. Various other rough spots can be identified in the table. Some adjustments seem to be indicated. These are probably best made by systematically examining the differences between entries in each row and column and adjusting them until they progress in a smooth and orderly fashion. Thus the differences in the illustration are shown by the values *not* in parentheses in the accompanying table.

	9	9–10	10	10–11	11	11–12	12
75		15 (16)		16 (13)		7 (10)	
70 to 75	22 (15)		15 (13)		10 (11)		12 (10)
70		8 (14)		11 (11)		9 (8)	
65 to 70	6 (14)		6 (12)		9 (10)		5 (9)
65		8 (13)		14 (10)		5 (7)	
60 to 65	11 (12)		14 (11)		9 (9)		12 (8)
60		11 (12)		9 (9)		8 (6)	

If these are evened out, they take on some such values as those shown in parentheses. Keeping the average of all the scale scores unchanged, but making the successive differences correspond as closely as possible to those in the parentheses, one comes out with a set of standard scores that looks something like this:

	9	10	11	12
75	152	136	123	114
70	137	124	112	104
65	124	112	102	95
60	113	101	93	87

These values would seem to be more appropriate than the original values.

EQUATING

There are occasions when more than one form of a test have been prepared, all designed to measure the same latent attribute. Two or more forms may have been developed concurrently, in order that a user might have a choice of forms or use one form for an initial testing and another for a later testing. Or a new form (or forms) may be developed each year for use in a continuing testing program. Thus many forms of the College Entrance Examination Board's Scholastic Aptitude Test have been produced over the years in order to permit secure testing each time the test is given.

When multiple forms of the same test are developed, there is no guarantee that the same raw score will have exactly the same meaning on all forms. Though appropriate attention to the item statistics obtained in the tryout should permit selection of items that will control the raw-score distribution within fairly close limits (see Chapter 4, pages 76-79), the matching cannot be expected to be perfect. However, it is usually important that the examinee not receive a bonus or a handicap by reason of having taken one form of the test rather than another. Accordingly, we must have some way of equating the raw scores on the several forms of the test. Equating sometimes means converting raw scores on the alternate test forms directly into the equivalent raw scores on the anchor form that is being used as the basic point of reference. But more often, scores on all forms are translated into some type of converted score, with the converted-score scale having been established initially in reference to the anchor form of the test.

In the rigorous sense, equating is possible only when all the tests in question are equally precise measures of exactly the same attribute. This means that forms yield the same reliability coefficient, or preferably the same standard error of measurement at each pair of equivalent scores, and that each have the same correlation with a measure of any other given attribute. In general, the conditions are met only when the tests are the same length and do not differ markedly in mean and standard deviation.

When tests meet the above conditions, the conversion from the raw-score scale of one form to the raw-score scale of the other should be invariant from one population to any other. If tests differ appreciably in the definition of the latent attribute that they are measuring, such an invariant relationship cannot be guaranteed. Consider, for example, two reading tests. Test X consists solely of paragraphs and questions to be answered relating to them. Test Y also includes a subtest involving knowledge of word meanings when the words are presented in isolation. Though scores on the two tests would certainly show a high correlation, the two do not have identical significance. Test X assesses solely those abilities involved in comprehending connected prose, whereas test Y gives substantial weight to knowledge of isolated word meanings. Suppose that population A, used for score equating, had received extensive vocabulary-building drill in school and that population B, to which the equating was being applied, had been instructed at length in the skills of reading connected prose. It is then entirely likely that population B would do less well than expected on test Y, relative to its performance on test X, and that scores that had been established as equivalent in population A would turn out not to be equivalent in population B. It is always possible to express in common terms degree of excellence in relation to a *specific* reference population, even for very different tests. Thus one could determine 10-year-old percentiles for Reading Test P and for Arithmetic Test Q and say that a reading score of 28 and an arithmetic score of 36 both fell at the 60th percentile *in that population*. But this provides no guarantee that these two scores will fall at the same percentile in any other age group or in a group defined in any other way.

Let us assume that we have two or more forms of a test that were built to the same specifications as measures of the same attribute and that the several forms have been shown or can be assumed to be closely similar in precision and in relationships to any measures of other attributes with which they have been correlated. How shall we go about the process of equating scores?

Ordinarily it makes sense to use one form as the anchor or reference form and to equate all other forms to it. Often the reference form is the one that was developed first. Sometimes the reference form is the one on which the most extensive normative data are available. Our task is to equate the other forms to the one that we have selected as the anchor.

The problem has two aspects. On the one hand, we must decide what data are to be collected in order to permit the equating. On the other hand, we must determine what statistical procedures are to be applied to the data once they have been gathered.

The primary objective of the data-collection phase is to assemble data from which an equating can be carried out that will be (1) free from bias and (2) as precise as possible for a given cost in money and/or effort. Three data-collection models will be considered. In the first model, random fractions of a group take the alternate forms—halves of the group if there are only two forms, smaller fractions if there are more than two. In the second model, all examinees take both (or all) forms, but the order in which the forms are taken is systematically rotated to make it possible to eliminate the effects of practice. Thus half would take form X first and half form Y. If the number of forms is more than two, constraints of time usually require that the group be divided into fractions; each fraction takes the anchor test together with one other form. In the third model, a bridging test, often fairly short, is given to each group. Each group also takes one complete form—either the anchor form or one of the other forms being equated to it. Let us now consider each model in turn, reviewing its merits and limitations and examining the statistical procedures involved in using it.

MODEL I

The chief advantages of the first model, in which the group is divided into random fractions and each person takes a single form of the test, are simplicity and convenience. It is necessary to persuade the school, company, or other agency to release only enough time for the administration of one form of the test. And it is not necessary to sustain examinee cooperation through a second testing. The one crucial condition in data collection is that the fractions taking the several forms be *truly* random fractions of the total, so that no systematic bias can creep in. This makes it almost essential that test forms be rotated in some way *within* each classroom or other unit tested, because different groups may differ systematically in the attribute being measured. Forms can be assembled in ABC, ABC, ABC order and passed out in order within each classroom or other subgroup. It is unlikely that the periodicity in the test forms will correspond to any systematic variation represented in the seating plan of the examinees, but this possibility should not be overlooked.

Unfortunately, though testing random fractions is a sound way of avoiding systematic bias, it is a relatively inefficient way of achieving precise equating. The standard error of linear equating for this model is given by the equation

$$S.E._{Y*} = \sqrt{\frac{2S_Y^2(z_X^2 + 2)}{N_t}}$$ (5.7)

where N_t = total number in groups X and Y combined
            z_X = $(X - \overline{X})/s_X$.
      $S.E._{Y*}$ = standard error of Y when the deviation from the mean of X equals z.

As this equation brings out, the accuracy of linear equating is greatest at the mean (where $z_X = 0$) and decreases as one departs from the mean in either direction. This is because sampling errors can affect estimates of both the mean and the standard deviation and because errors in estimating the standard deviation have greater and greater impact the further one departs from the mean. We will compare the precision of this model with that of each of the other models after the statistical procedures for applying each model have been presented.

In general, equating can be either linear or equipercentile. In linear equating, one determines the mean and standard deviation of scores for each group and uses the relationship

$$\frac{X - \overline{X}}{s_X} = \frac{Y - \overline{Y}}{s_Y}$$

to identify the equation of the straight line relating one form to the other. This equation says, in effect, that scores that differ from the mean by the same number of standard deviation units can be considered equal. Letting Y be the anchor test and solving for Y, we can convert X scores into Y scores by the equation

$$Y = \overline{Y} + \frac{s_Y}{s_X}(X - \overline{X})$$ (5.8)

This equation appears repeatedly in the statistics of score conversion.

It is appropriate to use a linear conversion whenever the distribution of item difficulties, and consequently the shape of the raw-score distribution, is substantially the same for both forms of the test that are being equated. This will usually be the case if they have been prepared following a common set of specifications. If the shapes of the raw-score distributions are likely to be appreciably different, it may seem more appropriate to use equal-area or equipercentile equating. This procedure defines as equal those raw scores corresponding to selected percentiles, say the 2nd, 5th, 10th, 25th, 50th, 75th, 90th, 95th, and 98th for each group. The raw scores corresponding to the same percentile for the two forms being equated would be defined as being equal to each other. A plot of the corresponding raw scores would be made, with X on one axis and Y on the other; a

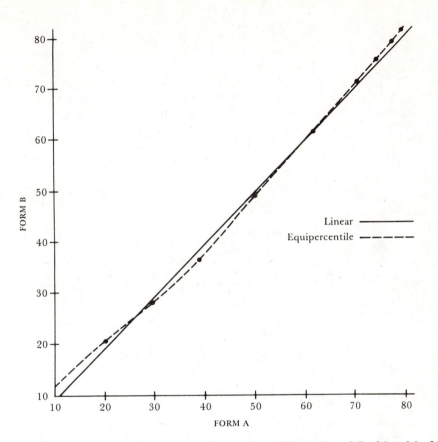

Figure 5.3   Linear and equipercentile equating of Forms A and B of Level 3 of Lorge-Thorndike Intelligence Tests.

smooth curve drawn through the points; and, for each X score, the corresponding Y score read off the graph.

Table 5.10 and Figure 5.3 provide an illustration of equating both by a linear conversion and by an area conversion. The solid line in Figure 5.3 represents the linear conversion and the dotted line the area conversion. In this example, the two correspond very closely. It is clear that the relationship of form B to form A is, to a close approximation, linear.

MODEL II

In the second model all examinees are required to take both forms of the test, but the order is reversed for approximately half the cases. It is not crucial that the two halves of the sample be precisely matched, so testing can ordinarily be carried out in intact groups, some taking the tests in one order and some in the

Table 5.10 Calculations for Equating Forms A and B of Level 3 of Lorge-Thorndike Intelligence Tests

CLASS INTERVAL	FREQUENCY DISTRIBUTION		CUMULATIVE FREQUENCY		SELECTED PERCENTILES	
	Form A	Form B	Form A	Form B	Form A	Form B
80–84	17	38	1000	1000		
75–79	89	92	983	962		
70–74	176	157	894	870	P_{98} 79.3	81.9
65–69	152	148	718	713	P_{95} 77.6	78.8
60–64	128	126	566	565	P_{90} 74.3	76.1
55–59	106	107	438	439	P_{75} 70.4	70.7
50–54	85	83	332	332	P_{50} 61.9	61.9
45–49	76	78	247	249	P_{25} 49.7	49.6
40–44	54	44	171	171	P_{10} 38.5	36.6
35–39	39	46	117	127	P_{05} 29.5	28.3
30–34	28	26	78	81	P_{02} 20.2	20.6
25–29	18	21	50	55		
20–24	14	18	32	34		
15–19	11	16	18	16		
10–14	7		7			
Mean	58.76	58.93	$A = 58.76 + \dfrac{14.90}{15.20}(B - 58.93)$			
S.D.	14.90	15.20	$A = 0.98B + 1.01$			

other. The advantage of this model is the greatly increased precision that results from having identical persons taking the two forms of the test. Sampling errors, which are the major source of inaccuracy in equating, are completely eliminated, and only the measurement error for specific individuals remains. The gain shows up in the equation for the standard error or equating:

$$S.E._{Y^*} = S_Y \sqrt{(1 - r_{XY}) \left[\frac{z_X^2(1 + r_{XY}) + 2}{N_t} \right]} \qquad (5.9)$$

The standard error of measurement, which is given by $S_Y\sqrt{1 - r_{XY}}$, is the dominant element in formula 5.9. Consider a case in which $r_{XY} = .90$ (a reasonable expectation for a good ability test) and $N_t = 200$. The standard errors of equating for the two models that we have considered so far are shown below for several values of z_X.

z_X	MODEL I	MODEL II
0.0	$.14S_Y$	$.032S_Y$
1.0	$.17S_Y$	$.044S_Y$
2.0	$.24S_Y$	$.070S_Y$
3.0	$.32S_Y$	$.098S_Y$

Under the conditions of our illustration and given the same size of sample, model II achieves about 4 times as great precision as model I. Expressing the relationship in a different way, model II could produce the *same* precision as model I with roughly 1/16 as many examinees.

The chief limitation of model II is the often overpowering one that it requires us to obtain enough testing time to give each examinee two forms of the test. There is also, in some situations at least, the possibility that motivation may degrade in a second testing.

Estimating score equivalents by the linear method when forms have been rotated requires that an appropriate adjustment be made for practice, so that all estimates can be those that would apply to an initial testing. It usually seems reasonable to assume that the gain in form X from having taken form Y will be equal to the gain in form Y from having taken form X, if both gains are expressed in standard deviation units. Thus,

$$P = \frac{G_X}{s_X} = \frac{G_Y}{s_Y}$$

where P = the practice effect
           G_X = gain in form X from having taken form Y
           G_Y = gain in form Y from having taken form X
Hence $G_X = s_X P$ and $G_Y = s_Y P$.

Then

$$P = \frac{1}{2}\left(\frac{\overline{X}_{\mathrm{II}} - \overline{X}_{\mathrm{I}}}{s_X} + \frac{\overline{Y}_{\mathrm{II}} - \overline{Y}_{\mathrm{I}}}{s_Y} \right) \qquad (5.10)$$

where $\overline{X}_{\mathrm{II}}$ = mean of form X when taken second
              $\overline{X}_{\mathrm{I}}$ = mean of form X when taken first

similarly for form Y, and s_X and s_Y are standard deviations for the total group.

The estimate of what the mean of form X and of form Y for the total sample would have been if all examinees had taken the test in question first is given by

$$\overline{X}_t = \frac{1}{2}(\overline{X}_{\mathrm{I}} + \overline{X}_{\mathrm{II}} - G_X)$$

$$(5.11)$$

$$\overline{Y}_t = \frac{1}{2}(\overline{Y}_{\mathrm{I}} + \overline{Y}_{\mathrm{II}} - G_Y)$$

and the estimate of the standard deviation in the total group is

$$s_X = \sqrt{(s^2_{X_{\mathrm{I}}} + s^2_{X_{\mathrm{II}}})/2}$$

$$s_Y = \sqrt{(s^2_{Y_{\mathrm{I}}} + s^2_{Y_{\mathrm{II}}})/2}$$

Having estimates of the two means and standard deviations, we can now return to our basic formula 5.1 for linear equating and solve the equation

$$Y = \overline{Y} + \frac{s_Y}{s_X}(X - \overline{X})$$

If an area or an equipercentile method of equating is used, it suffices, for each test, to pool the raw-score distributions when taken first and when taken second. The composite distributions of each test can be considered to be equally affected by practice. Percentiles can then be calculated for each combined distribution and plotted against one another in the manner shown in Figure 5.3.

MODEL III

The third model proceeds by administering each form to a fraction of the sample — and also administering a common bridging test to all fractions. The bridging test may be a separate and distinct short test or a common set of items that are actually included as an integral part of each of the tests. In either case, it should be given at the same point in the testing sequence for each of the forms, so that any practice or fatigue effects are similar for all forms. The effectiveness of a bridging test depends on its correlation with each of the tests being equated, so the bridging test should ordinarily be identical to or at least very much like the tests that are being equated. It should also be long enough to have fairly good reliability; low reliability limits its correlation with the tests being equated. The use of a bridging test is a very versatile procedure, because it does not require that both (or all) test forms be administered at the same time or to the same groups. If a new form of a test is produced at some later date, it can be equated to an earlier form by including, in the later testing, a bridging test that was incorporated in or administered with the earlier test. The scores on the bridging test make it possible to adjust for moderate differences between means and standard deviations of samples that have taken different forms of the test.

In this procedure, the means and standard deviations of the samples taking each one of the test forms are adjusted to what they would have been for the total group. This is done by using the data for the bridging test, which we shall designate as U, the data for each of the subgroups, and the regression of score on test X or test Y on bridging test U. The equations become

$$\hat{\bar{X}}_t = \bar{X}_a + r_{XU}\frac{s_x}{s_U}\left(\bar{U}_t - \bar{U}_a\right)$$

$$\hat{\bar{Y}}_t = \bar{Y}_b + r_{YU}\frac{s_y}{s_U}\left(\bar{U}_t - \bar{U}_b\right)$$

$$\hat{\sigma}_X^2 = S_{X_a}^2 + r_{XU}^2\frac{S_X^2}{S_U^2}\left(S_{U_t}^2 - S_{U_a}^2\right)$$

$$\hat{\sigma}_Y^2 = S_{Y_b}^2 + r_{YU}^2\frac{S_Y^2}{S_U^2}\left(S_{U_t}^2 - S_{U_b}^2\right)$$

(5.12)

In these expressions, a subscript t refers to the total group taking both (or all) forms of the test, and a subscript a or b refers to the group taking a specific test form. The values with the superscript $\wedge$ represent estimated values for the total group, based on the regression on test U.

Once the adjusted values have been obtained, they can be entered into the standard equation

$$Y = \bar{Y} + \frac{s_Y}{s_X}(X - \bar{X})$$

to provide a linear equating of the two forms. The precision of the equating is estimated by the equation

$$S.E._{Y^*} = \sqrt{2\,\hat{\sigma}_Y^2(1 - \hat{r}^2)\frac{(1 + \hat{r}^2)z^2 + 2}{N_t}}$$

(5.13)

where $\hat{r} = \frac{1}{2}\left(r_{XU} + r_{YU}\right)$.

Obviously, the efficiency of this procedure very much depends upon the correlation between the bridging test and the two tests being equated. When this value is .70, a value that can usually be reached and often exceeded, the standard errors for $N_t = 200$ are as follows:

z_X	$S.E._Y$
0.0	$.10S_Y$
1.0	$.13S_Y$
2.0	$.20S_Y$
3.0	$.28S_Y$

Comparing these values with those in the short table on page 139, one can see that, with a correlation of .70, this third model is about twice as efficient as model I. That is, it can achieve the same precision with half as many cases. It is generally much less efficient than model II, in part because a kind of double equating is involved (X to U and U to Y), and in part because the correlations obtained for model III are generally smaller than those for model II. As equation 5.13 shows, the effectiveness of model III is critically dependent on the correlation between the bridging test and the tests that are being equated.

Equipercentile equating with this third model is possible by a procedure that would involve the following sequence of steps.

1. Prepare a score distribution of test U, the bridging test, for the total group, including those who had taken each of the tests being equated.

2. Find the score on U in this combined distribution corresponding to each of selected percentile points.

3. Prepare separate distributions of U for each of the subgroups that took a specific test form.

4. In each subgroup, determine the percentiles that correspond to each of the scores identified in step 2.

5. Find the X (or Y) score corresponding to each of the percentiles you found in step 4.

6. The X and Y scores corresponding to the same U percentile, as determined from the composite group, are considered equivalent scores and plotted against each other in a two-dimensional plot.

7. A smooth curve drawn through the points plotted in step 6 will provide the basis for reading off the Y equivalent of any X score.

Other variations of equating procedures are possible, and some are discussed by Angoff (1971).

Chapter 6
Reliability

Any test presents a set of tasks that sample from some universe of responses by the examinee. The universe corresponds, we hope, to the latent attribute in which we are interested. In evaluating a test we encounter two broad questions that are different but overlapping. A first question is how accurately the test sample represents the broader universe of responses from which it is drawn; a second is how faithfully that universe corresponds to the latent attribute in which we are interested. The first relates to what is commonly called the *reliability* of the test, the second to its *validity*. Collectively, they have been spoken of by Cronbach and others (1972) as the generalizability of the test score—the range of inferences that can be made from it. The distinction between the jump from test score to universe score and that from universe score to standing on the hypothesized latent attribute becomes a little fuzzy at times. Our hope is that it will become clearer as the presentation proceeds.

We give a test (for example, a 40-item test requiring the examinee to answer 5 questions on each of 8 reading passages) to an examinee on a certain day in October. Applying a pre-established key to the responses, we obtain a score that may be used as it stands or may be converted into some type of more interpretable scale and is used as a measure of the examinee's standing in "reading comprehension." Clearly, all we have is a fairly small sample of the individual's behavior. We are not interested in the sample per se, but rather in that score as representing what the individual could be expected to do on any sample of reading tasks that call for correct responses to questions on reading passages. We are also interested in evaluating how well answering questions on reading passages represents the construct "reading comprehension," but for the present let us concentrate on how accurately the limited sampling of responses corresponds to the universe of answers to questions on reading passages.

Even if we limit the universe to "answers to questions on reading passages," that universe is still large and somewhat undefined. Do we view the universe as including other types of questions on these passages? Questions on other passages? Questions on other sorts of passages? Passages presented on other occasions—a week later, a month later, six months later? The point is that there is no one "reliability" for a test, but only various estimates that we can make depending on which facets or dimensions of a universe we wish to include in our generalization.

There are typically three sides of the issue of reliability: the basic rationale, the procedures for data collection, and the statistical procedures for data analysis. These facets interact in that certain empirical data sets are appropriate for certain conceptions of the universe to which inference is desired, and the possible types of statistical analysis depend on the data at hand. Ideally, one would feel that the rational analysis of the universe to which generalization was desired should be primary and that data collection and statistical treatment should flow from this analysis. Realistically, however, practical considerations may limit the data that it is possible to collect, and these limitations may set boundaries on the universe to which inferences can logically be made and on the statistical analyses that can be carried out.

In this chapter, we shall start with a consideration of "classical" reliability theory. This is the true-score-and-error model of a test score that was presented by Spearman in 1904 and that provided the accepted theoretical model for discussions of reliability for the next 50 years. Next we will develop the multifacet model presented by Lindquist (1953) and elaborated by Cronbach and his associates (1972). Then we will return to discuss the practical issues involved in data collection and analysis. Finally, we will briefly consider internal-consistency estimates for speeded tests and the meaning of reliability in the context of domain mastery or criterion-referenced testing.

SOME USEFUL RELATIONSHIPS STEMMING FROM THE CLASSICAL RELIABILITY MODEL

The classical reliability model views a test score as having two additive components, the "true" score and a random "error." The error is defined as unrelated to the true score and as unrelated to the error that would occur in another measurement of the same attribute. The true score is defined as the value that the average of repeated measurements with the identical measure approaches as the number of measurements is increased without limit. The term *identical* implies that it is possible to measure an individual repeatedly without changing that individual—a condition that obviously cannot be achieved in the real world. Though the model is in this and some other respects an oversimplification and not a representation of reality, development of the model brings out a number of relationships that are instructive and useful in the design and construction of tests and in the evaluation of test scores. We shall therefore trace the development of a number of the relationships that are implicit in the assumptions of the model.

BASIC ASSUMPTIONS AND RESULTING RELATIONSHIPS

The basic assumptions of the model are as follows:

1. The obtained score is the sum of true score plus error; that is,

$$X_{\text{obt}} = X_{\text{true}} + X_{\text{error}}$$

We will use the subscripts o, t, and e for observed score, true score, and error, respectively.

2. Over the population, error is independent of true score; that is,

$$r_{te} = 0$$

3. In pairs of measures, the error in one measure is independent of the error in the other; that is,

$$r_{ee'} = 0$$

Given these assumptions, we can conclude that, as the number of persons or the number of measurements increases, the mean error approaches 0 as a limit. That is,

$$\bar{X}_e \cong 0$$

when the number of measures increases without limit. This follows from the definition of errors as *random* deviations from the true score that are equally likely to be positive or negative. Any consistent direction to "error" would be indistinguishable from, and hence assimilated as part of, the operational "true" score.

It follows that, in the limit, the mean of observed scores is equal to the mean of true scores. Because

$$X_o = X_t + X_e$$

and

$$\bar{X}_o = \frac{\Sigma X_o}{N} = \frac{\Sigma(X_t + X_e)}{N} = \frac{\Sigma X_t}{N} + \frac{\Sigma X_e}{N}$$
$$= \bar{X}_t + \bar{X}_e$$

and, as above,

$$\bar{X}_e \cong 0$$

we have

$$\bar{X}_o \cong \bar{X}_t \tag{6.1}$$

This relationship holds both for repeated measures of an individual and for the mean of a group. That is, as the number of observations increases, the observed mean approaches the mean of true scores and is an unbiased estimate of the true-score mean.

We show next that the variance of observed scores equals the true-score variance plus the error variance. In most of the development from here on, we will work with scores that are expressed as deviations from the mean; that is, $x = X - \bar{X}$. We have

$$s_o^2 = \frac{1}{N}\sum(x_t + x_e)^2$$

$$= \frac{1}{N}\sum(x_t^2 + x_e^2 + 2x_tx_e)$$

$$= \frac{1}{N}\sum x_t^2 + \frac{1}{N}\sum x_e^2 + \frac{2}{N}\sum x_tx_e$$

$$= s_t^2 + s_e^2 + 2s_ts_er_{te}$$

But by definition, $r_{te} = 0$, so we have

$$s_o^2 = s_t^2 + s_e^2 \tag{6.2}$$

We now show that the correlation between two equivalent test forms is equal to the true-score variance divided by the observed variance. We define equivalent forms as forms that have identical true scores and equal magnitude of errors. We have

$$r_{xx'} = \frac{\frac{1}{N}\sum xx'}{s_xs_{x'}}$$

From our definition of equivalent forms, $s_x = s_{x'}$, so

$$r_{xx'} = \frac{\frac{1}{N}\sum(x_t + x_e)(x_t + x_{e'})}{s_x^2}$$

$$= \frac{\frac{1}{N}\sum(x_t^2 + x_tx_e + x_tx_{e'} + x_ex_{e'})}{s_x^2}$$

$$= \frac{\frac{1}{N}\sum x_t^2 + \frac{1}{N}\sum x_tx_e + \frac{1}{N}\sum x_tx_{e'} + \frac{1}{N}\sum x_ex_{e'}}{s_x^2}$$

But because, by definition, error is independent of true score and of error on any other measurement, the three last terms of the numerator above approach zero as a limit, and we then have

$$r_{xx'} = \frac{s_t^2}{s_x^2} \tag{6.3}$$

Thus the alternate-forms reliability of a test equals true-score variance divided by observed variance. From this it follows that $s_t^2 = s_x^2 r_{xx'}$ and $s_t = s_x\sqrt{r_{xx'}}$. The standard deviation of true scores can be estimated by multiplying the observed standard deviation by the square root of the reliability coefficient.

Returning to equation 6.2 and transposing, we can get

$$s_e^2 = s_x^2 - s_t^2$$

But we have seen that $s_t^2 = s_x^2 r_{xx'}$, so we have

$$s_e^2 = s_x^2 - s_x^2 r_{xx'}$$

or

$$s_e = s_x \sqrt{1 - r_{xx'}} \tag{6.4}$$

Thus the standard error of measurement is estimated from the observed standard deviation and the alternate-forms reliability coefficient.

Next we can derive the correlation between observed score and true score, and the correlation between observed score and measurement error. Remembering that $x_o = x_t + x_e$, we have

$$r_{x_o x_t} = \frac{\frac{1}{N} \sum (x_t + x_e) x_t}{s_x s_t}$$

$$= \frac{\frac{1}{N} \sum x_t^2 + \frac{1}{N} \sum x_t x_e}{s_x s_t}$$

But the second term in the numerator approaches zero because of the independence of true score and error. Hence we have

$$r_{x_o x_t} = \frac{s_t^2}{s_x s_t} = \frac{s_t}{s_x} \tag{6.5}$$

Referring to equation (6.3), we had found that $r_{xx'} = s_t^2/s_x^2$ so $r_{x_o x_t} = \sqrt{r_{xx'}}$. The correlation of an observed measure with the underlying true score is equal to the square root of the alternate-forms reliability coefficient.

Turning to observed score and error, we have

$$r_{x_o x_e} = \frac{\frac{1}{N} \sum (x_t + x_e) x_e}{s_x s_e}$$

$$= \frac{\frac{1}{N} \sum x_t x_e + \frac{1}{N} \sum x_e^2}{s_x s_e}$$

Once again referring to the independence of true score and error, we see that the first term of the numerator approaches 0, and we have

$$r_{x_o x_e} = \frac{s_e^2}{s_x s_e} = \frac{s_e}{s_x}$$

But we can see from equation (6.4) that $s_e / s_x = \sqrt{1 - r_{xx'}}$ so we have

$$r_{x_o x_e} = \sqrt{1 - r_{xx'}}$$

This correlation of observed score with error is a specific example of the more general expression $\sqrt{1 - r_{xy'}}$ which has been called the coefficient of alienation when predicting y from x.

EFFECTS OF INCREASING OR DECREASING TEST LENGTH

We turn now to the effects of increasing (or decreasing) the length of a test, considering en route the general expressions for the correlations of sums (and differences; a difference is, algebraically speaking, still a sum).

The equation for the mean of the unweighted sum of two or more variables is simply

$$\text{Mean}_{(x_1 + x_2 + \cdots + x_k)} = \overline{X}_1 + \overline{X}_2 + \cdots + \overline{X}_k$$

Illustrating with the case of two variables, we have

$$\overline{X}_{(1+2)} = \frac{1}{N} \sum (X_1 + X_2)$$
$$= \frac{1}{N} \sum X_1 + \frac{1}{N} \sum X_2$$
$$= \overline{X}_1 + \overline{X}_2$$

If X_1 and X_2 are equivalent forms of the same test, each will have the same mean, because in each case the observed mean will equal the true-score mean, and we can write

$$\text{Mean}_{2X} = 2 (\text{Mean } X)$$

When we double the length of a test by adding equivalent items, we can expect to double its mean. More generally,

$$\text{Mean}_{kX} = k (\text{Mean } X)$$

If the variables are combined with different weights, we get

$$\text{Mean}_{\text{wtd sum}} = \sum W_i \overline{X}_i \qquad (6.6)$$

Turning now to the variance of a sum, we have

$$s^2_{(x_1 + x_2)} = \frac{1}{N} \sum (x_1 + x_2)^2$$
$$= \frac{1}{N} \sum x_1^2 + \frac{1}{N} \sum x_2^2 + \frac{2}{N} \sum x_1 x_2$$
$$= s_1^2 + s_2^2 + 2 s_1 s_2 r_{12}$$

It is sometimes instructive to write this sum as a pooling square in the form

$$s^2_{(1 + 2)} = \begin{vmatrix} s_1^2 & + \; r_{12}s_1s_2 \\ + \; r_{21}s_2s_1 & + \; s_2^2 \end{vmatrix}$$

or

$$s^2_{(1 + 2)} = \begin{vmatrix} C_{11} & C_{12} \\ C_{21} & C_{22} \end{vmatrix}$$

where C stands for a covariance, with the special case of the diagonal terms, C_{ii}, representing variances. In more general terms,

$$s^2_{(1 + 2 + \cdots + k)} = \begin{vmatrix} C_{11} & C_{12} & \cdots & C_{1i} & \cdots & C_{1k} \\ C_{21} & C_{22} & \cdots & C_{2i} & \cdots & C_{2k} \\ \vdots & \vdots & & \vdots & & \vdots \\ C_{j1} & C_{j2} & \cdots & C_{ji} & \cdots & C_{jk} \\ \vdots & \vdots & & \vdots & & \vdots \\ C_{k1} & C_{k2} & \cdots & C_{ki} & \cdots & C_{kk} \end{vmatrix} \tag{6.7}$$

This can be written in summation notation as

$$s^2_{(1 + 2 + \cdots + k)} = \sum_{i=1}^{k} C_{ii} + \sum_{i=1}^{k}\sum_{j=1}^{k} C_{ij} \qquad i \neq j \tag{6.8}$$

If differential weights are to be applied to the scores being combined, then the expression can be written

$$\text{Variance}_{\text{wtd sum}} = \sum_{i=1}^{k} w_i^2 C_{ii} + \sum_{i=1}^{k}\sum_{j=1}^{k} w_i w_j C_{ij} \qquad i \neq j$$

Coming back to the situation in which we are dealing with equivalent forms of the same test, let us ask what the effect of doubling the length of the test will be. We then have

$$s^2_{(x + x')} = s_x^2 + s_{x'}^2 + 2r_{xx'}s_x s_{x'}$$

But because the test forms are equivalent, and so have the same standard deviation, we have

$$s^2_{(2x)} = 2s_x^2 + 2r_{xx'}s_x^2$$

$$= s_x^2(2 + 2r_{xx'})$$

and

$$s_{2x} = s_x \sqrt{2 + 2r_{xx'}} \tag{6.9}$$

In general terms, when the length of a test is increased by a factor of k, we may expect the variance to be increased by a factor of $k + k(k - 1)r_{xx'}$, so that we have

$$s_{kx} = s_x\sqrt{k + k(k - 1)r_{xx'}}$$

The rate at which the standard deviation increases as the length is increased depends on the correlation between unit-length tests. At one limit, as the correlation approaches .00, the increase is proportional to $\sqrt{k}$. At the other, as the correlation approaches 1.00, the increase is proportional to k.

Though we speak of covariance and correlation between *tests*, we could speak in terms of average inter-item covariance or correlation. The relationships developed between unit-length tests and longer tests also apply at the limit where the unit is a single item, and the k-length test is a test composed of k items.

What happens to the variance of true scores and to the variance of errors when the length of the test is doubled? Using equation 6.9 and remembering that the correlation of true scores on alternate forms is 1.00, we find that

$$s_{(2t)}^2 = 2s_t^2 + 2r_{tt}s_t^2 = 4s_t^2$$

$$s_{(2t)} = 2s_t$$

For the variance of errors, remembering that the correlation of errors on alternate forms is by definition 0, we have

$$s_{(2e)}^2 = 2s_e^2 + 2r_{ee'}s_e^2 = 2s_e^2$$

$$s_{(2e)} = s_e\sqrt{2}$$

In the general case of increasing test length by a factor k, we have

$$s_{kt}^2 = k^2 s_t^2$$

$$s_{kt} = ks_t$$

and

$$s_{ke}^2 = ks_e^2$$

$$s_{ke} = s_e\sqrt{k}$$

Thus we see that true-score variance increases as the square of test length, whereas error variance increases only as a linear function of test length. This relationship accounts for the progressively greater reliability of a test as its length is increased.

Next we ask what will happen to the intercorrelations when the length of the tests in question is increased. Let us start by expressing the general form of the correlation of sums. First, consider the situation when the sum of the variables x_1 and x_2 is correlated with the sum of the variables y_1 and y_2. We have

$$r_{(x_1 + x_2)(y_1 + y_2)} = \frac{\frac{1}{N}\sum(x_1 + x_2)(y_1 + y_2)}{\sqrt{s_{x_1}^2 + s_{x_2}^2 + 2r_{x_1x_2}s_{x_1}s_{x_2}} \cdot \sqrt{s_{y_1}^2 + s_{y_2}^2 + 2r_{y_1y_2}s_{y_1}s_{y_2}}}$$

$$= \frac{\frac{1}{N}\sum x_1y_1 + \frac{1}{N}\sum x_1y_2 + \frac{1}{N}\sum x_2y_1 + \frac{1}{N}\sum x_2y_2}{\sqrt{s_{x_1}^2 + s_{x_2}^2 + 2r_{x_1x_2}s_{x_1}s_{x_2}} \cdot \sqrt{s_{y_1}^2 + s_{y_2}^2 + 2r_{y_1y_2}s_{y_1}s_{y_2}}}$$

This can be written in the form of pooling squares as

$$\frac{\begin{vmatrix} C_{x_1y_1} & C_{x_1y_2} \\ C_{x_2y_1} & C_{x_2y_2} \end{vmatrix}}{\sqrt{\begin{vmatrix} C_{x_1x_1} & C_{x_1x_2} \\ C_{x_2x_1} & C_{x_2x_2} \end{vmatrix}} \cdot \sqrt{\begin{vmatrix} C_{y_1y_1} & C_{y_1y_2} \\ C_{y_2y_1} & C_{y_2y_2} \end{vmatrix}}}$$

More generally, when there are m elements in the first sum and n elements in the second, the correlation of sums can be written

$$\frac{\begin{vmatrix} C_{x_1y_1} & \cdots & C_{x_1y_j} & \cdots & C_{x_1y_n} \\ \vdots & & \vdots & & \vdots \\ C_{x_iy_1} & \cdots & C_{x_iy_j} & \cdots & C_{x_iy_n} \\ \vdots & & \vdots & & \vdots \\ C_{x_my_1} & \cdots & C_{x_my_j} & \cdots & C_{x_my_n} \end{vmatrix}}{\sqrt{\begin{vmatrix} C_{x_1x_1} & \cdots & C_{x_1x_i} & \cdots & C_{x_1x_m} \\ \vdots & & \vdots & & \vdots \\ C_{x_ix_1} & \cdots & C_{x_ix_i} & \cdots & C_{x_ix_m} \\ \vdots & & \vdots & & \vdots \\ C_{x_mx_1} & \cdots & C_{x_mx_i} & \cdots & C_{x_mx_m} \end{vmatrix}} \sqrt{\begin{vmatrix} C_{y_1y_1} & \cdots & C_{y_1y_j} & \cdots & C_{y_1y_n} \\ \vdots & & \vdots & & \vdots \\ C_{y_jy_1} & \cdots & C_{y_jy_j} & \cdots & C_{y_jy_n} \\ \vdots & & \vdots & & \vdots \\ C_{y_ny_1} & \cdots & C_{y_ny_j} & \cdots & C_{y_ny_n} \end{vmatrix}}}$$

or

$$r_{(x_1 + \cdots + x_m)(y_1 + \cdots + y_n)} = \frac{\sum_{i=1}^{m}\sum_{j=1}^{n}C_{x_iy_j}}{\sqrt{\sum_{i=1}^{m}\sum_{k=1}^{m}C_{x_ix_k}}\sqrt{\sum_{j=1}^{n}\sum_{l=1}^{n}C_{y_jy_l}}} \qquad (6.10)$$

A variety of interesting relationships can be derived from this very general formula. Consider first the case in which there is the same number of elements in each sum and in which all of both the x's and the y's represent equivalent forms of the same test. Then, if the tests are in fact equivalent, all the covariances will be equal, except for sampling fluctuations, and the same will be true of all the variances. We then get

$$r_{(1 \text{ to } m)(1 \text{ to } m)} = \frac{m^2 \overline{C}_{ij}}{\sqrt{m\overline{V}_i + m(m-1)\overline{C}_{ij}}\sqrt{m\overline{V}_i + m(m-1)\overline{C}_{ij}}}$$

$$= \frac{m\overline{C}_{ij}}{\overline{V}_i + (m-1)\overline{C}_{ij}}$$

$$= \frac{m\overline{s_i^2 r_{ii'}}}{\overline{s_i^2} + (m-1)\overline{s_i^2 r_{ii'}}}$$

$$= \frac{m\overline{r}_{ii'}}{1 + (m-1)\overline{r}_{ii'}} \qquad (6.11)$$

This is the general form of the Spearman–Brown Prophecy Formula to estimate the reliability of a test the length of which has been increased by a factor of m. When $m = 2$, we have

$$r_{2x} = \frac{2r_{xx'}}{1 + r_{xx'}} \qquad (6.12)$$

This is the specific form for a double length test. It is most frequently encountered in adjusting a split-half reliability coefficient obtained by correlating score on odd-numbered items with score on even-numbered items to give the reliability of the complete test.

When all the x's are to be considered equivalent forms of one test and all the y's equivalent forms of another test, we can use equation 6.10 to provide an estimate of the correlation when one or both of the two tests are lengthened. If both are lengthened, we get

$$r_{(x_1 + \cdots + x_m)(y_1 + \cdots + y_n)}$$

$$= \frac{mn\overline{C}_{xy}}{\sqrt{m\overline{V}_x + m(m-1)\overline{C}_{x_i x_k}}\sqrt{n\overline{V}_y + n(n-1)\overline{C}_{y_j y_l}}}$$

$$= \frac{mn\overline{s}_x\overline{s}_y\overline{r}_{xy}}{mn\overline{s}_x\overline{s}_y \sqrt{\frac{1}{m} + \left(\frac{m-1}{m}\right)\overline{r}_{xx'}}\sqrt{\frac{1}{n} + \left(\frac{n-1}{n}\right)\overline{r}_{yy'}}}$$

$$= \frac{\overline{r}_{xy}}{\sqrt{\frac{1}{m} + \left(\frac{m-1}{m}\right)\overline{r}_{xx'}}\sqrt{\frac{1}{n} + \left(\frac{n-1}{n}\right)\overline{r}_{yy'}}} \qquad (6.13)$$

This equation permits us to estimate what the effect would be on the correlation between any two variables, say a predictor test and some type of criterion measure, if more (or less) data were gathered for either or both. Suppose, for example, we had found that the correlation between two forms of an aptitude test was .80, the correlation between two independently obtained supervisory ratings was .60, and the correlation of a single test with a single rating was .25. We might ask what the correlation would be between a test twice as long and the average of 5 ratings. We would find, as an estimate,

$$r_{2x \cdot 5y} = \frac{.25}{\sqrt{\frac{1}{2} + \frac{1}{2}(.80)} \sqrt{\frac{1}{5} + \frac{4}{5}(.60)}}$$

$$= \frac{.25}{\sqrt{(.90)(.68)}} = \frac{.25}{.78}$$

$$= .32$$

If one of the tests, say x, remains of unit length while the length of the other is changed, we have

$$r_{x(y_1 + \cdots + y_n)} = \frac{\overline{r_{xy}}}{\sqrt{\frac{1}{n} + \frac{n-1}{n}r_{yy'}}}$$

If the length of y is now increased without limit, giving in effect the correlation between x and y_t, the true score on y, we have

$$r_{xy_\infty} = r_{xy_t} = \frac{r_{xy}}{\sqrt{r_{yy'}}}$$

Finally if, in equation 6.13, the length of both tests is allowed to increase without limit, we get

$$r_{x_\infty y_\infty} = r_{x_t y_t} = \frac{r_{xy}}{\sqrt{(r_{xx'})(r_{yy'})}} \tag{6.14}$$

This is the general form of the correction for attenuation. It provides an estimate of the correlation between true scores on x and y, or measures that are of such a length that measurement errors are negligible. Taking the values from our previous illustration, we would have

$$r_{x_t y_t} = \frac{.25}{\sqrt{(.80)(.60)}} = \frac{.25}{.693} = .36$$

PROBLEMS IN DEFINING TRUE SCORE AND ERROR

True score and error, of course, are not observables. We observe behavior samples, and from these observations we make inferences about the constructs of "true score" and "error." And the inferences that we can legitimately make depend on the nature of the samples of behavior that we observe. Consider the following example.

A supervisor observes a nursing trainee administer a hypodermic injection to a patient and rates the performance on a 9-point scale ranging from "Near perfect" to "Completely unacceptable." We want to determine to what extent such a rating reflects "true score" for the trainee and to what extent it reflects "error." Consider each of the following steps that we could take and the implications of each for the definition of error.

STEP TAKEN	DEFINITION OF ERROR
1. A second supervisor also observes and independently rates the same performance.	1. The idiosyncrasy and instability of a single supervisor's ratings—in general and in relation to the specific trainee.
2. A second supervisor immediately observes the trainee giving that injection to a different patient.	2. All of the foregoing plus the inconsistency of the trainee from moment to moment *and* any idiosyncrasy in the reactions of the trainee to the specific patient.
3. A different supervisor observes the trainee giving an injection to a new patient a week later.	3. All of the foregoing plus any changes in the trainee in the course of a week—possibly representing learning or forgetting—and any day-to-day variations in mood or alertness.
4. The trainee is observed giving any one of two or three procedures, each to a different patient, and after each observation is rated by a different rater on "quality of patient care." The ratings are averaged for a final pooled rating.	4. All of parts 1 and 2 plus *specific* skills that affect only a single procedure. "True score" on the pooled rating is defined as common core of judged competence running through a number of specific procedures.

In effect, each of these steps results in a different definition of the universe from which one is sampling—and consequently a different definition of what constitutes true score and what should be considered error.

In step 1, the universe includes only the one specific bit of behavior by one trainee. "True score" would be defined as the average value approached by the rating of that specific behavior sample for that trainee, as the number of (presumably competent) supervisors judging the behavior was increased without limit. "Error" is the difference between a single judge's rating and that average value. Error variance is the variance of the distribution of ratings by a group of judges around the average value, as the number of judges is increased without limit. True-score *variance* is the variance of the mean rating for a set of trainees, all presented with exactly the same task (something that would be very difficult to achieve in real life).

In step 2, the universe has been expanded to include other samples of behavior by the trainee, involving other patients and possible momentary fluctuations in alertness, technique, and "luck" in getting the needle adroitly into the proper place. With this broader universe, "true score" is defined as an average not only over supervisors, assuming that we continued to have multiple supervisors doing the rating, but also over repetitions of the skill—at that point in time. "Error" represents the difference between a specific act of giving a hypodermic injection, as rated by a particular judge, and the average of all acts of giving a hypodermic injection, rated by all judges. Error variance includes *both* variation among supervisors in their rating of a performance *and* variation by a trainee in actual quality of successive performances.* If there were only a single supervisor doing the judging on all the occasions, of course error variance could not include the systematic differences between judges, but it would include the erratic inconsistency of a given judge. That is, a given performance might receive a high rating in part because it was actually better than the trainee's average performance and in part because it hit the supervisor at a lenient moment. True score for this broader universe of raters and acts is estimated from the average rating received by each trainee, but now averaged over both the pool of supervisory raters and the set of specific acts.

Because the inconsistency of the trainee (which in step 1 was lost in, and not separable from, the estimate of that trainee's true score) is now treated as error variance, we should expect that in step 2 the error variance would be larger and consequently that the estimated precision of a score (a single rating of a single action) would be lower. The single score is less adequate to represent this more broadly defined universe.

In step 3 we have introduced the dimension of time and have broadened the universe to include a span of days, weeks, or possibly even months. If there is systematic variation in the trainee's performance over this time span (over and above the fluctuation that occurs from trial to trial and from moment to moment), it constitutes an additional source of error variance. This diurnal variation was previously buried in and treated as part of the true score, but when we study the consistency of measures taken at different points in time, the day-to-

---

* It also includes, as a possible minor component, any tendency for a particular judge to react *especially* favorably or unfavorably to any given performance.

day variation is viewed as error. As the error variance gets further augmented, the precision of a single score as representing this still more inclusive universe becomes less, and a correspondingly lower index is obtained to express that score's reliability.

Finally, in step 4, the universe was broadened markedly to include not just a single skill but a range of different skills that are collectively deemed to represent the more inclusive construct "quality of nursing care." Whereas the attribute of the trainee previously being assessed was "skill in giving hypodermic injections," we have now moved to a much broader, less clearly defined attribute that is inferred from a sampling of different specific skills. As we pool these, it is the common core that runs through all of them that becomes our "true score," and *specific* facets of skill, which apply to only one procedure and not to the others, are a source of inconsistency from one treatment to the next. They must be thought of as "error" and treated as such in analysis of the results.

Though perhaps more dramatically different, the different procedures to be mastered by a nursing trainee can be thought of as analogous to passages with different content in a reading test or even items based on different word meanings in a vocabulary test. The point is that a universe has a dimension of *content* as well as one of trials or occasions and/or one of judges or appraisers, and variable performance arises in part from the extent of variation in the specific content in terms of which the universe is assessed. Content may be defined quite narrowly, as when all the words in a vocabulary test are drawn from a single area of knowledge such as biology, or broadly to cover the whole of a field. The universe may be defined solely in terms of content, or it may also be limited in terms of format — as when the measure of vocabulary consists only of words out of context presented in pairs, with the examinee to judge whether the members are synonyms or antonyms. As the definition of the universe is broadened, any single task or narrow sampling of tasks becomes less adequate to represent that universe. The key point is that any estimate of reliability for a testing procedure appropriately refers to its precision as estimating some *particular* universe score, and it will depend as much on the definition of the universe as on the instrument.

RELIABILITY ESTIMATES AND VARIANCE COMPONENTS

The classical definition of reliability was framed in terms of true score and error variance and took the form

$$r_{xx'} = \frac{\sigma_t^2}{\sigma_t^2 + \sigma_e^2}$$

We have noted that what is included under the heading "error variance" depends on how the universe that the test score is presumed to represent is defined, with certain sources of variance being treated as error under one definition of the universe and as true score under another definition. In theory, at least, an ideal set of data and an ideal analysis would be those that permitted us to estimate the magnitude of each possible component of variance, so that estimates could be made of the reliability of an instrument as representing universes defined in various ways, and so that we could compare the effectiveness of various alternative strategies for increasing the reliability of generalization to a particular universe score. To return to our illustration based on the nursing trainee, what would be the gain from increasing the number of applications of a treatment by a trainee, compared to increasing the number of supervisors making ratings of a single sample? What is the relative efficiency of having two supervisors rate the same application of a treatment, as opposed to having each rate a different application?

If we have identified the different facets that are likely to be sources of variation in the resulting score, the theoretically ideal data-gathering and data-analysis design for getting information about the sources of error in an instrument or procedure would seem to be that of a completely crossed multidimensional analysis of variance.

. Let us start with a two-dimensional illustration. Suppose that each of N examinees has written answers to m test questions. Each answer has been evaluated by the same single reader. We then have an $N \times m$ data matrix that can be represented by the entries in the box

$$
\begin{array}{ccccc}
X_{11} & \cdots & X_{1j} & \cdots & X_{1m} & \quad X_{1.} \\
\vdots & & \vdots & & \vdots & \quad \vdots \\
X_{i1} & \cdots & X_{ij} & \cdots & X_{im} & \quad X_{i.} \\
\vdots & & \vdots & & \vdots & \quad \vdots \\
X_{N1} & \cdots & X_{Nj} & \cdots & X_{Nm} & \quad X_{N.} \\
\\
X_{.1} & \cdots & X_{.j} & \cdots & X_{.m} & \quad X_{..}
\end{array}
$$

The border entries represent summations, where a subscript of a dot (.) indicates summation over that facet. In our matrix, each row represents a person and $X_{i.}$ is the sum over questions for person i, whereas each column represents a question and $X_{.j}$ represents the sum over all persons for question j. By the usual computations for analysis of variance (see Winer, 1972, for example), we have

$$
\text{Total sum of squares} = \sum_{1}^{N} \sum_{1}^{m} (X_{ij})^2 - (X_{..})^2 / mN
$$

Persons sum of squares $= \dfrac{1}{m} \sum_{1}^{N} (X_{i.})^2 - (X_{..})^2/mN$

Questions sum of squares $= \dfrac{1}{N} \sum_{1}^{m} (X_{.j})^2 - (X_{..})^2/mN$

Residual sum of squares $=$ (Total SS $-$ persons SS
$\qquad\qquad\qquad\qquad\quad\, -$ questions SS)   (6.15)

and then

Persons mean square $\quad=$ (persons sum of squares)$/(N - 1)$

Questions mean square $=$ (questions sum of squares)$/(m - 1)$ (6.16)

Residual mean square $\;=$ (residual sum of squares)$/[(N - 1)(m - 1)]$

A numerical illustration is shown below, in which each of a group of six examinees responded to the same set of four questions. All were evaluated by one exam reader.

		QUESTIONS			
EXAMINEES	1	2	3	4	SUM
1	9	6	6	2	23
2	9	5	4	0	18
3	8	9	5	8	30
4	7	6	5	4	22
5	7	3	2	3	15
6	10	8	7	7	32
Sum	50	37	29	24	140

$\sum (X_{ij})^2 = 972 \qquad \sum (X_{i.})^2 = 3486$

$\sum (X_{.j})^2 = 5286 \qquad\quad (X_{..})^2 = 19{,}600$

Total SS $= 972 - 19{,}600/24 = 155.3$

Examinees SS $= 3486/4 - 19{,}600/24 = 54.8$

Questions SS $= 5286/6 - 19{,}600/24 = 64.3$

Residual SS $= 155.3 - 54.8 - 64.3 = 36.2$

Examinees MS $= 54.8/5 = 10.96$

Questions MS $= 64.3/3 = 21.43$

Residual MS $= 36.2/(3 \times 5) = 2.41$

We can now ask about the precision of the scores that result from a test composed of a set of m questions. Note that the only facet of the domain that we can study is that of questions rated by a single rater. We have no evidence on the variability that would be introduced if the examinees were tested on different occasions or if the questions were rated by different judges. To obtain evidence on these facets, we would have to introduce them systematically into the data-gathering and data-analysis design.

In this context, the usual situation is that all examinees respond to the same questions. When that is the case, "questions" becomes a fixed condition, does not vary, and consequently introduces no variance. Then the only source of error variance is the residual term: the interaction between persons and questions—that is, the fact that each examinee does better on some questions and worse on others than would be expected in light of that person's average performance and the difficulty of a given question for all examinees. The *observed* variance among persons includes both "true" between-persons variance and error, so we must subtract the error to get an estimate of σ_t^2. We have, therefore,

$$\sigma_t^2 = \text{examinees MS} - \text{residual MS}$$

and hence

$$\text{Reliability} = \frac{\text{examinees MS} - \text{residual MS}}{\text{examinees MS}} \qquad (6.17)$$

In our illustrative example, this becomes

$$\text{Reliability} = \frac{10.96 - 2.41}{10.96} = .78$$

and the standard error of measurement is $\sqrt{2.41} = 1.55$.

The foregoing estimate applies to the total score, in this example the score based on four questions. It is also possible to estimate the average error variance and the average reliability of a single element, in this illustration the response to a single question. The relationships are as follows:

$$\sigma_E^2 = \text{Residual MS}/m$$

$$\text{Reliability} = \frac{\text{Examinees MS} - \text{residual MS}}{\text{Examinees MS} + (m - 1)\,\text{residual MS}} \qquad (6.18)$$

For our illustrative example, the values come out

$$\sigma_E^2 = 2.41/4 = 0.60$$

$$\text{Reliability} = \frac{10.96 - 2.41}{10.96 + 3(2.41)} = .47$$

and the standard error of measurement equals $\sqrt{.60}$ = .77. Naturally, a score based on just a single question provides a much less accurate estimate of the universe score than one based on the pooling of a number of questions.

It is possible, of course, that questions are not uniform across examinees, and that we do not know which from a pool of possible questions a given examinee is going to encounter.* If that is so, and the questions vary from examinee to examinee, "questions" variance becomes part of error and must be so treated. There are then only two distinguishable components, examinees and residual, and we have

$$\text{Total SS} = \Sigma \; \Sigma \; (X_{ij})^2 \; - \; (X_{..})^2 \; / \; mN$$
$$\text{Persons SS} = \frac{1}{m} \; \Sigma \; (X_{i.})^2 \; - \; (X_{..})^2 \; / \; mN$$
$$\text{Residual SS} = \text{total SS} \; - \; \text{persons SS}$$
$$\text{Persons MS} = \text{persons SS}/N \; - \; 1$$
$$\text{Residual MS} = \text{residual SS}/N(m \; - \; 1)$$

Applying these relationships to our illustrative example, we have

$$\text{Examinees SS} = 54.8$$
$$\text{Residual SS} = 100.5$$
$$\text{Examinees MS} = 54.8/5 = 10.96$$
$$\text{Residual MS} = 100.5/18 = 5.58$$

$$\text{Reliability of total score} = \frac{10.96 \; - \; 5.58}{10.96} = .49$$

$$\text{Reliability of single item} = \frac{10.96 \; - \; 5.58}{10.96 \; + \; 3(5.58)} = .19$$

The reduction in reliability is quite dramatic in this example — and rightly so, because the questions obviously differed widely in their mean score for this group of examinees.

The approach to reliability through analysis of the facets of variance can be quite instructive, as the example brings out. It tells us in this case that a great deal of precision will be lost if different examinees are given different questions. However, for this conclusion to be dependable, it is important that the sample of questions be representative of the universe of admissible questions. Of course, if the estimate of examinee variance is to be meaningful, it is also important that the sample of examinees be representative of the population of examinees to which we want to generalize. However, research workers in general and test makers in particular are used to worrying about their sample of persons. We

---

* This possibility becomes a good deal more real if we shift to a different context. Consider supervisory ratings. Here, in a large organization, different workers are normally rated by different supervisors.

point out that, if estimates are to be made about the size of effects from varying any other facet of the situation, *equal attention must be devoted to sampling from the other facet*. It may be desirable to have as large a sample from the facet of questions, or of raters or of observation periods, as from the facet of persons.

THE GENERAL MULTIFACET MODEL

Up to this point we have considered an illustration in which only one facet of the domain was varied — the facet represented by questions. Let us turn now to a two-facet problem. Suppose that each of the questions had also been read by a second reader and that this reader had assigned scores as shown on the right below. (The scores assigned by the first reader are repeated on the left.)

Question: Examinee	FIRST READER				SECOND READER				SUM		
	1	2	3	4	1	2	3	4	First Reader	Second Reader	Both Readers
1	9	6	6	2	8	2	8	1	23	19	42
2	9	5	4	0	7	5	9	5	18	26	44
3	8	9	5	8	10	6	9	10	30	35	65
4	7	6	5	4	9	8	9	4	22	30	52
5	7	3	2	3	7	4	5	1	15	17	32
6	10	8	7	7	7	7	10	9	32	33	65
Sum	50	37	29	24	48	32	50	30	140	160	300

Item sum for both readers 98   69   79   54

The actual scores on single questions are enclosed in the two boxes. The sums over questions and over questions and readers are shown at the right. The sums over examinees and over examinees and readers are shown at the foot of the table.

We now have the raw material for a three-way analysis of variance and the possibility of obtaining estimates of seven distinct components of variance. If we designate the facet that is represented by raters as k, we have sums as follows:

$$\sum_i \sum_j \sum_k (X_{ijk})^2 = 2,214 \qquad \text{squares of single observations}$$

$$\sum_j \sum_k (X_{.jk})^2 = 12,014 \qquad \text{squares of sums over persons}$$

$$\sum_i \sum_k (X_{i.k})^2 = 8,026 \qquad \text{squares of sums over questions}$$

$$\sum_i \sum_j (X_{ij.})^2 = 4,258 \qquad \text{squares of sums over readers}$$

$$\sum_k (X_{..k})^2 = 45,200 \qquad \text{squares of sums over both persons and questions}$$

$$\sum_k (X_{..k})^2 = 45,200 \qquad \text{squares of sums over both persons and questions}$$

$$\sum_i (X_{i..})^2 = 15,878 \qquad \text{squares of sums over both questions and readers}$$

$$(X_{...})^2 = 90,000 \qquad \text{square of grand sum}$$

From these sums, we move to the sum of squares associated with each component.

$$
\begin{aligned}
\text{Total sum of squares} &= 2214 - 90,000/48 &&= 339.0 \\
\text{Persons sum of squares} &= 15,878/8 - 90,000/48 &&= 109.8 \\
\text{Questions sum of squares} &= 23,522/12 - 90,000/48 &&= 85.2 \\
\text{Readers sum of squares} &= 45,200/24 - 90,000/48 &&= 8.3 \\
P \times Q &= 4258/2 - 90,000/48 - 109.8 - 85.2 &&= 59.0 \\
P \times R &= 8026/4 - 90,000/48 - 109.8 - 8.3 &&= 13.4 \\
Q \times R &= 12,014/6 - 90,000/48 - 85.2 - 8.3 &&= 33.8 \\
P \times Q \times R &= 339.0 - (109.8 + 85.2 + 8.3 + \\
& \quad\ 59.0 + 13.4 + 33.8) &&= 29.5
\end{aligned}
$$

From here, we proceed to the mean squares for each of the seven components, dividing by the number of degrees of freedom.

SOURCE	SUM OF SQUARES	DEGREES OF FREEDOM	MEAN SQUARE
Persons	109.8	5	21.96
Questions	85.2	3	28.40
Readers	8.3	1	8.30
$P \times Q$	59.0	15	3.93
$P \times R$	13.4	5	2.68
$Q \times R$	33.8	3	11.27
$P \times Q \times R$	29.5	15	1.97

We need now to estimate the seven variance components. To do this, we must note that each mean square at a given level already includes, within itself, variance represented in the higher levels of interaction. That is, the persons-by-questions mean square includes a contribution from persons × questions × readers, and the persons mean square includes contributions from persons × questions and from persons × readers. We must also note that our mean squares represent the values that attach to a sum of several observations. For example, the mean square for persons is a sum over four questions each read by two readers. If we want the variance component for a single observation, we have to divide the given value by the number of observations on which it is based.

Taking these two points into account, we get the following set of equations from which the variance components can be determined:

$$\sigma^2_{pqr} = MS_{pqr}$$

$$\sigma^2_{pq} = \frac{1}{n_r}(MS_{pq} - MS_{pqr})$$

$$\sigma^2_{pr} = \frac{1}{n_q}(MS_{pr} - MS_{pqr})$$

$$\sigma^2_{qr} = \frac{1}{n_p}(MS_{qr} - MS_{pqr})$$

$$\sigma^2_{p} = \frac{1}{n_q n_r}(MS_{p} - MS_{pq} - MS_{pr} + MS_{pqr})$$

$$\sigma^2_{q} = \frac{1}{n_p n_r}(MS_{q} - MS_{pq} - MS_{qr} + MS_{pqr})$$

$$\sigma^2_{r} = \frac{1}{n_p n_q}(MS_{r} - MS_{pr} - MS_{qr} + MS_{pqr}) \tag{6.19}$$

In our problem, the values become

$$\sigma^2_{pqr} = 1.97$$

$$\sigma^2_{pq} = \frac{1}{2}(3.93 - 1.97) = 0.98$$

$$\sigma^2_{pr} = \frac{1}{4}(2.68 - 1.97) = 0.18$$

$$\sigma^2_{qr} = \frac{1}{6}(11.27 - 1.97) = 1.55$$

$$\sigma^2_{p} = \frac{1}{8}(21.96 - 3.93 - 2.68 + 1.97) = 2.16$$

$$\sigma^2_{q} = \frac{1}{12}(28.40 - 3.93 - 11.27 + 1.97) = 1.26$$

$$\sigma^2_{r} = \frac{1}{24}(8.30 - 2.68 - 11.27 + 1.97) < 0$$

The values for the seven components of variance provide estimates of how important the various facets will be in producing variation in our estimates of a given examinee's ability. It will pay to examine these values with some care.

First, note that we get an estimate of less than zero for readers. Of course, variation less than zero is meaningless. What this value points out is that we are, after all, dealing with *estimates*. These estimates may in some cases fall above the universe value and in some cases below. Furthermore, the estimates are often (and certainly in our data) based on a small number of degrees of freedom and are correspondingly unstable. We had only two readers. It happened that these two were similar in the overall severity of their grading standards (though they differed rather markedly in their severity on *specific* questions), and when account was taken of the interactions of readers with questions and with examinees, the residual contribution of readers per se appeared to be nil.

The result on readers points out the need, in studies of the importance of different variance components, to sample adequately from each of the facets—in this case examinees, questions, and readers. Practical realities often make it difficult to get as large or as well-designed a sample from such facets as test tasks, evaluators, and occasions as the sample we can get of examinees, but the need is as great in the one case as in the other.

Returning to our table of variance components, we note with satisfaction that the largest single component is that for persons (or examinees). This is the component that represents "true score" or "universe score" and is what we are primarily interested in assessing. The next largest component is that designated σ^2_{pqr}. This should more accurately be labeled $\sigma^2_{pqr} + \sigma^2_{e}$, because it incorporates both the second-order interaction of person × question × reader and the random "error" in its purest form. With only one observation in each $p \times q \times r$ cell of our data matrix, it is impossible to separate these two elements. In most instances it will happen that at the highest level of interaction there *will* be only a single observation, so that "error" and this highest interaction will be confounded.

The next three components, in order of size, are question-by-reader interaction (1.55), questions (1.26), and person-by-question interaction (0.98). All these involve the sampling of questions, and collectively they indicate that the particular set of questions included in the test is a very potent determiner of the score that a given examinee will achieve. From the viewpoint of a strategy for accurate measurement, the size of these components indicates that it will be important (1) for all examinees to answer the same questions and (2) for the number of questions to be large.

We can see the importance of the different variance components more clearly if we calculate the "coefficient of reproducibility," the ratio of expected true score or universe variance to expected observed variance. Universe variance for score that is the sum of observations on n_q questions, each rated by n_r readers, is given by

$$\sigma^2_{\text{true}} = (n_q n_r)^2 \sigma^2_p \tag{6.20}$$

where σ^2_p is our estimate of the *persons* variance component. This follows from the formula given on page 150, because to add questions and readers is in effect to increase the length of the behavior sample. The expected observed variance is given by

$$\sigma^2_{\text{obs}} - (n_q n_r)(n_q n_r \sigma^2_p + n_q \sigma^2_r + n_r \sigma^2_q + n_q \sigma^2_{pr} + n_r \sigma^2_{pq} + \sigma^2_{qr} + \sigma^2_{pqr})$$
$$(6.21)$$

With appropriate divisions in both numerator and denominator, the coefficient of generalizability becomes

$$\frac{\sigma^2_{\text{true}}}{\sigma^2_{\text{obs}}} = \frac{\sigma^2_p}{\sigma^2_p + \dfrac{\sigma^2_q}{n_q} + \dfrac{\sigma^2_r}{n_r} + \dfrac{\sigma^2_{pq}}{n_q} + \dfrac{\sigma^2_{pr}}{n_r} + \dfrac{\sigma^2_{qr}}{n_q n_r} + \dfrac{\sigma^2_{pqr}}{n_q n_r}} \qquad (6.22)$$

From our data we have

$$\frac{\sigma^2_{\text{true}}}{\sigma^2_{\text{obs}}} = \frac{2.16}{2.16 + \dfrac{1.26}{4} + \dfrac{0}{2} + \dfrac{0.98}{4} + \dfrac{0.18}{2} + \dfrac{1.55}{8} + \dfrac{1.97}{8}}$$

$$r_{xx'} = \frac{2.16}{3.25} = .66$$

This coefficient is an estimate of the correlation that would be obtained between two sets of scores for a group of examinees, when each examinee is tested with a random set of four questions chosen independently for that examinee and rated by a random two readers also chosen independently for each examinee.

Looking only at the denominator, one can see where most of the "error variance" comes from. We have

$$\sigma^2_{\text{obs}} = 2.16 + (0.32 + 0 + 0.24 + 0.09 + 0.19 + 0.25)$$
$$\phantom{\sigma^2_{\text{obs}} = 2.16 + (}p \qquad q \qquad r \qquad pq \qquad pr \qquad qr \qquad pqr$$

One can see that the largest components of the error variance, in order of size, are questions (0.32); the interaction of persons, questions, and readers (0.25); and the interaction of persons and questions (0.24). The strategy for reducing all these would be to increase the number of questions. This would increase the divisors in the largest terms of the denominator of equation 6.22 — and hence would reduce those largest terms and increase the precision of the resulting score. If the number of questions were doubled, we would have

$$\sigma^2_{\text{obs}} = 2.16 + (0.16 + 0 + 0.12 + 0.09 + 0.10 + 0.12) = 2.75$$

$$r_{xx'} = \frac{2.16}{2.75} = .79$$

By contrast, if the number of readers were doubled without any change in the number of questions, we would have

$$\sigma^2_{\text{obs}} = 2.16 + (0.32 + 0 + 0.24 + 0.04 + 0.10 + 0.12) = 2.98$$

$$r_{xx'} = \frac{2.16}{2.98} = .72$$

and the gain in precision would be a good deal less.

NONRANDOM QUESTIONS AND READERS

Up to this point, we have assumed that both the questions facet and the readers facet have been sampled at random, such that a given examinee could have any four questions drawn from the universe of admissible questions rated by any two readers drawn from the universe of admissible readers. It is a good deal more common for the set of questions (and possibly the readers) to be the same for all examinees. If the set of questions will be uniform for all examinees, the variance component associated with questions (σ^2_q) disappears, and we have

$$\sigma^2_{\text{obs}} = 2.16 + (0.24 + 0.09 + 0.19 + 0.25) = 2.93$$

$$r_{xx'} = \frac{2.16}{2.93} = .74$$

Naturally enough, our estimate of a person's standing in the group is appreciably more precise when we know that all members of the group will take the same test. If it is *also* known that the readers will be the same for all examinees, two other variance components (σ^2_r and σ^2_{qr}) drop out of our observed variance, and we have left

$$\sigma^2_{\text{obs}} = \sigma^2_p + \frac{\sigma^2_{pq}}{n_q} + \frac{\sigma^2_{pr}}{n_r} + \frac{\sigma^2_{pqr}}{n_q n_r} \tag{6.23}$$

For our data, this becomes

$$\sigma^2_{\text{obs}} = 2.16 + (0.24 + 0.09 + 0.25) = 2.74$$

$$r_{xx'} = \frac{2.16}{2.74} = .79$$

Thus, in our illustrative example, keeping the questions and readers uniform for all examinees raises the true-score variance, as a percentage of the total, from 66 to 79.

It is also possible that we may be interested only in a *specific set* of test questions, considering these to be the universe to which we want to generalize. The questions facet then becomes a *fixed* facet, rather than one that is sampled randomly from some larger universe. Considering a certain facet to be fixed has two effects: (1) The interaction between persons and that fixed facet, σ_{pq}^2 in our illustration, is treated as a component of true score rather than error. (2) The component associated with that fixed facet (σ_q^2) disappears. Thus we have

$$\sigma_{\text{true}}^2 = \sigma_p^2 + \frac{\sigma_{pq}^2}{n_q}$$

$$\sigma_{\text{obs}}^2 = \left(\sigma_p^2 + \frac{\sigma_{pq}^2}{n_q} \right) + \left(\frac{\sigma_r^2}{n_r} + \frac{\sigma_{pr}^2}{n_r} + \frac{\sigma_{qr}^2}{n_q n_r} + \frac{\sigma_{pqr}^2}{n_q n_r} \right)$$

$$\sigma_{\text{true}}^2 = 2.16 + 0.24 = 2.40$$

$$\sigma_{\text{obs}}^2 = 2.40 + (0 + 0.09 + 0.19 + 0.25) = 2.93$$

$$r_{xx'} = .82$$

If we had been interested in generalizing only to this set of questions as appraised by these specific readers, we would have had

$$\sigma_{\text{true}}^2 = 2.16 + 0.24 + 0.09 = 2.49$$

$$\sigma_{\text{obs}}^2 = 2.49 \qquad\qquad + 0.25 = 2.74$$

$$r_{xx'} = .91$$

CONFOUNDING

In all of our analyses, we have dealt with the situation in which the design for *collection* of the original data was completely "crossed" — that is, every examinee answered every question and every response was evaluated by every rater. Collection of the original data in this format has very real advantages in that it allows us to generate estimates (though somewhat fragile ones because of small n's for some of the facets) of *all* the variance components. However, it may not always be possible to gather such data. Thus the readers might vary from one examinee to another and we might not know which reader had read a particular examinee's paper. We might know only that two from a sizable universe of readers had read a given paper. In this case, reader is said to be "nested within persons." When we do not know which readers have read a given examinee's paper, certain of the variance components become confounded and cannot be separated from one another. Specifically, we cannot separate reader variance (σ_r^2) from the interaction between reader and examinee (σ_{pr}^2), because information for a particular pair of readers can be identified only within the data for a single examinee. Similarly, σ_{qr}^2 and σ_{pqr}^2 cannot be separated. Thus we have, as identifiable variance components, only σ_p^2, σ_q^2, σ_{pq}^2, $(\sigma_r^2, \sigma_{pr}^2)$, and $(\sigma_{qr}^2, \sigma_{pqr}^2)$. For our illustrative problem, the data are analyzed as follows:

COMPONENT	SUM OF SQUARES	NUMBER OF DEGREES OF FREEDOM	MEAN SQUARE
P	109.8	5	21.96
Q	85.2	3	28.40
$(R, P \times R)$	8.3 + 13.4	6	3.62
$P \times Q$	59.0	15	3.93
$(Q \times R, P \times Q \times R)$	33.8 + 29.5	18	3.52

Note that both the sum of squares and the number of degrees of freedom collapse for the two components that are confounded and cannot be separated.

The analysis of variance components also reduces to just the five that can be isolated, and we have

$$\sigma_{qr,\,pqr}^2 = MS\,(Q \times R, P \times Q \times R)$$

$$\sigma_{pq}^2 = \frac{1}{n_r}\,[MS\,(P \times Q) - MS\,(Q \times R, P \times Q \times R)]$$

$$\sigma_{r,\,pr}^2 = \frac{1}{n_q}\,[MS\,(R, P \times R) - MS\,(Q \times R, P \times Q \times R)]$$

$$\sigma_q^2 = \frac{1}{n_p n_r}\,[MS\,(Q) - MS\,(P \times Q)]$$

$$\sigma_p^2 = \frac{1}{n_q n_r}\,[MS\,(P) - MS\,(P \times Q) - MS\,(R, P \times R)$$

$$+ MS\,(Q \times R, P \times Q \times R)] \qquad (6.24)$$

For the data of our example, this becomes

$$\sigma_{qr,\,pqr}^2 = 3.52$$

$$\sigma_{pq}^2 = \frac{1}{2}(3.93 - 3.52) = 0.20$$

$$\sigma_{r,\,qr}^2 = \frac{1}{4}(3.62 - 3.52) = 0.02$$

$$\sigma_q^2 = \frac{1}{12}(28.40 - 3.93) = 2.04$$

$$\sigma_p^2 = \frac{1}{8}(21.96 - 3.93 - 3.62 + 3.52) = 2.24$$

The analyses of true score and observed variances parallel the development previously given, except that the confounding prevents us from testing some of the models that we might be interested in. Thus, for generalization to a situation in which each examinee is tested with a random set of four questions drawn from the universe of admissible questions, we have

$$\sigma^2_{\text{true}} = 2.24$$

$$\sigma^2_{\text{obs}} = 2.24 + \left(\frac{2.04}{4} + \frac{0.02}{2} + \frac{0.20}{4} + \frac{3.52}{8}\right)$$

$$= 2.24 + (0.51 + 0.01 + 0.05 + 0.44) = 3.25$$

$$r_{xx'} = \frac{2.24}{3.25} = .69$$

If we knew that all examinees would have the same questions, we would have

$$\sigma^2_{\text{obs}} = 2.24 + (0.01 + 0.05 + 0.44) = 2.74$$

$$r_{xx'} = \frac{2.24}{2.74} = .82$$

If we were interested only in generalizing to a universe of scores on these specific questions, we would have

$$\sigma^2_{\text{true}} = 2.24 + 0.05 = 2.29$$

$$r_{xx'} = \frac{2.29}{2.74} = .836$$

We cannot analyze the effects of uniform readers or a universe of only specified readers, because the required variance components involving readers are confounded.

It is even conceivable that both questions and readers could be confounded with persons (though it is unlikely that data would be gathered in this form). This would occur if all we knew was that, in our original analysis of the test, each examinee had taken *some* form of a test composed of four questions and that each person's paper had been read by *some* pair of readers. Confounding then becomes complete, and all we can isolate are between-persons and within-persons components of variance. We have

COMPONENT	SUM OF SQUARES	NUMBER OF DEGREES OF FREEDOM	MEAN SQUARE
p	109.8	5	21.96
Within p	229.2	42	5.46

$$\sigma_p^2 \;=\; \frac{1}{m_q n_r} \left[MS(p) \;-\; MS\,(\text{within}) \right]$$

$$ \;=\; \frac{1}{8} \,(16.50) \;=\; 2.06$$

$$\sigma_{\text{obs}}^2 \;=\; 2.06 \;+\; \frac{5.46}{8} \;=\; 2.06 \;+\; 0.68 \;=\; 2.74$$

$$r_{xx'} \;=\; \frac{2.06}{2.74} \;=\; .74$$

Our estimate is that, for a randomly chosen four-question test read by two randomly chosen readers, 74% of the variance is true-score or universe variance of persons and the other 26% is contributed by the composite of all other components. No further analysis of the situation is possible. This value may be compared with the 66% we found on page 165, which results from the variance components of the completely crossed data. That the agreement is not better than this must be attributed to the small number of degrees of freedom underlying several of the specific variance components.

We have explored this two-facet illustration of the variance-components approach to analysis of reliability and the precision of measurement in some detail, because it serves to exhibit both the logic and the empirical possibilities of the method. The same type of approach is possible with three or more varied facets, but the number of variance components approximately doubles each time a facet is added. In such multifacet studies, obtaining the full set of completely crossed data becomes quite an undertaking. Furthermore, obtaining samples of adequate size and of suitable randomness for each facet can present serious practical difficulties.

The variance-components model is one into which practically all the conventional procedures for gathering data on reliability can be fitted, and understanding any procedure is enhanced by seeing how it handles the several components of variance. The simplest procedure is to test each examinee with two forms of a test, giving everyone form A followed by form B — either immediately or at some later date. It has then been the usual procedure to compute the correlation between form A and form B. This is a single-facet problem, but the facet is a compound one that we could designate test-form-confounded-with-order. Thus there are three variance components: (1) persons, (2) test-form-and-order, and (3) the interaction of components 1 and 2. Component 2 shows up as a difference between mean scores on the two forms and does not influence the correlation, because product-moment correlations are based on deviations from the respective group means. Thus,

$$r_{AB} \;=\; \frac{\sigma_{\text{persons}}^2}{\sigma_{\text{persons}}^2 \;+\; (\sigma_{(\text{persons} \,\times\, \text{forms})}^2 \,/\, 2)}$$

(We divide by 2 because the persons-by-forms components is based on two forms.)

Coefficient alpha and its special case, Kuder–Richardson Formula 20, are also single-facet approaches in which analysis is carried out at the item level. Thus, we have (1) a between-persons variance component, (2) a between-items component, and (3) an interaction-of-persons-with-items component. Once again, items are thought of as a fixed effect and we come out with the analysis shown in equations 6.6, 6.7, and 6.8. The results from this analysis can be shown to be algebraically equivalent to coefficient alpha, computed by the formula

$$\alpha = \frac{n}{n-1}\left(1 - \frac{\sum_{i=1}^{m} s_i^2}{s_x^2}\right) \qquad (6.25)$$

where s_i^2 is the variance of item i and s_x^2 is the variance of test x.

Incidentally, the development beginning on page 157 makes it clear why coefficient alpha tends to become meaningless if a test is appreciably speeded and there are a number of students who do not have time to attempt a number of items. Then, in the persons-by-items data matrix, there are a number of empty cells. In effect we assign a value of zero to each of these empty cells, but we do it in the absence of data. The series of zeroes for a given examinee produces a kind of spurious consistency in his or her scores on the later items and consequently inflates to some degree our estimate of the reliability coefficient.

RELIABILITY WITH CONVENTIONAL DATA-COLLECTION STRATEGIES

Carrying out a systematic analysis of variance components is the most instructive way to obtain a complete understanding of the sources of error in a measurement procedure. However, collecting the data for such a complete analysis is rarely practical and perhaps not really necessary. The circumstances of life usually *do* make it possible (1) to give two presumably equivalent forms of a test and study the correlation between the resulting two sets of scores, (2) to give the same test form on two separate occasions and study the correlation between the results from the two testings, or (3) to give a single test form consisting of several sections or a number of items and study the consistency of performance over the sections or items. Much of the evidence on test reliability stems from one or another of these procedures.

The foregoing procedures permit the allocation to error of only certain components of variance. Consequently each provides a somewhat different and a somewhat limited definition of the universe being sampled by the test. However, each offers some information about the generalizability from a testing procedure.

When two presumably equivalent forms of a test are given, the common universe sampled by each is that defined by the blueprint of the test. That is, whatever is peculiar to that blueprint is considered to be part of the true score measured by the test. (If the test were correlated with a different test designed to appraise the same general domain or the same latent attribute, some of the elements common to alternate forms might function as error.) And, of course, if the two forms are given on the same day, the attribute is operationally defined as the individual's status on that attribute at that point in time. With this last procedure, any day-to-day variation in level of performance is absorbed into true score and cannot be separately identified. Only if the two forms are separated by some span of days is day-to-day variation treated as error and the universe defined as the individual's stable position on the latent attribute specified by the common blueprint.

If the *same* form of a test is repeated after an interval, the universe is defined as just the specific test exercises included in that form of the test. To the extent that test items depend on quite specific bits of information or elements of skill, those specifics are treated as elements of true score rather than as error. If the specifics account for an appreciable amount of variance, consistency on repeated testing can be a substantial overestimate of the consistency that would be found in the broader universe where separate forms of a test sample independently from the defined universe. In this procedure for data collection, day-to-day variation *is* allocated to error, so the procedure *does* allocate to error the facet of variability over time, but identity of content means that inferences on precision of measurement are limited to inferences about that specific set of test tasks.

A further disadvantage of basing inferences on retesting is that one does not know how memory of responses on the prior testing may affect the subsequent performance. Memory effects can vary, depending on the type of task and on the length of the interval between testings; they are more severe the more distinctive the task and the shorter the interval. The effect may be on the responses directly, as when the prior choice is remembered and repeated without further consideration. Or it may be on motivation, as when examinees can see no sense in retaking a questionnaire or inventory that they completed a few weeks ago and hence may respond hurriedly and superficially.

If a single test form is given and the internal consistency of response to the separate items serves as evidence of reliability, the universe is obviously defined as one of performance at a specific point in time. Day-to-day variations have no chance to show themselves as a source of error variance. Furthermore, the universe is defined as that which is common to the several items or exercises, so whatever is specific to particular exercises is allocated to error. If all the exercises in a test are designed to measure the same attribute, consistency in responding to the different items in the test seems quite reasonable as an index of how accurately the exercises do in fact accomplish this. However, if a test is composed of parts that are thought to differ somewhat from one another, the internal analysis should be carried out separately for each part and the results from the parts combined (using the formula for the correlation of sums) to provide an estimate of consistency for the more complex universe represented by the total test.

A major limitation of procedures that estimate reliability from the internal consistency of performance on the exercises of a test is that these procedures are not directly applicable to speeded tests. One can observe consistency of performance on a pair of test exercises only if the examinee has had an opportunity to attempt both exercises. If time limits are such that a number of examinees have not reached one or both of the exercises, the data are incomplete and standard procedures of analysis are not applicable. This consideration, together with testing being limited to a single point in time, makes the use of internal-consistency analysis meaningful only in appraising the precision of current status on an unspeeded test.

RELIABILITY ESTIMATED FROM EQUIVALENT FORMS

If two equivalent forms of a test are administered (forms that are measures of the same latent attribute and that can both be expected to measure it with the same precision), the correlation between them serves as an estimate of the reliability coefficient. That is, it can be shown that, if the foregoing conditions hold,

$$r_{12} = \frac{\sigma^2_{\text{true}}}{\sigma^2_{\text{observed}}} = \frac{\sigma^2_{\text{true}}}{\sigma^2_{\text{true}} + \sigma^2_{\text{error}}}$$

The value obtained for this coefficient is critically dependent on the heterogeneity of the group to which the two forms are administered — that is, on the size of σ^2_{true}. For this reason, an estimate of the error variance or of its square root, called the standard error of measurement, is often a more serviceable statistic. It is a good deal less sensitive to the range of talent in the sample on which the reliability estimate is based. This standard error of measurement is given by

$$\sigma_{\text{meas}} = \sigma_{\text{obs}} \sqrt{1 - r_{xx'}}$$

So far we have spoken as though the error variance kept the same value at all levels of the latent attribute. Of course, this is not necessarily the case. A test often measures more accurately within certain limits on the latent attribute than it does at other points; the location of higher accuracy depends on the way in which the items that compose the final test were chosen. (See the discussion of the information function in Chapter 4.) The standard error of measurement, estimated from the correlation between two forms of a test, is a kind of pooled overall estimate of precision, an estimate that is often better replaced by estimates at each of a number of different score levels. A procedure for obtaining those estimates is outlined below.

1. Find the average score of each examinee on the two forms combined. This average score represents our best estimate of where the individual stands on the latent attribute.

2. Group together all cases that fall between specified limits on this average score. Thus, for a 100-item test, it would probably be satisfactory to set up groupings 5 points or 10 points in width.

3. For each group, make a distribution of the score differences between form 1 and form 2—that is, a distribution of $X_1 - X_2$. Find the mean and the variance of the distribution of differences for each score group separately.

4. Divide the variance of the differences by 2 to get the error variance for a single test form.*

5. Take the square root to get the standard error of measurement at that score level.

The values obtained for the standard error of measurement at each score level will be expressed in raw-score units. Often (perhaps usually) raw-score units do not correspond to the same distance on the scale of the latent attribute at all points on the raw-score scale. Therefore, it is usually desirable to translate the raw-score standard errors to some converted-score scale designed to provide equal units throughout its length. Procedures for developing such score scales were discussed in Chapter 5. The raw-score standard errors can be multiplied by the factor that, at each score level, represents the number of points of converted score per point of raw score. This will translate the standard errors to the presumed equal-unit scale. A set of such standard errors is very informative in describing the precision of an instrument at different ability levels.

Often it is found that a test is most accurate in the middle range of scores, with the precision dropping off noticeably toward either extreme. The standard error of measurement at a given score level, when it is expressed in units of an interval scale, is proportional to the reciprocal of the square root of the information function of the test at that level. Where the information is greatest, the standard error of measurement is least.

The fact that the mean difference $\overline{X}_1 - \overline{X}_2$ obtained in step 3 above is rarely equal to zero arises from (1) the order in which the two test forms were administered, (2) differences in the difficulty of the two forms, or (3) both these considerations in some proportion. In a complete components-of-variance analysis, this difference would appear as a component associated with test form.

---

*If split-half procedures for estimating reliability have been used, the error variance is given directly by the variance of differences between the two half-test scores.

When all examinees are tested with the same form(s), this component becomes a constant and does not appear as a source of variance.

RELIABILITY ESTIMATED FROM RETESTING

As indicated on page 171, an alternative data-gathering strategy is to use one specific measure of a latent attribute and to repeat the identical measure after an interval. This is a reasonable strategy if (1) all test exercises are so similar in content or function that any one sample of exercises is equivalent to any other and (2) the exercises are so numerous and/or nondescript that, at the second testing, there will be little or no memory of the responses given on the initial testing. Specific memory will, of course, become less and less of a problem as the interval between the two testings is lengthened. However, as the time interval is lengthened, the variation from one testing to the other reflects in increasing proportion the impact of intervening experiences or of differential rates of growth. The variation then becomes, in increasing proportion, an indicator of instability of the underlying attribute over a time span, rather than of lack of precision in the measuring instrument.

The standard error of measurement at each score level can appropriately be obtained from retesting with the identical test. It now provides information about the consistency with which persons at different ability levels respond to the test tasks. The difference in mean score between the first and second testing constitutes a variance component reflecting some mixture of practice effect and growth between the two testings. The two are not separable, but the relative importance of each can be inferred at least crudely from the length of the interval between testings.

RELIABILITY ESTIMATED FROM INTERNAL CONSISTENCY

The third data-collecting strategy relies on the internal analysis of a single test administration. This has *very* great practical advantages, because (1) it requires development of only a single form of the test and (2) cooperation of examinees is required for only a single period of testing. These practical advantages have led test makers and research workers to use procedures of internal analysis frequently, in spite of their fairly severe theoretical limitations. One limitation is, of course, that all testing is done within a single brief period, so that no evidence can be obtained on diurnal variability—changes in individual performance from one occasion to the next. Another limitation is that the estimates of reliability become more and more inflated as the test is speeded. We shall return to this issue after the basic procedures have been set forth.

The early procedure for extracting reliability estimates from a single administration of a test form was to divide the test items into equivalent fractions, usually two equivalent halves, and obtain two separate scores—one for each fraction. The correlations between the sets of scores were then obtained and were corrected by the Spearman–Brown Prophecy Formula to give an estimate of the reliability coefficient for the full-length test. As indicated on page 152, when the test is divided into halves, the correction formula becomes

$$r_{11} = \frac{2r_{\frac{1}{2}\frac{1}{2}}}{1 + r_{\frac{1}{2}\frac{1}{2}}}$$

When items are numerous and arranged either by subarea or in order of gradually increasing difficulty (or by increasing difficulty within subareas), putting alternate items into alternate test forms has often seemed a sound strategy for achieving equivalence. Hence the odd–even correlations often reported. An investigator or test maker must decide in each case whether this or some other procedure is the most reasonable way to define equivalent halves for the instrument she or he is studying.

In recent years, those extracting reliability estimates from a single test administration have tended increasingly to base the estimates on analysis-of-variance approaches, in which single items constitute the units on which the analysis is based. The analysis is built on the assumption that all items are measures of the same underlying attribute — that is, that the test is homogeneous in content. For this reason, when a test is composed of two or more diverse subtests, it is usually necessary to apply the analysis to each subtest separately and then to use the formula for the correlation of sums (see page 151) to estimate the reliability of the total. Analysis-of-variance procedures do not depend on any particular choice in subdividing the items, and they approximate an average of all the possible correlations that might have been obtained by different ways of assigning items to alternate forms. When the assumption of homogeneity of function measured is justified, this would appear to be the most objective way to determine consistency across the items of the test.

The most general form of the analysis of item variance is provided by Cronbach's coefficient alpha (Cronbach, 1951), the formula for which is

$$\alpha = \frac{n}{n - 1}\left(1 - \frac{\Sigma s_i^2}{s_t^2}\right) \tag{6.26}$$

where n = number of items in the test

s_i^2 = variance of item i

s_t^2 = variance of the total test

This expression is quite general in its application. It will handle test exercises in which score can take a range of values, as in essay tests or in inventories that provide multiple levels of response. It can even be applied when the "items" are themselves groups of test exercises.

When all the items are scored either 0 or 1, coefficient alpha reduces to the form reported earlier by Kuder and Richardson (1937) and known as Kuder–Richardson Formula 20. It is

$$\text{Reliability} = \frac{n}{n-1}\left(1 - \frac{\Sigma p_i q_i}{s_t^2}\right) \tag{6.27}$$

A lower-bounds estimated of this value, which is exact if all items are of the same difficulty, is provided by Kuder-Richardson Formula 21, which takes the form

$$\text{Reliability} = \frac{n}{n-1}\left(1 - \frac{\Sigma n\bar{p}\bar{q}}{s_t^2}\right)$$

where $\bar{p}$ = mean percent of correct responses

$\bar{q}$ = mean percent of incorrect responses

K.R. 21 can also be expressed as

$$\text{Reliability} = \frac{n}{n-1}\left(1 - \frac{\bar{X} - \frac{(\bar{X})^2}{n}}{s_t^2}\right) \tag{6.28}$$

This formula provides a convenient way to get a quick, conservative estimate of coefficient alpha, because it requires information only on the mean, standard deviation, and number of items in the test. It differs from the full formula by the amount

$$\frac{ns_p^2}{s_t^2}$$

where s_p^2 = the variance of the item difficulty indices, p. For a test of 50 or more items, this element is likely to be no greater than .02 or .03. For example, if the items have a range of p-values from .30 to .90 with a standard deviation of .10, and the test's standard deviation is 6 points (a realistic figure), for a 50-item test we have

$$\frac{50(.10)^2}{6^2} = \frac{.50}{36} = .014$$

Thus, with tests of a length commonly encountered in practice, formula 6.28 provides a very serviceable approximation.

We indicated earlier that coefficient alpha in its standard form is applicable only to homogeneous tests in which all items are designed to measure the same common latent attribute. When test items are not designed to be measures of a single homogeneous attribute, a test may often be divided into subtests each of which *is* designed to be homogeneous in what it measures. Then formula 6.26, 6.27, or 6.28 can be applied to each subtest separately to estimate the reliability (in the internal-consistency sense) of the subtest. Finally, formula 6.10 can be applied to the set of reliability estimates, subtest intercorrelations, and subtest variances to obtain an estimate of the reliability of the total test. An illustration for a two-part test follows.

SUBTEST	K.R. 20	S.D.	INTERCORRELATION
Vocabulary	.78	5.1	.58
Number Series	.73	4.8	

Calculating variances and covariances, we have

$$\text{Variance V} = 26.01$$
$$\text{Variance N} = 23.04$$
$$\text{Covariance V vs. N} = 14.20$$
$$\text{Covariance V vs. V}' = 20.29$$
$$\text{Covariance N vs. N}' = 16.82$$

Remembering that the two forms are assumed to be exactly parallel, and hence to have identical variances and covariances, we have

$$\frac{\begin{vmatrix} 20.29 & 14.20 \\ 14.20 & 16.82 \end{vmatrix}}{\begin{vmatrix} 26.01 & 14.20 \\ 14.20 & 23.04 \end{vmatrix}} = \frac{65.51}{77.45} = .846$$

Here the numerator is the covariance of the two parallel forms, and the denominator is the variance of either of them.

INTERNAL-CONSISTENCY ESTIMATES FOR SPEEDED TESTS

We have said that internal-consistency procedures for estimating reliability (split-half, coefficient alpha) give spuriously high values when applied to speeded tests. But the fact that a test is given with a time limit does not necessarily mean that speed of work is a significant source of variance in the resulting test scores. The time limits *may* be long enough so that the great majority of examinees have time to attempt all of the items for which they know the answers and so that the only nonattempted items are items with which the examinees would have little prospect of success. One would like some statistic that would indicate how much of the variance in individuals' test scores can be attributed to variation in speed of work from one test administration to another.

For tests in which the items are arranged approximately in order of difficulty, Cronbach and Warrington (1951) have provided a procedure that yields an estimate of the maximum amount of variance that can be attributed to speeding—and through this a lower bound to coefficient alpha. The obtained alpha and this bound may be thought to define a band within which the correct value of alpha lies. When this band is narrow, one can be content that one has located alpha within useful limits. Otherwise, one must regard an obtained alpha as relatively meaningless.

The Cronbach and Warrington estimation procedure assumes two inequalities, both of which seem intuitively reasonable. They can be stated as follows:

1. The variance from one testing to another within a single individual in number of items attempted is no greater than the variance among persons at a single testing.

2. The probability of success on items just not reached is no greater than the achieved proportion of successes on the last items attempted.

We now show the steps by which these two assumptions are used to arrive at a maximum for speededness variance and hence a lower bound for internal consistency.

1. For the set of test papers, a frequency distribution of number of items not reached at the end of the test is prepared.

2. It is assumed that, among those attempting all items, a number m just equal to the number omitting the one last item should be considered to have just barely finished, and hence to be likely not to finish an alternate form of the test. This number m of 0 scores is entered in the distribution of number not reached.

3. The variance of this distribution of not-reached items is calculated.

4. Considering the last two items actually answered, a count is made of the number of answer sheets with 0, 1, and 2 correct. This is done separately for (a) those not attempting all items and (b) those attempting all items.

5. The score variance per item contributed by these final items is estimated by multiplying frequencies by square of proportion gotten right. This is done separately for groups (a) and (b) in step 4.

6. Results from groups (a) and (b) are combined, weighting group (b) by the

ratio m/n, where m is the number omitting the last item and n is the number attempting all items.

7. The results from steps 3 and 6 are entered in the expression

$$\frac{s^2_{F(a)} \dfrac{\sum\limits_{1}^{N(a)} x^2_{\lambda_p}}{N}}{s^2_t} \tag{6.29}$$

where $s^2_{F(a)}$ = variance in number attempted, as calculated in step 3

$\displaystyle\sum_{1}^{N(a)} x^2_{\lambda_p}$ = sum of frequencies times square of proportion of correct answers as calculated in step 6

N = total number of cases

s^2_t = score variance for total test

   The value obtained in formula 6.29 is the correction for speededness that is to be subtracted from coefficient alpha to provide a lower-bound estimate of internal consistency. The steps in the calculation can be clarified by an example.

   For a 20-item test with a score variance of 9.78 and an uncorrected alpha of 0.637, the distribution of number not reached was as follows:

Number	0	1	2	3	4	5	6
Frequency	60	20	8	5	3	2	2

On the last two items attempted by each examinee, the frequency distribution of number of correct answers was, respectively, for those who did not and those who did attempt all items:

NUMBER CORRECT	PERCENT CORRECT	$F(a)$	$F(b)$
0	0	19	33
1	50	15	15
2	100	6	12

Based on the first distribution, and counting 20 of the 60 completing the test as just barely finishing, we calculate the variance of number not attempted to be

$$\frac{257}{60} - \left(\frac{85}{60}\right)^2 = 4.45 - (1.42)^2 = 2.44$$

Based on the second distribution, and weighting the completed cases by 20/60, we get, for (a) and (b) respectively,

p^2	$p^2f(a)$	$p^2f(b)$	Sum
.00	0	0	0
.25	3.75	1.25	5
1.00	6	4	10
			15

Entering these results in formula 6.29 yields

$$\frac{2.44(15/100)}{9.78} = .037$$

$$\text{Alpha}_{\text{corrected}} = .637 - .037 = .600$$

Thus, in this test, speededness did not seem to be a very important factor in determining score, and the rather narrow band from .60 to .64 appears to express its possible effects.

RELIABILITY IN THE CONTEXT OF DOMAIN MASTERY OR CRITERION-REFERENCED TESTS

In our discussion of reliability up to this point, we have been concerned with the precision with which an individual can be located on the scale of a latent attribute through the administration of a test. Within limits, this conception can still be applied to a domain mastery test. The adaptation that may be required is to think of the attribute as having a limited range, because the tasks that fall within a precisely defined domain may have a limited range of difficulty. Within that range, correlations may be attenuated because of the presence of substantial numbers of perfect (or zero) scores. Such scores indicate individuals who fall at the boundaries of the difficulty range of the domain and who are in a sense not fully measured. The presence of such scores acts to attenuate correlation coefficients. The location of these extreme cases on a continuous scale representing the domain is in a sense indeterminate, so it is difficult to estimate a meaningful standard error of measurement for them.

Within the domain mastery model, interest usually focuses on some one level of performance—often 80% or 90% of correct answers—that has been defined as constituting "mastery" of the domain. When this is the case, the critical issue so far as reproducibility of results is concerned would appear to be whether another sample from the domain would lead to the same decision (mastery or nonmastery, as the case may be) for each individual.

The most direct approach to answering the question of consistency in the critical decision is to obtain two test scores for each individual by administering two equivalent test forms—equivalent in that each sampled by the same rules from the defined domain. The two could be given concurrently or with a lapse of time, depending on the nature of the universe to which one wished to generalize. From the test results, one could produce a 2 × 2 table such as the one shown here.

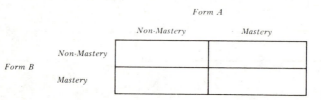

The table would present the basic data on consistency, but finding a statistic that adequately evaluates the test is not easy. The simple percentage of cases with consistent decisions depends on the range and level of talent in the group. In the extreme case, if we are dealing with a group for whom the domain is completely new and untaught (no one approaches mastery), we will get an appearance of a very accurate test, because all cases will fall in the upper left-hand cell. Of course, consistency of performance could also appear if the test were extremely easy for all members of the group. Furthermore, if the group were extremely varied in competence (including a number for whom the test was very hard, a number of others for whom it was very easy, and very few who were just about at the threshold of mastery), high consistency of placement would be the rule. In all of these cases, consistency in placement reflects properties of the groups tested rather than excellence of the test. Furthermore, in the intermediate range of excellence of examinees, both percentage of agreement and the point correlation represented in the phi-coefficient are sensitive to the proportional split between the two groups.

If the two forms of the test have been equated for difficulty and if it is reasonable to assume that, within the domain as defined, competence shows a normal distribution, then one can postulate a normal bivariate distribution of competence underlying the score distribution on the tests, and one can appropriately calculate a tetrachoric correlation for the fourfold table. This should be relatively independent of the average *level* of ability in the group tested, though it would be sensitive to the variability in the ability being studied and would be higher for a group that is more heterogeneous in ability. However, the tetrachoric correlation will not be sensitive to differences in the proportion achieving the criterion score level on form 1 and form 2. If these differences appear to be due to something in the forms themselves, rather than to the sequence of testing, the tetrachoric will yield an overestimate of the test's reliability.

Various measures that have been proposed for use with criterion-referenced tests depend in some way on the average of squared deviations of test scores from the established "mastery" level, developed as formulas analogous to those for error variance. However, these formulas are substantially (perhaps even primarily) dependent on level of competence within the group of examinees, and they reveal little about the properties of the test as a testing instrument. They seem to be going off in an unproductive direction.

If one is dissatisfied with the conventional reliability coefficient when a test is being used for mastery decisions, perhaps the best alternative is the standard error of measurement for scores within a range of a few percentage points above and below the critical percentage that is defined as "mastery." This is one index that does *not* depend to any substantial degree on the range or level of talent within the group, but solely on consistency of performance from trial to trial. Though this statistic might be difficult to interpret in terms of proportion of cases receiving the same decision on two testings (that *does* depend on the nature of the group), the standard error would permit comparison of one test with another.

The procedures for calculating a standard error of measurement at a specific score level are set forth on pages 173–174, and these procedures can be applied in the present case. The form that the results might take can be illustrated for a triad of tests (unfortunately not designed to be mastery tests) for which standard errors by score level happen to be available. Consider the Cognitive Ability Tests at Level A. Standard errors of measurement based on a sample of 500 and expressed as percentage of items gotten right were as follows for examinees with an *average* score of from approximately 70% to 90% percent of correct answers:

Verbal Test	3.96%
Quantitative Test	3.99%
Non-Verbal Test	3.15%

Within the limits of the data, these results would be interpreted as showing that the Verbal Test and the Quantitative Test are quite comparable in the precision with which a judgment can be made that a person has achieved "mastery" of their domain, but that the Non-Verbal Test permits this decision to be made with appreciably greater precision.

Chapter 7
Validity

When we inquire about the validity of a test, we are asking what generalizations can appropriately be made from scores on that test. As we saw in the preceding chapter, those generalizations are always limited by the imperfect *precision* with which a sample from any universe of behavior represents the universe from which it was drawn. But now we ask about broader aspects of generalizability. The questions are of three types:

1. How representative is the behavior sample of the universe that it was intended to represent?

2. What does that behavior signify so far as underlying attributes of the individual are concerned?

3. To what extent can that test behavior predict some life performance of special interest, most often success in some type of training program or performance in some specific job?

These three types of question correspond to what have been designated respectively *content* validity, *construct* validity, and *predictive* validity. We will consider in turn the issues that arise in evaluating each of these.

CONTENT VALIDITY

Especially when a test has been designed to appraise degree of mastery of some domain of knowledge or skill, we ask how well the tasks in the test do in fact match the definition of that domain. If we had identified "capitalization" as a subdomain of the larger domain designated "punctuation" and had developed a capitalization test, the question would be whether the sample of capitalization tasks that we had generated covered the same range of situations (beginning of sentences, proper names, quotations, and so on) that had been specified in the definition of the domain.

Obviously, both the person who is trying to achieve content validity in constructing a test and the person who is trying to evaluate the content validity of an existing test need a clear, detailed, and explicit definition of the domain that is to be appraised. If the domain can be broken down into the specific elements of which it is composed, and if the relative emphasis on each in instruction or use can be specified so that a weight can be attached to each, then the test can be analyzed to see which elements are in fact included in it and with what frequency. The congruence between the content of the domain and the content of the test can be made quite explicit.

Frequently, however, the boundaries of a domain, or even of a subdomain within a broad domain of content, may be far from explicit or clear-cut. Consider a unit on "communicable diseases" within a course on "human biology" or "health and hygiene." What belongs in such a unit, and with what weight? Which diseases? How much on causal agents? How much on preventive measures? What on identification and symptoms? What on treatment? Clearly, it would take a detailed and extended blueprint covering content and objectives to define this subdomain at all adequately, and even such an outline could only suggest some of the many specifics.

A detailed outline is crucial. For the curriculum planner and teacher, such an outline provides a detailed guide for the development of curricular materials and instructional procedures. For the test maker, it becomes the blueprint that guides construction of test exercises. Only as a full and detailed outline has been developed on *both* sides can the content validity of a test be satisfactorily appraised. That is, the match of a test blueprint to curricular objectives can only be appraised when those objectives are themselves clearly and explicitly defined.

There has been relatively little attempt to develop quantitative indices of content validity. Test evaluators have generally been satisfied with making a subjective and qualitative evaluation of the congruence between curricular objectives and test content and expressing their evaluation in narrative form, pointing out the areas of congruence and the points of mis-match between the test and the curricular objectives as they view those objectives. So there is not a great deal to be said about a theory or a methodology for evaluating content validity. Cronbach (1971) has suggested that a relevant procedure might be to have two independent teams of test makers each prepare a pair of forms of a test on a defined domain. (He suggests, as his illustration, the automobile driver's manual.) If all four forms were then given to a group of examinees, the average of the cross-team correlations could be compared with the within-team correlations to provide an index of the uniformity or objectivity of the definition of the domain. Thus the index would be

$$r_{A_\infty B_\infty} = \frac{r_{A_1 B_1} + r_{A_1 B_2} + r_{A_2 B_1} + r_{A_2 B_2}}{2(r_{A_1 A_2} + r_{B_1 B_2})}$$

where A and B refer to the two teams of test makers, 1 and 2 refer to the two test forms made by a team, and $r_{A_\infty B_\infty}$ indicates the correlation between perfectly reliable tests from the two teams.

If the corrected cross-team correlation approaches unity, it is clear that the two teams are producing functionally equivalent tests. However, the proposed procedure would be quite laborious and has seldom if ever been tried. It seems unlikely that a commercial publisher would find it practical to carry through. As of now, we have had too little experience with this index to know what levels of

$r_{A_\infty B_\infty}$ are likely to be encountered or what represents a "good" correlation when it falls somewhat short of unity.

CONSTRUCT VALIDITY

If, as is frequently and perhaps usually the case, we think of a test as designed to measure some latent trait or characteristic of a person, the most basic question about the test is: What trait (or traits) does it measure? How well does it measure them?

This is not an easy question to answer. The trait is a *latent* attribute—a concept that we have constructed to describe or account for certain recurring characteristics of a person's behavior. We cannot assess it directly. (If we could, we wouldn't need a test.) But we do have, at some level of sophistication, a "theory" of the attribute. That is, we do have ideas about where it should display itself, what types of life performances should be facilitated by possession of the attribute, what subgroups in the population should possess it to a high or low degree, and what conditions should favor or inhibit its expression. The "theory" of the attribute or construct suggests what types of test tasks should be appropriate for eliciting the attribute. It also suggests kinds of evidence that should be relevant for assessing how well the test under study does, in fact, elicit or depend on the construct.

Generally speaking, evidence on the construct validity of a measure tends to be of four types.

1. Judgmental comparison of the nature of the task with our conception of the construct.

2. Correlational data, showing correlations between the test under study and other measures (tests or life events) believed to reflect or depend on the attribute in question.

3. Group difference data, comparing test scores of subgroups that might be expected to differ on the attribute.

4. Data showing the effects of treatments or experimental interventions that might be expected to influence expression of the attribute.

We shall discuss each of these sorts of evidence in turn.

COMPARISON OF TEST TASKS WITH
CONCEPTION OF ATTRIBUTE

A first and most obvious question to ask about a test is: Do the test tasks *appear* to call for the trait or attribute in question? Do they "make sense"? Is the content of the test reasonable to elicit the trait that we are trying to assess?

Many traits, especially those involving an ability, carry in their very designation some implication of the test tasks that would be appropriate to assess them. It seems axiomatic that the way to appraise a person's "reading comprehension" is to give that person material to read and then to ask questions to evaluate comprehension of what has been read. We naturally tend to test "verbal ability" with tasks involving the manipulation of words and "quantitative ability" with numerical tasks. So our first query is one that comes close to those we raise in relation to the content validity of a test. Do the test tasks match our conception of the trait?

This one criterion is in no way conclusive. Just as the height of a column of mercury bears no direct resemblance to heat, measures of psychological attributes of persons may, too, be indirect. Use of perception of the vertical in the face of contradictory cues as a measure of "field dependence" or of movement responses in a Rorschach protocol as an indicator of "creativity" has no immediate or obvious appropriateness. But such indirect measures may have validity as indicating the stated characteristic of a person. Where the sign has no obvious relationship to the attribute it is alleged to measure, the burden falls with extra weight on the test maker to demonstrate that the sign does in fact signify that attribute.

Though a surface correspondence between test task and our description of the attribute carries an implication that the test is a measure of that attribute, this is not necessarily the case. There have been reading tests in which the questions could be answered on the basis of common background knowledge with no necessity of reading the passage! Other examples could certainly be cited in which the function actually tapped by a test was not what it superficially seemed. So congruence of content is only a probable indicator of the essential nature of a test. But it *is* a relevant and a natural first thing to look at.

CORRELATIONAL EVIDENCE OF CONSTRUCT VALIDITY

A new test is not born into a vacuum. There are likely to be in existence other tests designed to appraise the attribute under study, as well as other possibly related attributes. The test in which we are interested may be correlated both with other tests designed to assess the same attribute and with tests designed to measure other attributes that, one fears, may contaminate the new test as a measure of the attribute it was designed to measure. One's test should show substantially higher correlations with other measures designed to assess the same attribute than with measures designed to assess other attributes. This can be formalized through the procedures of factor analysis, in which measures designed to appraise the same attribute should load on a common factor.

The type of analysis may be illustrated with data from an early instrument designed to measure the construct "social intelligence." This test was composed of five subtests. If these subtests all were, at least in part, expressions of social intelligence, they should have correlated appreciably with each other. Administered together with the "social intelligence" subtests was a set of subtests designed to measure abstract or verbal intelligence. These should also have correlated with each other. And if the two constructs were really distinct and different, the cross-correlations from measures of the one construct to measures of the other should have been distinctly lower than the internal correlations among subtests designed for one specific construct. The results were as follows:

Average correlation among social intelligence subtests .335

Average correlation among abstract intelligence subtests .390

Average cross-correlation of social versus abstract subtests .344

The results from a factor analysis of the matrix of correlations among all the subtests produced loadings as follows:

| | FACTOR | | |
	I	II	III
Abstract			
Vocabulary	.768	−.122	.307
General information	.472	−.121	.422
Learning ability	.605	.000	.350
Arithmetical reasoning	.276	.044	.368
Comprehension	.669	.237	.070
Social			
Judgment in social situations	.547	−.196	−.005
Recognition of mental state	.574	−.192	.010
Observation of human behavior	.682	−.208	−.007
Memory for names and faces	.399	.154	.009
Sense of humor	.588	.262	−.015

The average cross-correlation is just about the same size as the average within-test correlation. And the factor analysis shows a single general factor running through all ten subtests. There is a slight suggestion of a minor factor common to the first four of the abstract subtests, but there is no evidence of a factor common to the five subtests designed to measure social intelligence. Thus there is little evidence that the social intelligence subtests measure anything distinctive that is not measured by the tests of abstract intelligence. Because (1) abstract intelligence is a much more firmly established construct than social intelligence and (2) the content of most of the subtests is verbal and somewhat abstract, the most defensible conclusion is that the alleged social intelligence test does not appear to measure any general construct other than abstract verbal ability.

Table 7.1   Correlations Among Three Traits Assessed by Three Different†
Procedures (Decimal points are omitted.)

		1	2	3	4	5	6	7	8
1. D.O.T.*	sociable	—							
2.	cheerful	13	—						
3.	impulsive	−10	−05	—					
4. Self-rating	sociable	64	13	−02	—				
5.	cheerful	31	46	−10	34	—			
6.	impulsive	20	12	47	−20	−15	—		
7. Peer rating	sociable	40	06	13	¢	¢	¢	—	
8.	cheerful	15	29	−05	¢	¢	¢	34	—
9.	impulsive	24	04	37	¢	¢	¢	60	15

*Dimensions of Temperament
¢ Correlation not available
†Selected correlations reproduced by permission from the Manual for the Thorndike Dimensions of Temperament. Copyright © 1966 by The Psychological Corporation, New York, N.Y. All rights reserved.

The type of analysis we have just illustrated is an attempt to assess the convergent and the discriminant validity of the so-called social intelligence test. *Convergent validity* would be indicated by relatively high correlations among those measures designed to assess a common construct. *Discriminant validity* would be indicated by much lower correlations between those measures and ones designed to measure some other construct. We must conclude that this test of social intelligence has failed to demonstrate the required pattern.

In a more systematic approach, convergent and discriminant validation can take the form of applying each of several methods to each of several traits and examining the matrix of correlations among the scores that result. If the proposed construct does have some independent reality, the correlations among measures of that trait by different methods should be relatively high, and correlations among measures of different traits should be low even when the same method of eliciting them is applied. Then most of the covariance is attributable to the common trait and relatively little to the common data-gathering method. Some illustrative data are shown in Table 7.1 for a personality inventory called the Dimensions of Temperament. The three methods of measurement used here were the inventory, self-rating on a rating scale, and pooled peer ratings. (Correlations were not available between self-ratings and peer ratings.) Though none of the correlations are dramatically high, the correlations for the same trait as measured by different procedures are generally the highest, and the three traits of "sociable," "cheerful," and "impulsive" seem clearly to represent different constructs. There is some slight evidence of a "method" covariation in the correlations among the three ratings, but not in the other procedure. Such a multitrait, multimethod matrix has been proposed by Campbell and Fiske (1959) as an appropriate way to assess the identifiability of a proposed construct.

High correlations among different tests designed to be measures of a common construct do tend to support the claim of each to be a measure of that construct. This is especially true if the tests have been developed by different persons and if they are different in their superficial characteristics (item type, content, format, and so on). However, these *are* all tests. It is important that a test display reasonable correlations with nontest indicators that are deemed to be related to the construct. Certainly, one's "theory" of abstract verbal ability would imply that it should be related to academic success or to mental alertness as rated by teachers. One might hypothesize (perhaps somewhat less securely) that a measure of social intelligence should correlate appreciably with volume of life insurance sold. A test of mechanical comprehension might be expected to correlate with an adequate performance measure of trouble-shooting an engine or some other mechanical device.

In all of these illustrations, we have made a judgment about the nature of certain life activities and about the abilities required to perform them successfully. If the relationships that we have predicted on the basis of our theory appear, our confidence is strengthened both in the validity of our test and in our conception of the abilities required in the life task. If the relationship fails to appear (given adequately reliable measures of the life performance), then we are forced to decide either that the test is not a valid measure of the construct it was designed to measure or that our "theory" stating that the attribute is required for a specific life performance is at fault. If only one or two of a number of predicted relationships fail to appear, we may be inclined to question those facets of the "theory." But if a number of predicted relationships are not found, it seems appropriate to doubt the validity of the test as a measure of the attribute that it was intended to measure.

GROUP DIFFERENCES AS EVIDENCE OF CONSTRUCT VALIDITY

A group difference may be thought of as analogous to a correlation, but with a dichotomous variable to be predicted. We have considered dichotomous variables in the context of relationships between a test score and responses to a single test item. Now we encounter them in the context of being identified as, for example, a librarian versus an insurance salesperson. Our theory of social intelligence and our experience of the roles of librarian and insurance salesperson might suggest that social intelligence would be more at a premium in the latter occupation than in the former, and hence that the insurance salesperson could be expected to score higher on the alleged social intelligence test. Once again, in testing predictions of this sort, we are simultaneously testing the construct validity of the test and the sagacity of our analyses of the characteristics of groups. Positive results affirm both, but negative results may stem from a shortcoming of either.

If group differences are to provide incisive evidence on the validity of a test, the groups must be ones that would *not* be expected to differ (or that would be expected to differ in the reverse direction) on other attributes that the test might be thought to measure. This is another instance of discriminant validation. Thus, as evidence of the validity of the social intelligence test, it was reported that managerial personnel surpassed routine clerical employees on the test. However, it is highly likely that the managerial employees would also prove superior on measures designed to appraise abstract intelligence. No evidence was offered that this was not the case. Hence the evidence reported did not exclude the possibility that it was primarily (or solely) abstract intelligence that the test was measuring.

Once again, the evidence from group differences is cumulative. If all but one or two predictions hold up, it is primarily the rationale for those one or two predictions that becomes suspect. But if a number of the predictions fail to be confirmed, we must question the interpretation that has been made of the test.

TREATMENT EFFECTS AS EVIDENCE OF CONSTRUCT VALIDITY

As we use the term *treatment* here, we refer to any experimentally introduced intervention or any naturally occurring change in conditions that might be expected to influence the attribute we are studying. Thus Buhler (1953) postulated that an imminent minor operation should raise a person's level of anxiety, and he compared performance on a test that had been proposed as an indicator of anxiety (rate of flicker fusion) before the operation and at a later time when no operation was in prospect. The lower scores found before the operation were in the predicted direction and were interpreted as supporting the validity of the test as an indicator of anxiety.

It is not easy to think of an intervention that would be expected to modify an individual's "social intelligence." One might perhaps argue that a series of sessions of role playing or group therapy, designed to improve "insight" and "self-awareness" should affect the person's sensitivity to and effectiveness in interacting with others. It seems that these qualities might be aspects of, or at least related to, social intelligence. One could, then, compare scores before and after such a program of training. But if one came out with negative results, one would have to ask whether these were due to the ineffectiveness of the training, to an inappropriate hypothesis that the training *should* affect social intelligence, or to inadequacy of the test as a measure of that attribute.

At this point it is appropriate to contrast those attributes that are intended to refer primarily to *states* of the individual with those that are intended to refer primarily to *traits* of the individual. (Of course, many attributes refer in some degree to both.) Anxiety can be thought of as primarily a state attribute in the sense that a person's level of anxiety may change radically from one time to another. Of course, there is a trait aspect to anxiety; some people seem typically to operate at a high anxiety level, whereas for others the anxiety level is typically low. It is primarily *state* attributes that should be sensitive to interventions and for which the modification of prior or current conditions should be expected to modify test score.

To the extent that a test is viewed as a trait measure, indicating some persisting characteristic of the individual, it should be expected to be relatively impervious to manipulations of background conditions or the circumstances of measurement. If social intelligence, for example, is a stable individual trait, then scores on a test of it should not easily be changed by the temporary state of the individual or the circumstances surrounding the testing. To the extent that scores *are* responsive to such peripheral influences, they are reflections of some temporary state rather than of a stable trait of the person being tested. For that reason, variations may be introduced in aspects of motivation or in circumstances of testing in order to determine how robust the test is as a measure of a stable, underlying trait in the individuals being studied. Responsiveness to situational factors is then viewed as evidence not of validity, but of fragility of the test as a measure of that which it was intended to measure. Thus research on the impact of examiner differences, of incentive conditions, or of "coaching" explores possible limitations on the construct validity of a test as a measure of something important and enduring in the persons tested.

THE ROLE OF COUNTERHYPOTHESES

Whenever a test author makes an assertion about what a test measures, a fruitful way to test that assertion is to propose a set of possible counterhypotheses. Thus, for the suggested measure of social intelligence, we proposed the counterhypothesis that it measured primarily (or solely) abstract or verbal intelligence. One subtest of the social intelligence test involved remembering the name presented along with a picture of a face. A counterhypothesis might be that this subtest measured merely short-term memory of figural material. Another subtest required choice of the adjective to describe the mental state represented in a quoted phrase or sentence. A counterhypothesis might be that this is primarily a test of vocabulary and/or reading comprehension.

The appropriate follow-up of a counterhypothesis is to propose the data that would permit one to decide between the hypothesis espoused by the test maker and that proposed by the critic. So far as possible, the data should yield sharply different results under the two hypotheses. One might, for example, compare scores on the alleged social intelligence test for (1) engineers, (2) lawyers, (3) mechanics, and (4) salespersons. A social intelligence hypothesis would *seem* to require relatively high scores for groups 2 and 4 and lower scores for groups 1 and 3. An abstract intelligence hypothesis would seem to require high scores for groups 1 and 2 and lower scores for groups 3 and 4. The hypothesis that the names-and-faces test measured simply short-term memory of figural material could be tested by developing other memory tests using visual figural material, administering all the tests together in a battery, and determining by correlational analysis whether the names and faces measured anything different from the other memory tests.

The more complete the set of counterhypotheses is that one generates and the more crucial the data one collects are to a decision between the construct proposed by the test author and that suggested by a counterhypothesis, the more confident one can be as to what attribute the test really does measure.

Clarifying both what constructs are useful for understanding human behavior and which one or ones of these are assessed by a given test is a never-ending process. It is, in fact, coterminous with the whole development of psychological theory. Every research study that is made using a certain measurement procedure adds a small brick to the structure that constitutes the meaning of that procedure—our understanding of what the measure signifies.

PREDICTIVE VALIDITY

Much of the use of tests over the years has been to guide the selection, classification, and placement of persons into specific training programs or jobs. In that context, the validity of a test has meant its effectiveness in *predicting* success in the job or training program in which the investigator is particularly interested. The typical statistic to express that effectiveness has been the correlation between test score and standing on some criterion indicator that serves to represent success. Of course, correlations with training and job performance indices can also add to the body of information about the construct validity of a test, insofar as they confirm or fail to support our "theory" of what the test measures. But at this juncture our interest centers on the pragmatic concern of identifying those persons who are likely to do well if they are employed in job A or are admitted to educational program B.

A prime focus of concern in studies of predictive validity is the criterion indicator of success with which the predictor test is to be correlated. What *does* constitute success as a college student? As a secretary? As a life insurance salesperson? As a physician?

One thing is certain. Success is complex and many-faceted and it unfolds only gradually. It is difficult even to formulate any complete definition of successful performance on a job, much less to develop a measure that adequately represents it. To take a job with which every student has had at least some contact, what constitutes degree of success as a college teacher? How much of it is mastery of a field of knowledge? How much is effectiveness of exposition? How much is sensitivity to student difficulties and student interests? How much is skill in arranging learning tasks? How much is working effectively with colleagues? The list goes on and on.

And the complete story of effectiveness is displayed in a life career, not at one specific moment in time. Though we would anticipate a degree of consistency over time, a short cross section is clearly a partial picture. The conscientious young instructor may get lazy with the passing years. Conversely, the poorly organized beginner may "get his act together" and prove an effective teacher later on. Any short-term perspective is at best a partial and incomplete view of the lifetime effectiveness of an individual in that person's field of work.

The point is that any score we may use as an indicator of success in a job or training program provides an incomplete picture of a person's effectiveness — incomplete in its range and incomplete in the time span that it covers. It is important to realize that we are dealing with *partial and fallible indicators* of success, not with the thing itself.

Sometimes it may seem that we are getting fairly close to the essence of "success," as when grades and grade point averages are used as criterion indicators of success in school or college. Pragmatically, these *do* define *failure* and possible rejection and do serve as currency to buy certain "goods" such as eligibility for athletic teams, admission to advanced courses, or admission to graduate school. But most educators would protest vehemently that "mere grades" are a very imperfect and incomplete index of what a person has learned and accomplished at any level of education. Their great practical advantage is that they are usually routinely recorded as an aspect of the educational scheme of things and are available ready-made for the researcher to use in studying the validity of some test as an academic selection device.

Such ready-made criterion indicators are rarely found outside the academic setting. The naive test validator may expect to find some existing output measure or supervisory evaluative rating ready at hand to serve as a criterion score. Typically, such a measure will be either nonexistent or unsatisfactory. The search for and/or development of suitable criterion scores against which tests may be evaluated is at once the most demanding and the most frustrating aspect of the test researcher's task. Let us consider some of the shortcomings that tend to plague criterion indicators and some of the types of criterion indicators that are often encountered or developed.

SHORTCOMINGS OF CRITERION INDICATORS

We shall consider five shortcomings of criterion indicators: incompleteness, misweighting, intrusion of irrelevant factors, bias, and low reliability.

Incompleteness

No criterion indicator covers all aspects of the job or the learning enterprise. If nothing else, the indicator deals with a limited time span and reflects performance only over that period. Usually, however, the criterion indicator is incomplete in other respects as well. College grades reflect only those aspects of learning within a course that are evaluated by the instructor, and the composite of grades in all courses tells nothing about the learning that has gone on that was not related to particular courses — learning through reading, through participation in extracurricular activities, through informal interaction with faculty and peers. Supervisory ratings reflect only those aspects of job performance that are considered significant by (and that are observed by) a particular supervisor. A record of sales volume fails to reflect quality of relationships with other employees, clerical errors made in handling transactions, and frequency of customer dissatisfaction. One needs to ask of any such criterion indicator: What is missing? What has been left out? Is it important? If so, is there some further indicator that can be obtained, with reasonable effort, to fill the gap?

Mis-weighting

The ideal criterion score should weight the different elements or facets of job performance in proportion to their importance for effectiveness in the job. Of course, we do not know in any ultimate sense what the "true" importance of different facets of performance is. But we can make a thoughtful analysis of the job or training program and pool judgments about what importance the different facets have. After we have done so, we can check to see whether the weights received by the elements in existing criterion indicators come anywhere close to matching what we have judged to be desirable.

Some of the most dramatic illustrations of mis-weighting have come from training school grades in various schools of the armed forces. Typically, these schools have had an academic component involving a good deal of verbal learning *about* the job and the equipment used in it. In addition, there has usually been a performance component involving use of the equipment in situations somewhat similar to those that will be encountered in the field. The academic part has been fairly thoroughly and reliably assessed with paper-and-pencil tests. All too frequently, however, appraisal of the performance component has been subjective, casual, and of questionable reliability. Often, the dispersion of grades on the academic part has been large and that on the performance part small. The result has been that the academic component has loomed much larger than the performance component in the final school grade. This has usually happened without the school authorities being aware of it or intending it. One of the services that psychometricians have been able to perform for the military has been to point this out and to help remedy the situation by improving procedures for assessment of the performance component. But so long as training school grades, whether military or civilian, give disproportionate weight to easily evaluated "book learning," those grades will be deficient as criterion indicators to assess the validity of selection tests. They will favor tests that predict academic performance at the expense of those that predict field performance on the job.

In the foregoing illustration, and in other instances in which one is evaluating the balance of factors in a criterion indicator, it is crucial that one attend to the real *effective* weight of a component (as distinct from its nominal weight). This means that one must attend to the standard deviation of each component as it is weighted in a criterion composite.

Often the factors entering into a criterion indicator cannot be separated into discrete elements, as they can if separate marks are given on specific tests or ratings of performance. When this is so, the evaluator of the criterion indicator may have no guidance other than personal judgment as to what, for example, a supervisory rating represents. Even there, however, it may be possible to obtain and analyze ratings of specific qualities in a subordinate, in relation to the overall judgment of effectiveness, to get a sense of what qualities are most closely related to, and hence seem to get the most weight in, the summary judgment. One should seek any leads that will yield a better understanding of what a criterion indicator represents and how well the weighting of factors in it matches what is judged to be the most suitable representation of effective performance.

Intrusion of Irrelevant Factors

Here we are really speaking of an extreme case of mis-weighting—of an instance in which weight is given to a factor that really should receive a 0 weight. It is frequently debatable whether a factor should be *completely* excluded from appraisal of a person's effectiveness as a student or worker. But one becomes concerned when it appears that factors of handwriting or spelling (or even worse, cleanliness, orderliness, and personal attractiveness) influence a teacher's judgment of the competence of a child as a student of history or science, for example. And rather generally, personal attractiveness is irrelevant, if not to effectiveness in a job, then at least to those aspects of effectiveness that one hopes to be able to predict with a test or a battery of tests. The intrusion of such factors tends to dilute and attentuate the relevance of the criterion indicator as a target representing that which we hoped to be able to predict.

Various devices have been used to try to squeeze the irrelevant variance out of criterion appraisals, especially those that depend on ratings by instructors or supervisors. One approach, developed quite extensively in the years following World War II, was the *forced-choice* format for ratings. In this format, statements are presented in blocks, often blocks of four, and the rater is required to select from each block a specified number of statements that are most (or one most and one least) characteristic of the ratee. The statements within a block have been matched on the basis of previously collected data for general favorableness, but they are differentiated as sharply as possible for relevance to effective performance on the job. Criterion score is the number of *relevant* desirable statements (sometimes less the number of relevant undesirable statements) that are selected as most characteristic of the candidate.

An alternative procedure, in some ways simpler and more appetizing for the rater, would be to have each candidate rated on a number of characteristics—some judged to have high job relevance and some to have low or negligible relevance, but all socially desirable. A composite "relevant goodness" score and a composite "irrelevant goodness" score could be calculated for each student or employee. Techniques of partial correlation could be used to determine the correlation between test score and job-related excellence after the influence of general enthusiasm for the candidate had been removed.

A somewhat different type of intrusion can occur when variance in criterion score is due to persons or conditions outside the worker or student being evaluated. These include differences in severity of standards applied by different instructors or supervisors. The substantial variation in grading standards among instructors in even a single school or department is a commonplace to anyone who has examined academic grading practices. Variation among rating standards of job supervisors is equally common. Outside conditions also include differences in setting for different workers (such as wealth of a sales territory for salespersons) and dependence of the outcome on other members of a working team. A criterion measure must be scrutinized for such extraneous influences, and an attempt must be made to adjust for them or to minimize their impact.

Bias

One specific type of nonrelevant variance that merits separate mention is bias. We tend to use the term *bias* in referring to prejudicial attitudes held by evaluators toward individuals or groups. Prejudicial attitudes toward ethnic, sex, or age categories on the part of supervisors or other evaluators are a real possibility and must be reckoned with. More specific biases toward particular individuals because of their dress, manner of speaking, appearance, or other personal characteristics are also a possibility.

However, bias may also arise in relatively impersonal criterion indicators. Volume of sales by a soap salesperson may be biased by the presence or absence of soot or of hard water in his or her territory; that of an insurance salesperson may be biased by the economic level of the surrounding community. Performance measures for a weaver may be biased by the quality of maintenance of the loom or by the illumination level at the work station. As we look at any potential criterion indicator, it is important that we ask what factors there are that may bias the score for an individual and that, having identified them, we seek ways to minimize or circumvent them.

Low Reliability

A final limiting factor on the predictability of any criterion indicator is low reliability. Conventional personnel ratings have long had a bad reputation because of low reliability. As far back as 1931, Symonds, summarizing the available evidence, estimated the reliability of the typical personnel rating to be no more than about .50, and there seems to be no reason to raise that estimate. As one turns to performance samples, one realizes that in many cases the sampling is quite limited and that the samples' reliability in representing the universe of job behavior is probably quite low.

Of course, low reliability limits the correlations that can be obtained between any predictor and that criterion variable. The correlations will be attenuated by a factor equal to $\sqrt{r_{cc'}}$. However, it is possible to estimate the correlation of a predictor with a perfectly reliable criterion score using the relationship

$$r_{tc_\infty} = \frac{r_{tc}}{\sqrt{r_{cc'}}} \qquad\qquad (7.1)$$

Note, though, that the precision of the estimate of validity is reduced as reliability is reduced. When a correlation is inflated by the correction factor given in equation 7.1, the standard error of that correlation is proportionately inflated. In addition, there is a sampling error in the reliability coefficient itself, and this serves to reduce further the precision of the corrected estimate. We must remember that significance levels of validity coefficients should always be derived from the *uncorrected* values. And, because these are attenuated if the reliability of the criterion measure is low, larger samples are required in order to determine the "true" validity coefficient with as great precision as would be obtained with a more reliable criterion measure.

Low reliability results in a loss of sensitivity in validity studies, but it is possible (at least in theory) to compensate for this by increasing sample size. A more troublesome situation arises when the reliability of the criterion indicator is unknown. Then it is impossible to determine to what extent low test–criterion correlations are due to the fact that the test is useless as a predictor of that criterion variable and to what extent they are due to the fact that the criterion measure itself is very unreliable. Unfortunately, it is not always easy to get sound estimates of the reliability of criterion indicators. When ratings are being used as criterion measures, only one supervisor may be closely enough in touch with the work of a given employee to offer a sound evaluation of it. And if more than one are available, there is a real possibility that the two or more raters may have discussed the employee's performance or in other ways shared common information so that their judgments are not experimentally independent. Performance records may not be kept in such a way that it is possible to get scores for two or more independent segments of the record. But whatever the difficulties, it is important for the investigator to do everything possible to generate a sound estimate of the reliability of a criterion score that is proposed for use, so that obtained validity data can be appropriately interpreted.

TYPES OF CRITERION INDICATORS

The two most commonly encountered types of criterion indicators are grades in an educational or training program and ratings by an instructor, supervisor, or other person in a position to judge the examinee's subsequent performance. In addition, one can sometimes make use of proficiency test results or of some type of performance record. We shall consider each of these in turn.

Grades in Training

Sometimes we are interested in school grades for their own sake, when the purpose of a test is to predict success in schooling. In other cases, a training program is a prerequisite to entry into a particular job, and success in that program is the first indication of whether and how well a person will succeed in the job. In a negative sense, a trainee's elimination from the training program may preclude the individual's ever having an opportunity to perform in the actual job, so that at least minimal success in the training program is a necessary condition to being a successful worker on the job.

Grades are usually a convenient criterion indicator, because they are likely to be routinely recorded for the internal use of the program itself. Furthermore, they involve the least delay between time of testing and availability of a criterion score. Often, though not always, grades are based on fairly objective and reliable evidence—from tests, exercises, and other samples of the student's work. However, the bases that are being used to evaluate student performance need to be scrutinized with care, because that which receives major weight in the evaluation may be quite remote from the realities of job performance. There is likely to be an over-weighting of "book learning" at the expense of the practical performance skills that are closer to actual job tasks. Grading practices can appropriately be scrutinized to determine what types of competence are being evaluated and how the different aspects are actually weighted.

Grades in a training program undertake to assess the cognitive skills, and perhaps the performance skills, that underlie job performance. They assess some of the "can do" but not the "will do" of worker performance. Temperamental and motivational elements and interpersonal skills that may be very important when a person enters the actual world of work are hardly represented. And, of course, for many jobs there are no specific, formalized training programs. Thus grade in a training program or successful completion of training is a convenient and moderately relevant criterion indicator for some jobs, but for only a limited fraction of them.

Supervisory Ratings

By all odds the most common of criterion indicators are supervisory ratings, and this is in spite of their very serious technical limitations. Their great appeal lies in their apparent simplicity and near universal applicability. Practically every worker entering a field of work has a "boss"—someone who tells him or her what to do and checks, at least to a degree, to see that it is done. Of course, supervision may be quite casual, and the supervisor may not keep close track of the worker's performance, but at least nominally a supervisor is there.

Unfortunately, ratings by supervisors suffer from all the shortcomings that ratings are heir to. The evidence on which the ratings are made is often casual and unsystematic. The supervisors have other responsibilities and often consider the making of ratings a bothersome and unpleasant chore. Different supervisors have different standards of rating—both in severity and in what is given weight in their evaluation. Supervisors are influenced by the attractiveness (or unattractiveness) of the person rated. Ratings often have little dispersion and are afflicted with halo and generosity effects. The supervisor may feel personal loyalty to his or her subordinates and little real commitment to the personnel office or other agency that has imposed the rating task. The net result is that ratings tend to be rather low in reliability and of limited relevance so far as identifying real differences in effectiveness of job performance.

Over the years, personnel psychologists have tried various procedures in an attempt to overcome the limitations of ratings. Mention was made earlier of forced-choice formats that require the rater to pick from among a set of statements, balanced for general desirability but differentiated for job relevance, the ones most descriptive of the ratee. Another form of forced choice requires the supervisor to rank the individuals in the group of subordinates with respect to their effectiveness. Often the procedure calls for an "alternation ranking" starting with the best, then indicating the worst, and working in from the two extremes. Attempts have been made to move away from simple adjectival labels (superior, excellent, very good, good, fair, poor) to statements describing actual behaviors in response to job demands. Here the supervisor picks from a set the statement that best describes how the worker would respond to that particular job demand. Many of these procedures call for a substantial commitment to developmental work by the personnel psychologist, and they often present a fair-sized clerical chore for the supervisor. They do appear to reduce some of the individul idiosyncrasy of raters, but they cannot overcome a supervisor's lack of familiarity with the work of subordinates due to limited contact with them or limited interest in the quality of their performance.

There are many jobs in which no tangible record of the individual worker's performance is maintained. The work may be highly diverse, it may deal with persons rather than things so that no countable product is produced, or maintaining "production" records may be prohibitively involved and costly. Most office jobs, technical jobs, service jobs, and professional jobs are of this sort. In such jobs, there may be little that one can turn to for a criterion indicator other than a rating — in spite of ratings' subjectivity, modest reliability, and susceptibility to bias and intrusion of irrelevant factors. When the job is sufficiently important, a good deal of effort may be warranted to try to make ratings more objective and behaviorally oriented, but the ability and willingness of a diverse group of supervisors to make discriminating appraisals of their subordinates will always be limited and will always limit the effectiveness of any rating procedure.

Proficiency Tests

For a good many types of training programs, as well as some jobs, a proficiency or performance test may represent one useful type of partial criterion indicator. Whenever the training program is designed with the objective of developing performance skills, a test of those skills is appropriate. A well-designed skills test presents a standard task or set of tasks with uniform instructions, conditions that are as uniform as possible from one examinee to another, and a standard set of procedures for evaluating the product. In some cases, developing a performance test is fairly straightforward, as in the case of typing tests or transcribing tests.

Often, a good deal more developmental work may be involved to generate a task or series of tasks that corresponds realistically to on-the-job duties, that can be presented in a limited test period, that can be scored objectively, and that provides a reliable index of individual performance. Promising types of measures are those that call for diagnosis and trouble-shooting in the case of mechanical or electronic technicians and those that call for fabrication of a standard object in the case of skilled tradespeople such as carpenters, electricians, or machinists.

Performance and proficiency tests seem most clearly applicable as a major element in appraisal at the end of a standard program of training. Their reliability needs to be determined in each instance, but their relevance as appraising at least one segment of the desired training outcomes seems high. Giving a performance test and evaluating the product is likely to be time-consuming and hence is not something to be entered upon lightly. The most serious limitation on the use of this type of criterion indicator is that there are relatively few jobs in the entire world of work for which a performance test is feasible and appropriate.

Performance Records

Some types of jobs may generate a routine record of the performance by individual workers. Sales and commissions recorded for individual salespersons, accident records of individual truck or taxi drivers, and production records of individual typists in a typing pool are cases in point. Where such a record exists, it represents an attractive possibility as a criterion indicator. The questions one asks are: (1) Do uniform conditions for different workers assure that performance is a function primarily of the individual worker? (2) How reliably does the sample of behavior for a period of time represent the overall performance of the individual? (3) How large a fraction of total competence is represented in that which is recorded?

Unfortunately, the proportion of jobs for which any quantitative record of performance is available is quite small. Where such a record can be found it merits investigation, but the probability of finding one is not high.

PRACTICAL PROBLEMS IN EMPIRICAL VALIDATION

We have considered in some detail the problems that arise in relation to criterion indicators. These loom large among the practical difficulties an investigator faces in developing worthwhile estimates of predictive validity. However, it is also important to mention some other problems. We shall consider briefly (1) the numbers of cases available, (2) heterogeneity of tasks and functions in instances of what are ostensibly a common job, and (3) preselection of cases in unknown amounts and on unknown grounds.

Number of Cases

There are many life situations in which the flow into a specific job or training program is small. This is especially true in small and medium-sized companies, but it is also true of many jobs that occur infrequently even in large companies. The standard error of a correlation coefficient of zero is $1/\sqrt{N-3}$, so, with a sample of 25 cases, it is quite possible to get sample correlations of .30 or even .40 when the true population correlation is zero. Even with samples of 100, sample correlations can deviate from the population value by as much as .20.

These variations seem troublesome enough when one is considering a single predictor test taken in isolation. They become very much more disturbing when one is trying out an extended set of predictors and knows that one or two of them are almost certain to look promising just because of the idiosyncrasies of the present sample. Before embarking on an empirical validation study, one always needs to ask: Will the flow of cases into this position be great enough so that, within reasonable time limits, it will be possible to generate a sample large enough to yield dependable results? If the answer is no, it may be better to invest one's effort in a more profound study of the job and of possible tests, in an attempt to match job demands and test functions on a rational basis.

Job Heterogeneity

It is also important to know to what extent jobs that bear the same label are indeed the same. If a single title covers a number of positions in which the duties and demands are radically different, data obtained by pooling those positions in a single validation study may be meaningless or downright misleading. In general, the effect will tend to be an attenuation of any genuine validities. Once again, thorough study of the work situation is called for to determine to what extent it will be legitimate to pool, for analysis, test and criterion data from a range of different positions, whether or not they are included under a common job title.

Preselection

Persons admitted to a training program or to employment have almost always been preselected to some degree and on some bases. If we know how much and on what bases, we can make adjustments for the selection effects, as we shall see later in this chapter. But often the amount and type of preselection are not clear. It then becomes very difficult to estimate how data obtained on an accepted group should be adjusted to make them applicable to a group of candidates. Study of the process of entering into a training program or into employment may help clarify the nature and degree of preselection. Such understanding is vital if we are to apply validation data realistically to future applicant groups.

If conditions are sufficiently unfavorable with respect to these three conditions, and/or if the possibilities of getting relevant and reliable criterion indicators appear sufficiently poor, it may be better to abandon empirical prediction studies. Having no data may be preferable to having data that are inadequate or misleading.

The Matter of Time

In everyday speech, the term *predict* means to forecast something that is to happen at some future date. But statisticians use the term without reference to time to indicate a dependence existing between two variables. When tests are used as predictors, it is ordinarily in the common sense: a forecast from a prior testing to subsequent success in training or on a job. The realistic concern of the test user is to be able to make a forecast of performance months, perhaps years, later. But to wait months or years for criterion scores to mature presents a serious problem. One wants answers as soon as possible. Thus, as a compromise with practical pressures, the investigator is likely to settle for those criterion indicators that are available in the shortest time span. These are necessarily incomplete and often of limited relevance.

One compromise that may be made to adjust to practical pressures is to test persons already employed on the job or already completing the training program. This yields what is usually called "concurrent validation." To infer prediction over a time span from such concurrent validation data involves several assumptions that are often seriously suspect. The first is that relative standing on the attribute measured by the predictor test is stable and will not be significantly distorted by a period of experience on the job. For example, if actual job experience leads those persons who do well at it to develop interest in that job, while those who do poorly tend to acquire an aversion, the relationship of interest patterns to success on the job might be quite different in experienced workers from what it would be in applicants. A second, possibly important difference between applicants and employed workers lies in their differing motivation to excel on the tests. Employed persons may see little reason to put forth maximum effort on a test that they know will have no influence on their own futures. For these and other reasons, concurrent validation must always be considered to provide only suggestive data. It is always necessary to confirm them via data from tests given at the point and under the conditions that will prevail in operational use.

STATISTICS OF VALIDITY

The statistic commonly used to express the validity of a test is the correlation between test score and some criterion measure or measures being used to represent degree of "success" in the job or training program. Issues relating to the choice or development of measures to serve as criterion indicators were discussed in the previous section. For the present discussion, the criterion measure is taken as given, and the discussion centers on the various issues that arise in connection with using the test as a predictor. We will consider each of the following issues:

1. Expressing validity when the criterion variable is dichotomous — for example, pass–fail in some training programs.

2. Estimating the validity coefficient when data are available only from the tails of a distribution.

3. Estimating the validity coefficient when data are available only from a systematically curtailed distribution.

4. Identifying nonlinear relationships and dealing with them.

5. Strategies for decision when several partial criterion measures are available.

6. Dealing with taxonomic (group-membership) criterion indicators.

7. Use of evidence on test and criterion reliability in interpreting validity coefficients.

8. Practical implications of validity coefficients.

DICHOTOMOUS CRITERION VARIABLES

Correlation indices appropriate to dichotomies have already been presented in the context of item selection. The issues involved in the choice between biserial and point-biserial correlations were considered at that time. The same logic applies when the dichotomy appears in a variable that is being used as a criterion indicator. Most commonly, the division by some means is into two groups, one of which is identified as "successes" and the other as "failures." We must decide whether we should think of the categorization as qualitative and absolute or quantitative and essentially arbitrary. If the former, a point biserial is the appropriate correlational statistic; if the latter, a biserial. A slightly different way of expressing the issue is to ask whether we are interested only in the *fact* of being identified as "successful" or are also concerned with degree of excellence. The former focus of interest would be compatible with a point biserial, the latter with a biserial.

In many (perhaps most) job or training programs, performance is viewed as a continuum, with variations in degree. Level of excellence is significant, and the boundary line between success and failure is viewed as at least somewhat arbitrary, shifting with the pressures of supply and demand. Standards for "success" vary from time to time and from place to place. Especially when data are to be pooled from different schools or companies, in which different proportions of trainees are allocated to the "success" category, it seems more appropriate to use the biserial correlation as the index of validity for a predictor variable.

Occasionally one must deal with a situation in which both predictor and criterion variable appear as dichotomies. Thus one might have as a predictor married versus nonmarried and as a criterion variable pass or fail in a training program. When the data occur in this form, one has three possible ways of viewing them.

1. Both variables may be viewed as true dichotomies between qualitatively distinct categories.

2. One variable may be viewed as a true dichotomy and the other as an arbitrary division of a basically continuous variable.

3. Both variables may be viewed as basically continuous.

In the case of a *predictor* variable, the key consideration is whether, in the real-life prediction situation, that predictor will continue to appear and have to be used as a dichotomy. If so, it must be treated as a true dichotomy. Considerations relating to the criterion variable have already been commented on.

In case 1 in the foregoing list, the appropriate statistic is the phi-coefficient. This is the product-moment correlation between two 0–1 variables, and it is given by the formula

$$\phi = \frac{ad - bc}{\sqrt{pqp'q'}}$$

when the proportions of cases are represented in a 2 × 2 table as shown below.

	0	1	Total
1	c	d	p
0	a	b	q
Total	q'	p'	

Case 2 is a hybrid that we call biserial phi, and can be expressed by the formula

$$\phi_{\text{bis}} = \frac{ad - bc}{\sqrt{pq}} \cdot \frac{\sqrt{p_i q_i}}{y'}$$

where p and q relate to the truly dichotomous variable

p' and q' relate to the continuous variable

y' = the ordinate of the normal curve at p' (or q').

Case 3 calls for a tetrachoric correlation. The tetrachoric correlation is the estimated value of the product-moment correlation between two normally distributed continuous variables that have been split in such a way as to yield the entries shown in the 2 × 2 table. Computation of the tetrachoric requires the iterative solution of a power series involving powers of r. However, various procedures have been developed for providing approximations to the full computation. One very convenient procedure (Davidoff and Goheen, 1953) uses simply the ratio ad/bc and reads the approximate tetrachoric from a brief table, reproduced in this book as Appendix B. If the ratio is less than unity, the reciprocal (bc/ad) must be used to enter the table, and the correlation is then negative.

The important thing in reporting correlations among variables is that the nature of each dichotomous variable be decided on and that an internally consistent set of procedures be used in the correlation of dichotomous variables with continuous and with other dichotomous variables. Thus, if a dichotomy is treated as real and categorical, its correlations with continuous variables should be point biserials and its correlations with other dichotomies should be phi-coefficients or biserial phi's, depending on whether the second variable is considered a real or an artificial dichotomy. Conversely, if a certain dichotomy is considered an artificial division of a continuous variable, correlations with continuous variables should be biserials and those with other dichotomies should be either biserial phi's or tetrachorics. The situation is displayed in tabular form below.

	VARIABLE 1		
VARIABLE 2	Continuous	Artificial Dichotomy	Real Dichotomy
Continuous	product moment	biserial	point biserial
Artificial dichotomy	biserial	tetrachoric	ϕ_{bis}
Real dichotomy	point biserial	ϕ_{bis}	ϕ

CORRELATIONS ESTIMATED FROM TAILS OF A DISTRIBUTION

Sometimes when one wishes to estimate the correlation between two variables, it may seem to be sound strategy to measure the whole group on one variable (which we will designate X) and then to measure only those who fall at the extremes on X with the other variable Y. This strategy is a reasonable one to adopt when

1. It is reasonable to assume a nearly linear relationship between X and Y.

2. It is reasonable to assume to a reasonably close approximation that, in the complete group, the joint distribution of X and Y is bivariate normal.

3. It is either (a) only feasible to classify cases on variable X into three groups (the high, the low, and the undifferentiated in between) or (b) much more expensive to measure variable Y than to measure variable X. The former case might be illustrated by peer nominations, in which peers might be able (or willing) to identify one or two in their class or work group as outstandingly high or outstandingly low on some characteristic such as "effectiveness as a leader." The latter case might be illustrated by a situation in which a paper-and-pencil test is being related to an elaborate job sample.

In the first case, members of the middle group's status on variable X may be so ill-defined that it seems inappropriate to assign them any score on that variable, and one works only with the extreme groups whose status is somewhat more clearly defined. In the second case, limited time and funds are more efficiently spent in getting a score on Y for those who are known to be extreme on X. One can then get greater precision in one's estimate of the correlation per dollar or hour expended by gathering information on the expensive variable only for those who get extreme scores on the cheap measure. The expensive measure might represent a criterion measure for which the data would be expensive or difficult to obtain. Thus we might be interested in a multiple-choice test of English usage as a predictor of competence in public speaking. To obtain a reliable appraisal of performance in public speaking could be laborious and costly, requiring that each examinee give three or four speeches and that each speech be evaluated by a panel of competent judges. In this case one *might* elect to pick, from among those given the paper-and-pencil test, those who fell in the top and bottom tenth of the group and then generate, for each member of this subsample, the criterion score for competence in public-speaking.

If data of this type are to be analyzed, the appropriate statistic is the biserial correlation from widespread classes. (See Peters & Van Voorhis, 1940, pages 384–391.) The formula is

$$ r = \frac{(\overline{Y}_U - \overline{Y}_L)\, P_U P_L}{S.D._Y(P_U Z_L + P_L Z_U)} \tag{7.2} $$

where $\overline{Y}_U$ and $\overline{Y}_L =$ mean scores on Y of cases from the upper and lower tails of the X distribution

             P_U and $P_L =$ percent of the cases in the X distribution included in the upper and lower tails, respectively

                      $S.D._Y =$ standard deviation for the total distribution of Y

            Z_u and $Z_L =$ ordinates of the normal curve corresponding to P_U and P_L, respectively

Using this formula is a little awkward, because it *does* involve the standard deviation of the Y variable in the *total* group. Estimates of this standard deviation might be available from previous work or might be obtained by getting Y scores for a modest-sized sample of the total group representing all levels of X.*

We illustrate the procedure with a numerical example. Suppose that criterion public speaking scores had been obtained for all persons in the highest and

---

* The standard deviation in the total group can be estimated from the Y scores of those in the tails of the distribution (see Peters and Van Voorhis, 1940).

lowest 10% on an entrance examination in "correctness of English expression." In addition, suppose that scores had been obtained for a random 5% of the total group and that these had given an estimate of s_Y of 8.5. The mean criterion score for the upper test-score group was found to be 74.6 and for the lower group 61.2. From these figures we calculate as follows:

$$r_{tc} = \frac{(74.6 - 61.2)(.10)(.10)}{8.5\,[(.10)(.1755) + (.10)(.1755)]}$$

$$= \frac{.134}{8.5(.0351)} = \frac{.134}{.298} = .45$$

If one is willing to accept the assumption of a normal bivariate distribution of the two measures and wishes to maximize precision for a constant total cost, Abrahams and Alf (1978) provide a table indicating the optimum percentage of the group to be measured in each tail with the second measure, for various ratios of cost of the second measure to cost of the first measure. A few selected values are shown below.*

COST RATIO OF MEASURE 2 TO MEASURE 1	PERCENTAGE IN EACH TAIL TO RECEIVE MEASURE 2
1.0	21.5
2.0	16.1
4.0	11.4
8.0	7.7
16.0	5.0

As one would expect, the proportion to be tested decreases as the cost ratio increases. Note that there is a gain from testing only a fraction of the cases, even when the costs of the two measures are equal. However, this gain is counterbalanced by the inability to check whether the data really conform to the assumed bivariate normal distribution.

CURTAILMENT

When criterion data are collected for persons on a job or in a training program, those for whom criterion data become available have usually been selected on some basis from among the total group who were candidates for the job. In the simplest case, a *cutting score* has been set on some one predictor variable, and

---

* From N. M. Abrahams and E. F. Alf, Jr., "Relative Costs and Statistical Power in the Extreme Groups Approach." *Psychometrika*, 1978, 43, 11–18. Used by permission.

Table **7.2**   Effect of Mean and Standard Deviation of Excluding
Certain Stanines

ACCEPTED STANINES	MEAN	STANDARD DEVIATION	REJECTED STANINES
8–9	8.36	0.51	1–7
7–9	7.65	0.77	1–6
6–9	6.95	1.00	1–5
5–9	6.30	1.23	1–4
4–9	5.79	1.45	1–3
3–9	5.42	1.65	1–2
2–9	5.17	1.82	1
1–9	5.00	1.96	none

all candidates scoring below the cutting score have been rejected and all above
have been accepted. Often the basis for selection has been more complex and/or
more ambiguous. But let us consider the simple case first, turning later to some
of the complications.

If a cutting score has been set, and only those falling above the cutting score
are accepted for employment or training, the range of scores and the variance of
scores on the predictor will be reduced. This can be illustrated for a set of
stanine scores—normalized standard scores with mean of 5 and standard deviation of approximately 2. Table 7.2 shows the effect of excluding those with
stanines of 1; 1 and 2; 1, 2, and 3; and so forth. The progressive reduction in
variability shows clearly.

If we can assume (1) that in the bivariate frequency distribution for predicting
the criterion variable, here called C, from a predictor, here called P, the standard error of estimate of C estimated from P is uniform for all values of P
(homoscedasticity) and (2) that the relationship is linear (an equal increase in C
for a given increase in P at all points on the scale of P), then a reduction in the
variability of P will result in a reduction in the correlation coefficient between P
and C. This occurs because the variance of predicted criterion scores is reduced
in proportion to the reduction in the variance of predictor scores, whereas the
variance of errors of estimate remains (by assumption 1) unchanged. The effects
on the correlation depend on which variable has been curtailed. We shall discuss
three different cases.

Case A. The *predictor variable* has been directly curtailed, and correlation
between predictor and criterion is to be corrected for the effect of the curtailment.

Case B. The *criterion variable* has been directly curtailed, producing indirectly a reduction in predictor variability, and the correlation is to be corrected for the effect of this curtailment.

Case C. A predictor variable has been directly curtailed, resulting in the indirect curtailment of some other research or predictor variable, which we shall identify as R, and a correction is to be made to the correlation between R and C to take care of the indirect effect of the curtailment on predictor variable P.

Case A

This is the straightforward situation of direct curtailment. Typically a test has been given, a minimum qualifying score has been set, and all those who reached or exceeded the minimum qualifying score have been accepted. A criterion score is obtained for all those accepted, and the correlation is obtained between the predictor test P and the criterion score C. The standard deviation of the predictor test is known, both for the total group of applicants and for those accepted for training or employment. We wish to know what the correlation would have been in the total applicant population. The formula for estimating the correlation in the total group is

$$R_{pc} = \frac{r_{pc}\left(\frac{S_p}{s_p}\right)}{\sqrt{1 - r_{pc}^2 + r_{pc}^2\left(\frac{S_p}{s_p}\right)^2}} \tag{7.3}$$

where
R_{pc} = correlation in the total group
r_{pc} = correlation in the curtailed group
S_p = standard deviation of the directly curtailed variable in the total group
s_p = the corresponding standard deviation in the curtailed group

Thus, if a stanine of 4 or better (stanines being based on the applicant group) had been required for acceptance in a job or training program, and if the validity within the accepted group had turned out to be .45, we would have

$$R_{pc} = \frac{.45\left(\frac{1.96}{1.45}\right)}{\sqrt{1 - (.45)^2 + (.45)^2\left(\frac{1.96}{1.45}\right)^2}}$$

$$= \frac{.45\,(1.352)}{\sqrt{1 - (.45)^2 + (.45)^2(1.352)^2}}$$

$$= \frac{.608}{\sqrt{1.168}}$$

$$= .563$$

The correlation that was .45 in the curtailed sample is estimated to have been .56 in a group with variability equal to that of the total group.

It is, of course, *possible* that the group for which criterion data were obtained was *more* variable than the total original group. This could occur if some group were tested and then a second measure (which we have been calling a criterion score) were obtained only for samples chosen because they were at one extreme or the other on the predictor test. This might happen if the second (or criterion) measure was very costly to obtain — something like a work sample observed and rated by a panel of several raters. Then if the basic assumptions of homoscedasticity and linearity hold, a more precise evaluation of the relationship, per person evaluated on the criterion measure, would be obtained by using widely separated cases. Suppose that we gave a predictor test to a total group, then ruled out of further consideration those with stanines of 4, 5, or 6 (in relation to that group), and obtained a criterion measure from a sample drawn randomly from the two tails of the predictor distribution. We would then have $S_p = 1.96$ while $s_p = 2.76$. Here s refers to the incomplete distribution, in this case the one with the middle dropped out. If $r_{pc} = .45$ for *this* distribution, we have

$$R_{pc} = \frac{.45\,(1.96/2.76)}{\sqrt{1 - (.45)^2 + (.45)^2 (1.96/2.76)^2}}$$

$$= \frac{.320}{.948}$$

$$= .337$$

The correlation for the total group is estimated to be noticeably *less* than that actually calculated from the two tails.

Let us see why anyone might use this strategy of omitting the middle cases. Let us compare the results from completing criterion scores for a sample of a given size (say 100), drawn in the one case at random from the total group and in the other case at random from the two tails of the predictor distribution. The standard error for testing the null hypothesis that the correlation did not differ from zero would, in either case, be $1/\sqrt{N - 3}$. But observed correlations from the tails of the distribution (for this degree of expansion of predictor variability) are about a third larger than those from the total distribution. If a correction formula is applied that "shrinks" each obtained value by 25% (approximately), the standard error is also shrunk by 25%, and the estimate of correlation in the total group is achieved with an error of estimate only about 75% as great as would be the case if the same number of criterion cases had been drawn randomly from the total tested group. Or, the same precision could have been achieved with a sample $(.75)^2 = .56$ times as large.

Remember that these formulas to adjust for changes in dispersion of scores in the predictor variable *assume a linear relationship* between the two variables throughout the range on the predictor. No good check on this assumption is possible when criterion scores are not available for part of the range. So the correction formulas must be used and interpreted with some caution.

Formula 7.3 can appropriately be used when cases from all parts of the predictor score range are available but certain segments have been sampled more heavily than others. In the problem just described, for example, criterion scores might have been obtained for all cases with predictor scores falling in stanines 1, 2, 8, and 9, but for only 25% of those with stanines of 3, 4, 5, 6, and 7. We would then find that the standard deviation of predictor scores in the selected subsample would be 2.63. If r_{pc} were .45 for such a sample,

$$R_{pc} = \frac{.45\,(1.96/2.63)}{\sqrt{1\, -\, (.45)^2\, +\, (.45)^2\,(1.96/2.63)^2}}$$

$$= \frac{.335}{.954}$$

$$= .351$$

In situations such as this, it is crucial that cases be drawn *randomly* from the subsampled section of the score range of the directly curtailed test, so that the assumptions of linearity and homoscedasticity are met. (Incidentally, when *some* cases are available for all parts of the score range, data are available that make it possible to check on those assumptions.) If some outside factor has produced some sort of systematic selection of those cases accepted from a certain part of the score range, then the linearity and homoscedasticity conditions are likely to be violated and formula 7.3 will not apply. For example, if persons with low predictor-test scores were given employment *if* they had had previous successful work experience in a similar job, criterion scores for these individuals might turn out to be substantially higher than would have been predicted simply on the basis of their test scores.

Case B

Sometimes we encounter a situation in which curtailment has taken place on the variable that we have designated variable C, but the standard deviation for total group as well as curtailed group is known only for the other variable that we have designated variable P. As an illustration, suppose that end-of-year freshman grade point average was being used as a criterion variable. But some students might have been screened out at mid-semester or mid-year because of poor academic work. For them, no end-of-year grades would be available. However, an admissions test or a research test might have been given to *all* entering students. Then the test standard deviation would be available both for the total group and for those who survived and received year-end grades. In this case, the curtailment formula becomes

$$R_{pc} = \sqrt{1\, -\, (s_p^2/S_p^2)\,(1\, -\, r_{pc}^2)} \tag{7.4}$$

The notation remains the same, but in this case variable P has been *indirectly* curtailed as a result of the direct curtailment on variable C. Because the curtailment has been indirect, its effect on the standard deviation of P tends to be less. Thus it might turn out that S_p was 1.96 while s_p was 1.85. If r_{pc} = .45, we would then have

$$R_{pc} = \sqrt{1 - (1.85/1.96)^2 (1 - .45^2)}$$

$$= .538$$

Even a fairly small difference between the standard deviations leads to a rather substantial change in the correlation.

Instances of case B are not likely to arise often in practice, but it is important that one be prepared to handle them when they do occur.

Case C

We deal now with the very common case in which direct curtailment has taken place on one variable (which we will continue to designate P) but our interest lies in the correlation of the criterion variable (variable C) with some third variable, perhaps a research test, which we shall call variable R. A situation that may often occur is that variable P is actually a composite score derived from the combination of two or more tests. Thus a college might use a combination of the verbal and quantitative scores on the College Board SAT, employing some such formula as $2V + Q$ as the basis for a cutting score. It might then want to determine the validity of some new research test (or of V or Q taken singly) as predictors of a criterion measure such as grade point average.

The formula applicable in this case is

$$R_{rc} = \frac{r_{rc} + r_{pr} r_{pc} \left(\dfrac{S_p^2}{s_p^2} - 1 \right)}{\sqrt{1 + r_{pr}^2 \left(\dfrac{S_p^2}{s_p^2} - 1 \right)} \sqrt{1 + r_{pc}^2 \left(\dfrac{S_p^2}{s_p^2} - 1 \right)}} \qquad (7.5)$$

where P refers to the directly curtailed variable and R and C refer to variables that are indirectly curtailed as a result of the curtailment on P.

Returning to our illustration on page 000, where S_c = 1.96, s_c = 1.45, and r_{pc} = .45, let us assume that we have a research test for which r_{pr} = .60 and r_{rc} = .40. Entering equation 7.5, we get

$$R_{rc} = \frac{.40 + (.60)(.45) \left(\dfrac{1.96^2}{1.45^2} - 1 \right)}{\sqrt{1 + (.60)^2 \left(\dfrac{1.96^2}{1.45^2} - 1 \right)} \sqrt{1 + (.45)^2 \left(\dfrac{1.96^2}{1.45^2} - 1 \right)}}$$

$$= \frac{.40 \ + \ (.60)\,(.45)\,(.827)}{\sqrt{1 \ + \ (.36)\,(.827)} \ \ \sqrt{1 \ + \ (.2025)\,(.827)}}$$

$$= \frac{.623}{(1.139)\,(1.080)}$$

$$= \ .506$$

It is instructive to examine how the impact of curtailment is affected by the relationship of the "research" test to the measure that has been directly curtailed. The following table of values of R_{rc} shows the impact of degree of curtailment and degree of relationship. Throughout, r_{pc} is assumed to be .45 and r_{rc} to be .40.

Ratio S_p/s_p	r_{pr}				
	.20	.40	.60	.80	.95
1.1	.409	.422	.431	.437	.440
1.2	.417	.444	.462	.472	.477
1.3	.427	.466	.492	.506	.511
1.5	.447	.490	.547	.566	.572
1.8	.478	.571	.620	.641	.648
2.0	.499	.609	.662	.683	.689

It is apparent that the correlation between the directly curtailed variable P, and the other variable, R, is critical in determining the amount of effect from curtailment. The effect increases continuously as the correlation increases, but the increase up to .60 or so is particularly important.

Formula 7.5 is, in a way, a generalization of the formula for partial correlation. If S_p becomes zero (that is, if the variable P is held constant) the expression $(S_p^2/s_p^2) \ - \ 1$ becomes -1 and formula 7.5 is exactly the formula for partial correlation.

Complications

The most common problem in applying the formulas that correct for curtailment is that it is not clear on just what basis curtailment has taken place. Decisions on admission or employment are often made by a director of admissions or a personnel officer. The decision may be based on a variety of considerations combined intuitively with unspecified and largely unknown weights. Some way must be found to convert the judgment into a definable continuous variable. This can be done if the person making the acceptance-rejection decision can be persuaded to record, for each candidate, a multicategory judgment on that candidate's desirability as a student or employee. Thus one might use some such scale as

1. Outstandingly desirable
2. Very good
3. Fairly acceptable
4. Marginally acceptable
5. Marginally unacceptable
6. Poor candidate
7. Very obvious reject

Letting such a scale constitute the variable P, and treating it as an interval scale, we can get values to represent S_p, s_p, and r_{pr}. Given a criterion variable C for those accepted for education or employment, and hence being able to calculate values of r_{pc} and r_{rc}, we can use equation 7.3 to get an estimate of R_{pc}, the validity of the admissions officer's selection decision as a predictor of success, and equation 7.5 to get an estimate of R_{rc}, the validity of some other variable that was used (or might have been used) with some weight by the selector in arriving at a selection decision.

Another possible complication is that curtailment may have taken place independently on two or more variables. Thus a college might specify as requirements for admission a score of 450 on V (verbal) and 420 on Q (quantitative), and exclude applicants who failed to pass *either* hurdle. Generalizations of the curtailment formulas are available for direct curtailment on two or more variables, and these will be presented in Chapter 9 as part of the general discussion of multivariate methods in psychometrics.

Nonlinear Relationships

Most statistical analysis of test results is based on the assumption that the relationship between the pair of variables can be represented as a straight line. This may not always be the case. In particular, there are a number of situations in which it seems likely that the relationship between a predictor and a measure of job success is nonlinear. Thus some degree of reading ability might be important for a mechanic, but additional increments above that required degree might add little to effectiveness on the job. It is even conceivable that an exceptionally good reader might (perhaps because of competing interests) be a poor worker in a mechanical job. The relationship might be as shown below.

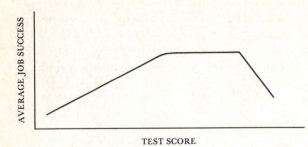

The first problem is to determine whether the relationship is significantly nonlinear. The measure of nonlinear relationship is called the *correlation ratio* and represented symbolically with the lowercase Greek letter eta (η). Calculations from the bivariate frequency distribution are displayed in Table 7.3. The mean of each column of the distribution is calculated,* and the between-columns variance is related to the total variance in the vertical variable. The formula is

$$\eta = \sqrt{\frac{\Sigma n_k(\overline{Y}_k)^2 - N(\overline{Y})^2}{Ns_y^2}} \qquad (7.6)$$

where n_k = number in column k
             $\overline{Y}_k$ = mean score for column k
             N = total number of cases
             $\overline{Y}$ = total group mean
             s_y^2 = total group variance

For the illustrative example, the linear correlation is .267 and the correlation ratio is .325. At this point, the question is whether the increase as one goes from the limitation of a linear relationship to the greater freedom of the correlation ratio is significantly greater than 0. A chi-square is computed by the formula

$$\chi^2 = (N - k) \frac{\eta^2 - r^2}{1 - \eta^2} \qquad (7.7)$$

where the number of degrees of freedom is $k - 2$, k being the number of columns in the data matrix. For our illustrative example, with $N = 100$, we have

$$\chi^2 = (100 - 5) \frac{.1058 - .0714}{.8942} = 3.65$$

---

* Columns and rows can be interchanged to yield a second and usually different correlation ratio.

Table 7.3 Illustration of Calculation of Nonlinear Relationship

			X			
	1	2	3	4	5	
5			3	1		
4		4	9	5	3	
Y 3	3	6	16	8	4	r_{xy} = 0.267
2	4	6	9	5	3	
1	3	4	3	1		
$\overline{Y}_k$	2.0	2.5	3.0	3.0	3.0	$\overline{Y}$ = 2.8
n_k	10	20	40	20	10	N = 100
$N_k(\overline{Y}_k)^2$	40	125	360	180	90	S_y = 1.02

$$\eta_{yx} = \sqrt{\frac{795 - 784}{100(1.02)^2}} = 0.325$$

With df $= 5 - 2 = 3$, the probability of the obtained chi-square falls between .50 and .30, and the nonlinearity is not significant. If the same eta had been obtained with 1000 cases, we would have had a χ^2 of 38.28, and the nonlinearity would have been significant at the .01 level.

If a relation *does* display a statistically significant nonlinearity, the next question is whether the nonlinearity makes any sense. Is it regular and systematic, or haphazard? If systematic, what type of more complex function can represent the data? We may try fitting some more complex function to the column means and seeing whether fit to the data is significantly improved. Curve-fitting procedures are described in the SPSS Manual (Nie et al., 1975, pp. 368–372). If a more complex function, such as a second-degree polynomial or a logarithmic function, provides a significantly improved fit to the data, a new variable U in which $U = f(X)$, such as

$$U = a + bX + cX^2$$

can replace X as the predictor variable, and any future analysis can be made with the new variable.

Before attempting to fit a more complex function, it usually pays to prepare and inspect a plot of the column means. If their deviation from a straight-line relationship appears erratic and meaningless, we are not likely to find a function that improves the linear one, even though eta may meet statistical tests as being significantly greater than r.

PARTIAL CRITERION MEASURES

Any measure that one can develop is an imperfect and usually incomplete in-dicator of success in an educational program or effectiveness on a job. Grades are not the only indicators of what one has learned in college. In the purely cognitive area, one might point to performance on such post-college tests as the Graduate Record Examination or the Medical College Admissions Test. And there are extra-class activities in music, art, journalism, student government, and even athletics. The effectiveness of a secretary might involve not merely amount of correspondence typed, its neatness, and freedom from errors, but also adroitness in handling people who come to the office; meticulousness in main-taining records and remembering appointments; judgment in setting work priorities, allowing access to the executive(s) worked for, and arranging travel plans; and maintenance of good working relations with others in and around the office.

Whenever a number of different criterion indicators are or can be obtained, one encounters the problem of deciding how the multiple items of criterion in-formation should be used. The problem involves two facets. We will call them understanding and decision.

To improve our *understanding* of what it is about an educational or job situa-tion that can be predicted by a given predictor or different ones of a set of predictors, it often pays to obtain a number of relatively specific criterion in-dicators and to relate each indicator to each of the predictor measures. Thus, rather than simply relating overall GPA to the College Board SAT verbal and quantitative scores, it is more informative to keep separate the grades in specific courses (English, foreign language, math, science, history) and to examine the correlations of each predictor with each course. Again, if we are able to generate, for a student nurse, separate (and adequately reliable) appraisals of performance in specific academic courses and performance with patients in a clinical setting, then we can develop a better understanding of which aspects of performance in the training program are predicted by tests or other types of in-formation gathered before the start of training. The more precisely delimited and defined the criterion indicators are, the more instructive they will be in tell-ing us just what a specific test is able to predict — that is, in helping us define the construct validity of the test.

In the context of *decision,* we must proceed in a rather different way. Decision is an all-or-none matter. Either we admit (or employ) the candidate, or we reject that candidate. We cannot admit the high secretarial skills and reject the abrasive personality. They are inseparable. Our decision must be made in rela-tion to the whole person. How shall we best use the information from partial criterion indicators in validity research oriented toward this decision?

It is possible that we might still want to keep the criterion indicators separate and do prediction studies on the predictability of each. If we found that typing, spelling, and editing tests gave usable predictions of a secretarial applicant's per-formance at the typewriter, while an employment interviewer's ratings gave some prediction of his or her later success in getting along with fellow employees, we might want to set *separate* minimum standards on each of these types of predictors and require that a job applicant come up to that minimum on *both* before being offered a job. Conversely, we might accept very minimal predicted performance in relation to one criterion indicator when prediction of some other aspect of the criterion was very high — as when a very promising high school football player who might turn out to be a star wide receiver is given preference over other candidates, even though the prediction is that academic performance will be only barely acceptable.

However, we might decide that we wanted to combine the partial criterion indicators in some uniform way that would give a uniform "best" approximation to the complete and ultimate index of training or job success. If we decide to generate a uniform composite criterion index, how is it to be done?

One possibility is to try to identify the criterion composite that is *most predictable* and to settle for that. If we think of a single predictor measure and multiple criterion indices, this problem can be attacked by conventional multiple correlation methods (see Chapter 9), reversing the role of test and criterion. That is, one determines the weights to be applied to the separate facets of the criterion so that the weighted composite will have the highest possible (linear) correlation with the predictor test. Such a procedure *may* be instructive in adding some clarification to just what it is that the test predicts, but weights assigned in this way to criterion components are likely to bear little or no relationship to the judged importance of the components. Thus, in our illustration of the training program for nurses, it is almost certain that the classroom component that is likely to be relatively reliably assessed by examinations will be much more predictable (especially by admissions tests) than hospital performance in relation to actual patients. If this is so, academic performance will get the swamping weight and clinical performance, which may well be considered more central to later performance on the job, may receive a minimum weight.

A partial criterion indicator's value as a component of a composite that will correlate maximally with some complete and "ultimate" criterion is a joint function of that criterion indicator's relevance to the ultimate criterion and its reliability. In the limit, if *either* the relevance or the reliability is zero, the correlation will be zero. The reliability of a criterion indicator is an empirical matter and can, in theory at least, be determined by one or another of the procedures discussed in Chapter 6. (In practice, getting adequate data to permit an estimate of the reliability of a criterion score is often a sticky matter.)

In certain (relatively rare) cases, some evidence on the relevance of a criterion indicator may be obtained from the correlation of that indicator with later, and presumably more nearly ultimate, indicators. This occurs, for example, when training school grades are correlated with some subsequent on-the-job appraisal of performance. In most instances, however, estimation of the relevance of criterion indicators must rest on human judgment. Some degree of consensus can probably be achieved on the relative relevance of different criterion measures as indicators of the complete construct "effective job performance." The ideal scale on which to express such judgments would be a scale representing the correlation that would in theory be found between a perfectly reliable measure of that facet of performance and "effective job performance." It is likely to be difficult to make such a scale clear to the rater, but *relative* ratings of different kinds of criterion indicators might be feasible. The pooled average of such ratings would then need to be tempered by evidence on reliability (that is, by the square root of the reliability coefficient). Suppose the pooled rating of the "relevance index" was .45 for academic course average and .60 for performance in the hospital as judged by clinical supervisors. Suppose evidence indicates the reliability of the *actual measures* of academic performance to be .80 and that of rated clinical performance to be .40. We would then have, as relevance indices for the actual measures,

$$\text{Academic performance} = .45 \sqrt{.80} = .40$$
$$\text{Clinical performance} = .60 \sqrt{.40} = .38$$

To know how best to weight these and perhaps other partial criterion indicators in such a way as to give maximum correlation with the complete criterion of "effective job performance," we would need to know the correlations among the partial indicators. Multiple regression weights could then be calculated, following the procedures set out in Chapter 9.

GROUP MEMBERSHIP AS A CRITERION VARIABLE

One type of evidence of the relevance of a particular test for choice of occupation and/or survival in the occupation is the difference between average test scores for persons in different occupations. We can speak of this as *taxonomic validity*, by contrast to the predictive validity that we have considered up to this point.

If we have to deal with only two groups, say a group of lawyers and a group of engineers, then ability of a test to differentiate between the two groups can be expressed as a point-biserial correlation. If, on a test of spatial visualizing, the mean of 200 engineers was 105, the mean of 100 lawyers was 90, and the standard deviation of the total group was 20, we would have

$$r_{\text{pbis}} = \frac{105 - 90}{20} \sqrt{(200/300)(100/300)} = .353$$

The square of the point biserial corresponds exactly to the ratio of the between-groups variance to the total variance.

In more general terms, we can compute the between-groups variance for any number of different occupations (or other subgroups) and express it as a proportion of the total variance. Thus, suppose that we had three groups with the means and numbers shown below and that the standard deviation of the total group was still 20.

	MEAN	N
Engineers	105	200
Lawyers	90	100
English teachers	80	100
Total	95	400

We would then have, for the between-groups variance,

$$200(105 - 95)^2 + 100(90 - 95)^2 + 100(80 - 95)^2 = 45,000/400$$
$$= 112.5$$
$$\text{Total variance} = (20)^2 = 400$$

The ratio of between-groups variance to total variance is 112.5/400 = .28125. That is, 28.125% of the variance stems from differences between groups. If we needed an index analogous to the point biserial, we might take the square root of this figure, yielding an index of 0.530.

One can calculate the proportion of between-groups variance (and can, of course, take its square root) for any number of groups and get an index of the effectiveness of a test in differentiating among the members of that set of groups. The usual significance tests from analysis of variance can be applied to determine whether the spread of group means is greater than might have arisen just from sampling fluctuations. Usually the differences are clearly non-chance. The issue is, rather, one of judging whether the degree of differentiation is sufficiently great to be helpful for classification or guidance decisions. Even when a substantial part of the variance is between-groups variance, specific groups show substantial percentages of overlap, and our judgments and decisions concerning the group to which a candidate belongs must be tentative.

Our concerns, as we deal with taxonomic validity, focus less on the statistic to express differentiation than on the legitimacy of existing group differences. When we use taxonomic differences as a basis for judgments about the future, we are saying, in effect, "Things should be as they now are." Thus, if we find (as we very well may) that persons in a skilled trade fall below average on verbal ability, we may be tempted to conclude that it is *desirable* that persons below average on verbal ability go into skilled trades. We may neglect the possibility (the probability) that verbally fluent persons were academically successful and were attracted to and able to qualify for positions in various types of professional jobs, and that the relatively low scores of persons in skilled trades are the indirect result of selection *into* other occupations. The interpretation of group differences for low-scoring groups is particularly suspect, though high scores in an occupation need not indicate that the ability in question is demanded in that occupation. Occupational test-score levels may reflect artificial educational barriers, or other historical accidents, rather than the essential demands of the job. However, having noted these cautions, we may still find group differences worth examining as indicators of the significance of a test score.

RELIABILITY AND THE INTERPRETATION
OF VALIDITY COEFFICIENTS

Validity coefficients obtained in predictive validity studies are often discouragingly small, indicating that only a small amount of the variance in the criterion measure is shared with the predictor. However, the fault does not lie solely with the predictor. Part, sometimes a good part, of the deficiency stems from unreliability of the criterion measure. A predictor cannot be expected to predict the part of the criterion measure that is error variance. It is the correlation between the predictor and "true score" or "universe score" on the criterion that is the proper measure of the effectiveness of a test. To arrive at this, we need an adequate appraisal of the reliability of the score that we are using as a criterion measure.

Problems of estimating reliability were discussed rather fully in Chapter 6, primarily in the context of tests. The various problems become especially acute as we turn our attention to criterion indicators. How shall we define the universe from which we draw a criterion sample? What is it feasible to do to get independent samples from that universe? What components of variance creep into our criterion score, and how should these be allocated between "true score" and "error"? We must do the best we can to get sound estimates of criterion reliability, but it won't be easy.

Once we have done our best to generate an estimate of criterion reliability, use of that statistic is simple and straightforward. We have

$$r_{tc_\infty} = \frac{r_{tc}}{\sqrt{r_{cc'}}} \tag{7.8}$$

where r_{tc_∞} = correlation of test with "true score" on the criterion variable

r_{tc} = obtained test–criterion correlation

$r_{cc'}$ = criterion score reliability

Thus, if $r_{tc} = .40$ and $r_{cc'} = .64$, we have

$$r_{tc_\infty} = \frac{.40}{\sqrt{.64}} = .50$$

Of the criterion "true score" variance, 25% is predictable by the test, compared with 16% of the variance in the observed criterion score. The 25% is a much more appropriate statement of the test's level of effectiveness.

VALIDITY AND PRACTICAL UTILITY

The validity coefficient is a very convenient statistic, but it leaves a good deal to be desired when it comes to expressing the practical value of a test as an instrument for personnel decisions. And it does not convey a great deal of meaning to the lay person who may need to decide whether a test is to be used or need to interpret such validity statistics. Some better approach is required for expressing the practical significance of a test as a predictor.

A first step toward making the practical value of a test explicit is to display the full bivariate table of test scores versus criterion scores. This is often called an *expectancy table;* a table that shows what has occurred in the past provides one basis for anticipating what may be expected to occur in the future. Table 7.4 shows such a table, obtained when the Spatial Relations test of the Differential Aptitude Tests was used to predict grades in a watch repair school. The first form of the table presents numbers of cases, and the second gives percents of cases.

There is something down-to-earth and convincing about a table showing actual results with actual numbers of cases. However, such a table reproduces all the chance fluctuations and idiosyncrasies of the specific sample. If tests for linearity (see page 216) indicate no significant nonlinearity in the relationship, it may be more applicable to future groups to base the expectancy table on the properties of the normal bivariate frequency distribution. We would divide the score range on the predictor into a manageable number of intervals, selecting a score to represent the midpoint of each. Expressed in standard scores, the average expected criterion score at predictor score level a is given by

$$\tilde{z}_{c(a)} = r_{xc} z_{x(a)} \tag{7.9}$$

The percents of cases in the total group falling above specified criterion levels can be determined and these in turn converted into normal deviates. Thus, in our illustrative example, the percentages and corresponding normal deviates are:

GRADE	PERCENT	NORMAL DEVIATE
A	11.7	1.190
A or B	49.5	0.012
A, B, or C	78.4	-0.786
A, B, C, or D	92.8	-1.461

For a score at a given (standard-score) level, the normal deviate value for a specified criterion level becomes

Table **7.4** Expected Success in Watch Repair School at
Different Score Levels on Spatial Relations Test*

SCORE	OBSERVED FREQUENCY OF FINAL GRADE				
	E	D	C	B	A
80–99				3	6
60–79			7	19	7
40–59	1	8	17	17	
20–39	3	5	4	2	
0–19	4	3	4	1	

	OBSERVED PERCENT OF EACH FINAL GRADE				
	E	D	C	B	A
80–99				33	67
60–79			21	58	21
40–59	2	18	40	40	
20–39	21	36	29	14	
0–19	33	25	33	9	

	PERCENTS ESTIMATED FROM BIVARIATE NORMAL DISTRIBUTION				
	E	D	C	B	A
80–99			6	40	54
60–79		4	19	54	23
40–59	4	15	36	40	5
20–39	19	30	34	16	1
0–19	49	30	18	3	

* Reproduced by permission from the Fourth Edition Manual of the Differential Aptitude Tests. Copyright © 1966 by The Psychological Corporation, New York, N.Y. All rights reserved.

$$\frac{z_c - \tilde{z}_{c(a)}}{\sqrt{1 - r_{cx}^2}} \tag{7.10}$$

Thus, in our illustration, the predictor-score mean is 51.8 and the standard deviation is 21.6, so a score of 89.5 has a standard-score value of 1.88. Entering this number in equation 7.9, we get a value of 1.28 for $\tilde{z}_{c(a)}$, the mean criterion score at that predictor-score level. If we put this value and the predictor-criterion correlation of .68 in formula 7.10, we can enter the values from the foregoing table and determine the normal deviate dividing A's from B's, B's from C's, and so forth. These can be converted back to percents of cases at that test-score level expected to receive a criterion score in or above the designated category. The computations for a score of 89.5 are illustrated below.

DIVIDING BETWEEN	$\dfrac{z_c - \tilde{z}_{c(a)}}{1 - r_{cx}^2}$	CUMULATIVE PERCENT OF CASES	PERCENT IN GRADE ABOVE DIVIDING LINE
A and B	− .113	54	54
B and C	− 1.595	94	40
C and D	− 2.599	99.5	5.5
D and E	− 3.488	99.97	.47

From calculations for a selection of predictor-score values, we can synthesize a complete table of percents of cases expected in specified criterion ranges that preserves the marginal test score and criterion distribution of the original data but is free from any trivial and meaningless idiosyncrasies of the limited set of cases. Such a table is shown at the bottom of Table 7.4.

If evidence on criterion unreliability is available, the corrected validity coefficient may be used in equation 7.9 and formula 7.10 to yield an expectancy table showing the mean and dispersion of "true" criterion scores to be expected at each test-score level.

If one can assume that the criterion scale is fixed and will not drift with changes in input (as academic grades are inclined to do), one can display the predicted effect of progressively higher selection standards on output. This has been done for our illustration in Table 7.5. It should be emphasized that these predicted outcomes do assume that the standards for evaluating performance will remain unchanged.

A further step in trying to express the practical usefulness of a test for personnel selection decisions requires that we set up some decision rule based on test scores and then try to appraise, in some common unit, the gain that would result from applying that rule. The gain must be relative to the efficiency of random selection or selection based on some test or other procedure of known but lower validity. This is a very difficult step to take, because it requires that we be able to express the gains (utility) and losses (cost) from the application of our decision rule. As a crude first approximation, we may recognize just four outcomes of the decision rule:

1. A person is accepted who becomes successful.
2. A person is accepted who fails on the criterion.

Table **7.5**   Estimated Grade Distribution in Percentages for Different
Admission Standards

MINIMUM	GRADE				
SCORE	E	D	C	B	A
0	7.2	14.4	28.8	37.8	11.7
20	4.4	12.0	27.4	41.2	14.9
40	2.0	9.1	26.2	45.4	17.3
60		3.1	16.2	51.0	29.8
80			5.5	40.0	54.4

	GRADE		
	D or better	C or better	B or better
0	92.8	78.3	49.5
20	95.5	83.5	56.1
40	98.0	88.9	62.7
60	100	97.0	80.8
80		100	94.4

3. A person is rejected who would have been successful.

4. A person is rejected who would have failed.

Somehow we must attach a value, expressed in some type of unit, to each possible outcome. A natural unit, though not easy to apply, is dollars. As a direct cost in all four categories, there is the per-person expense of maintaining the personnel recruitment and selection program. As a measure of gain or "utility" in category 1, we can try to estimate the cost of recruiting and training a replacement for a satisfactory employee. The gain or utility in category 4 would be the saving realized from not spending money to employ and train a person who would later have to be let go. The costs in category 2 would be those same training and employment costs. In category 3, direct costs are those general per-person costs of recruitment and testing with no offsetting gain.

Clearly, the costs and gains are difficult to estimate even in the simplified four-cell model that we have set up, which makes no provision for differences in degree of effectiveness within the accepted and successful group. And they are difficult to evaluate even in an employment context, in which the dollar is a fairly plausible unit of measure. Costs, and especially gains, are even harder to quantify in educational or public service settings, in which the outcomes are expressed in course grades received, educational levels completed, or gains in personal adjustment resulting from therapy. We have no accepted metric for measuring such social goods. Judging whether some procedure for selecting persons for education or for therapeutic or other intervention is worth the cost tends to bog down for want of a scale in terms of which to measure the gains that can be shown to result.

Chapter 8

The Issue of Bias in Testing

One topic that has been prominent in the literature on testing during the past 20 years is that of test bias. The concern has arisen most prominently in connection with the use of tests with members of ethnic minorities, but it is potentially involved whenever the group with which a test is used brings to the test a cultural background noticeably different from that of the group for which the test was primarily developed and on which it was standardized. However, it is often far from clear what is meant by bias. We must first examine the different ways in which the term is used. We can then turn our attention to different psychometric indicators of bias and to steps that can be taken, during the construction of tests and in the use of a test, to minimize its effects.

There are several levels of inference that can be made from a test score. Consider a reading comprehension test built on several passages drawn by an appropriate random sampling procedure from the articles appearing in *Reader's Digest*. Comprehension of each passage is tested by a set of multiple-choice questions, and score is the number of correct answers chosen. From a low score on this test we might wish to make the following inferences:

1. The examinee has a low level of understanding of these passages.
2. The examinee will have difficulty in understanding the contents of *Reader's Digest*.
3. The examinee is, in general, a poor reader.
4. The examinee is not likely to do well in college.

The first of these is a limited inference of narrow scope. Its acceptability depends primarily on the degree to which answering the test questions depends on understanding the passages in the test and on the extent to which the questions adequately sample the ideas expressed in the passage. (Sometimes questions on a reading test can be answered by general knowledge without the examinee's reading the passage, and sometimes very specialized knowledge is required in order to read a passage with understanding.) Whether inference 1 may fairly be made for groups different from the reference population on which items were selected and norms based depends, if the items were adequate for the reference population, only on whether the content and language of the test questions, as distinct from the passages themselves, are peculiarly difficult for that group. Although this is possible, it does not seem highly probable, and the first inference seems likely to be acceptable for almost any group.

The second level of inference involves, in addition, the character of the passages that were drawn in the sample. One may ask whether, through some fluke of sampling, passages were drawn that were peculiarly difficult (or peculiarly easy) for the culturally different group. Because the passages were, by definition, sampled at random, it could not have been a systematic biasing effect, but a chance difference could possibly put this level of inference in question. Again, this does not seem very likely, but we would want to scrutinize the passages with some care to see that they didn't appear to be a freakish sample.

When we proceed to the third level of inference, we are assuming that comprehension of *Reader's Digest* provides an adequate basis for inferring status on a considerably more general attribute—level of reading comprehension. Clearly, this represents a substantially greater leap from observed data to conclusion, and the adequacy of the sample of passages to represent this considerably broader attribute would call for our critical scrutiny for *any* group. In the context of test bias, the question would become: Are these passages as appropriate for probing the reading ability of special groups with deviating cultural background as they are for the general reference group? Do they handicap (or aid) these groups in comparison with the ability of mem ers of these groups to read other sorts of materials? Is *Reader's Digest* disproportionately tied to a white, middle-class culture? This seems to us a somewhat more likely possibility than that distortion would appear in inferences at the first and second levels. We would need to scrutinize critically the general character of the reading tasks presented by *Reader's Digest* to determine whether such a criticism might be justified.

Finally, with inferences of the fourth sort, we are using a test score to predict some qualitatively different type of life performance. This is a still greater inferential leap, and it is possible that a given test score has noticeably different implications for members of a special group than for members of the general reference population. Reading ability as measured by this test may be less (or more) relevant to college success for the special group members, so that the regression of success on test score is flatter (or steeper) than for the general reference group. Or there may be a systematic displacement of criterion scores in relation to the test scores so that, for a given test score, members of the special group have a higher (or lower) average college grade point average than members of the general reference group.

With this larger inferential leap, many other factors may enter in to modify the generally observed relationship. Motivation, study skills, knowledge background, and other academic experiences may operate differentially in the two types of groups. Particularly when the criterion being predicted is actual job performance, rather than academic achievement, this seems a likely possibility. Then inferences based on experience with a general group and applied to a special group with a different cultural background may be inappropriate and may not be fair to members of that special group.

The point is that unfairness tends to stem from the inferences that are made from a test score. When the inferential leap is a small one, there is still some possibility of unfairness in the inference, but the likelihood is relatively small. As the size of the inferential leap increases, the *possibility* of bias also increases, and the need to check on it and to take special precautions to avoid it increases correspondingly.

BIAS AT THE ITEM LEVEL

The initial point at which to identify and try to minimize bias is at the level of the individual test item. Single items are typically selected to be good indicators of the attribute measured by the test as a whole, and, as indicated in Chapter 4, items are typically evaluated in terms of their difficulty level and their correlation with a score intended to represent the latent attribute that the test is designed to measure. The typical statistical indications that an item is inappropriate for a culturally different group are that it is peculiarly difficult (or peculiarly easy) in that group, or that it shows a lower correlation with the underlying latent attribute. In other words, in terms of the latent trait model, it has a significantly different b_g parameter or a significantly lower a_g parameter in the special group.

A first step in avoiding biased items can be taken at the stage of item preparation. One can try to obtain perceptive item critics who are members of, or intimately acquainted with, the group for which one is concerned about bias and ask them to review the pool of available items. They will be asked to pick out any items that they believe would be inappropriate for the group in question because of special language problems or special aspects of the group's background as well as items that might in any way offend the group. By way of illustration, in a vocabulary test the word *alto* was identified as inappropriate for Hispanic children because of the range of different meanings that the word has in Spanish.

There is not a great deal of evidence to show how much correspondence there will be between perceived inappropriateness and statistical indications of unsuitability. However, this type of editorial review certainly serves a useful purpose in public relations with potential users of the test. It helps to weed out a certain number of items that are likely to *appear* inappropriate to other members of the group in question. And it may serve to screen out a few items that would show unacceptable statistical properties.

In order to obtain statistical evidence on the acceptability, for any given special group, of the items in a pool of test items, it is necessary to try the items out with an adequate sample of members of that group. This is more easily said than done. School systems are not uniformly eager to provide such samples for item tryout. In job settings the groups may be essentially unavailable. A substantial amount of extra time and effort may be required if one is to obtain the participation of the special groups with adequate numbers and representativeness. However, in our further discussion, we will by-pass these very real practical problems and assume that the sample has in fact been obtained.

At this point the statistics to be obtained consist of discrimination and difficulty indices item by item for each of the groups in which we are interested. The objective is to identify specific items that, on the basis of these statistics, seem inappropriate for the special groups. An item might be considered for rejection because it showed too flat an item characteristic curve (too little ability to differentiate between levels of ability on the latent attribute) in one or more of the groups, or because it was disproportionately hard (or easy) for the special group.

DISCRIMINATION INDICES

Turning our attention first to the discrimination indices, which are likely to be in the form of biserial correlations between item and total test score, we might first raise the question of whether the average of these indices is noticeably lower in the special group than in the general reference group. If this is found to be the case, it might mean (1) that the special group is fundamentally less variable than the reference group on the latent attribute or (2) that the items are less effective measures of the attribute in the special group. Unfortunately, there seems to be no simple way to choose between these two interpretations. If one had an existing measure that was known to be an equally good measure of the latent attribute in both groups (and how this would be known is a bit obscure), one could look at the variance of the two groups on this measure. If differences in variability were observed, the item correlations for the special group could be adjusted to the same variance as that of the reference group, using the formula for curtailment given in Chapter 7 (case 1).

We are more likely to obtain useful information by looking at the discrimination indices of specific items. Here, one or more of several criteria might be used for weeding out unacceptable items. Three possibilities may be considered.

1. An item might be rejected if it fell below some pre-established level of discrimination in *any* of the groups being considered. The level should probably be fairly low because of chance sampling fluctuations from group to group. A biserial correlation of .30 might be a reasonable value.

2. An item might be rejected if the average of its discrimination indices in *all* the groups fell below some pre-established level. The standard here could probably be set somewhat higher, possibly a biserial of .40 or .45.

3. An item might be rejected if the difference in discrimination indices between the groups was so large that it could hardly have occurred by chance. Perhaps the difference should be significant at the .01 level.

Some experience with sets of items suggests that criteria 1 and 2 are the most likely to be invoked. The rationale for them seems fairly straightforward. The item is either weak in general or clearly weak in some one group. The rationale for criterion 3 seems less clear, but such an item does appear to be functioning rather differently in the two or more groups, and perhaps it is not desirable that it be included in a test.

DIFFICULTY INDICES

Let us turn now to item difficulty, the index for which will either be or be derived from the percentage of examinees selecting the keyed answer. First of all, it must be made clear that a simple difference in *average* item difficulty cannot automatically be accepted as an indication of pervasive bias in the items. It cannot be assumed in advance that boys are just as good readers as girls or that Anglo-Saxon children are just as good in arithmetic as Orientals. To *assume* that there are *no* genuine group differences begs the question that a test may have been designed to investigate. Existence of genuine group differences in an attribute must be entertained as a possibility, though the existence of such differences provides no basis for an interpretation of their origin or their significance.

If the finding of an average difference in item difficulty cannot be used as the basis for inferring bias, what *can* be so used? The answer that is often given, and that seems generally reasonable, is that a marked deviation in the discrepancy for a specific item from the average discrepancy for all items may provide such evidence.

In order to compare the difficulties of the items in a pool of items for two (or more) groups, it is first necessary to convert the raw percentage of correct answers for each item to a difficulty scale in which the units are approximately equal. Procedures for doing this were discussed in Chapter 4. The simplest procedure is probably to calculate the Rasch difficulty scale values separately for each group. If the set of items is the same for each group, the Rasch procedure has the effect of setting the mean scale value of the common set of items at 0 within each group, and then differences in scale value for any item become immediately apparent. Those items with the largest differences in scale values are the suspect items.

Wright and Stone (1979) indicate that the standard error of the Rasch scale value of an item, in the logit units used in Rasch scaling, is equal to

$$\left(\frac{1 + s^2/2.89}{Np\,(1 - p)}\right)^{\frac{1}{2}}$$

where s = standard deviation of test measures in logits in the group
          p = proportion of correct answers to the item
        N = number of cases in the group.*

---

* From B. D. Wright and M. H. Stone, *Best Test Design*. Chicago: Mesa Press, 1979. Used by permission.

The standard error of the difference between scale values in two groups 1 and 2 can be estimated by

$$S.E._{\text{diff}} = \sqrt{S.E._1^2 + S.E._2^2}$$

We could set some standard, such as the .01 significance level, and reject all items for which the difference exceeded that level. Note that with two groups 1 and 2, such a procedure would reject not only those items that were unexpectedly difficult for group 1 but also those that were unexpectedly easy.

If bias affects only a certain fairly small fraction of the items and then only with respect to one of the groups being compared, we might anticipate a skewed distribution of the differences in Rasch scale values. The result might appear as shown in Figure 8.1. A cutoff at a difference as large as 2.58 standard errors (the .01 level) would pick up almost solely those items that were particularly difficult for the special group. One might then feel some conviction that these were distinctively inappropriate items. If, on the other hand, the distribution of differences was approximately symmetrical, and especially if the proportion of items showing differences significant at the .01 level was not much in excess of 1% of the total number of items in the pool, one might well feel that those few large differences were no more than accidents of random sampling. Such items might be excluded from the final test, but one suspects that doing this would have little impact on the "fairness" of the test as a whole.

Another way that has been suggested for looking at differences on specific items (see Ironson, 1980) is to divide the range of test scores into a number of slices and then to look at the percent of success on specific items for members of the two groups who received the same or nearly the same total test score. Each score level on the test provides data for a fourfold table showing numbers of successes and failures for each group. A chi square with one degree of freedom can be calculated for each slice, and the values totaled to give an overall chi square for the item with as many degrees of freedom as there are slices. The slices must be broad enough so that each includes a sufficient number of both successes and failures to make the calculation of chi square appropriate.

Items that yield significant chi squares appear to be discrepant, in that persons with the same or nearly the same level of total score have different levels of success on them. The percentages in the separate slices can be examined to determine the nature of the discrepancy. If one group is more successful at all score levels, this indicates that the item is peculiarly easy for that group, as compared with the other group. If the difference shifts systematically as one goes from a low to a high test score, this indicates that the item is more discriminating in the group that shows the more rapid shift.

Yet another approach (proposed by Coffman, 1978) that has the advantage of producing a statistic in which the standard error is the same for all items in a set (if N remains the same) is to convert the percentage values using an arcsin transformation. The transformation is

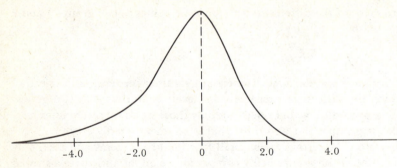

Figure **8.1** Hypothetical skewed distribution of scale differences.

$$\phi = 2 \arcsin p$$

The standard error of the transformed values is indicated to be $1/N$, and this does not depend on the original value of p. Once again, the standard error of the difference between the arcsin values for two groups is given by

$$S.E._{\text{diff}} = \sqrt{S.E._1^2 + S.E._2^2}$$

One can determine the mean difference for a set of items and then determine a range of values around that mean difference within which some specified proportion of the observed differences (.95 or .99) would be expected to fall. Thus the .99 confidence interval would be mean difference $\pm 2.58 \, S.E._{\text{diff}}$. An excess of large differences would indicate that the groups genuinely did perform in a distinctive way on specific items. A skewing of the differences to show more items peculiarly difficult for the special group might be taken as evidence of systematic bias.

Some results from the application of this arcsin transformation are shown in Figure 8.2. These were drawn from a study by Rusinah (1980) based on subsamples of 600 black and 600 white pupils at each of several grade levels. The subsamples were drawn from the norming groups used to norm the Cognitive Ability Tests, Form 3, and the items were the items in that test battery. The values reported represent the arcsin value for black examinees less the arcsin value for white examinees at a given age level. Vertical lines are drawn on the graphs to indicate the mean difference and the limits at $\pm 2.58 \, S.E._{\text{diff}}$.

The mean difference in arcsin value is substantial, and the negative value for the mean indicates a generally higher rate of success on these items for the white examinees. A substantial number of items deviate significantly from the mean difference. However, there is no evidence of skewness toward the minus end of the scale that would show a group of items that were peculiarly hard for black examinees. If anything, the skewness is in the opposite direction, with a long tail of items showing much smaller differences. There was a tendency for these very

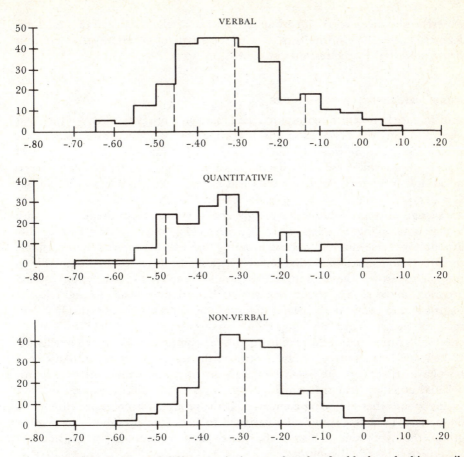

Figure **8.2** Distributions of differences in item scale value for black and white pupils (based on Arcsin Transformation). (Based on tables in Rusinah bt. Joned, A comparison of the performance of blacks and whites and of males and females on the items of the Cognitive Abilities Test, Form 3. Unpublished M.A. thesis, University of Iowa, 1980. Used by permission.)

small differences to appear on items that were extremely difficult for both groups, but it was hard to find any rationale for the items that showed especially large differences. The obtained type of distribution provides little basis for attributing bias to specific items.

BIAS IN A COMPLETE TEST

We turn now to the question of assessing bias in a total test—either an existing test or one that we may have just constructed. We shall need to look at (1) group differences in mean score, (2) group differences in reliability, and (3) group differences in the slope of the regression of some type of criterion variable that is being predicted by the test on test score.

GROUP DIFFERENCES IN MEAN SCORE

A difference between two groups in mean score on a test is an observed fact. It is absurd to deny the existence of a fact. Having observed the datum, we face the problem of deciding what the datum means — what inferences are to be drawn from it. As was indicated at the beginning of this chapter, there are several levels of possible inference. For many tests and in many countries (for example, see Comber and Keeves, 1973), girls do less well than boys on tests of science knowledge. Given this datum, one might choose to argue that the tests deal with a biased sampling of science knowledge, picking out that which is readily available and relevant for boys and avoiding that which is relevant and available for girls. This seems a somewhat unlikely hypothesis, but it would presumably be possible to test it. The appropriate test would be to try to identify, on rational grounds, any aspects of science knowledge that are most available and relevant to girls and to compare the performance of the two sexes on a test dealing with such knowledge. If girls do better than boys on this test, the possibility of biased selection is supported; if they fail to do so, the hypothesis is very much weakened. If the reversal takes place, the future task of the test maker is to see that science tests have an appropriate balance of male-oriented and female-oriented items.

This same logic and procedure apply to any area of ability measurement and to any groups that are being compared. If the group differences are eliminated or reversed by a test specifically designed to favor the previously low-scoring group, the hypothesis of bias in the test content receives support. If not, the hypothesis is largely demolished.

If the content of the science test exercises turns out to be essentially neuter, dealing with content that is neither particularly "masculine" nor particularly "feminine," one may be inclined to ascribe the differences in performance to differences between boys and girls in opportunity to learn about science or in motivation to learn about science. With this interpretation, the differences are accepted as real but are attributed to the effect of environmental forces. There is certainly a substantial amount of independent evidence that, on the average, boys and girls differ in the amount of science they have studied and in the extent to which they have engaged in science-related activities. This same type of inference might be made, and the relevant evidence marshaled to support it, to account for differences found in other subjects or other more general abilities, and for other types of groups.

It is far from easy to assemble crucial evidence either to confirm or to rebut such an explanation of observed differences. The relevant environmental and motivational variables are not easy to define and identify, and the size of their effects is not easy to assess, much less to measure or control. The body of research on relationships of environmental factors and environmental differences to ability measures is voluminous and confused, and we make no attempt to review or evaluate it here.

Some investigators might be inclined to draw, from the difference between boys and girls in average scores on science tests, the inference that girls will generally do less well than boys in science-related occupations. Such an inference implies that there is a substantial relationship between science test scores and subsequent entry into and success in science careers—and a relationship that holds equally for boys and girls. This is the issue of the validity of the test as a predictor, an issue that we shall consider in some detail later in the chapter. Such an inference might, of course, also be proposed with respect to any type of test and for any groups being compared.

Finally, one might propose to draw, from the difference in mean science test scores, the inference that girls, on the average, have inherently less potential than boys for careers in science. This inference requires not only that the test have validity as a predictor of future careers in science but that test scores be determined by *inherent* factors differing in the two groups—that is, determined by something in the basic biological constitution of males and females. This inference gets us into the whole involved field of behavior genetics and the role of genetic factors in determination of group differences, an enormous literature rife with controversy. The same type of inference, leading to the same type of controversy, can be proposed for differences between any types of groups on measures of any human attribute.

The fairness of test content to groups differing in sex, ethnicity, or background can be checked, in part at least, by the type of special test-construction experiment that we proposed on page 236. The validity of the test as a predictor of future outcomes in each group can, in theory at least, be verified by follow-up studies in each of the groups with which it is to be used. Determining the relative influence of various aspects of past histories and of biological constitution in producing observed differences between groups has proved, and will continue to prove, a most difficult and controversial enterprise.

GROUP DIFFERENCES IN RELIABILITY

Group differences in test reliability have typically received less attention than group differences in test score means or group differences in correlation with relevant external variables. They are a matter of some interest, however, because reliability differences may affect the correlation of test scores with other variables in which we are interested. If test reliability is low, the test's correlations with other variables tends to be depressed.

Reliability in group A may be lower than reliability in group B because group A is genuinely less variable in the attribute being measured than group B is. If between-persons variance is lower and other sources of variance remain the same, the ratio of between-persons to total observed variance will be less and a lower reliability coefficient will result.

Another way in which lower reliability can result for group A is if the difficulty of the items is less appropriate for group A than for group B. As we saw in Chapter 4, each item has its own distinctive information function, providing maximum information over a limited range of the attribute it is designed to measure. The information function of a test is a composite of the information functions of the items that have been chosen to go into it. If well designed, the test provides its highest level of information over the ability range within which most of the examinees are expected to fall. If that test is subsequently used with a group in which the average ability level is substantially different, the average information level—and hence the test's reliability—may be appreciably reduced. Thus, if group A has a substantially lower (or higher) mean ability level than the group for which the test was designed, the test may display appreciably lower reliability over this different ability range.

Finally, there may be some other reason why the test exercises depend less on a common attribute in group A than in group B. Lack of a common background of experiences, fluctuation of attention and effort, and greater tendency to guess blindly all might make certain items (and the test as a whole) a less homogeneous measure of a common attribute. The reasons for lowered reliability in a particular instance are not easy to determine. However, any such differences between two groups in reliability must always be taken into account in interpreting any differences between the groups in correlation of the test with other measures.

GROUP DIFFERENCES IN RELATIONSHIP
TO A "CRITERION" VARIABLE

Much of the discussion of "fairness" of tests has focused on their correlation with measures of school or job success that are thought of as criterion measures that the tests are expected to predict. In its traditional form, the question posed has been: Does a given test score correspond to the same average score on the criterion measure for both groups? If the question can be answered in the affirmative, the test has been considered "fair."

To answer this question, we must determine for each group separately the regression line for predicting the criterion variable from the test score. The equation for the regression line is given by

$$Y = r_{XY} \frac{s_Y}{s_X} (X - \overline{X}) + \overline{Y}$$

This is a straight line of the form

$$Y = AX + B$$

where

$$A = r_{XY} \frac{s_Y}{s_X} = \text{slope of the line}$$

$$B = \overline{Y} - r_{XY} \frac{s_Y}{s_X} \overline{X} = \text{intercept of the line on the } Y,$$
$$\text{or criterion variable, axis}$$
$$\text{when } X = 0.$$

The slope, A, indicates the degree of relationship between the test and the criterion variable. If the slope is significantly less for group 1 than it is for group 2, it indicates that, for some reason, the test is a poorer predictor of the criterion in group 1. It has less relevance for job success in that group, and its usefulness (if not its fairness) becomes subject to question.

Given equal slopes, any difference between the two intercepts indicates the difference in level of criterion performance between the two groups, given a specified level of test score. If group 1 has a higher intercept, members of that group who receive a given test score do better on the criterion measure, on the average, than the members of group 2 who receive that same test score. If this situation prevails, the test might be considered unfair to members of group 1 because, in relation to group 2, they do better on the job criterion than the test would predict. If the slopes are *not* equal, no general interpretation can be made of the difference between intercepts, because the regression lines are not parallel and may in fact intersect. Figure 8.3 shows several patterns that might be obtained for regression lines for two groups.

Diagram A in Figure 8.3 illustrates a situation in which the slopes are radically (probably unrealistically) different in the two groups. For group 2 the slope is very steep, and the test is correspondingly a very good predictor of the criterion variable. In group 1 the regression appears as an almost horizontal line, and the predicted criterion score changes only very slightly as one goes from a low to a high test score. The test is essentially useless as a predictor in group 1. It is not so much unfair as irrelevant. However, using the test to exclude persons from training or employment would do a considerable injustice to the low-scoring members of group 1. That low score does not indicate comparably poor criterion performance.

Diagram B illustrates a situation in which the slopes do differ somewhat for the two groups, but in which there is at all actual score levels a difference in criterion performance favoring group 2. That is, at any score level the average criterion score for group 2 members surpasses that for members of group 1. By the usual definition, using this test with a common qualifying score would penalize members of group 2 relative to members of group 1. Using group 1 as a standard of reference, members of group 2 do better on the criterion than would be predicted from their test scores. Only at *very* low test scores do the regression lines for the two groups approach one another.

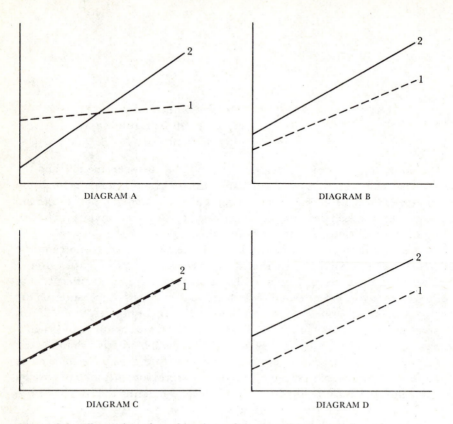

Figure **8.3**   Illustration of combinations of slopes and intercepts for two groups.

Diagram C illustrates a close approximation to the model of a fair test according to the definition given on page 238. The regression lines for the two groups
have nearly identical slopes and intercepts. The predicted criterion score will be
almost exactly the same no matter which group's regression equation is used.
From the point of view of an employer, it would make essentially no difference to
which group an applicant belonged. For a given test score, the predicted job performance would be the same. We will consider presently the "fairness" of this
situation from a somewhat different point of view.

Diagram D illustrates a case in which the slopes are the same for the two
groups but the intercepts are markedly different. In this illustration the regression lines are parallel, but one is well above the other. At all test score levels, the
average criterion score in group 2 falls well above that in group 1. Use of a common regression equation would be markedly disadvantageous to members of
group 2 and advantageous to members of group 1.

To provide an illustration from actual data, we show in Figure 8.4 the regression lines that were obtained for predicting grade point average from the verbal

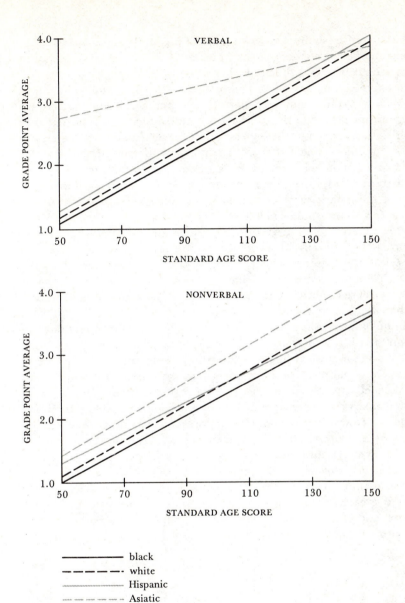

Figure 8.4   Regression lines for predicting GPA from Cognitive Ability Test scores for four ethnic groups.

section of the Cognitive Ability Tests for groups of black, Hispanic, Asiatic, and white students in one large school system. These can be compared with similar regression equations based on the nonverbal section.

For the verbal test, the regression lines for black, Hispanic, and white pupils are approximately parallel and very close to one another. Applying the appropriate significance tests* to the differences between them, we find that they are nonsignificant. By contrast, the regression line for the Asiatic group is clearly different from the others. The verbal test is a much less effective predictor in this group, and the regression line is relatively flat. Over most of the score range, the line falls well above that for the other three groups. By the standards of the white group, most of the Asiatics are "over-achievers," doing much better than the regression line for whites would predict.

For the nonverbal test, all four groups show essentially the same slope, so test scores appear equally relevant for school success in each of them. However, the Asiatic group still does better in school grades, in relation to test score, than the other groups. Though more relevant than the verbal test, the nonverbal test could still be considered somewhat unfair to Asiatics on the basis of the definition of fairness that we have considered up to this point.

The definition of fairness as equal predicted criterion score for equal test score is not the only possible definition. It can be demonstrated (Thorndike, 1971) that, when the same regression line is obtained for two groups (meaning equal criterion score for equal test score) but one group has a markedly lower mean score on the predictor test than the other group has, the fraction of the less able group accepted at any cutting score will be disproportionately small. That is, the overlap of the two groups in *predicted* criterion scores will be much less than the overlap in *actual* criterion scores. This discrepancy is a function of the amount of difference between the means of the two groups on the predictor, of the correlation between predictor and criterion, and of the minimum test score set as the standard to qualify. It will be greater when the difference between the two group means is greater, greater when the correlation between predictor and criterion is low, and greater when a high cutting score is used for admission to the training program or job. Table 8.1 shows the ratio of numbers admitted

---

* The error variance of the slope parameter is estimated by

$$s_A^2 = \frac{s_{y \cdot x}^2}{\Sigma \, (X_i - \overline{X})^2}$$

and the error variance of the intercept parameter by

$$s_B^2 = s_{y \cdot x}^2 \left(\frac{1}{N} + \frac{\overline{X}^2}{\Sigma \, (X_i - \overline{X})^2} \right)$$

The variance of the difference between the parameters of two groups is equal to the sum of the variances for the separate groups.

Table **8.1**   Ratio of Percent Reaching Criterion Standard to Percent Qualifying on Test

CORRELATION WITH CRITERION	FOR LOWER GROUP	CUTOFF SET AT MEAN OF HIGHER GROUP		
		DIFFERENCE IN MEAN PREDICTOR SCORE		
		0.3 SD	0.7 SD	1.0 SD
0.65	(1) Percent to qualify on test	38.2	24.2	15.9
	(2) Percent of total group to qualify on criterion	42.3	32.5	25.8
	Ratio (1)/(2)	.903	.745	.616
0.50	(2) Percent of total group to qualify on criterion	44.0	36.3	30.9
	Ratio (1)/(2)	.868	.667	.515
0.35	(2) Percent of total group to qualify on criterion	45.8	40.3	36.3
	Ratio (1)/(2)	.834	.600	.438
0.20	(2) Percent of total group to qualify on criterion	47.6	44.4	42.1
	Ratio (1)/(2)	.803	.545	.378

CUTOFF SET AT $+0.5$ S.D. of higher group

0.65	(1) Percent to qualify on test	21.2	11.5	6.7
	(2) Percent of total group to qualify on criterion	30.2	21.8	16.5
	Ratio (1)/(2)	.702	.528	.406
0.50	(2) Percent of total group to qualify on criterion	34.4	27.4	22.7
	Ratio (1)/(2)	.616	.420	.295
0.35	(2) Percent of total group to qualify on criterion	39.0	33.7	30.0
	Ratio (1)/(2)	.544	.341	.223
0.20	(2) Percent of total group to qualify on criterion	43.6	40.5	38.2
	Ratio (1)/(2)	.486	.284	.175

from the less able group to numbers of that total group who would reach a specified level of score on the criterion variable. The set of calculations is illustrated below for one illustrative case with the following values:

Low group mean is 1 S.D. below that of the higher group.

Correlation of test with criterion is .50 in each group.

Qualifying score for admission is set at the mean of the higher group, so expected criterion performance is also set at the mean of criterion performance in the higher group.

It is assumed that all distributions are bivariate normal, all standard deviations are 1.0, and all regressions are linear. The criterion score corresponding to a minimum qualifying score on the test is

$$Y_H - \overline{Y}_H = r_{XY} \frac{s_Y}{s_X} (X_H - \overline{X}_H)$$

$$= .50 (\overline{X}_H - \overline{X}_H) = .00$$

That is, the average criterion score for those with minimally acceptable test scores is at the average criterion performance for the upper group.

The mean criterion score for the lower group is then

$$Y_L - \overline{Y}_H = .50 (\overline{X}_L - \overline{X}_H) = .50$$

For the identical regression line to apply when the correlation of predictor and criterion is .50 and the group means on the predictor differ by 1.00 S.D. units, the difference in the criterion means can be only .50 S.D. units.

The proportion of the lower group reaching the qualifying score on the *test* is, from tables of the normal curve, .159, because the qualifying score is at $+1.00$ S.D. units for the lower group.

The proportion of cases in the lower group that would equal or exceed the average *criterion* score corresponding to the minimum acceptable test score is .309, because the two groups differ by only .50 S.D. units on the criterion scale. The ratio of the proportion qualifying on the test to the proportion reaching acceptable minimum performance on the criterion is .159/.309, or 515/1000.

Thus the definition that accepts a common regression line as marking a test as fair tends, in this instance, to admit to the program only about half as large a proportion of the lower group as would, if no selection were applied, reach the minimum acceptable criterion performance. In more extreme cases, where the admission standard is set higher and/or where the correlation is lower, the ratio drops below 2/10. One can see how this outcome would appear unfair to members of the lower-scoring group.

Of course, the proportions shown in Table 8.1 don't tell the *whole* story, because those qualifying in the higher-scoring group will surpass the minimum standard of criterion performance by a greater amount, on the average, than will the qualifiers in the lower-scoring group. The higher group, as defined by the test, will produce higher average criterion scores among those qualified by the test. However, the disparity between the proportion qualified by a test and the proportion reaching some minimum criterion standard does point out the possibility of other definitions of fairness. Minority group members and other concerned people might feel that ratios such as those reported in Table 8.1 should approach 1.00 if the test is to be applied to members of that minority group.

In the final analysis, what constitutes "fair" use of test results in qualifying members of different groups for admission to some desired educational program or job is less a problem of psychometrics than one of social values. If the important social value is to minimize the chance of admitting a person who will turn out to be incompetent, as it might be in the selection of airline pilots, then predicted criterion performance is *the* important consideration. If, on the other hand, an important consideration is equity for groups who will, for one reason or another, perform less well on a reasonably valid test, then attention must be paid to whether the test has the effect of disproportionately excluding members of that group. Some adjustment of standards of acceptance may have to be made to counteract the effect of the test. Test results can only give us information about the *probability* of various outcomes. The *utility* of those outcomes to society must be decided on other grounds.

Chapter 9
Using Multiple Measures

There are many occasions on which a user of test results may find it advantageous to use more than one instrument in research or in practical work. In a prediction problem there may appear to be several different attributes that have potential for predicting a criterion measure of success in training or on a job. In studies focused on differentiating among several occupational (or other) groups, the differences may appear to be multidimensional. When we try to understand or isolate some hypothesized attribute, a set of diverse measures may help to bring out the common underlying attribute and to separate it from other attributes that may also be of interest. Thus we may have occasion to use a set of different measures in studies designed (1) to predict, (2) to differentiate, and (3) to describe and understand. We shall direct our attention to each of these settings in turn.

MULTIPLE MEASURES IN PREDICTION

Success in most human endeavors is favored by a number of distinct personal characteristics. Academic performance depends on quantitative as well as verbal ability, to say nothing of conscientiousness and persistence. Learning to fly a light plane is facilitated by good eye–hand–foot coordination, as well as by a background of mechanical knowledge and a pervasive interest in flying. A candy packer will do better with good finger dexterity and with a tolerance for routine repetitive activity. Job analysis of almost any job will suggest a number of attributes that tend to facilitate (or interfere with) a person's learning of or performance on that job. The analysis can be tested out via validation studies in which test scores (or other types of measures) designed to appraise the apparently relevant attributes are validated against one or more criterion indicators of success in training or on the job. If we find two or more different measures that show appreciable correlations with the criterion, we must then decide how best to combine the information provided by the several measures to produce the most effective prediction of that criterion score.

As indicated in the last chapter, the evidence for validity of a single measure is ordinarily expressed as a correlation coefficient, and this in turn is translated into the coefficient of a linear equation for predicting the criterion variable from the test score. If both are expressed in standard-score form, we have

$$\tilde{z}_c = r_{tc} z_t$$

where r_{tc} = test-versus-criterion correlation
z_t = standard score on the test
$\tilde{z}_c$ = predicted standard score on the criterion

If we deal with data expressed as raw scores, we have

$$\tilde{X}_c = r_{tc} \frac{s_c}{s_t} (X_t - \overline{X}_t) - \overline{X}_c$$

As indicated in Chapter 7, if the relation of test score to criterion is not linear, some function of the raw scores can be identified that does show a linear relationship, and this function can become the variable that is used in the regression equation. However, nonlinear relationships seem to occur relatively infrequently.

When two or more predictors each make a distinct contribution to the prediction of a criterion score, the simplest and most natural way to combine the information from the set of predictors is once again to express it as a simple linear composite, in which each predictor score is given an appropriate weight and the weighted scores are combined additively. We get an expression of the type

$$\tilde{X}_{ci} = b_1 X_{1i} + b_2 X_{2i} + \cdots + b_m X_{mi} + C$$

where $\tilde{X}_{ci}$ = predicted criterion score of person i
$b_1, b_2, \ldots$ = raw-score regression weights for the corresponding predictor variables
C = an additive constant

Our problem is to determine the set of weights for the several predictors that will most accurately reproduce the actual criterion scores. "Most accurate" is defined in the least-squares sense, to mean the set of weights for which

$$\sum_{i=1}^{N} (X_{ci} - \tilde{X}_{ci})^2$$

is a minimum. Working with standard scores, where

$$\sum_{1}^{N} (z_{ci} - \tilde{z}_{ci})^2 = \text{minimum}$$

we have

$$\sum_{1}^{N} (z_{ci} - \beta_1 z_{1i} - \beta_2 z_{2i} - \cdots - \beta_m z_{mi})^2 = \text{minimum}$$

where the β's are weights to be applied to standard scores on the predictor measures.

To make a function a minimum, we set its derivative with respect to each of the unknowns equal to zero. This gives us a set of m equations of the form

$$\sum_{1}^{N} [-2z_i (z_c - \beta_1 z_1 - \beta_2 z_2 - \cdots - \beta_m z_m)] = 0$$

or

$$-2 \sum_{1}^{N} z_i z_c + 2 \sum_{1}^{N} \beta_1 z_i z_1 + 2 \sum_{1}^{N} \beta_2 z_i z_2 + \cdots + 2 \sum_{1}^{N} \beta_m z_i z_m = 0$$

Because $\sum_{1}^{N} z_i z_j = N r_{ij}$, we have equations of the form

$$-2N r_{ic} + 2N \beta_1 r_{i1} + 2N \beta_2 r_{i2} + \cdots + 2N \beta_m r_{im} = 0$$

Dividing by $2N$ and transposing r_{ic}, we get the set of equations

$$
\begin{aligned}
\beta_1 + \beta_2 r_{12} + \cdots + \beta_i r_{1i} + \cdots + \beta_m r_{1m} &= r_{1c} \\
\beta_1 r_{21} + \beta_2 + \cdots + \beta_i r_{2i} + \cdots + \beta_m r_{2m} &= r_{2c} \\
&\vdots \\
\beta_1 r_{i1} + \beta_2 r_{i2} + \cdots + \beta_i + \cdots + \beta_m r_{im} &= r_{ic} \\
&\vdots \\
\beta_1 r_{m1} + \beta_2 r_{m2} + \cdots + \beta_i r_{mi} + \cdots + \beta_m &= r_{mc} \qquad (9.1)
\end{aligned}
$$

The self-correlations r_{11}, r_{22}, . . ., r_{mm} are, of course, equal to unity, so the diagonal terms become simply β_1, β_2, β_3, and so on.

Thus we wind up with a set of m linear equations in m unknowns (β_1, β_2, . . ., β_m) that, when applied to the test results in standard scores, most accurately reproduce the standard scores on the criterion measure c. Weights to be applied to raw scores are obtained by multiplying the beta weights by the ratio of the two standard deviations. That is,

$$b_i = \beta_i \frac{s_c}{s_i}$$

In the present day and age, solving even very large sets of linear equations is a trivial exercise for a computer, and programs to handle smaller sets are available for use on programmable calculators. The widely used SPSS program package deals with the solutions of such sets of equations in the program Multiple Regression Analysis: Subprogram Regression, which appears on pages 320–367. Small predictor sets can be handled conveniently by an iterative procedure that is described in Appendix C of this book. This is a convenient procedure if no computer or programmable calculator is readily available.

At this point we can appropriately ask how good the prediction is that is obtained from the team of predictor variables. What is the size of our errors of prediction? In the case of a single predictor variable, the variance of errors of prediction is equal to

$$s_e^2 = s_c^2 (1 - r_{ct}^2)$$

or

$$r_{ct}^2 = 1 - \frac{s_e^2}{s_c^2}$$

Similarly,

$$R_{c(t_1, t_2, \ldots, t_m)}^2 = 1 - \frac{s_e^2}{s_c^2} \qquad (9.2)$$

where $R_{c(t_1, t_2, \ldots, t_m)}$ is the multiple correlation (that is, the correlation of the criterion with the weighted composite of the test scores) and $e = (x_c = \tilde{x}_c)$ is the discrepancy between actual criterion score and criterion score predicted from the weighted composite.

The formula for computing the multiple correlation is

$$R_{c(t_1, t_2, \ldots, t_m)}^2 = \sum_{i=1}^{m} \beta_i r_{ic} \qquad (9.3)$$

The squared multiple correlation corresponds exactly to the proportion of the variance in the criterion score that is predictable from the team of predictors. It is worth noting that the multiple correlation is nothing more than the simple correlation between the criterion score and the score that is obtained by combining the predictors with the specified weights.

Some of the properties of regression weights and multiple correlations can be illustrated by a small example. The example shows the correlations of a verbal, a quantitative, and a spatial ability test with each other and with a measure of academic performance, grade point average, as follows:

	VERBAL	QUANTI-TATIVE	SPATIAL	GPA
Verbal	1.00	.71	.64	.55
Quantitative	.71	1.00	.58	.49
Spatial	.64	.58	1.00	.44

Note that in this illustrative example, as is often the case, the predictor tests correlate substantially with each other. This limits the prediction that can be achieved with the team, because the variance in individual GPA that is accounted for by each test is in considerable part the same variance that is accounted for by the others.

In this example, the beta weights of the three predictors are $\beta_1 = 0.36$, $\beta_2 = 0.17$, and $\beta_3 = 0.11$, respectively. That is,

$$\tilde{z}_c = 0.36z_V + 0.17z_Q + 0.11z_S$$

Note that the weights vary substantially more than the original validity coefficients. Because of their overlap, the most valid test absorbs much of the prediction that would have been possible from the others, which then have relatively little to add.

The squared multiple correlation is equal to

$$R^2 = (.36)(.55) + (.22)(.49) + (.11)(.44) = .330$$

Thus 33% of the variance in the criterion measure can be predicted by the team of three predictors. This can be compared with $(.55)(.55) = .3025$, which is the proportion predicted by the one best predictor. Adding the other two predictors adds only a further 2.75% to the predictable criterion variance.

It is instructive to see what happens to the regression weights and multiple correlation if the correlations among the predictors are lower. Suppose that each of the three correlations among predictors were lower by .10.

	VERBAL	QUANTI-TATIVE	SPATIAL	GPA	BETA
Verbal	1.00	.61	.54	.55	.34
Quantitative	.61	1.00	.48	.49	.20
Spatial	.54	.48	1.00	.44	.16
				$R^2 =$	.355

The weights and squared multiple correlation are shown in the last column. Note, in the first place, that the squared multiple correlation has increased from .330 to .355. With the lower overlap among the predictors, the same validity coefficients account for another 2.5% of the criterion variance. In the second place, the three regression weights have become more nearly equal. The most valid test robs less of the predictive power from the tests with lower validity.

In the unlikely event that the correlations among the predictors had been zero, the regression weight of each would have been identical to its validity, and the squared multiple correlation would have been

$$(.55)^2 + (.49)^2 + (.44)^2 = .736$$

or more than double what it was with the given correlations. This illustrates the very large role that predictor intercorrelations play in any prediction undertaking and the great importance of trying to identify relatively different and independent measures to put together in a team of predictors.

Frequently, a battery including a fairly large number of predictors may be tried out when one is attempting to predict a criterion score, and many of the predictors may add very little to the prediction.* Below, as an illustration, we show correlations among six factor scores from the U.S.E.S. General Aptitude Test Battery and the correlation of each with a criterion measure of grades in dental assistant training. The regression weights for the six predictors are in the column at the far right. (Decimal points have been omitted from the table.)

	1.	2.	3.	4.	5.	6.	GRADES	BETAS
1. Verbal	100	42	40	34	29	−03	32	08
2. Quantitative	42	100	34	42	42	−03	40	28
3. Spatial	40	34	100	48	26	01	51	45
4. Form perception	34	42	48	100	66	27	28	−16
5. Clerical perception	29	42	26	66	100	20	22	02
6. Finger dexterity	−03	−03	01	27	20	100	21	25

Note first that "form perception," in spite of its positive correlation with the criterion, appears in the regression equation with a negative weight. This is due to its substantial correlation with other more valid measures, especially the spatial factor. "Form perception" functions here as what is sometimes called a *suppressor variable*. It appears to measure something common to the first three variables that is *not* related to the criterion, and its negative weight serves to partial out some of this nonvalid variance. However, negative weights must be viewed with some skepticism. Often they fail to hold up in new samples of cases.

Note second that "clerical perception" receives a very small weight—so small that it is probably not significantly different from zero. The squared multiple for all six variables is .3814 ($R = .616$), and the squared multiple for the five variables (omitting clerical perception) is .3811. To three decimal places, the sixth variable has contributed nothing to the prediction.

Because it is possible to drop one predictor with no apparent loss in the predictive effectiveness of the battery, we are led to ask what would happen if we dropped still more of the variables in the set. How much of the battery would be

---

* In the limit, a predictor may get a zero regression weight and make no addition at all.

worth keeping for further use? The usual approach to answering this question has been called *stepwise regression*. This procedure starts with the one best predictor and partials out the effect of this variable from the column of validity coefficients and the matrix of predictor intercorrelations. An examination of the partial validity coefficients, in relation to the partial variances in the diagonal terms, identifies the variable that will add the most to the already predicted variance, and appropriate weights are determined for this variable together with the initial variable. The multiple correlation is computed for the pair of variables. We then repeat the process, looking for the third variable that will add the most to the first two, and so on until either all the variables have been added or the next variable adds too little, by some criterion, to make it worth continuing. The result for this process for our illustrative example is as follows:

ORDER OF ENTRY	REGRESSION WEIGHTS AND MULTIPLE CORRELATIONS BY NUMBER OF VARIABLES				
	2	3	4	5	6
3. Spatial	.42	.42	.47	.45	.45
2. Quantitative	.26	.26	.31	.28	.28
6. Finger dexterity		.21	.26	.26	.25
4. Form perception			−.15	−.15	−.16
1. Verbal				.08	.08
5. Clerical perception					.02
R^2	.318	.364	.377	.381	.3815
Multiple correlation	.564	.604	.614	.6173	.6176

One basis for deciding whether to add an additional variable is to check on whether the beta weight for that variable is significantly greater than zero. This can be done by comparing the multiple correlation when the predictor in question is added with the multiple correlation without that predictor. The significance test takes the form of an *F*-test, in which

$$F = \frac{R^2_{inc} - R^2_{rem}}{(1 - R^2_{rem})/(N - k - 1)} \tag{9.4}$$

where R^2_{inc} = multiple correlation including the variable in question
R^2_{rem} = multiple correlation based on the remaining variables
k = number of remaining variables
N = number of cases in the sample

Degrees of freedom for the *F*-ratio are 1 and $N - k - 1$.

In our illustrative example, let us assume that the data were based on a sample of 50 cases. Then for variable 5, "clerical perception," we have

$$F = \frac{.3815 - .3811}{(.6189)/44} = \frac{.0004}{.0141} = .028$$

The increment is obviously not significant, and by extension neither is the regression coefficient that produced it.

Checking the increment for variable 1, "verbal," we have

$$F = \frac{.381 - .377}{(.623)/45} = \frac{.004}{(.623)/45} = .29$$

still not a significant increase, and hence not a significant regression weight. If, however, we had been working with a sample of 500, we would have had

$$F = \frac{.004}{(.623)/495} = 3.17$$

a value that, for degrees of freedom $= 1,495$, is clearly significant.

Library programs for stepwise regression are available in most computer centers. The SPSS program, a representative one, will, at each stage, (1) check the significance level of the beta weight for each variable, (2) if any variable now in the predictor set has an F-ratio lower than some predetermined critical value, drop the variable in the set with the lowest F-ratio, (3) check whether any variable *not* now in the set comes up to some specified F-ratio and, if so, add the one with the largest F-ratio, and (4) if no variable meets either the criterion for deletion or the criterion for addition to the set, terminate the program. It will occasionally happen that a variable that looked promising early in the stepwise solution loses its effectiveness as more variables are added, because it overlaps in part each of the added variables. The computer program makes it possible to reverse an earlier decision and drop out a variable that has lost much of its unique predictive value.

SHRINKAGE, CROSS-VALIDATION, AND POPULATION WEIGHTS

A multiple regression solution based on a sample of cases exploits the idiosyncrasy of that particular sample of cases. The sample validity coefficients differ by varying (and unknown) amounts from their true population values. Variables for which the sample value exceeds the population value tend to be overweighted, and those with sample values below the population value tend to be underweighted so far as prediction of new cases is concerned. The sample weights differ from the population regression weights, so the correlation resulting from the application of sample weights tends to be less in the population than in the sample on which they were derived. The effect of sample idiosyncrasy is more pronounced when (1) the sample is small and (2) the number of predictors is large. This becomes evident as one looks at the significance test to test whether the sample multiple correlation might have arisen from a population in which the multiple correlation was zero. The test is an F-test, where

$$F = \frac{R^2}{1 - R^2} \frac{N - p - 1}{p} \tag{9.5}$$

and there are p and $N - p - 1$ degrees of freedom. In this expression, p is the number of predictors and N is the number of cases. It is instructive to observe what size the multiple correlation must display if it is to differ significantly from zero at the .05 level for different sample sizes and different numbers of predictors. Selected values are shown in the following table.

NUMBER OF PREDICTORS	SAMPLE SIZE				
	25	50	100	200	400
2	.486	.345	.245	.173	.122
5	.644	.464	.331	.235	.166
10	.806	.579	.419	.299	.213
20	.983	.744	.545	.391	.278

One step that is often informative is to hold out part of one's available sample of cases, to calculate validities, intercorrelations, and regression weights on the balance of the sample, and to apply the resulting regression equation to the hold-out group to see what level of validity is obtained for those cases that were not used in determining the regression equation. This procedure is called *cross-validation* and is recommended whenever one wants an unbiased estimate of the validity of a predictor battery.

An elaboration of the cross-validation model, designated *double cross-validation*, proceeds by splitting the original sample into random halves, which we may designate A and B. A regression equation is determined on sample A and then applied to sample B, while one determined on sample B is applied to sample A. The average of the two resulting multiple correlations provides an estimate of the validity in the population of a prediction equation derived from samples of the size of A and B. As a final step, it would seem desirable to determine a new regression equation based on the total sample, A + B. This could be expected to show validity in new samples *from the same population* at least as high as, and probably a bit higher than, the average cross-validational validities based on the smaller split samples.

With current computer facilities, a further refinement of cross-validation procedure, sometimes called *jack-knifing*, is possible. This procedure calls for a computer program that computes validity coefficients, intercorrelations, and regression coefficients on all cases except one. The criterion score is predicted for that one case, and the error of prediction is recorded. The procedure is repeated as many times as there are cases, getting an error of estimate for each case. The average of squared errors of estimate provides an unbiased value for the variance of estimate, and subtracting this value from the total observed criterion variance gives an estimate of the squared multiple correlation. This procedure is particularly appropriate when the sample is relatively small, and it is important to use all of the available data to estimate regression weights.

Basing regression weights on the specific sample of cases tends to produce predicted criterion scores that are less than optimal when applied to new samples. Persons with extreme scores on overweighted variables tend to receive predicted criterion scores that are more extreme than their expected population values, as do persons extremely high (or extremely low) on most or all of the weighted variables. A good deal of thought has been devoted in recent years to appropriate ways to temper regression estimates so as to minimize the discrepancies between estimated and actual criterion scores in the population (as distinct from the sample on which the weights were determined). Several possibilities are discussed by Darlington (1978).

One procedure simply reduces all the validity coefficients by a constant factor. This has the effect of reducing each regression weight by the same factor and moving each estimated criterion score back toward the population mean of criterion scores by that factor. The "shrinkage" factor depends on the size of the sample, the number of predictors, and the size of the multiple correlation. The factor that has been proposed (Stein, 1960) is

$$S = \frac{p - 2}{N - p + 2} \cdot \frac{1 - R^2}{R^2} \tag{9.6}$$

where p = number of predictors
          N = number of cases in the sample
          R = obtained multiple correlation

Thus, if the correlations in our illustrative example on page 250 had been based on 50 cases, so that $p = 6$, $N = 50$, and $R = .616$, we would have

$$S = \frac{4}{46} \cdot \frac{.621}{.379} = .142$$

All regression weights would be multiplied by $1 - .142 = .858$. Applying such a factor to the weights has the effect of regressing all predicted criterion scores back toward the mean of the group by this same proportion. Note that the "shrinkage" becomes greater when (1) the number of cases is small, (2) the number of predictors is large, and (3) the multiple correlation is small.

If one has some substantial basis for making a *priori* estimates of the regression weights (as from previous studies with a similar criterion variable and similar tests), one can refine this procedure by regressing each of the weights toward the a *priori* value rather than toward zero. The procedure is to use the a *priori* weights to get an estimated criterion score for each individual in the original sample of cases. One then calculates the discrepancy between the estimated and the actual criterion scores. This discrepancy value becomes the new criterion score to be predicted. Regression weights are determined for each predictor variable as a predictor of this discrepancy score. The regression of each variable as a predictor of the residual is multiplied by the appropriate shrinkage factor, determined by equation 9.6, and this "shrunken" adjustment is added to the original *a priori* weight for that variable. When the *a priori* estimates are good, there will be little basis for predicting the discrepancies; R^2 will be small; S will be relatively large, so the shrinkage on the adjustments to the *a priori* weights will be large; and adjustments to those weights will be minor. If the *a priori* weights are likely to be little if any better than chance, it is advisable not to use this procedure.

A third possibility is to replace the single test scores by their successive principal components (see the section beginning on page 277; and especially page 284) and to use some small number of component scores as predictors. The rationale for doing this is the belief that most of what is stable and meaningful in the typical set of predictor variables can be represented by a small number of independent dimensions and that the composite scores representing these dimensions, based as these composites are on all the tests in the battery, are less subject to fluctuations in validity from sample to sample than the scores for single tests. By their very nature, component scores have zero correlations with each other, so the regression weight for any component score is its zero-order correlation with the criterion score. One anticipates that most of the validity will be concentrated in the first few principal components, so that only the weights for these will need to be used.

A fourth alternative, also based on component scores and called *ridge regression*, applies a shrinkage factor to the component regression weights. This factor is a function of the correlation of that component with the criterion variable. The shrinkage factor takes the form

$$\frac{1}{1 + k/\lambda_j}$$

where λ is the eigenvalue of component j and k is constant for all components and depends on p, N, and R^2. Computationally, ridge regression is equivalent to multiplying all the intercorrelations and validity coefficients by $1/(1 + k)$ and then solving the set of linear equations based on these new correlations. The problem is to choose an appropriate value of k, and no definitive answer for this problem appears to be at hand.

NONLINEAR EXPRESSIONS

If one feels that a simple linear combination of predictors does not adequately express the predictive potential that resides in a set of predictor variables, it is always possible to add to the predictor set more complex functions of the separate variables. Thus one could generate variables that were higher powers of the original variables. Or one could generate variables that represented products of two or more variables or products of powers of two or more variables. These new variables could be added to the set of predictors, and the augmented set could be analyzed to determine whether the addition of these more complex functions did in fact significantly improve prediction. Our suggestion would be to work with the residuals from the simple linear prediction and see whether the more complex functions correlated with those residuals at a level significantly different from zero.

There is, unfortunately, no limit to the number of more complex functions of predictor variables that can be dreamed up, and shrinkage from sample to population in an extended set of such variables is likely to be very large. Consequently, analysis of more complex functions should probably be undertaken (1) only when there is a good *a priori* reason to expect some specific complex function or functions to be useful predictors, (2) only for those selected functions, and (3) only when N is large.

LOSS FROM APPROXIMATE WEIGHTS

Exact regression weights represent the mathematically elegant way to combine information from a set of predictor variables in the prediction of a criterion score. However, one may ask how much actual gain in predictive effectiveness results from this elegance—even in the original sample of cases. We have already seen the need to temper those sample weights in order to optimize prediction for new cases drawn from the basic population. Some sense of the magnitude of gain can be obtained by comparing the multiple correlation from the best two-digit weights with those resulting when the weights are rounded to a single digit and with those resulting when the weights are made all equal. The comparisons for our two illustrative examples follow.

THREE-VARIABLE ILLUSTRATION	R
Two-digit weights: $V = .36$, $Q = .22$, $S = .11$	.5745
One-digit weights: $V = .4$, $Q = .2$, $S = .1$	.5738
Equal weights: $V = 1$, $Q = 1$, $S = 1$	.5651
SIX-VARIABLE ILLUSTRATION	
Two-digit weights: .08, .28, .45, $-.16$, .02, .25	.6176
One-digit weights: .1, .3, .4, $-.2$, .0, .2	.6111
Equal weights: all $= 1$	.5026

We see that the drop in multiple correlation occasioned by shifting from two-digit to single-digit weights appears only in the third decimal place. This difference can be considered to be of no practical significance, especially when the weights are to be applied to some new sample other than the one on which they were established. The effect of going to equal weights is greater and rather different in the two illustrations. In the first example, in which the three tests did not differ greatly in validity and all received positive weights, the effect is still small. In the second example, in which the range of validities was greater and one test received a substantial negative weight, the drop is considerably greater. Even here, however, the equally weighted sum of the various tests is still approximately as valid as the best single test.

SELECTION OF ITEMS TO MAXIMIZE VALIDITY

Sometimes one has a varied pool of items, each of which has been separately validated against some outside criterion, and one wishes to determine which items to retain in a score that is to predict that criterion. The problem is analogous to that of stepwise regression, with single items taking the place of complete tests. However, an additional difference is that simplicity of procedure leads one to plan to use uniform unit weights for each item. With adequate computer facilities, a procedure that closely resembles stepwise regression can be applied.

The initial analysis will be to compute the complete interitem covariance and correlation matrices and the vector of item-versus-criterion covariances and correlations. (Interitem correlations will be phi-coefficients, and item-versus-criterion correlations will ordinarily be point-biserial correlations.) A prudent first step before carrying out any further analyses will be to examine the complete vector of item validity coefficients to determine whether the distribution of values differs significantly from what might be expected to have arisen by chance sampling variations in a population in which all the true correlations are zero. One possibility would be to apply a chi-square test to the complete set of item validities. If the distribution of values does not differ significantly from that to be expected from chance sampling in a population for which the values are zero, and especially if there is a negligible surplus of large correlations, then it seems unlikely that the validity of any selection of items would hold up in a new sample.

Another somewhat more laborious, but perhaps more definitive, procedure would be to split the sample into two halves, obtain item validities from each half, and find the correlation between the two sets of validity coefficients. If the correlation is very low and not significantly different from zero, and if the mean value of the correlations in each half centers around zero, there would seem to be little profit in proceeding further.

If the deviations from a chance distribution *are* significant, it is appropriate to continue with the analysis. The sequence of steps, which is analogous to stepwise regression, is as follows:

1. Pick the item that has the largest correlation (positive or negative) with the criterion. We will refer to this item as X_1.

2. Compute partial correlations of the remaining items with the criterion, C, holding X_1 constant.

3. Locate the item with the largest partial correlation. Call this X_2. This will be added with unit weight to X_1. For any item that shows a negative correlation with the criterion, the weight will be -1, in effect reversing the direction of the item.

4. Compute the correlation with the criterion, C, of the sum $X_1 + X_2$. In terms of item covariances, this is given by

$$r_{(1\,+\,2)c} = \cfrac{C_{1c} + C_{2c}}{\sqrt{\begin{vmatrix} C_{11} & C_{12} \\ C_{21} & C_{22} \end{vmatrix} \cdot s_c^2}}$$

Continue only if $r_{(1+2)c} > r_{1c}$

5. Compute the correlations of the remaining items with $X_1 + X_2$. For item i, this is given by

$$r_{(1\,+\,2)i} = \cfrac{C_{1i} + C_{2i}}{\sqrt{\begin{vmatrix} C_{11} & C_{12} \\ C_{21} & C_{22} \end{vmatrix} \cdot s_i^2}}$$

6. Compute partial correlations of the remaining items with the criterion variable C, partialing out the "test," $t = X_1 + X_2$.

7. Repeat steps 3 through 6, adding a third item, X_3.

8. Continue additional cycles until r_{tc} no longer increases, or starts to decline.

9. It will be prudent to hold out some fraction of the available cases to use as an independent sample for cross-validation. As items are added, the validity of the "test" should be checked in the cross-validation sample. The test length should presumably be that which maximizes validity in the cross-validation sample.

EFFECTS OF CURTAILMENT ON MULTIPLE MEASURES

In Chapter 7 we explored the effect of curtailment on some one variable upon the correlations among variables. The curtailment effects are especially important for multiple regression problems because these effects can severely distort the pattern of regression weights. If values obtained from a curtailed group are used, those variables most severely affected by curtailment tend to be underweighted in the prediction equation, often by a substantial amount. Therefore, to the extent that it is practical, all validity coefficients and intercorrelations should be corrected for curtailment before a regression analysis is carried out. One should attempt to achieve estimates of the correlations that would prevail in the complete applicant group from which selection decisions will be made.

Formulas appropriate for use when curtailment has taken place with respect to a single variable were presented in Chapter 7. It is also possible that curtailment may have taken place on two or more variables, each having been considered without regard to the other. Thus an employer might have set minimum qualifying scores both on an ability test and on a rating by an employment interviewer. Applicants might be employed only if they reached a qualifying score on both of these hurdles, and they might be uniformly offered employment if they did reach qualifying scores. The personnel psychologist might wish to determine the optimum weights for these two and for several research tests, and he or she would need estimates of validities and intercorrelations in the applicant population.

The formulas given in Chapter 7 can be generalized to multiple curtailment, maintaining the same basic assumptions:

1. The regression slopes for the directly curtailed variables are the same in the curtailed and the uncurtailed groups.

2. The error in predicting any of the *indirectly* curtailed variables from those that were directly curtailed is the same in the curtailed and the uncurtailed groups.

The formulas needed to deal with multidimensional curtailment can be conveniently expressed only as matrix equations. In the equations that follow, a lower case letter refers to data from the curtailed group and a capital letter to data from the complete uncurtailed group. The directly curtailed variables are denoted by X and the indirectly curtailed variables by Y. As information available to us, we have

c_{xx} = matrix of covariances of x variables in the curtailed group

C_{XX} = matrix of covariances of X variables in the complete uncurtailed group

c_{xy} = matrix of covariances between x and y variables in the curtailed group

c_{yy} = matrix of covariances of y variables in the curtailed group

Our problem is to estimate C_{XY} and C_{YY}, the covariance matrices involving the indirectly curtailed variables for the complete uncurtailed group.

The weights for predicting y variables from x variables in the curtailed group are given by the matrix equation

$$w_{xy} = c_{xx}^{-1} c_{xy} \qquad (9.7)$$

where w_{xy} = matrix of regression weights

c_{xx}^{-1} = inverse of the covariance matrix of x variables

c_{xy} = matrix of covariances of x with y variables

For the uncurtailed group, the covariances of X with Y variables are given by

$$C_{XY} = C_{XX}w_{xy} \qquad (9.8)$$

That is, the matrix of covariances of X with Y variables in the complete uncurtailed group is found by multiplying the covariance matrix of X by the matrix of weights for estimating y variables from x variables. For the uncurtailed group, the covariances among Y variables are given by

$$C_{YY} = c_{yy} + w'_{yx}(C_{XY} - c_{xy}) \qquad (9.9)$$

That is, the covariance matrix of Y variables in the complete uncurtailed group is found by adding to the covariance matrix in the curtailed group an amount obtained by premultiplying a difference matrix obtained for the xy covariances by the transpose of the matrix of the weights for predicting y from x.

Once all the covariances (including the variances as diagonal terms) have been obtained for the complete uncurtailed group, the table of correlations can be computed and regression weights determined.

In the small illustrative example that follows, data were available for two variables in both the complete and the curtailed groups. For another set of three variables, data were on hand only for the curtailed group. The correlation matrix and standard deviations in the curtailed group were

	1	2	3	4	5	S.D.
1	1.00	.74	.52	.30	.49	1.58
2		1.00	.50	.46	.49	1.37
3			1.00	.59	.66	2.32
4				1.00	.69	2.14
5					1.00	1.42

For variables 1 and 2 in the uncurtailed group, the values were

	1	2	S.D.
1	1.00	.90	1.91
2		1.00	1.90

The corresponding covariance matrices become

		1	2	3	4	5	
C_{xx}	1	2.51	1.60	1.92	1.00	1.10	c_{xy}
	2		1.88	1.61	1.34	0.96	
	3			5.40	2.94	2.17	
	4				4.56	2.10	c_{yy}
	5					2.01	

and

$$
\begin{array}{c|cc}
 & 1 & 2 \\
\hline
1 & \underline{3.65} & 2.92 \\
2 & & \underline{3.61}
\end{array} \; C_{XX}
$$

The variances, which appear in the diagonal cells, have been underlined.

Applying one of the standard procedures for calculating the inverse of a matrix, we get

$$
c_{xx}^{-1} = \begin{vmatrix} 0.88 & -0.75 \\ -0.75 & 1.17 \end{vmatrix}
$$

and the product

$$
\begin{vmatrix} 0.88 & -0.75 \\ -0.75 & 1.17 \end{vmatrix} \cdot \begin{vmatrix} 1.92 & 1.00 & 1.10 \\ 1.61 & 1.34 & 0.96 \end{vmatrix}
$$

gives

$$
w_{xy} = \begin{vmatrix} 0.48 & -0.13 & 0.24 \\ 0.44 & 0.81 & 0.30 \end{vmatrix}
$$

Then

$$
\begin{vmatrix} 3.65 & 2.92 \\ 2.92 & 3.61 \end{vmatrix} \cdot \begin{vmatrix} 0.48 & -0.13 & 0.24 \\ 0.44 & 0.81 & 0.30 \end{vmatrix} = \begin{vmatrix} 3.05 & 1.90 & 1.77 \\ 3.00 & 2.56 & 1.80 \end{vmatrix} = C_{XY}
$$

Next, $C_{XY} - c_{xy}$ becomes

$$
\begin{vmatrix} (3.05 - 1.92) & (1.90 - 1.00) & (1.77 - 1.10) \\ (3.00 - 1.61) & (2.56 - 1.34) & (1.80 - 0.96) \end{vmatrix}
$$

and $w_{xy}'(C_{XY} - c_{xy})$ is

$$
\begin{vmatrix} 0.48 & 0.44 \\ -0.13 & 0.81 \\ 0.24 & 0.30 \end{vmatrix} \cdot \begin{vmatrix} 1.13 & 0.90 & 0.67 \\ 1.39 & 1.22 & 0.84 \end{vmatrix}
$$

which equals

$$
\begin{vmatrix} 1.16 & 0.98 & 0.07 \\ 0.98 & 0.88 & 0.60 \\ 0.70 & 0.60 & 0.42 \end{vmatrix}
$$

Finally, adding this to c_{yy} gives

$$
\begin{vmatrix} \underline{6.56} & 3.92 & 2.87 \\ & \underline{5.44} & 2.70 \\ & & \underline{2.45} \end{vmatrix} = C_{YY}
$$

Putting the pieces of our matrix together, we have, as the covariance matrix for the complete uncurtailed group,

	1	2	3	4	5
1	3.65	2.92	3.05	1.90	1.77
2		3.61	3.00	2.56	1.80
3			6.56	3.92	2.87
4				5.44	2.70
5					2.45

Converting back from a covariance to a correlation matrix, we have, as estimates of the values in the uncurtailed group,

	1	2	3	4	5	S.D.
1	1.00	.90	.62	.43	.59	1.91
2		1.00	.62	.58	.61	1.90
3			1.00	.66	.72	2.56
4				1.00	.74	2.33
5					1.00	1.57

ALTERNATIVES TO MULTIPLE REGRESSION

Various alternatives have been proposed to additive linear combination of scores from a set of predictor variables. We shall give some consideration to three: (1) multiple cutoffs, (2) unique patterns, and (3) combination by clinical judgment. In addition, we shall comment briefly on the concept of the moderator variable.

MULTIPLE CUTOFFS

With this procedure, minimum qualifying scores are set for *each* of the predictors, and any candidate who surpasses *all* the specified minima is accepted. Because one usually has a quota of positions to be filled, one cannot set unrealistically high standards, and any increase in the minimum score to qualify on one predictor must be balanced by a reduction in the qualifying score on some other. The problem may be expressed: How shall we set the qualifying scores on predictors X_1, X_2, . . . X_k under the condition that P percent of applicants will be qualified, so that the maximum proportion of those who qualify will be successful on the criterion (or so that the average level on the criterion of those who qualify will be a maximum).

In general, there is no analytic mathematical solution to this problem. This is true particularly for those conditions in which a multiple cutoff procedure is likely to yield superior results—conditions of sharply nonlinear relationships between the criterion and one or more predictor variables. Thus determination of the optimal combination of cutting scores is a trial-and-error proposition in which various combinations are tried, the yield of qualified candidates from each combination is calculated, and the proportion (or level) of success among those who qualify is determined. The set of cutting scores will have been manipulated to maximize success in the analyzed sample of cases, so verification in a new sample is required if one is to have an unbiased estimate of the effectiveness of the procedure.

A simple diagram helps make explicit the manner and extent to which multiple cutoffs differ from multiple regression. The illustration for two predictors is shown in Figure 9.1. Separate cutting scores are shown for variables X_1 and X_2. Persons qualifying by multiple cutoff are those in the upper right-hand quadrant, above both lines. The diagonal line represents the linear combination of X_1 and X_2 specified by the multiple regression equation. Persons above and to the right of this line would be qualified by the multiple regression procedure. (The line would be so placed as to qualify the same proportion of candidates as were qualified by the cutoffs.) Persons falling in the horizontally hatched region would be qualified on the basis of the two cutoffs but would fail to qualify by multiple regression. Persons in the vertically hatched areas would qualify by multiple regression but would be rejected on the basis of one or the other of the two cutoffs.

We see from the diagram that, for most persons, the verdict will be the same by both procedures. They will be rejected by both or accepted by both. Those for whom the decision differs tend to be marginal cases, close to the threshold of decision by both procedures. Multiple regression will accept persons who are exceptionally high on one predictor but slightly below the cutoff on the other. The implication is that exceptional capability in one respect can compensate for some deficiency in the other. By contrast, the multiple cutoff procedure would be logically appropriate when, below a certain level on trait X_1, no amount of some other ability could compensate for that lack. Thus we might conceive that there is some minimum level of visual acuity that is necessary for an automobile driver, and that no amount of manual dexterity or of planning and foresight can take its place. In the extreme (and somewhat trivial) case, we would probably agree that a blind person could not drive safely, no matter what other exceptional capabilities that person might have. Whether the conclusion holds for some lesser degree of visual defect is, of course, more debatable.

The existence of a sharply nonlinear relationship between score on some measure and success on a criterion variable assumes a highly reliable measure. If the reliability is only moderate, so that a good deal of score variance is contributed by measurement error, any nonlinearity that might exist between true criterion score and true score on the underlying attribute will be badly blurred. It will then be difficult to justify any specific level of test score as essential for satisfactory criterion performance.

Certain practical circumstances can argue in favor of separate cutting scores on separate predictor variables. One of these is marked difference between the cost of applying the several measures. If one predictor is simple and inexpensive to apply, whereas the other is complex and costly, practical considerations might dictate that a preliminary screening be done on the inexpensive measure, so that

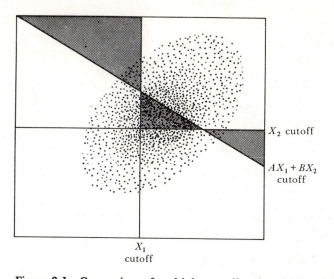

X_2 cutoff

$AX_1 + BX_2$
cutoff

X_1
cutoff

Figure **9.1** Comparison of multiple cut-off and multiple regression procedures.

the costly one would have to be applied only to a reduced sample of candidates. Thus a college that considered it necessary to interview any applicant before the candidate was accepted might plausibly exclude, on the basis of a scholastic aptitude test, some substantial percentage of the lowest-scoring candidates and then interview only the remainder. Applying cuts sequentially does not in any way alter their effect.

Another practical consideration that might favor successive cutoffs is simplicity of application of the procedure by personnel with limited training and sophistication. It is relatively simple to instruct a clerk: Accept only applicants with scores above A on Test X_1 *and* above B on Test X_2. Generally speaking, using multiple cutoffs is likely to be justified more on practical grounds than on any demonstration of improved prediction efficiency.

Multiple cutoff procedures have a number of very real limitations. Manipulating qualifying scores in such a way as to maximize validity and still maintain a given yield of qualifying applicants becomes extremely cumbersome when the number of predictors exceeds two or three. There are just too many interacting components to be adjusted. Again, applying multiple cutoffs serves merely to categorize applicants as qualified or not qualified. The procedure yields no quantitative estimate of level of promise and hence no basis for selecting the best from among those qualified. If the supply of good applicants exceeds the number of positions to be filled, use of predicted criterion scores based on multiple regression makes it simple to select those with the highest predicted criterion scores, and hence the greatest promise, but no comparable index results from the application of multiple cutoffs. It is not easy to adapt the cutting scores in an efficient way to changed supply–demand conditions.

UNIQUE PATTERNS

Some clinically minded test users like to contend that it is the pattern of test scores, rather than any one mechanical combination of them, that provides the most powerful information about an individual's probable success in training, in therapeutic treatment, or on the job. This position is, in a sense, an extension of the notion of multiple cutting scores and a further rejection of the mechanical combining of test scores via a regression equation.

Before it is possible to test out this position, it is necessary to be somewhat clearer about what is meant by a unique pattern. For the proposition to be testable, the patterns must be objectively definable and of a manageable number. If patterns are truly "unique," in that a given pattern never recurs, no research on patterns is possible. It is possible to define patterns in terms of score ranges on each of two or more predictors. Thus, if we had 2 predictors, each divided into thirds, it would be possible to encounter any of the 9 patterns shown below.

		X_2		
		Low	Medium	High
	High	H_1L_2	H_1M_2	H_1H_2
X_1	Medium	M_1L_2	M_1M_2	M_1H_2
	Low	L_1L_2	L_1M_2	L_1H_2

The 9 cells in this diagram define 9 patterns. With 3 variables and 3 levels, there could be 27 patterns, such as $L_1M_2H_3$, and with 4 variables there could be 81. Some such objective definition of patterns is essential if they are to be subjected to study.

It is immediately apparent that the number of patterns increases rapidly and soon reaches unmanageable proportions as either the number of predictors or the number of levels that are identified for each is increased. If stanine scores (1 to 9) were used for only 3 predictor variables, we would have 729 possible patterns. In order to get stable estimates of average criterion score (or percent passing) for each cell, where each cell was considered to be a different pattern, one would require a sample of thousands of cases. It is therefore no wonder that there has been little definitive work on the effectiveness of unique patterns as predictors of criterion scores.

One study by Tucker (1950), based on Air Force data from shortly after World War II, illustrates the form the analysis must take and the type of results that might be anticipated. Two analyses were carried out, one of pilots in primary training and one of students in clerk–typist school. The criterion in the first case was graduation versus elimination from the training program; in the second case, it was final training school grade. In each case, weights to be used were determined on an initial sample, and the effectiveness of those weights was judged in a cross-validation sample. For the unique pattern approach, various numbers of patterns were established by dividing the score range of each predictor into 2, 3, 4, or 9 levels and considering all possible combinations of levels. The score value assigned to each cell as a prediction of criterion performance was the actual performance of cases in that cell in the initial sample—the percent passing in the case of pilots and the mean final grade in the case of clerk-typists. In the case of pilots there was, in addition to test scores, a three-category measure of previous flying experience. Sample sizes were as follows:

	ORIGINAL	CROSS-VALIDATION
Total pilot group	1001	569
Pilots — no flying experience	648	385
Clerk-typists	804	400

Correlations between predicted outcome and actual outcome in the cross-validation sample are shown below

	TOTAL PILOT GROUP			
	9 levels	4 levels	3 levels	Regression
2 tests	.364	.415	.415	.435
1 test + PFE	.407	.421	.426	.429
3 tests		.390	.391	.460
2 tests + PFE		.472	.453	.466
3 tests + PFE			.485	.475
4 tests			.508	.496
	PILOT GROUP — NO PREVIOUS FLYING			
2 tests	.272	.324	.317	.359
3 tests		.296	.293	.365
4 tests			.422	.406
	CLERK–TYPIST GROUP			
	4 levels	3 levels	2 levels	Regression
3 tests	.551	.563	.538	.610
4 tests		.552	.573	.644
5 tests			.602	.659
6 tests			.590	.658

These tables have a number of interesting features. In the first place, for a given number of predictor variables, combining test scores by linear regression was almost universally better than *any* procedure based on assigning predicted scores to each separate cell. In the second place, a fairly fine subdivision that resulted in 64 or 81 cells was generally less valid in the cross-validation sample than a somewhat coarser division. Finally, quite a crude division on 3 or 4 predictor variables, into no more than 2 or 3 score levels, permitted predictions almost as valid as those that were possible with any finer division.

Of course, even with a sample of 1000 cases, the cell frequencies become quite small when one uses several predictors and several levels of each, so that cell means become erratic and validity shrinks markedly on cross-validation. This is part of the basic reality of any procedure that tries to weight separately each unique combination of scores.

CLINICAL VERSUS ACTUARIAL COMBINATION OF DATA

The unique-pattern approach described in the previous section still falls somewhat short of satisfying the conviction of the clinically oriented person that there is something that the skills of the trained clinician* can do that cannot be reduced to any form of stereotyped actuarial procedure. We must inquire what this might be and what the evidence is for its effectiveness. We can entertain three somewhat different possibilities.

1. The clinician might make an effort to take the standard items of information that are available for each candidate and to weight them more judiciously for the individual case than can be done by actuarial use of a standard procedure— regression equation, multiple cutoff, or unique-pattern score. It is hard to provide any convincing rationale why this should be the case, and the weight of evidence that has accumulated from studies in which clinical combination has been compared with actuarial combination (Meehl, 1954; Sawyer, 1966) is that it does not occur.

2. The clinician might be able to assimilate and react to nonstandard items that appear only occasionally in the records of candidates or that appear in such varied form that no standard quantitative treatment of them seems possible. It is likely that, in some situations at least, such nonstandard idiosyncratic information might permit judgments that have some (and perhaps substantial) validity. The question then becomes how this information should be combined with standard information (as from a test or tests) uniformly available for all candidates.

Because the evidence suggests that the human brain is less efficient than a computer-based regression equation in using standard information, it seems

---

* The term *clinician* is used here quite broadly to refer to anyone whose special training or experience might lead one to expect that person to be qualified to judge the suitability of a candidate for a job or that of a patient for a treatment.

reasonable that the clinical judgment be kept as a separate datum. Then the composite prediction from a regression equation and the prediction made by the clinician from nonstandard items of information could be thought of as two distinct data sets. The weights appropriate for combining these could be empirically determined, and the two could finally be combined with optimal weights. Such a procedure implies that clinicians can be treated as interchangeable and that the weight should be equal for each clinician. However, it would not be completely impossible to establish an individual weighting factor for each clinician, if each had evaluated enough cases to provide some reasonable data base. Or the weight to be allocated to the clinical appraisal might be varied as a function of the clinician's level of confidence about a given case, if the evidence showed that such a refinement was merited.

3. Finally, it is possible that the clinician might actually generate new data to be used in the prediction process. This could occur if the clinician interviewed or observed the candidate and arrived at judgments about certain of the candidate's characteristics on the basis of the interview or observation. These judgments could be recorded as ratings on specific characteristics, or they could be merged into a prediction of probable success. In either case, one or more new predictor scores would be generated in this way for each candidate. Whether these scores did in fact have validity, or could add to the prediction possible from more objective data, would be an empirical matter to be determined in an appropriate validation study. The point is that here we are thinking of the clinician primarily as the generator of a new predictor variable, rather than as a synthesizer and weighter of scores already available from more objective sources.

As we have indicated, the first of the three roles described above for the clinician is not a promising one. The other roles have been less thoroughly studied in the prediction context, but it seems likely that, in at least some prediction situations, they would yield significantly positive results.

MODERATOR VARIABLES

It has been reported from time to time that scholastic aptitude tests give a more accurate prediction of grade point average for women than they do for men. The implication is that a different regression equation is needed for each sex. If this is true, sex operates here as a *moderator variable*. A moderator variable in psychometrics is like a catalyst in chemistry. Without being directly involved in the reaction, it determines how well the reaction will go. That is, the moderator variable does not itself receive a weight in the prediction equation, but it indicates which set of weights the predictor variables should have.

It is, of course, possible that any test might itself function as a moderator. For example, it is conceivable that the validity of a spatial relations test as a predictor of success in engineering school might differ depending on whether a candidate was high or low in verbal ability. (The *a priori* rationale would be that the high-verbal students attack the learning problems in engineering school in verbal terms, while the low-verbal students use spatial visualizing.) However, there are so many possible interactions of a given test's validity with different other tests and at different test-score levels that one should view evidence on such interactions with considerable skepticism until they have been confirmed with new data on new samples.

Moderator effects seem most likely to be sustained when they refer to groups that are categorically distinct—sex groups, ethnic groups, socioeconomic groups. Here too, verification of observed effects is needed with new samples of cases. Unless there is strong *a priori* reason to expect differences of a specific kind, finding a difference between groups in test validities or regression weights should be thought to be hypothesis generating rather than hypothesis testing. To test the truthfulness of that hypothesis, the investigator should subject the moderator effect to verification in a new set of data.

MULTIPLE MEASURES IN DIFFERENTIATION

We turn now to those situations in which we are interested in differentiating categorically distinct groups. The groups may be identified as men and women; Republicans, Democrats, and noncommitted; lawyers, doctors, engineers, and bankers; or any other set of groups where each individual belongs in one and only one of the groups. We may ask how well each of a set of measures does in fact differentiate between the groups and how the measures should be combined to separate the groups most sharply.

When we take one measure at a time on the groups, sharpness of differentiation may be expressed as the proportion of the variance that is between-groups variance. Suppose that we had the following data for a measure of mechanical knowledge:

	MEAN	S.D.	VARIANCE	N
Lawyers	30	5	25	100
Doctors	35	8	64	100
Engineers	45	6	36	100

The mean score for the total group is $(30 + 35 + 45)/3 = 36.67$, and the variance for the total group is given by

$$\frac{(25 + 64 + 36)}{3} + \frac{(30 - 36.67)^2 + (35 - 36.67)^2 + (45 - 36.67)^2}{3}$$

or $41.67 + 38.89 = 80.56$. The first term represents the pooled within-group variance, and the second term is the between-groups variance. In this instance, we have $38.89/80.56 = .483$ as the proportion of variance that represents difference between the three groups, and this serves as an index of the effectiveness of the test in separating the groups from one another. At one extreme, if all members within each group received the same score, all the variance would be between groups and the index would equal 1.00. At the other extreme, if all the groups had the same mean value and variation occurred only within groups, the index would equal zero. Thus this index has some of the same properties as a correlation coefficient. In fact, when only two groups are to be differentiated, the statistic is identically the squared point-biserial correlation coefficient. More generally, the statistic will be spoken of as a *discriminant*.

If only two groups are to be differentiated through use of a number of tests, the computational procedures can be identically the same as those developed in the previous section, the only difference being that the correlations with the criterion dichotomy (that is, group A versus group B) must be point-biserial correlations. The determination of that set of weights that will most effectively separate the two groups can then be carried out by standard multiple-regression procedures. These procedures identify that linear combination of the set of measures for which the between-groups variance is maximized relative to the within-group variance.

When the data involve both a number of predictor variables serving to predict group membership and a number of groups to be differentiated, the logic remains the same but the computations rapidly become more complex. The logic specifies that we identify the linear combinations of predictor variables that will maximize the between-groups variance and minimize the within-group variance. The computations require that one solve a matrix equation that takes the form

$$(W^{-1}A - \lambda I)V = 0 \qquad (9.10)$$

where W = matrix of within-groups sum of deviation squares and cross products

       A = matrix of between-groups sum of deviation squares and cross products

       I = identity matrix

       λ = successive characteristic roots of the equation

       V = vector of weights for the predictor variables

The computations are practical only for a computer and will not be further elaborated here. Programs for discriminant function appear in such standard computer library packages as SPSS and BioMed. The person faced with a problem in discriminant analysis should investigate the facilities for this type of analysis at a local computer center.

By contrast to multiple regression, which generates just one set of weights, discriminant analysis generates a succession of sets of discriminant weights. The possible number is equal to the number of predictors, or to 1 less than the number of groups, whichever is less. The vectors of weights are extracted in the order of their importance. The first set is *the one set* that produces a score that *most sharply* differentiates the groups. The second is that set that produces a score orthogonal to (that is, uncorrelated with) the score from the first set of weights and accounts for as much as possible of the remaining differences among the groups, and so on for successive discriminants.

The flavor of discriminant analysis can be conveyed more effectively by looking at some of the results of an analysis by Richard Wolf (unpublished) of data on the effectiveness of the U.S.E.S. General Aptitude Test Battery in differentiating among over 400 jobs for which test-score means and standard deviations were available. Using the reported standard-score means and standard deviations for the job groups and the defined population means and standard deviations, Wolf estimated the within-group (W) and among-groups (A) covariance matrices for the 8 tests of the GATB and, from these, the weights for each of the 8 possible discriminants. The weights for the first discriminant are shown below in the column on the left.

		WEIGHT	CORRELATION WITH DISCRIMINANT
V	(verbal)	.14	.71
N	(numerical)	.87	.94
S	(spatial)	.30	.71
P	(form perception)	.10	.63
Q	(clerical perception)	−.30	.54
K	(motor coordination)	.08	.38
F	(finger dexterity)	−.01	.24
M	(manual dexterity)	−.07	.21

These indicate how standard scores on the 8 variables should be weighted to yield a score that provides sharpest separation of the occupational groups. The second column (which can be obtained by using the general formula for the correlation of sums given in Chapter 6, p. 151) shows the correlation of each of the 8 separate variables with this composite and helps to sharpen the descriptive picture of the nature of the composite. Note that, though the discriminant weights vary widely from one variable to another, all of the single variables show positive correlations with the weighted composite. This occurs because these 8 scores of the GATB are themselves positively correlated. Naturally, the best representation of the first discriminant is provided by the numerical score, which is so heavily weighted in the discriminant. However, the verbal and spatial scores are also substantially correlated with the discriminant, as are, to a slightly lesser degree, the perception measures. Thus the picture of the first discriminant is of a general cognitive measure that especially emphasizes the quantitative. This interpretation is supported by the finding that the occupational groups with highest means on this discriminant are mathematician, systems analyst, and programmer.

The second discriminant, which is uncorrelated with the first and represents another way in which occupational groups differ from one another, produced the weights for separate tests and correlations of tests with the composite shown below.

	WEIGHT	CORRELATION WITH DISCRIMINANT
V	−.22	.04
N	−.41	.04
S	.24	.29
P	.03	.42
Q	.63	.56
K	.07	.40
F	−.36	.04
M	.41	.57

Once again, the weights show a wide range, and the correlations of tests with the discriminant composite are more subdued, being nearer zero or moderately positive. Largest correlations are with perceptual and manual dexterity tests, all of which appear to place a good deal of emphasis on speed of perception and/or response.

The successive discriminants are extracted in the order that corresponds to the amount of between-groups variance accounted for. For example, in the illustration above, the 8 discriminant dimensions accounted, respectively, for 37.3%, 24.6%, 15.1%, 7.5%, 6.0%, 4.7%, 2.5%, and 2.4% of the explainable between-groups variance. One would ordinarily decide that some number of the later discriminants were trivial, either arising by chance or accounting for so little variance as to suggest that they be ignored. One would then concentrate on the interpretation and use of the first few discriminants.

Discriminant analysis serves to provide a type of simplified framework in terms of which the characteristics of different groups may be viewed. By way of illustration, the mean scores of 10 occupational groups on the first two GATB discriminant dimensions are shown in Table 9.1 and Figure 9.2. This is a simpler pattern to comprehend than the group profiles on 8 correlated variables that make up the original data. To the extent that the main differentiations of the original data are preserved in this simplified structure, the essential group differences are more incisively presented. Thus for these groups (and, in fact, for the complete set of groups), the substantial group differences are on the first discriminant, which has been characterized as general cognitive ability with a

Table **9.1**   Mean Discriminant Scores of Selected Occupations

	DISCRIMINANT DIMENSION I	DISCRIMINANT DIMENSION II
Cabinetmaker	114.6	46.6
Candy packer	85.1	40.4
Dental lab technician	103.9	46.9
Dentist	141.7	49.3
Engineer	125.3	56.8
Food service worker	89.9	46.4
Inspector–packer	84.7	35.7
Service station attendant	105.8	47.6
Teacher, elementary or secondary	125.8	38.3
Welder, production line	90.1	48.1

somewhat quantitative slant. Most of these differences would seem reasonable in terms of the educational and task demands of the occupations in question. Differences on the second discriminant are not so easy to describe or so obviously sensible. However, it seems reasonable that engineering draws candidates with greater perceptual–motor skills than does school teaching.

If it were desired to abbreviate a test battery used for group differentiation, the discriminant analysis would provide some suggestions about which tests to keep for the purpose of maintaining the maximum amount of differentiation. Thus, in the present instance, the test with the highest loading on discriminant I is N (number) and on discriminant II is Q (clerical perception) together with M (manual dexterity). The mean standard scores (scale of 100 and 20) of the 10 occupations on these tests are as follows:

	N	Q	M
Cabinetmaker	100	99	113
Candy packer	86	90	97
Dental lab technician	97	99	110
Dentist	121	114	111
Engineer	114	114	124
Food service worker	85	91	97
Inspector–packer	84	84	89
Service station attendant	97	97	115
Teacher	110	115	88
Welder	82	98	89

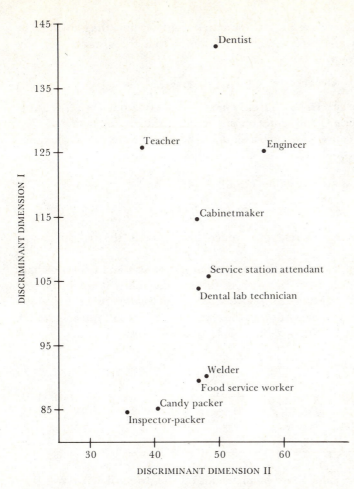

Figure 9.2   Mean discriminant scores of selected occupations.

In varying degrees and in different combinations, this set of 3 tests does provide a fair amount of differentiation among the samples in these 10 jobs.

As applied to the scores of an individual, discriminant analysis addresses itself to the question of how closely the individual resembles those persons in one or several different occupations. To this end the individual's score on a given discriminant is found by applying the discriminant weights to the individual's raw score on the several measures. One can look simply at the distance of the individual from the centroid* of each group, expressed in terms of a general measure of distance based on the variance in all groups concerned, or one can consider the person's status in relation to each group relative to the dispersion in that group.

---

* The group average on each of the discriminant dimensions.

Discriminant dispersions have a certain simplicity in describing the individual in that the dimensions are uncorrelated. This means that the distance, for any given person and group, is

$$\text{Distance} = \sqrt{\Sigma \, (\text{Ind}_j - \text{Group}_j)^2}$$

where j refers to the successive discriminants. Thus, using our GATB illustration, suppose that Susie Q had scores on the two discriminants of 98 and 45. We ask how similar (or, conversely, how dissimilar) she is to the average teacher and the average dental technician in the USES sample. We find

$$\text{Distance}_{\text{teacher}} = \sqrt{(98 - 125.8)^2 + (45 - 38.3)^2} = 28.6$$

$$\text{Distance}_{\text{dent tech}} = \sqrt{(98 - 103.9)^2 + (45 - 46.9)^2} = 6.2$$

and conclude that Susie Q resembles much more closely the typical dental technician.

This conclusion might be modified somewhat if teachers and dental technicians differed in their dispersion on these dimensions. Then it would be appropriate to express the distance for each occupation in relation to the dispersion within that occupation. It happens that the standard deviations for teachers and for dental technicians on the two dimensions are as follows:

	DISCRIMINANT I	DISCRIMINANT II
Teachers	14.75	10.67
Dental technicians	17.38	10.76

The teachers are noticeably more homogenous on the primarily cognitive first discriminant dimension. If we express Susie's distance from the centroid of each of the two groups in relation to the dispersion of the groups, we have

$$\text{Distance}_{\text{teacher}} = \sqrt{\left(\frac{98 - 125.8}{14.75}\right)^2 + \left(\frac{45 - 38.3}{10.67}\right)^2} = 1.99$$

$$\text{Distance}_{\text{dent tech}} = \sqrt{\left(\frac{98 - 103.9}{17.38}\right)^2 + \left(\frac{45 - 46.9}{10.76}\right)^2} = 0.38$$

The distance measures can be thought of as multivariate analogues of normal deviates, and the ordinates at these distances can be considered the relative frequency of numbers of the two (or more) occupational groups at these distances. Values of the multivariate normal density give ordinates of .029 and .060, respectively. Thus a dental technician could be considered .060/.029 = 2.1 times as likely as a teacher to display this particular score pattern.

A distance measure can be obtained directly from the multivariate score distribution of the set of test variables. In that case, it is necessary to take account not only of the variances but also of the covariances of the several measures in the group. The formula for calculating the distance is

$$D = X_i' C^{-1} X_i \qquad (9.11)$$

where X_i is the vector of score deviations for individual i, and C^{-1} is the inverse of the covariance matrix of the tests in the group in question. The multivariate density function is proportional to

$$\frac{1}{|C|} e^{(-X_i' C^{-1} X_i)/2} \qquad (9.12)$$

where $|C|$ is the determinant of the covariance matrix C.

Measures of the relative probability of a member of different groups falling at the particular score point in the test or the discriminant space corresponding to an individual's scores have not received much practical use before now. In the past, the computational hurdles for routine use of such an analysis have been prohibitive, but the increasing availability and decreasing cost of high-speed computers are largely overcoming this obstacle. More serious for the future is the lack of an adequate data base from which could be obtained measures of similarity to a group or frequency of such a score pattern occurring in the group. The practical problems of accumulating data on samples in different occupations that are adequate in size and representativeness are very great indeed. Furthermore, the characteristics of occupational groups are subject to progressive change over time. And the assumption that the present group membership defines the *desirable* characteristics for the group is open to serious question. For these reasons, multiple discriminant analysis has received limited use in applied psychometric work.

MULTIPLE MEASURES IN DESCRIPTION

Just as overlap on the one hand limits the predictive effectiveness of a team of variables, and on the other reduces the number of significant dimensions by which those measures serve to differentiate among groups, this overlap also muddies the significance of multiple measures as descriptions of distinct attributes of persons. It would make for clarity of description if each score that we had for a person represented a clearly distinct attribute not correlated with the attributes represented by other scores. But the data provided by tests are scores that are in varying degrees correlated—overlapping and redundant. We would like to analyze those overlapping, redundant scores to try to find an underlying structure, hoping to identify a small number of more fundamental trait dimensions. The complex edifice of component and factor analysis has been built up in order to accomplish this.

A factor is a new variable generated by a linear combination of the original test scores. The hope is that a small number of such linear composites can incorporate nearly all the information that is provided by the original, much larger set of test variables and can hence simplify our description of each individual's characteristics. The hope is, further, that judicious development of the factors can produce variables that imply a clear and meaningful psychological construct, so that our description of a person is not only simpler but also clearer and more incisive.

Factor-analytic procedures serve initially to improve our understanding of the instruments with which we work — and thus indirectly to improve our procedures for describing individuals. For example, if we find that a number of tests designed to elicit reasoning in different forms and with different materials overlap in a way that would suggest a common ability running through all of them, we may wish to use a pooled score from two or three of the set of measures to distill out the common reasoning ability. Such a composite may then serve to characterize the reasoning ability of an applicant for some type of training or employment.

The literature of component and factor analysis has become very large, both the literature elaborating variations of statistical methodology and the literature of substantive results. We shall be content here to illustrate with a small example one of the simplest of factor-analytic procedures. Actually, most computational work for component and factor analyses is now done using standard library programs and high-speed computers. The illustration is intended only to provide a little more sense of what lies behind the computer-generated results. Any reader who wants to go into the procedures in depth should refer to one of the standard texts (Comrey, 1973; Harman, 1976; Guertin and Bailey, 1970).

The basic data for studying the overlap and structure of a set of measures is a score matrix providing a score for each individual on each one of the measures. From this data matrix, the usual procedure is to calculate the matrix of correlations among the measures. Analysis of this matrix of intercorrelations becomes the heart of the matter. We show below a correlation matrix derived from the scores of 2857 fifth-grade pupils on 7 subtests of the Cognitive Abilities Test, Form 3.

SUBTEST	1	2	3	4	5	6	7
1. Vocabulary	(.744)	.712	.744	.696	.477	.517	.482
2. Sentence completion	.712	(.724)	.720	.724	.502	.548	.463
3. Verbal classification	.744	.720	(.756)	.756	.560	.603	.543
4. Verbal analogies	.696	.724	.756	(.756)	.611	.681	.566
5. Figure classification	.477	.502	.560	.611	(.654)	.654	.543
6. Figure analogies	.517	.548	.603	.681	.654	(.681)	.592
7. Figure synthesis	.482	.463	.543	.566	.543	.592	(.592)

We have here a set of variables that all show positive correlations with each other, so we can expect that they will all show positive loadings on a common factor. In the analytic procedure that we shall illustrate, if any variable showed a predominance of negative correlations with the other variables, we would have to *reflect* it—that is, turn it end-for-end so that what was originally a high score becomes a low score. Though negative correlations are rare for ability measures, they may often appear for personality measures, which are typically bipolar. Thus a scale for "sociability" can be reversed to make it a scale for "solitariness." Our first analysis will be directed at determining how completely each variable can be accounted for by the principal common factor. We will calculate a kind of average of the correlations of each variable with all the other variables.

At this point, a comment is required about the diagonal elements in the correlation matrix, the ones enclosed in parentheses in our illustration. These are estimates of the *communality* of each variable—the proportion of its variance that it has in common with some other one of the variables in the set. As a first approximation, we take as an estimate of communality for each variable its largest correlation with any of the other variables. We may wish to refine these estimates at a later stage. By using communality estimates as diagonal entries, we indicate that we wish to analyze only the common or shared variance. Component analysis places unity in each diagonal cell, including in addition to shared variance specific as well as error variance in the analysis, and looks for the structure to account for *all* the variance of the set of variables. This procedure will not be illustrated.

In the procedure that we shall illustrate, called the *centroid* method, one starts by summing the values in each column of the correlation table. Then one sums the column totals to get the grand sum and takes the square root of this grand sum. The column sums are divided by this square root value, and the resulting values (the sums of the correlations for a given variable divided by the square root of the sum of all the correlations in the table) provide the *loadings* on the first centroid factor. The calculations are shown below.

	1	2	3	4	5	6	7	TOTAL
Column sums	4.372	4.393	4.682	4.790	4.001	4.276	3.781	30.299
						Square root =		5.504
Sums ÷ 5.504	.794	.798	.851	.870	.727	.777	.687	

As could be expected from an inspection of the original correlation table, all variables show substantial positive loadings on the first common factor. The factor loadings are to be thought of as the correlation of each measure with a perfect, pure measure of the common factor.

The correlation between any pair of variables can be represented by the sum of the products of the loadings of those two variables on all the common factors required to account for the complete correlation matrix. That is,

$$r_{ij} = f_{1i}f_{1j} + f_{2i}f_{2j} + \cdots + f_{ki}f_{kj}$$

if there are k common factors.

In general, procedures for extracting factors extract them in the order of their importance, as represented by the amount of variance each one explains. As a result, many of the later factors are usually of no consequence and can be ignored. Removing the effect of the first factor from the intercorrelations, we have

$$r_{ij} - f_{1i}f_{1j} = f_{2i}f_{2j} + \cdots + f_{ki}f_{kj}$$

That is, if we subtract from the original correlations the product of the loadings on factor 1, the remainder represents the amount of correlation between the variables to be accounted for by all the remaining factors. So, for variables 1 and 2, we have

$$r_{12} - f_{11}f_{12} = .712 - (.794)(.798) = .078$$

and similarly for the other variables. The matrix of first-factor residuals, representing the correlation among variables to be accounted for by later factors, is as follows:

	1	2	3	4	5	6	7
1	(.114)	.078	.068	.005	−.100	−.100	−.063
2	.078	(.087)	.041	.030	−.078	−.072	−.085
3	.068	.041	(.032)	.016	−.059	−.058	−.042
4	.005	.030	.016	(.000)	−.021	.005	−.032
5	−.100	−.078	−.059	−.021	(.125)	.089	.044
6	−.100	−.072	−.058	.005	.089	(.077)	.058
7	−.063	−.085	−.042	−.032	.044	.058	(.120)

It is obvious from inspection that, in this set of data, these residual values are *very much* smaller than the original correlations. A very large proportion of the shared variance of the seven variables is accounted for by the one common factor, with which all seven tests show quite substantial correlations. However, we shall continue to extract some additional factors to try to account for the remaining pattern of relationships.

It is inherent in this procedure for extracting factors that the sum of the residuals for each variable is zero, except for rounding errors. The first factor does, on the average, account for each variable's correlations with the remaining variables. Hence, if we are to proceed further, we must reflect (reverse the signs of) some of the variables. Usually one starts by reflecting the variable for which the sum of absolute values is greatest (in this case variable 5) and continues by reflecting all columns (and rows) for which the sum is then negative. In the present instance, this means reflecting variables 5, 6, and 7. The table then becomes

	1	2	3	4	$\left(\dfrac{-}{5}\right)$	$\left(\dfrac{-}{6}\right)$	$\left(\dfrac{-}{7}\right)$
1	(.114)	.078	.068	.005	.100	.100	.063
2	.078	(.087)	.041	.030	.078	.072	.085
3	.068	.041	(.032)	.016	.059	.058	.042
4	.005	.030	.016	(.000)	.021	− .005	.032
(−)5	.100	.078	.059	.021	(.125)	.089	.044
(−)6	.100	.072	.058	− .005	.089	(.077)	.058
(−)7	.063	.085	.042	.032	.044	.058	(.120)

Repeating the process of summing columns and dividing by the square root of the grand sum, we get

Sum	.528	.471	.316	.099	.516	.449	.444	Total = 2.823
								Square root = 1.680
Factor 2	.314	.280	.181	.059	− .307	− .267	− .264	

Because of the reversals of sign for those variables, the loadings for variables 5, 6, and 7 must be thought of as negative.

A table of residuals can again be calculated, removing the correlation among variables that is accounted for by the second factor. For second-factor residuals we get, for example,

$$[r_{12} - f_{11}f_{12}] - f_{21}f_{22} = .078 - (.314)(.280) = -.010$$

The complete table of second-factor residuals is shown below.

	1	2	3	4	5	6	7
1	(.015)	−.010	.009	−.014	.004	.016	−.020
2	−.010	(.009)	−.012	.013	−.008	.003	−.011
3	.009	−.012	(−.003)	.005	.001	.008	−.008
4	−.014	.013	.005	(−.003)	.003	−.021	.016
5	.004	−.008	.001	.003	(.031)	.007	−.037
6	.016	.003	.008	−.021	(.007)	(.006)	−.012
7	−.020	−.011	−.008	.016	−.037	−.012	(.050)

These residuals are obviously very small, and it is questionable whether the remaining shared variance is enough in amount to be worth analyzing. However,
we did extract one additional factor. When this was done, the factor loadings for
the first three factors were as follows.

VARIABLE	FACTOR		
	I	II	III
1. Vocabulary	.794	.314	.119
2. Sentence completion	.798	.280	−.089
3. Verbal classification	.851	.118	.040
4. Verbal analogies	.870	.059	−.072
5. Figure classification	.727	−.307	−.115
6. Figure analogies	.777	−.267	−.099
7. Figure synthesis	.687	−.264	.208
Total variance accounted for	4.35	0.45	0.10

In the last row of the table, we show the total amount of variance in the set of
tests accounted for by each factor. This is equal to the sum of the squared
loadings for a given factor, summed over all the variables. The total variance for
each variable is unity, so the *total* variance for the set is 7, and the percentages of
the total variance accounted for by the factors are, respectively, 62.1, 6.4, and
1.4. The amount of *common factor* variance in the set of variables is equal to the
sum of the communalities. In this illustrative example, it is estimated to be
4.907. That is, the common factor variance is 4.907/7 = 69.9% of all the
variance in the set. The first factor accounts for 4.35/4.907 = 88.6% of the
common factor variance; the second and third factors account for 9.2% and

2.0%, respectively; and the three factors together account for 99.8% of the shared variance of the set of tests.

By looking at the individual factor loadings and at the variance accounted for, one can see that the third factor is of very little consequence and that any further factors would reflect little more than chance sampling fluctuations in the correlation matrix.

The procedures that we have used have been designed to extract factors that have the mathematical property of accounting, at each stage, for the greatest amount of shared variance. But usually the result is not in a form that is psychologically most meaningful. The first factor is a kind of grand average of shared relationship, but the later factors must be equally divided into positive and negative values and appear as *differences between* subsets of variables. Such a difference factor is hard to give meaning to as a basic psychological construct. What kind of an attribute of a person is it that makes that person perform better on a figure classification test than on a vocabulary test?

It may be more meaningful to apportion the variance between factors in such a way that each contributes only in a positive sense, and only to performance on certain of the tests. If we remember that each of our factors was defined so as to be independent of, and hence orthogonal to, each of the others, we can plot pairs of factor loadings on orthogonal coordinates and view the factor pattern.

This has been done for factors I and II in Figure 9.3. There is nothing sacred about the position of the axes in such a plot, and we can account for the same amount of relationships equally well by a new pair of orthogonal axes in the two-dimensional space. These have been designated I′ and II′, and the loadings of the variables on these new axes are shown below.

	I′	II′
1. Vocabulary	.615	.590
2. Sentence completion	.633	.560
3. Verbal classification	.742	.432
4. Verbal analogies	.780	.390
5. Figure classification	.789	−.012
6. Figure analogies	.820	.050
7. Figure synthesis	.736	.018

We now have a configuration in which the first factor has substantial loadings on all seven tests but the second factor has appreciable loadings only on the tests involving verbal material. A possible interpretation is that there is a general cognitive ability called for by all the tasks but that the first four tests also call on the individual's store of, or ability to manipulate, verbal symbols. We may feel

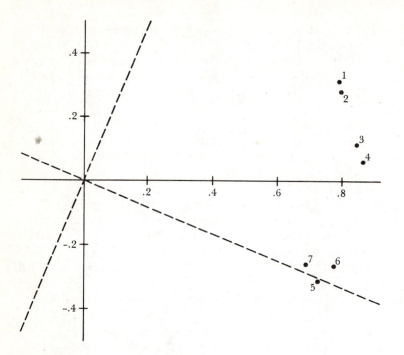

Figure 9.3   Factor structure, showing possible rotation.

that the rotated factors permit a more meaningful interpretation in terms of useful psychological constructs.

In the example that we have provided, as in many of its other applications, factor analysis is used to verify or check on the structure of the attributes that the investigator had intentionally built into a set of measures. It thus provides a check on the construct validity of one or more of the measures in the set, clarifying the degree to which it fits into a pattern of relationships in the expected way. At other times, factor analysis is used in a more exploratory way, to examine a largely unmapped domain in order to see what structure emerges within it. Often a study involves a little of each: exploration *and* verification.

In addition to determining the factor loadings of tests, in order to gain a better understanding of the tests' nature, one may be interested in estimating factor *scores* for each individual. Factor scores tell where the individual stands on the composite attribute or construct that the combination of tests assesses. The optimal weighting of the separate tests to provide an estimate of individual factor scores can be determined by applying the multiple regression procedures described in the first section of this chapter, remembering that factor loadings can be thought of as "validity coefficients"—that is, as correlations of the tests with an ideal perfect measure of the factor. Applying these procedures to the present table of correlations and set of factor loadings, we get the following weights as the best estimates of individual standing on each of the factors.

TEST	FACTOR I	FACTOR II	FACTOR III	FACTOR I$'$	FACTOR II$'$
1	.15	.40	.35	$-.02$	.50
2	.15	.36	$-.27$	.01	.45
3	.20	.27	.12	.17	.07
4	.23	.01	$-.21$	.13	.15
5	.15	$-.40$	$-.20$	.30	$-.31$
6	.18	$-.40$	$-.20$	.30	$-.26$
7	.12	$-.32$	.45	.24	$-.24$
Multiple Correlation	.95	.77	.44	.94	.79

There may be situations in which one would prefer to use an individual's factor score on one or more of the common factors, rather than his or her score on a single test, to describe an attribute of that person.

It is of some interest to estimate the reliability of individual factor scores, because this information may provide guidance as to their usefulness either in theoretical studies or as practical indices to describe an individual. The reliabilities may be estimated, given the reliabilities of the component tests, by the formula

$$\frac{\displaystyle\sum_{i=1}^{m}\sum_{j=1}^{n} w_{x_i}w_{y_j}C_{x_iy_j}}{\sqrt{\displaystyle\sum_{i=1}^{m}\sum_{k=1}^{m} w_{x_i}w_{x_k}C_{x_ix_k}} \cdot \sqrt{\displaystyle\sum_{j=1}^{n}\sum_{\ell=1}^{n} w_{y_j}w_{y_p}C_{y_jy_p}}} \tag{9.13}$$

for the correlation of weighted sums. In general, we would expect the reliabilities of successive factors to decline fairly sharply as the factor loadings become smaller and as a number of them become negative. This is borne out in the present illustration; the reliabilities of the weighted combinations that estimate scores on the three factors are .92, .59, and .28, respectively. Rotation redistributes the variance among the factors, and hence the reliability, so, for the first two factors after rotation, the reliabilities are .89 and .62. Though our illustrative example may be a bit extreme in its concentration of variance in the first factor, these figures are still useful to emphasize the fragility of scores on later factors and their limited utility as descriptors of individual examinees. At the same time, the first factor score provides a descriptor that is a more stable indicator than score on any of the component tests. At times, such a factor score or an approximation to it may serve as a useful index in descriptive and predictive studies of individuals.

ISSUES TO BE DEALT WITH
IN FACTOR ANALYSES

We have illustrated one procedure for estimating factor loadings and for rotating them to a potentially more meaningful structure for describing individual differences. As indicated, there are many variants of procedure for both factor or component extraction and rotation. We will conclude by identifying some of the issues that the investigator must resolve before embarking on this type of analysis.

How large a sample of cases is necessary to yield meaningfully stable results? In factor analysis one is always estimating a large number of parameters — as many as there are factors times the number of test variables. With so many unknowns to be estimated, it seems clear that a sizable sample will be required. No rigid minimum can be set, but accepted practice calls for at least ten times as many cases as there are variables entering into the correlation matrix. Elaborate analyses of small samples is more likely to confuse than to enlighten because of the unstable and erratic values that may result.

What values should be used as diagonal entries in the correlation matrix? The choice is between unities, estimates of test reliability, and estimates of test communality. Those with a mathematical bent tend to prefer unities, which say in effect that we will analyze everything about a test, including not only variance shared with other tests but also variance specific to that one test and even error variance. This analysis (called principal component analysis) is mathematically cleaner, and it avoids the possibility of certain mathematical anomalies. Those oriented primarily toward the substantive meaning of the final structure tend to get uncomfortable at the thought of incorporating in one's factor solution the error variance and perhaps at including variance specific to a single test. They are likely to prefer, as the diagonal entry, some estimate of communality — of the variance shared with other measures.

When the number of variables being analyzed is large, what entries are put in the diagonal cells makes relatively little difference in the results obtained. Then the very large number of off-diagonal covariance terms tends to swamp any effect from the diagonal entries. But if unities are used with small matrices, one may find rotated factors that are determined primarily by a single variable, including the unique and error variance on that variable.

How many factors should be extracted and subsequently rotated? Once again, one is in a trade-off situation. If too few factors are extracted, it may be impossible to represent fully the structure of a given set of variables. But, as we have illustrated, there is a progressive decline in the variance accounted for by successive factors and in the reliability of successive factor scores. The drop will often not be so precipitous as it was in our illustration, but it will always be there. Of course, when factors are rotated into positions that are thought to be psychologically more meaningful, the amount of variance accounted for by each factor is somewhat evened out, and the error variance gets distributed more evenly between factors. But if 75% or 80% of what is incorporated in a factor before rotation is random error, it seems questionable that the factor will really contribute to clarification of the field that is being studied.

Fortunately, when factors are being extracted by computer, the computations to extract many more factors than are likely to be meaningful can be done in short order. One can then scan the results and see how rapidly the variance accounted for by successive factors shrinks to trivial amounts. For rotation, one can instruct the computer to retain and rotate only a specified number of the largest factors. The number can be varied, and one can compare the rotated structures with different numbers of factors to see which one appears to provide the most sensible and coherent picture.

Should rotated factors be orthogonal or oblique? In all of our discussion up to this point, we have spoken only of orthogonal factors, where each factor is completely distinct from and independent of all the others. There is an appealing economy and simplicity to uncorrelated constructs. Each one represents entirely new information, and we do not have to be aware that both represent in part the same thing. Certainly, when measures to which different names are attached have high correlations with each other, one's thinking about them is likely to get muddy. The history of attempts to draw distinctions between aptitude and achievement is full of such murky thought. So a case can be made for dealing solely with orthogonal rotations that maintain the independence of our factors.

But nature is not necessarily orthogonal. It may be that a group of measures of physical speed, for example, is in fact correlated with a group of measures of physical strength, though each group forms a clear and distinct cluster and each cluster seems to represent a meaningful construct. Do we make for clarity (and possibly for understanding of the biological bases of the two clusters) by constraining our analysis to an orthogonal framework? Should we, rather, let our dimensions be determined by the apparent clustering in our data and recognize (and perhaps study) the relationships of the clusters to one another?

Multivariate correlational analysis is at best a descriptive approach to relationships among variables and constructs as they exist. We must conclude by reiterating the adage that "correlation is not causation." We need to dig beneath the surface of relationships to understand the biological and experiential bases of the structures of relationship that we observe.

Chapter 10

Bayesian Approaches and Testing

It was in 1763 that the formal statement of Bayes' theorem of inverse probability appeared in print, but only in the past 15 or 20 years has the theorem or the type of thinking that it represents started to have much of an explicit impact on the development of testing procedures or the interpretation of test results. For many years Bayes' theorem was either ignored or actively rejected by statisticians as being in some sense intellectually disreputable. Recently, however, interest in the Bayesian approach has undergone a strong revival, and it appears to offer some significant contributions to the design of testing procedures and to thinking about test results. The Bayesian approach is based on two key ideas that are stated and somewhat elaborated below.

First, we have the concept of *prior probability*. For almost any event in which we may be interested, we have *some* notion, in advance of the collection of new data, of the probability distribution for that event. If the event is a dichotomy, we do have some belief about the likelihood that the event will turn out to be A rather than B. Thus, knowing only that a pregnancy has occurred, we have a well-founded belief that the odds are approximately equal that the offspring will be female. More relevant to psychometric studies, we approach most measurement situations with some beliefs, based on our history of past experience or our acquaintance with an accepted literature, about the distribution of the measure in the population with which we are concerned. So an even moderately sophisticated mental tester, testing with, say, the WISC-R a child about whom absolutely nothing is known, would believe that the most likely IQ for that child is approximately 100 and that there are about 2 chances in 3 that the IQ will fall between 85 and 115. Moreover, if the mental tester knew that a Binet testing 2 or 3 years earlier had yielded an IQ of 80 for that child, the tester's beliefs about what the WISC-R would yield would be substantially modified. The most likely value might now appropriately be thought to be about 85 in this case, and the range within which there were 2 chances in 3 that the new IQ would fall might be narrowed to 75 to 95.

Even in matters about which we know very little, we often have *some* prior beliefs, though all values within a considerable range may be viewed as equally likely. Thus, though I have no direct information on the pulse rate of elephants, I may be willing to express a belief that it is almost certainly (say with .95 probability) between 20 and 100 beats per minute. Even in situations such as this, the Bayesian would feel that prior beliefs can be expressed and quantified.

Second, there is the concept that prior beliefs are modified by data according to specifiable rules. The outcome is the *posterior belief,* and Bayes' theorem is a formal statement of the relationship between the prior belief, the data, and the posterior belief. Bayesian statistics is the development of rational quantitative methods for combining data with prior beliefs to arrive at posterior beliefs.

Naturally, as the data become more and more extensive, they take a more and more predominant role in determining the posterior belief, and differences between persons in their prior belief systems become less and less important. On the other hand, the more the prior beliefs are themselves based on adequate prior data, the more resistant they should be to change by additional data. What Bayesian methods of analysis try to do is to provide an optimal procedure for weighting the prior information system together with the new data that have been collected so as to produce the most appropriate statement of posterior probabilities.

Bayesian thinking has implications for both test interpretation and test construction. In the matter of test interpretation, it undertakes to provide us a guide for making the best possible estimate of an examinee's standing on some latent attribute, given everything we know about the individual's past history, as well as his or her current performance on some test or tests. In the matter of test construction, it offers the rationale for the selection of test materials that will provide the greatest amount of information at each stage of testing—and hence increase as rapidly as possible the precision of our posterior estimate of an examinee's position on some latent trait. This lies at the heart of adaptive or tailored testing, a current development of outstanding interest.

BAYES' THEOREM

A formal statement of Bayes' theorem is as follows: The posterior probability of a specific outcome, given a certain datum, is equal to the prior probability of that outcome times the likelihood of the datum occurring, given the outcome, divided by the base-rate likelihood of the datum.

We can illustrate this in the simplest case, in which both the outcome and the datum are dichotomous. Suppose that we know that 50% of students recommended by their high school principal successfully complete the freshman year at Bacon College and that, of those who complete the freshman year successfully, 60% got scores on the APL Admissions Test of 500 or over. We also know that 40% of all those recommended by their principal got scores of 500 or over. We ask: What is the probability that a student who has been recommended *and* gets a score over 500 will successfully complete the freshman year? Bayes' theorem applied to this situation gives

$$\text{Posterior probability} = (.50)(.60)/(.40) = .75$$

Expressed in symbolic notation,

$$P(H/E) = \frac{P(H) \cdot P(E/H)}{P(E)}$$

where $P(H/E)$ = posterior probability of the hypothesized outcome, given the specified event

$P(H)$ = prior probability of the outcome, knowing nothing about the event

$P(E/H)$ = likelihood of the event among all those who have achieved the hypothesized outcome

$P(E)$ = the overall likelihood of the event in the base population

In our illustration, H corresponds to successfully completing the freshman year, E corresponds to a score of 500 or over, and the base population is all students recommended by their principal.

From time to time we are interested in dichotomous outcomes and dichotomous events, but it is much more usual for us to have an outcome that is expressed as a continuous variable (for example, freshman grade point average) and an event that is expressed as a particular score value on some continuous score scale. In that case, we can speak of

$P(\theta/X)$, the posterior conditional frequency distribution or density function of the score θ, given that the relevant event has the value X

$P(X)$, the frequency distribution or density function of the event X in the base population

$P(\theta)$, the prior frequency distribution or density function of the score θ

$P(X/\theta)$, the frequency distribution or density function of the event X, given a specific value of θ

Bayes' theorem can now be expressed

$$P(\theta/X) = \frac{P(\theta) \cdot P(X/\theta)}{P(X)}$$

or

$$P(\theta/X) \propto P(\theta) \cdot P(X/\theta)$$

where the symbol $\propto$ means "is proportional to." Because both X and θ are now continuous distributions, our concern is to estimate the parameters of the posterior distribution, $P(\theta/X)$, when we have information on the prior distribution, $P(\theta)$, and on the frequency distribution of the event for a given value of θ, $P(X/\theta)$.

Working out Bayesian problems can lead into rather complex mathematics, so we shall limit ourselves to two of the simplest ones. Then we shall follow these up with some applications to specifically psychometric problems. The two relatively straightforward applications of Bayesian procedures that we shall consider are (1) estimating the probability of some dichotomous event and (2) estimating the mean of a subpopulation when the standard deviation in that subpopulation is assumed to be known. We shall describe and illustrate these, to bring out the type of thinking and sequence of steps involved. For more complex applications, interested readers should refer to one of the texts devoted specifically to Bayesian methods (Novick and Jackson, 1974; Phillips, 1973).

Case 1

Suppose that we wish to determine what proportion of fifth-graders in our school system can correctly complete the number series

$$26 \quad 22 \quad 19 \quad 15 \quad 12 \quad \underline{\hspace{1cm}} \quad \underline{\hspace{1cm}}$$

We happen to know that, in a national sample of 500 fifth-graders, the percentage succeeding was 65, and we suspect that our school is a little above the national average. These items of information constitute the basis for our prior probabilities. On the basis of this information we can sketch a graph of our prior estimate of what the percentage in our school is most likely to be and what it possibly could be. The graph might look like Figure 10.1. We consider 70% the most likely figure and are nearly certain (with perhaps a .95 probability) that the percentage lies between 50 and 85.

The sampling distribution for a dichotomous event with a given population value p takes the form of what is known as the Beta function. Tables and graphs of this function are available for different values of the frequency of a, occurrence of the event, and b, nonoccurrence of the event being studied. These tables appear in texts presenting Bayesian statistics. (If a and b are both equal to 0, the graph is a straight line, indicating that all values of p, the probability of the event, are equally likely.) Specifically, there are tables that show the values of p that bound the 95% credible interval (in conventional statistics, the 95% confidence interval). The range 50 to 85 we specified corresponds approximately to the 95% interval of a Beta function in which a equals 17 and b equals 8. Thus our prior range of credible values of p corresponds to the range of results one would get from samples of 25 drawn from a population in which the event occurred 17 times out of 25, or 68% of the time.

Bayesians suggest that we check the reasonableness of such an interpretation by dividing the range of possible values into three segments that we would perceive to be equally likely. That is, we should create a division such that, if we had to place a 1-to-2 bet on a segment, we would not care which segment was assigned to us. Considering the prior evidence and my graph, perhaps I set my dividing lines at .65 and .74. Checking against tables dividing the Beta function into equal thirds, I find that a curve with mode at 0.7 and values of a and b of 15 and 7, respectively, divides into thirds at 0.64 and 0.73. This is reasonably consistent with the 17 and 8 derived from the 95% interval, so I can feel that I have been consistent and that a Beta(17,8) does quite reasonably represent my prior probabilities. I have expressed a view that is consistent with a mean value of p of .68, based on a sample of 25 observations.

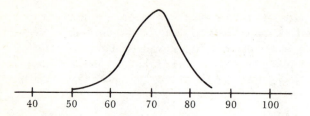

Figure 10.1   Prior probability of success on test item.

If the 95% interval had been larger, it would have reflected less prior certainty on my part, and vice versa. For example, a range from .30 to .95 would correspond to Beta(9,4), or information equivalent to a sample of 13 cases.

Having made explicit the nature and strength of my prior beliefs, I am now ready to go out and collect some data. I administer the item to a *representative* sample of, say, 20 fifth-graders in my school system. (Bias in the sampling procedure can distort the results from a Bayesian analysis, as from any other.) Suppose that 15 of the 20 pass the item and 5 fail it. Then my posterior values for the parameters a and b are, respectively,

$$a = 17 + 15 = 32 \qquad b = 8 + 5 = 13$$

The information from the data is added to the information contained in my prior estimate to yield the posterior estimate, and this is Beta(32,13). The 95% credible interval for Beta(32,13) is from .58 to .84. The mean, mode, and standard deviation of a Beta function are, respectively,

$$\text{Mean} = \frac{a}{a+b} = \frac{32}{32+13} = 0.711$$

$$\text{Mode} = \frac{a-1}{a+b-2} = \frac{31}{43} = 0.721$$

$$s = \sqrt{\frac{ab}{(a+b)^2\,(a+b+1)}} = \sqrt{\frac{416}{93,150}} = .067$$

In the example as given, our prior information was held with enough certainty (as represented by a fairly narrow range of credible values) to carry somewhat more weight than the data for 20 cases. If the prior certainty had been enough less to correspond to Beta(9,4), we would have had for our posterior values of a and b, respectively, $9 + 15 = 24$ and $4 + 5 = 9$. And for the posterior Beta(24,9), we would have had

$$\text{Mean} = \frac{24}{33} = 0.727$$

$$s = \sqrt{\frac{216}{37026}} = .076$$

The mean of our posterior distribution of credible values of p is now somewhat higher, reflecting the relatively greater influence of the data sample, and the dispersion is somewhat greater, reflecting our somewhat lower posterior certainty.

Case 2

The second manageable type of situation is one in which we are willing to accept that the scores we are interested in have (at least approximately) a normal distribution and that the standard deviation in the population is known. Our concern is to estimate the mean score in some subpopulation, combining our prior knowledge about the measure in question with such data as we have gathered from a sample of that group.

Let us say that school system X wants to estimate the mean Standard Age Score on the Cognitive Abilities Test, Verbal, for fifth-graders in the system. It is known that, in a national sample, the Standard Age Score of fifth graders has a mean of 101 and a standard deviation of 16. Allowing for the greater homogeneity of a single community, testing personnel in system X are willing to accept 14 as the standard deviation in their community.

Once again, our first step is to establish prior probabilities, and we ask the testing personnel in system X to prepare a graph of their prior expectations, indicating what they consider to be the most likely average S.A.S. for their community and the limits within which that value would almost certainly fall (say with probability of .999). They gave 99 as their most probable value and the range as extending from 93 to 105. We may consider the standard deviation of their expectation of their group's mean to be roughly one-sixth of the total range, or 2 points, and the variance to be 4.* Now the variance of the distribution of Standard Age Scores was accepted as being $(14)^2 = 196$. The variance of a mean is given by

$$s^2_{\text{Mean}} = \frac{s^2}{N} \quad \text{and hence} \quad N = \frac{s^2}{s^2_{\text{Mean}}}$$

In the present case this gives $N = 196/4 = 49$, so the prior expectations of the testing personnel in system X have a precision corresponding to that from a sample of 49 cases.

We now proceed to get some data by testing a representative sample from the school system, say a sample of 100 fifth-graders. Let us suppose that the mean for this sample turned out to be 102. Then we have, as a posterior estimate,

$$\text{Mean}_{\text{Post.}} = \frac{N_{\text{Prior}}(\text{Mean}_{\text{Prior}}) + N_{\text{Data}}(\text{Mean}_{\text{Data}})}{N_{\text{Prior}} + N_{\text{Data}}}$$

---

* In this case also, we could check on their estimate by asking them to divide the possible range into three equally likely segments. The portion of a normal curve including the middle third of the cases extends from -0.43 to $+0.43$ standard deviations. If they are consistent, they should identify the equally probable intervals as below 98, 98 to 100, and above 100.

$$s^2_{\text{Mean}_{\text{Post.}}} = \frac{s^2}{N_{\text{Prior}} + N_{\text{Data}}}$$

In our example, we have

$$\text{Mean}_{\text{Post.}} = \frac{(49)(99) + 100(102)}{49 + 100} = 101.0$$

$$s^2_{\text{Mean}_{\text{Post.}}} = \frac{196}{149} = 1.315$$

$$s_{\text{Mean}_{\text{Post.}}} = 1.147$$

The posterior estimate that takes into account both the prior judgment and the data from a sample of cases is that the mean is 101.0, and the precision of that estimate is represented by a dispersion of 1.147.

SOME MEASUREMENT APPLICATIONS

There are several kinds of measurement applications in which Bayesian thinking either clarifies the interpretation of tests that we have been making or suggests useful new interpretations. We shall consider (1) estimating "true score" on a latent attribute, (2) combining information from earlier testing with the results from a present test, (3) using collateral information from other tests to modify the score estimated from a specific test, and (4) using information from other individuals (or groups) to modify one's estimate based on test results for a specific individual or group.

ESTIMATING "TRUE SCORE"

In practically every instance in which a test is administered to a person, we have *some* prior knowledge of what the parameters are for that test in the group to which the present examinee belongs. Usually the precision of our prior knowledge increases as we are able to define the group more completely. The standard deviation for very specific groups is usually less than for the general population, and, of course, the group mean often differs from the general population mean. Thus we may know that the average standard score on the General Aptitude Battery N (Numerical Aptitude) is 100, with a standard deviation of 20, for a general adult sample. But we may also have information that the mean is 110 and the standard deviation 13 for a sample of drafting trainees. Before we test a specific trainee, we can define our distribution of prior probabilities as one with a mean of 110 and a standard deviation of 13.

An actual measurement yields a specific score with a known (or knowable) standard error of measurement. Given the prior mean and standard deviation for the group, together with the obtained score for the individual (with its standard error), we can find the best posterior estimate of the person's status on that measure by applying

$$\widetilde{X}_t = \frac{\dfrac{\overline{X}_G}{s_G^2} + \dfrac{X_M}{s_{e_M}^2}}{\dfrac{1}{s_G^2} + \dfrac{1}{s_{e_M}^2}}$$

where
$\widetilde{X}_t$ = best estimate of person's true score on measure X
$\overline{X}_G$ = prior group mean score on X
s_G^2 = group standard deviation on X
X_M = actual individual score on X
s_{e_M} = standard error of measurement on X

Thus the evidence suggests that the standard error of measurement on the N scale is about 5.6, giving a measurement error variance of about 32, so that our posterior estimate of the trait score for a trainee who obtained a test score of 130 would be

$$X_t = \frac{\dfrac{110}{(13)^2} + \dfrac{130}{(5.6)^2}}{\dfrac{1}{(13)^2} + \dfrac{1}{(5.6)^2}} = \frac{\dfrac{110}{169} + \dfrac{130}{32}}{\dfrac{1}{169} + \dfrac{1}{32}}$$

$$= \frac{0.651 + 4.062}{.0059 + .0312} = \frac{4.713}{.0371} = 127.0$$

The variance of this estimate would be $1/.0371 = 26.95$.

Thus the use of prior knowledge about the distribution of an attribute in a specific type of population permits us to adjust our posterior estimate based on a test result and also to increase (slightly) the precision of that estimate. The prior knowledge is weighted by the reciprocal of the variance in the group, and the measure itself is weighted by the reciprocal of the variance of measurement. When a measure is very reliable, the adjustment is usually quite minor. But if the measure has a sizable measurement error and/or the group in which the person can be located is quite homogeneous with respect to the attribute, the prior information may receive considerable weight.

COMBINING INFORMATION FROM EARLIER TESTING
WITH PRESENT TEST RESULTS

When current test results are obtained for a person, earlier test data are often available also on the same or a similar test. Earlier results usually show a substantial correlation with present test scores. If we know to a reasonable approximation what this correlation is for a group of specified variability, we can calculate from the earlier test a predicted present true score with an associated standard error of estimate for predicting true score at the moment of the present test. That is,

$$\tilde{X}_{M_\infty \cdot E} = \frac{r_{ME}}{\sqrt{r_{MM'}}} \frac{s_M}{s_E} (X_E - \overline{X}_E) + \overline{X}_M$$

where $\tilde{X}_{M_\infty \cdot E}$ = present true score estimated from earlier test

r_{ME} = correlation between present measure M and earlier measure E

$r_{MM'}$ = reliability of present measure

We also have

$$\tilde{s}_{M_\infty \cdot E} = s_M \sqrt{1 - (r_{ME}^2 / r_{MM'})}$$

where $\tilde{s}_{M_\infty \cdot E}$ = error variance of estimating true present status from an earlier test

Given these two values, we can combine them with data from the present testing to give a best estimate of true present status. That is, we have

$$\tilde{X}_t = \frac{\dfrac{\tilde{X}_{M_\infty \cdot E}}{\tilde{s}_{M_\infty \cdot E}^2} + \dfrac{X_M}{s_{e_M}^2}}{\dfrac{1}{\tilde{s}_{M_\infty \cdot E}^2} + \dfrac{1}{s_{e_M}^2}}$$

Suppose the standard deviation (in a common-score scale) is 20 for both the earlier and the present test, correlation between the two tests is .80, and reliability of the present test is estimated to be .90. In that case we would have $s_{e_M}^2 = 20^2(1 - .90) = 40$, and $\tilde{s}_{M_\infty \cdot E}^2 = 20^2(1 - 0.64/.90) = 116$. Suppose an examinee had scored 1 standard deviation below the reference group mean at the time of the earlier test, so that

$$\tilde{X}_{M_\infty \cdot E} = (.80/\sqrt{.90})(-1.00) = -0.84$$

If that examinee now scored 0.5 S.D.s above the mean on the present testing, our best estimate of her or his present true status would be

$$\frac{\dfrac{-0.84}{116} + \dfrac{0.50}{40}}{\dfrac{1}{116} + \dfrac{1}{40}} = \frac{-.00724 + .0125}{.0336} = +0.16 \text{ S.D.s}$$

The error of estimate for this value would be $\sqrt{1/.0336} = 5.46$, compared with a standard error of measurement for the present test of 6.32. We considerably modified our estimate of present status and also improved its precision somewhat by taking account of the earlier test results.

USING COLLATERAL INFORMATION FROM OTHER MEASURES

Of course, we can get a predicted value for true score on test X from measures of *any* other variables that are correlated with X. The supplementary information need not be from an earlier testing with X or a test very similar to X. Suppose we have scores on the Verbal, Quantitative, and Non-Verbal sections of the Cognitive Ability Tests and want to make our best estimate of *true* standing on whatever is measured by the type of tasks contributing to the Verbal score. We can determine the regression equation for predicting true Verbal score from the other two scores, and we can determine the multiple correlation of true Verbal score with a weighted composite of the other two scores. The formulas from the previous section still apply, with the modification that we must replace r_{ME} by the multiple correlation of true score on the predicted test, M, with the composite of predictor tests.

In the illustration that we have proposed, the basic data are approximately

$$r_{V \cdot Q} = .74 \qquad r_{Q \cdot NV} = .71$$
$$r_{V \cdot NV} = .66 \qquad r_{VV'} = .94$$
$$S.D._V = S.D._Q = S.D._{NV} = 16$$

Given these values, we get

$$R_{V_\infty(Q, NV)} = .788 \quad \text{and} \quad \tilde{z}_{V_\infty} = .567 z_Q + .278 z_{NV}$$

It should be noted that, to compute the multiple correlation with estimated true score, we must adjust each of the correlations between observed scores by the formula $r_{M_\infty \cdot X} = r_{MX}/\sqrt{r_{MM'}}$. The variance of estimated true scores is equal to $s_M^2(1 - R^2)$ or, in this illustration, $(16)^2(1 - .788^2) = 97.04$, and the error variance for the Verbal score is $s_M^2(1 - r_{MM'})$, in this case $(16)^2(1 - .94) = 15.36$.

Suppose, now, that an examinee obtained the following standard age scores on the three tests:

Verbal	120
Quantitative	105
Non-Verbal	108

The standard-score scale has a mean of 100 and a standard deviation of 16. Estimating true score on the Verbal test from Q and NV, we would have

$$\tilde{V}_\infty = .567(105 - 100) + .278(108 - 100) + 100$$
$$= 105.1$$

Putting the values that we have determined into the equation for the posterior estimate, we get

$$\frac{\dfrac{105.1}{97.04} + \dfrac{120}{15.36}}{\dfrac{1}{97.04} + \dfrac{1}{15.36}} = \frac{8.896}{.07538} = 118.0$$

The standard error attached to this estimated value is $\sqrt{1/.07538} = 3.64$, a modest (7%) improvement over the standard error of 3.92 derived from the Verbal test alone.

Note that this procedure tempered the estimate of the score on V toward the average of the scores on all three tests. In the same way, the scores on Q and NV would be tempered (upward), so that the profile of estimated true scores is always flatter than the profile of observed scores.

USING INFORMATION FROM OTHER INDIVIDUALS OR GROUPS

This application has already been covered in part in (1) the procedures for estimating true score, in which we regressed the individual's score toward the mean of his or her specific group, and (2) the procedures for estimating a group's mean score, in which we used prior information about the mean and variance of the general population. More generally, we can use information of any sort that is available to us about groups we consider similar to our present group as a basis for generating a prior estimate of some parameter in which we are interested, and we may then collect data to modify that prior estimate.

As an example, we might wish to estimate as accurately as possible the correlation between SAT Verbal score in our small liberal arts college and freshman grade point average. The College Entrance Examination Board may have published a report in which correlations for 10 small liberal arts colleges were reported as follows: .35, .38, .42, .43, .45, .45, .48, .51, and .54. This information provides us with the basis for generating a prior estimate of what the correlation is in our college. On the basis of our judgment about how much faith we should have in the similarity of our college to this set, we might decide on a 95% credible interval for our prior estimate that has a range extending from .30 to .60 with a mean value of .45. Roughly, this corresponds to a distribution with a standard deviation of .075. The standard error of a correlation coefficient of zero is approximated by

$$S.E._r = \frac{1}{\sqrt{N - 3}}$$

Putting the value .075 for $S.E._r$ in this equation and solving for N, we get $N =$

180. That is, we have judged our prior data to have a degree of precision corresponding to a sample of 180 cases.

We are now ready to collect data from a sample (or all) of our own freshman class. Let us suppose that we have a freshman class of 150 and that, for this group, the correlation turns out to be .52. Our best posterior estimate for the value to be expected in similar freshman groups in our college would then be given by

$$r_{\text{Post.}} = \frac{(177)(.45) + (147)(.52)}{177 + 147} = \frac{156.09}{324} = .482$$

and its standard error by

$$S.E._{\text{Post.}} = 1/\sqrt{324} = .056$$

This same technique can be applied quite generally to any statistic that approaches a normal sampling distribution. We use the existing data, together with our judgment of its relevance, to generate a prior probability distribution, and we estimate how much that prior information is "worth" expressed as a sample size. We then combine our prior estimate with the results from a data sample to produce what appears to be our best posterior estimate.

TAILOR-MADE TESTING

A natural sequel to Bayesian thinking about estimation and to considering the information function of a test item (as was done in Chapter 4) is to try to design testing procedures so that, at each stage in testing, the next item is chosen in such a way as to yield the greatest possible amount of information, given the present estimate of the examinee's standing on the latent trait that is being measured. Thus we start with a prior estimate for an individual, based at least on the person's age or grade but also possibly giving some weight to socioeconomic level or to earlier tests taken by that individual. We then search our item file for the item that will provide the greatest amount of information for a person with that estimated value of the latent trait θ. If the examinee passes the item, we revise upward our estimate of his or her standing. If he or she fails the item, we adjust our estimate downward. The next item is then selected in the light of our revised estimate. The sequence continues, with a revised estimate made after each item and selection of the next item always based on the most up-to-date estimate of the individual's standing on the latent trait.

This is the full Bayesian attack on tailored testing—on the precise adjustment of task difficulty to the individual's estimated ability level. We will report the equations necessary for application of the procedure presently. It should be clear, however, that this approach is feasible only with computer-administered testing. The arithmetical speed and accuracy of the computer are needed to carry out the calculations involved in adjusting the prior estimate of ability level, and its memory storage and search capabilities are required for storing the pool of items, together with their statistical parameters, and for scanning the available pool and selecting the next item for administration. For this reason, a wide variety of simpler approximations to the full Bayesian approach have been suggested, and they have been tried out with varying degrees of thoroughness. We identify six here and describe them briefly. They will be dealt with more fully after we have presented the Bayesian formulas.

Multilevel Format

Here the choice of level to be administered is based solely on prior information. Some published tests (Iowa Tests of Basic Skills, Cognitive Ability Tests) have been produced in a modular format such that, in a subtest, each successive module is more difficult than the one that preceded it. For the lowest level of the test, the examinee begins with the easiest module and continues through a specified number of modules. Each higher level moves up one in both the starting and the finishing modules. Thus a series of eight or ten levels of a test can be produced, each slightly more difficult than the one next below it. Choice of level for an examinee has typically been based on age or grade, but this can be modified on the basis of that individual's earlier test or classroom performance.

Two-stage Testing

In this model, the testing is divided into two segments. The initial segment, often rather brief, is uniform for all examinees and is used to determine which second segment the examinee is to take. The second segment exists in several alternate forms that differ in level of difficulty. Score on the first segment provides a rough estimate of ability level, and this estimate is used to select that one of the later forms that can be expected to provide the most additional information about the individual's standing on the latent trait.

Self-selecting Testing

Because even a two-stage testing procedure presents logistical problems in getting an initial test segment scored and examinees directed to the proper second segment, it has been proposed that each examinee use his or her own experience of the difficulty of the test items to guide him or her to a set of test items of difficulty appropriate for him or her. Test items (or modules) are arranged in order of difficulty, and the individual is started on items of average difficulty for persons of that age or grade group. If those items are easy for the examinee in question, the examinee moves ahead to harder items; if they seem hard, the examinee can move back to easier items. The particular set of items answered by each examinee can thus be made up of the ones that the examinee finds challenging but not overwhelming.

Alternation Testing

Once again, items are arranged in order of difficulty, but the starting item is one in the middle of the difficulty range. From this starting point, two limbs of a V extend out like this:

```
                                              _____    Harder
                                  _____
                       _____
           Start   _____
                       _____
                                  _____
                                              _____    Easier
```

Instructions indicate that, if an examinee passes the first item, he or she is to proceed to the next more difficult item and, if this is passed, to continue on to the next more difficult item. The examinee continues up the side of harder items until one is failed. At that point, he or she shifts to the first item of the lower or "easier" wing and continues down that route until an item is passed. Whenever an item is passed, the individual switches to the first unattempted item of the upper wing; whenever an item is failed, the individual switches to the first unattempted item in the lower wing. Testing continues until the examinee has attempted a specified number of items.

Pyramidal (Multistage) Testing

This model requires a set of items prearranged by level of difficulty and order in the testing sequence. The typical pattern is illustrated below for a 5-stage pyramid.

	STAGE					
	I	II	III	IV	V	
	—	—	—	—	—	
					11	Difficult
				7		
			4		12	
		2		8		
Start	1		5		13	
		3		9		
			6		14	
				10		
					15	Easy

All individuals start with item 1. Those who pass item 1 go to item 2, while those who fail go to item 3. At each stage, those who pass move up to the somewhat more difficult item at the following stage, while those who fail move to the somewhat easier one. Note that a pool of 15 items is required for a 5-stage test, in which each examinee takes 5 items; 55 for a 10-stage test; and 120 for a 15-stage test. As the desired test length increases, the size of the necessary item pool (with items closely controlled for difficulty) expands rapidly.

Stradaptive Testing

The term *stradaptive* was coined by Weiss (1973) to designate a model in which items are grouped into strata, each stratum being homogeneous in difficulty. Testing for an individual begins with the first item of the stratum that is believed, on the basis of age, grade, or additional prior knowledge, to be appropriate for that examinee. If the item is passed, the examinee is given the first item of the next more difficult stratum. If it is failed, testing moves to the next easier stratum. Each time an item is passed, one moves up; each time an item is failed, one moves down. Within a stratum, the items are arranged in order, usually from the most to the least discriminating item. At any point in the testing, when testing moves to a given stratum, the first unused item in the list for that stratum is administered. Typically, testing oscillates between the two or three strata that are closest to the individual's ability level.

THE BAYESIAN MODEL

We will return now to the Bayesian model, elaborating it in some detail and giving the necessary equations for calculating the mean and dispersion of the posterior estimate of the examinee's ability at each stage in testing. After that, we will explore the administratively simpler alternative procedures, considering their practical advantages and limitations, the precision that they appear to make possible, and the issues and decisions that arise with each.

Before we begin to test a person, we have certain information about that person, even if it is no more than the age or grade group to which the person belongs. With only that information, our prior probability distribution corresponds to the known distribution of the ability in that group, and our best estimate of the person's ability is that it falls at the mean of the group. Because of the considerable variability within the group, the "credible interval" covers quite a range at, for example, the 95% level of belief. If we express the results for the group in z scores, our prior probability for each individual can plausibly be expressed as $N(0,1)$, a normal probability function with mean equal to the mean of the group and dispersion equal to the standard deviation in the group. With each successive item passed or failed, the mean and variance of this function are modified. The mean rises or falls depending on the success or failure of the examinee, but the dispersion of the posterior estimate continuously decreases as more information accumulates.

Equations provided by Owen (1975) permit calculation of the mean and dispersion of the posterior estimate of ability level after the addition of the $(m + 1)$th test item. Owen's* equations are

Following a right answer:

$$\mu_{m+1} = \mu_m + (1 - c_g) \left[\frac{\sigma_m^2}{\sqrt{\frac{1}{a_g^2} + \sigma_m^2}} \right] \left[\frac{\phi(D)}{c_g + (1 - c_g)\, \Phi(-D)} \right] \tag{10.1}$$

and

$$\sigma_{m+1}^2 = \sigma_m^2 \left\{ 1 - \left[\frac{1 - c_g}{1 + \frac{1}{a_g^2 \sigma_m^2}} \right] \left[\frac{\phi(D)}{A} \right] \left[\frac{(1 - c_g)\phi(D)}{A} - D \right] \right\}$$

Following a wrong answer:

$$\mu_{m+1} = \mu_m - \left(\frac{\sigma_m^2}{\sqrt{\frac{1}{a_g^2} + \sigma_m^2}} \right) \left(\frac{\phi(D)}{\Phi(D)} \right)$$

and

$$\sigma_{m+1}^2 = \sigma_m^2 \left[1 - \left(\frac{\phi(D)}{1 + \frac{1}{a_g^2 \sigma_m^2}} \right) \left(\frac{\phi(D) + D}{\Phi(D)} \right) \right] \tag{10.2}$$

where $\phi(D)$ = normal probability density function (that is, the ordinate of the normal curve) at point D

$\Phi(D)$ = cumulative normal distribution function (or area under the unit normal curve) up to the point D

$$D = \frac{b_g - \mu_m}{\sqrt{\frac{1}{a_g^2} + \sigma_m^2}}$$

$$A = c_g + (1 - c_g)\Phi(-D)$$

---

* From R. J. Owen, "A Bayesian Sequential Procedure for Quantal Response in the Context of Adaptive Mental Testing," *Journal of the American Statistical Association*, Vol. 70, 1975. Used by permission.

a_g, b_g, and c_g are, as in Chapters 1 and 4, the parameters of the item characteristic function for the $(m + 1)$th item.

Thus, when $m = 0$, $\mu_m = 0$, and $\sigma_m^2 = 1$, these define the starting prior distribution. The posterior distribution calculated after the addition of each item becomes the prior distribution for the addition of the next item.

To illustrate the operation of this system, assume that we have an unlimited pool of items, all with a discrimination parameter a_g of 1.00 and an asymptote parameter c_g of .20. Assume that we can, at each stage, select an item the difficulty of which exactly matches the prior estimate of the examinee's ability level — that is, $b_g - \mu_m = 0$. Suppose that, for a given examinee, we have the sequence of pass, fail, pass, pass, fail, fail for the initial six test items administered. Let us follow what happens to our estimate of ability level, both its mean value and its dispersion.

For the first item, we have

$$\mu_1 = 0 + (1 - 0.20)\ \left(\frac{1}{\sqrt{1+1}}\right)\left(\frac{0.3989}{0.20 + (0.80)(.50)}\right)$$

$$= 0.376$$

$$\sigma_1^2 = 1.0(1.0 - \left(\frac{1.0 - 0.20}{1.0 + \dfrac{1.0}{1.0}}\right)\left(\frac{0.3989}{0.20 + (0.80)(0.50)}\right)\left(\frac{(0.80)(0.3989)}{0.20 + (0.80)(0.50)}\right)$$

$$= 0.859$$

Thus, when we know that our examinee has passed the first item, we raise our best estimate of the examinee's ability to 0.376 (expressed in group standard deviation units of ability), and we reduce the dispersion of our beliefs to a variance of 0.859. Now, when he or she fails item 2, we have

$$\mu_2 = 0.376 - \left(\frac{0.859}{\sqrt{1.0 + 0.859}}\right)\left(\frac{0.3989}{0.50}\right)$$

$$= -0.127$$

$$\sigma_2^2 = 0.859\left\{1.0 - \left(\frac{.3989}{1.0 + \dfrac{1.0}{0.859}}\right)\left(\frac{.3989}{0.25}\right)\right\}$$

$$= 0.606$$

The complete results for the set of six items are as follows:

AFTER ITEM	RESPONSE	μ	σ^2	σ
1	pass	0.376	0.859	0.927
2	fail	-0.127	0.606	0.778
3	pass	0.127	0.541	0.736
4	pass	0.359	0.487	0.698
5	fail	0.040	0.385	0.620
6	fail	-0.221	0.317	0.563

It is worth noting that the items gotten wrong have more effect on both the mean and the dispersion than do the items gotten right. This is due to the possibility of getting an item right by guessing, represented in this illustration by a value of 0.20 for c_g. Basically, for this reason an item gotten wrong provides more information about an examinee's ability (or rather, lack of it) than does an item gotten right. If there were no guessing ($c_g = 0$) the effects of rights and wrongs would be symmetrical.

In our illustration, after six items we estimate that this examinee falls about one-fifth of the group standard deviation below the group mean, and this estimate has attached to it a standard error of estimate (or range of uncertainty) equal to $\sqrt{0.317}\sigma$, which is 0.563 as large as the group standard deviation that represented our initial standard error for estimating that person's score. When the test is computer-administered, the computer can be programmed to terminate testing either when the standard error of measurement drops below some specified amount that is deemed acceptable or after a specified number of items has been presented.

In the discussion so far, it has been assumed that our prior information was limited to the single fact that the examinee is a member of some general group— a 10-year-old or a fifth-grader, for example. When this is so, our prior probability distribution can be no more than the general distribution of the attribute in the total age or grade group. The distribution of our prior belief has the same mean and dispersion as those of the trait in that population. However, we often have some additional information that permits us to refine our prior belief, changing its mean and making it more precise. Thus, if we know that a year earlier Alice scored at $+1.00\sigma$ on a test that (with a one-year interval) correlates .90 with present status on the latent trait θ, we can apply a regression equation and the formula for the standard error of estimate to give us a prior of $N(0.90, 0.44)$. That is, we start with the belief that the most likely position for Alice on the trait is $+\frac{9}{10}$ of a standard deviation unit and the dispersion of our interval of belief is $\frac{44}{100}$ of a standard deviation unit.

This modified and more precise estimate constitutes our situation at stage m, and item $m + 1$, the first item in our current testing, operates to modify this initial situation. If the other assumptions of our illustrative example on page 304 remain unchanged and we have the same sequence of rights and wrongs, we get

$$\mu_{m+1} = 0.90 + (1.0 - 0.20)\left(\frac{0.19}{\sqrt{1.0 + 0.19}}\right)\left(\frac{0.3989}{0.20 + (0.80)(0.50)}\right)$$

$$= 0.90 + 0.092 = 0.992$$

$$\sigma^2_{m+1} = 0.19 \left\{1.0 - \left(\frac{0.80}{1.0 + \frac{1.0}{0.19}}\right)\left(\frac{0.3989}{.20 + (0.80)(0.50)}\right)\right.$$

$$\left. \times \left(\frac{0.80\,(0.3989)}{0.20 + (0.80)(0.50)}\right)\right\}$$

$$= 0.181$$

$$\mu_{m+2} = 0.992 - \left(\frac{0.180}{\sqrt{1.0 + 0.180}}\right)\left(\frac{0.3989}{0.50}\right)$$

$$= 0.992 - 0.132 = 0.859$$

$$\sigma^2_{m+2} = 0.181 \left\{1.0 - \left(\frac{0.3989}{1.0 + \frac{1.0}{0.18}}\right)\left(\frac{0.3989}{.25}\right)\right\}$$

$$= 0.163$$

For a set of six items with the sequence C, X, C, C, X, X, the results are as follows:

AFTER ITEM	RESPONSE	μ	σ^2	σ
$m + 1$	pass	0.992	0.181	0.425
$m + 2$	fail	0.859	0.163	0.404
$m + 3$	pass	0.939	0.157	0.396
$m + 4$	pass	1.017	0.151	0.389
$m + 5$	fail	0.905	0.138	0.371
$m + 6$	fail	0.802	0.127	0.356

The effect of adding data from six new items to the fairly substantial information provided by the earlier test is observable but modest. Not surprisingly, the mean of our final belief system is determined primarily by the earlier test, and the dispersion of our belief system is not greatly reduced by the six added items.

With whatever initial information is available to us, we should establish our most reasonable prior belief system. Equations 10.1 and 10.2 can then be applied to modify the belief system as we get the results of presenting new items to the examinee.

In our illustration we have presented a highly idealized and simplified picture of the testing process. Items are usually not all equal in their discrimination parameters. With a finite set of test items, it is rarely possible to find an item that exactly matches the current estimate of an examinee's ability, and difficulty of doing so is likely to increase as testing continues and the pool of items is depleted. Consequently, reduction of the standard error of measurement is likely to proceed somewhat more slowly than in this ideal example—though a good deal faster per item than would be the case if a uniform test were presented to all examinees.

As indicated earlier, the fundamental difficulty with this complete Bayesian approach is that it is feasible only when adequate examinee computer terminals and adequate computer memory are available so that completely computerized testing is possible.

ALTERNATIVE TESTING PROCEDURES

We turn now to the various approaches that have been tried to simplify adaptive testing procedures, while maintaining as much as possible of the improved efficiency. Some of these, at least, may be practical for administration by a human examiner and even (perhaps) for group administration.

MULTILEVEL TEST FORMAT

It is a relatively simple matter to prepare a test in the form of a series of modules, each one at a higher difficulty level than the one before it. The level of test administered can then be determined by the module at which the individual enters the test and the module at which she or he terminates. For example, each subtest of the Cognitive Abilities Tests is composed of 12 modules, each consisting of 3 to 5 items. There are 8 entry modules corresponding to the 8 levels of the test, A to H, and each test level consists of 5 modules.

With a multilevel format it is not possible to have all items at an optimal level of difficulty for an individual. However, it should be possible to choose a test level such that the middle module or modules are close to the optimal difficulty, while the first and last modules (though easy and difficult, respectively) still contribute some useful information toward appraisal of the examinee's ability level. The chief operational problem is to determine, for each examinee, the level of the test that will provide the maximum amount of information about that person.

Table 10.1   Standard Errors of Measurement for Four Test Levels, Expressed as Raw Scores and as Universal-Scale Scores*

RAW-SCORE LEVEL	RAW SCORE S.E._MEAS.				UNIVERSAL-SCALE SCORE CORRESPONDING TO RAW SCORE				UNIVERSAL-SCALE SCORE S.E._MEAS.			
	A	C	E	G	A	C	E	G	A	C	E	G
85	2.70	3.08	3.30	3.16	130	147	166	189	5.0	6.2	7.2	7.4
75	4.32	3.51	4.24	3.97	114	131	148	171	6.3	4.3	5.9	6.0
65	3.66	4.16	3.74	3.62	102	120	136	157	3.7	4.2	3.7	3.6
55	3.60	4.09	4.06	4.05	93	111	126	146	2.8	3.6	3.6	4.6
45	3.57	4.57	3.68	3.78	85	102	117	135	2.6	4.1	3.3	3.8
35	4.23	3.64	4.74	4.62	77	93	108	125	3.2	3.6	5.1	4.9
25	3.58	3.31	4.15	2.06	67	82	95	113	4.6	4.0	6.2	3.1

* From R. L. Thorndike and E. P. Hagen, *Cognitive Ability Tests.* Iowa City, Iowa: Riverside Publishing Co. Used by permission.

The first requirement for setting up a strategy for assigning examinees to test levels is that raw scores on all the different test levels be expressed in a common converted-score scale. Where most of the items in adjacent test levels are shared (80% of items in the case of the Cognitive Abilities Tests), the common items provide a bridging test through which this common conversion can be achieved via procedures set forth in Chapter 5 (pages 117–121). A standard-score scale can be set up, anchored to some middle level of the test series, and raw scores for each level can be expressed in terms of this universal standard-score scale.

If one is willing to accept its assumptions, the Rasch scaling procedure described in Chapter 4 (pp. 96 ff.) could also be used to establish a common universal-score scale, though it would be likely to prove quite laborious for tests of considerable length. Using the items common to adjacent levels, the mean difference in item scale value in the two test levels would provide an amount to be added to (or subtracted from) a given level to convert its scale to that of an adjoining level. By successive additions (or subtractions), the adjustment could be determined that bring all levels to the scale of one common, near-central level.

The next requirement is to determine the standard error of measurement at different raw-score levels for each test level. Procedures for doing this have been described in Chapter 6 (pages 173–174). These raw-score levels and raw-score standard errors can then be converted to and expressed in units of the universal standard-score scale. The result is a table like Table 10.1, which illustrates the procedure for Levels A, C, E, and G of the Cognitive Abilities Test, Verbal Form 1. (Material on Levels B, D, F, and H has been omitted to simplify the presentation.) In Table 10.1 the raw-score standard errors appear somewhat smaller at the extremes than in the middle range. However, when they are converted to

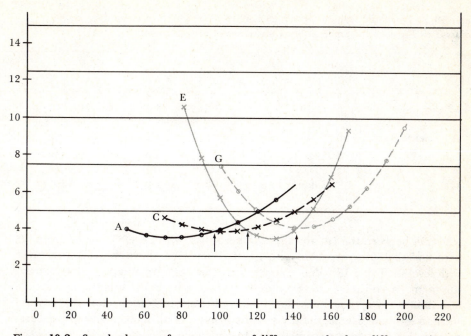

Figure **10.2** Standard error of measurement of different test levels at different universal scale scores.

universal-scale scores, the situation is generally reversed. The greater precision is now in the intermediate range. The set of values for each level is unfortunately somewhat erratic. (The calculations were based on 500 cases for each level of the test, but substantially larger numbers would be needed to produce stable estimates at each of 7 different score levels.) Some type of smoothing of the data is required, and so is something to provide an estimate of the precision at each point on the score scale. For that reason, a quadratic curve was fitted by least squares to the points calculated in Table 10.1 for each of the four levels of the test. The curves have been plotted in Figure 10.2, and these make it possible to determine the range of universal-scale scores for which each level provides the smallest standard error of measurement. In our illustration, Level A is optimal for universal-scale scores below about 97, Level C for scale scores from 97 to 115, Level E for scale scores from 115 to 142, and Level G for scale scores above 142. A comparison of the standard errors estimated by the curves indicates the amount by which the optimal level surpasses its nearest competitor.

The final step is to translate these optimal ranges into percentiles or standard scores for specific age or grade groups. This is done in Table 10.2, using the normative data obtained in the national standardization of the Cognitive Abilities Tests. If we take a 12-year-old as an illustration, a child who was estimated to fall below the 7th percentile would be most accurately tested with Level A, one

Table **10.2** Percentile Ranges for Which Each of Four Levels of Cognitive Ability Test Provides the Smallest Standard Error of Measurement

TEST LEVEL	AGE								
	8	9	10	11	12	13	14	15	16
A	below 81	−55	−31	−16	−7	−5	−3	−2	
C	81–96	55–84	31–52	16–40	7–25	5–14	3–10	2–6	1–4
E	97+	84–99	52–94	40–83	25–69	14–52	10–42	6–31	4–23
G			95+	84+	70+	53+	43+	32+	24+

who falls between the 7th and the 25th percentile with Level C, one between the 25th and the 69th percentile with Level E, and one above the 70th percentile with level G. Table 10.2 defines the optimal strategy for obtaining precise measurement, given that we have a sound prior estimate of the standing (percentile or standard score) of an individual in his or her age or grade group. The bases of such an estimate are potentially so varied that it is difficult to give any general prescription for how the estimate is to be arrived at. The most accurate estimate is likely to be based on some type of earlier test, especially a test similar to the one about to be given. If one knows or can make a good estimate of the correlation between the type of earlier test and the one about to be given, taking account of the age level of the examinee and the interval between testings, a simple and appropriate estimate is that the deviation on the new test, Y, will be equal to r_{xy} times the deviation on the earlier test, X, each expressed in standard deviation units. Less accurate estimates can be based on school marks, on teachers' estimates of ability, or on some selection or combination of demographic variables. In the last instance, estimated level of test performance should be set at the test score level of the most differentiating demographic category to which the examinee belongs.

Using prior information to select the most appropriate level of a multilevel test is certainly one of the simplest ways of adapting the test that is administered to the ability level of the examinee. It is practical for large-scale group test administration, because the only adjustment that needs to be made to ordinary group testing procedures is to regroup examinees prior to the test administration by level of test to be administered. The limitation—and it is a fairly serious limitation—is that the typical existing multilevel test, designed for administration to a whole grade group, is a fairly broad-band test with a rather flat-topped information function and relatively uniform standard error over quite a range. This is illustrated by the values in Table 10.1 and by the curves fitted to these points in Figure 10.2. The standard error of measurement curves are rather flat, and at many levels the difference in precision between adjacent test levels is quite small. Multilevel tests *could* be built having greater uniformity of difficulty within modules, larger modules, and larger gaps between modules. Each level of the test would then have a more peaked information function and hence be more efficient, but over a narrower range.

TWO-STAGE TEST ADMINISTRATION

Because prior score on a similar type of test, even one of only modest reliability, is usually the most accurate advance indicator of an individual's standing on the latent attribute that we want to measure, it has frequently been proposed that a brief initial test be used to determine which level of the main test an individual is to take. Such a procedure could be very effective when a main test already exists in a peaked multilevel format, and when the local situation makes it possible to give the routing test a few days in advance of the main testing, so that it could be scored and assignments made to levels of the main test. It could also be an effective model for individual testing, in which the examiner would first give the routing test and then, on the basis of the results from it, select the modules of items that were to make up the main test for the examinee.

More frequently envisaged and encountered is the situation in which (1) the routing test and the main test must be given at a single testing session, and (2) the several levels of the main test are distinct test forms developed specifically for the purpose of tailored testing. Under these conditions, a number of issues arise.

1. Given a fixed limit on time for testing, how much time should be devoted to the routing test and how much to the main test?

2. How many levels of the main test should there be, and how much should they differ in difficulty?

3. How can scores on the routing test be obtained quickly enough to make the procedure practical?

4. What decision rule should be applied to score on the routing test to determine the level of the main test to be administered?

5. Should score on the routing test be weighted with score on the main test to arrive at a final posterior estimate of ability level for the examinee, and if so how is that weighting to be determined?

6. What should be done so that performance on the several levels of the main test be expressed on a common score scale?

Length of Routing Test and Main Test

Given a fixed amount of time, which is the usual situation in testing, there is obviously a trade-off between time spent on the routing test and time spent on the main test. A longer routing test means a more accurate prior determination of ability level and correspondingly greater assurance that the examinee is routed to the main test that will yield the most information per item. A longer main test means more accurate measurement of those who take it. The best division of time would seem to depend on certain characteristics of the set of main tests — specifically, how many different levels there are to be and how widely they are to be spaced. It seems intuitively reasonable that, the fewer levels of the main test there are and the more widely they are spaced, the more important it will be to have a reliable routing test so that errors made in assigning examinees to a level of the main test are few and minor. It also seems reasonable that more time be allocated to the routing test if scores on that test will actually be weighted into the final estimate of the examinee's standing on the latent trait. We have no analytic solution of the problem nor any specific numerical guidelines at this time.

Number of Levels of Main Test, Variability of Item Difficulty, and Amount of Separation

In theory, at least, the more levels there are of the main test, the more exactly the test can be adapted to the estimated ability level of the examinee. This is the appeal of the modular multilevel format. However, when several distinct tests are prepared, and perhaps printed in separate booklets, there are very real practical limits to the number of test forms that can be printed up, and a practical limit may also be involved in handling the mechanics of testing. This may well dictate that we limit ourselves to 2, 3, or 4 levels of the main test.

Given a decision on the number of test forms, it may be intuitively plausible to set the *average* difficulty level of the forms so that they are centered in equal segments of the total ability range with which we are concerned. Thus, if we assume that we have a population with a range of 6 standard deviations on the latent attribute, it might be reasonable to plan average difficulty levels as follows:

2 levels	$-1.5\sigma, +1.5\sigma$
3 levels	$-2.0\sigma, 0.0\sigma, +2.0\sigma$
4 levels	$-2.25\sigma, -0.75\sigma, +0.75\sigma, +2.25\sigma$
5 levels	$-2.4\sigma, -1.2\sigma, 0.0\sigma, +1.2\sigma, +2.4\sigma$

Thus, if only 2 levels of the main test were prepared, the more difficult would be given to all persons falling above the group mean on the routing test and the easier to all falling below the mean. With 3 levels, the most difficult would be used for those with estimated standing on the latent trait above $+1.0\sigma$, the intermediate test for those estimated to lie between $+1.0\sigma$ and -1.0σ, and the lowest level for those estimated to lie below -1.0σ. These estimates would be based on the regression of the main test on the routing test.

In planning the spread of item difficulty within each level of the test, we might try to produce an information function that was highest at the middle and dropped off *only slightly* at the limits of the range of the latent attribute for which that test was to be used. This specifies that the highest and lowest levels of the test be nearly as effective at the extremes, where relatively few cases are found, as at intermediate levels. We might wish to temper the test design to allow somewhat more loss of efficiency at these extreme values. On the other hand, in some situations these may represent the part of the range within which key personal or personnel decisions are made. Only familiarity with the specific use situation can guide decisions about where high precision is most important. In general, a specification of equal information would imply approximately an even distribution of item difficulties over that segment of the latent attribute for which the test in question was to be used.

Obtaining Scores on the Routing Test

If the routing test is to be administered one or several days before the main test, it may well be feasible to use a conventional answer sheet and to have scoring done by hand or by an optical scanner. The resulting scores can be used to assign individuals to particular levels of the main test. If the routing test is to be given *immediately before* the main test, some form of immediate scoring is necessary, and each examinee's participation will be required to determine what score he or she got. The most satisfactory procedure would seem to be to use one of the *latent image* forms of printing on the answer sheet. In this case, the answer sheet is imprinted with an invisible chemical, coding whether a given answer choice is right or wrong. The chemical is activated by another chemical in a crayon or felt-tipped pen. When a particular answer space is marked with the pen, a reaction between the chemical on the pen and that on the paper develops the latent image, with the result that an R or a W, or some similar code, becomes visible in the marked area on the answer sheet. If instructions restrict the examinee to marking one choice per item, then a simple count of the number of R's (unless a correction for guessing is used) will give the examinee's score. The count can be done immediately by the examinee and the score recorded. This score can then be used to route the examinee to the proper level of the main test.

The Decision Rule

The correlation between raw score on the routing test and true position on the latent trait can be considered to be given by $\sqrt{r_{11}}$, where r_{11} is the reliability coefficient for the routing test. Thus, in standard-score form, an individual's estimated position on the latent trait would be given by

$$z_{\text{trait}} = \sqrt{r_{11}} \, z_{\text{routing test}}$$

Once one has an estimate of the individual's standing on the latent trait, one would presumably assign the test level designed, as indicated in the previous section, to provide maximum information at that ability level. Thus, with two symmetrically placed levels of the test, persons estimated to lie above the population mean on the latent trait would be assigned to the more difficult test, and those below the mean to the easier test. With 3 levels, assignment would be made to the lower level if the estimated trait standard score were below -1.0σ, to the middle level if the estimated trait score were between -1.0σ and $+1.0\sigma$, and to the highest level if the estimated trait score were above $+1.0\sigma$.

Using the Routing Test in the Final Score Estimate

It seems as though information from the routing test should generally be included in arriving at the *final* judgment about the examinee's standing on the latent trait. In effect, the routing test establishes a prior probability with a standard score mean of $z_r\sqrt{r_{11}}$, where z_r is the standard score on the routing test and r_{11} is the reliability of the routing test. The standard error of estimate of the trait score is $(1 - r_{11}^{1/2})^{1/2}$, and this represents the dispersion of the prior estimate. If we define the precision as the reciprocal of the variance in standard-score units, the precision of our prior estimate, based on the routing test, is $1/(1 - r_{11}^{1/2})$.

The routing and main tests are likely to be composed of items with about the same level of discrimination, as represented by the item discrimination parameter a_g. Hence the average precision of the two tends to be roughly proportional to the number of items in each. The information provided per item by the second-stage tests *should* be somewhat greater, over the ability range in which each is used, because more of the items should be appropriate in difficulty for each examinee. However, as a first approximation, estimates of θ from the routing test and the main test might be weighted in proportion to the number of items contained in each. That is, if the routing test contained 10 items and the second-stage test 30 items, the score would be

$$\theta_{tot} = \frac{\theta_r + 3\theta_s}{4}$$

where θ_r =   trait level estimated from the routing test
             θ_s =   trait level estimated from the second-stage test
             θ_{tot} =   final estimate of trait level

One could argue for giving somewhat greater weight than indicated here to the second-stage test to reflect the more appropriate difficulty level of the items, but this would become significant in practice only if the forms of the main test each covered a quite narrow band and the routing test covered a wide range of difficulty.

Defining a Common Score Scale for the Several Tests

Establishing a common score scale for the several second-stage tests, as well as the routing test, can be accomplished through procedures for item and score scaling set forth in Chapters 4 and 5. The simplest procedure is to assume the Rasch single-parameter model, in which all items are assumed to share the same steepness parameter and in which all lower asymptotes are assumed to be zero. For each of the second-stage tests, an internal Rasch scaling provides difficulty scale values for each of the items and ability scale values for each of the score levels. The problem is now to tie these separate scales together into a single common scale.

If there is some overlap of items in adjoining levels of the second-stage tests, those common items can be used to adjust the scale values of the tests to a common scale. This may often be the case. That is, it will seem appropriate to include some items designed to be the hardest items of the level 1 test as the easier items of the level 2 test, and similarly for any additional levels. Suppose we found the following average scale values for common items:

	COMMON TO LEVELS 1 AND 2	COMMON TO LEVELS 2 AND 3
Level 1	+ 1.50	
Level 2	− 1.00	+ 1.25
Level 3		− 0.75

Then, if we decided to base our common scale on level 2, all level 1 item difficulties and score ability levels would be reduced by 2.50, and all level 3 values would be increased by 2.00. A person who had taken level 1 and gotten enough items right to receive a score of + 2.00 on that scale would receive a score of − 0.50 on the common scale based on level 2.

If no overlap of items exists, some common anchor test must be administered to all the groups taking different tests, and the scale values of the items in the anchor test be determined separately for each of the groups. Differences between the groups in the average of the resulting *scale values* can then be used as described above.*

Similar procedures might be applied using the more complex three-parameter model, if the simple Rasch model is not considered appropriate. If the more complex model is used, large groups are required in order to get stable scaling.

SELF-SELECTED TESTING

A procedure that lets the examinee choose the level of test tasks that he or she considers most appropriate is based on the assumption that an examinee knows whether a test task is easy or difficult and will pick tasks at an appropriate level to provide approximately maximum information about his or her ability. There is relatively little information to show how generally this is true. Prestwood and Weiss (1977) provide some evidence that examinees see as suitable for them

---

* One caution: The routing test, if actually used to assign persons to groups, cannot at the same time serve as *anchor test*. Regression effects would distort the equating.

items that are really too easy to be efficient providers of information. It is possible, though the issue has been little investigated, that choice of items may depend on temperamental characteristics as much as on ability. The examinee with high test anxiety might well seek security in doing very easy tasks, almost all of which were gotten right. If this were so, the set of items would not be efficient ones to provide information about that person's ability level. It would be important for examinees to understand that their final score would not suffer if they attempted items near the limit of their ability. Following the directions for this model of test would appear to require some sophistication, so the procedure would probably not be suitable below the senior high school level.

To operate efficiently, self-selected testing would need modules such as those described in the section on multilevel tests. Modules would be arranged in order of difficulty, and the items in each module would be chosen to be quite homogeneous in difficulty level. The examinee would be required to try *all* the items in a given module and *then* would have the choice of whether to move up to a more difficult module or down to an easier one. After each module was completed, the choice would recur—to go up or to go down to an untried module. One would probably want to specify the number of modules to be completed, so that each examinee would take the same length of test.

Aside from the problem of instructing examinees and getting them to take an appropriate set of items, the main problem with this model of testing would seem to be that of assigning a score level to each examinee when various combinations of testing modules can occur. Assuming that difficulty scale values have been determined for each item referred to a common base population, the procedures described for equating the several levels of test in two-stage testing could be used to assign a scale value to any score from 1 to $n - 1$ items right (each module containing n items) for each of the modules. Thus an individual would receive scale scores on several of the modules taken. The most dependable information would come from modules in which the percentage of success (corrected for guessing) was near 50%, and one might choose to base the individual's final score on an average of the scale values from the 2 or 3 modules that came closest to this level. Or one could simply average the scale values for all the modules the individual attempted on which some but not all of the items were gotten right.

ALTERNATION TESTING

In this model, all examinees start at a common starting point. An examinee moves up to the next more difficult item if the first item is passed and keeps moving up the sequence of more difficult items as long as she or he passes. When an item is failed, the examinee switches to the lower limb of the V and attempts the first untried item on that limb, continuing down as long as the items are failed. Every pass switches the examinee to the upper limb, and every fail switches him or her to the lower limb. The examinee must keep track of which items have been attempted and must follow the procedural directions about which item is to be attempted next. This fact would seem to limit the model to types of examinees who can follow fairly complex directions.

Immediate feedback must be given on success and failure to guide subsequent item choices. This can probably be best accomplished by the use of latent image printing on the answer sheets. Instructions must specify when to stop. This would normally be after a specified number of items had been attempted, uniform for all examinees. Thus, if each limb of the V contained 24 items, all examinees could be instructed to complete 25 items. At one extreme, they could have passed the initial item and all items in the upper limb; at the other, they could have failed the first item and all items in the lower limb. Usually they would have shown a combination of passes and failures. A simple raw score would be the total number of items passed, and this would probably prove quite serviceable because for a given number of items passed, the items passed would be much the same for all examinees. This score could be converted into a percentile or standard score for some reference group.

The alternation pattern does tend to assure that at least *some* of the items are of a difficulty level appropriate for each examinee. However, rather than converging on the examinee's ability level and giving items more and more closely centered around that level, this pattern tends to lead to wider and wider oscillation of item difficulties as the test proceeds. For persons of average ability, one reaches a point where one is alternating between an item that is obviously too easy and one that is obviously too difficult. As items deviate markedly from the examinee's ability level, those items add little information and the test gains little in precision. In addition, it seems likely that the experience of wide swings in item difficulty might be disorganizing for some examinees.

THE PYRAMIDAL TEST

One of the most frequently proposed and studied of the adaptive testing models is the multistage pyramidal test. This starts with an entry item and presents a somewhat more difficult item as the second item if the first item is passed, a somewhat easier item if the first one is failed. The progress up or down is repeated at each stage of the pyramid. The pyramidal model is perhaps the closest approach to the full Bayesian model, because the adjustment at each stage can be approximately what would be dictated by the prior estimate of the examinee's ability based on the history of passes and failures at the earlier stages. It differs in that the location of the items in the pyramid is pre-established once and for all, so that an item can be used only at the one place in the pyramid where it has been placed. This tends to be wasteful of items and quite demanding on the test maker, who must produce enough items of specified levels of difficulty to complete the pyramid.

More information is available after each stage in the pyramid, so it seems logical, following the Bayesian model, that the intervals between adjacent items should become smaller at each stage. If one chose to have item difficulty match the posterior estimate of ability level, one could use the formulas given on page 303 to estimate how much the extreme items should increase or decrease in difficulty scale value at each stage, given that one could make a reasonable estimate of the typical item discrimination parameter a_g and the guessing parameter c_g. The intermediate items could then be evenly spaced between the extremes, representing a good approximation to the exact values that the formulas would call for. We will illustrate the model for a 10-stage pyramid in which it has been assumed that $\overline{a}_g = 0.7$ and $c_g = 0.0$ on page 319.

The numbers in parentheses for the first 3 stages refer to item numbers, whereas the figures represent the desired values of the difficulty parameter b_g on a scale on which the group's mean on the latent attribute serves as the zero point and the scale unit is equal to the standard deviation of the group.* Obviously, with a real pool of items it would never be possible to match a model such as this perfectly, but it illustrates the type of target that one might choose to aim at. In order to be able to approximate it at all closely, it would ordinarily be necessary to try out a substantial surplus of items.

Group administration of a pyramidal test would seem to be feasible if a suitable latent-image answer sheet were used. The answer sheet would have to provide space to print, for each answer choice, the number of the item that the examinee was to attempt next. Thus all examinees would start with item 1. Those who chose the right answer would read "2" in the answer space they had marked, this being an instruction to go next to item 2. Meanwhile, those who chose a wrong answer could see "3." At the next stage, those who picked the right answer to item 2 would see (4), while those who chose the wrong answer to item 2, as well as those who chose the right answer to item 3, would see "5," and so on. Of course, if the test had very many stages, the test booklet would tend to become somewhat bulky, but this proliferation of items is one of the problems inherent in a pyramidal test. The pyramidal test could readily be administered by computer, but for computer administration one would generally prefer the greater flexibility of a fully Bayesian model.

The test maker faces three main types of decisions in the construction of a pyramidal test: (1) how many stages there should be in the pyramid, (2) how widely the items in each stage should be spaced, and (3) how the performance of an examinee should be scored. We will consider each of these in turn.

Number of Stages

Deciding on the number of stages represents a compromise between desirable precision of measurement and practical size of the item pool. Some impression of

---

*If the c_g parameter is not zero, the pyramid will be asymmetrical. Thus, if $c_g = 0.20$, the items on the lower border will remain unchanged but the items on the top border will increase by smaller amounts. In stages 2, 3, and 4 of the pyramid they will become, respectively, 0.30, 0.58, and 0.85.

STAGE

1	2	3	4	5	6	7	8	9	10
(1) .00	(2) .46	(4) .84	1.16	1.44	1.68	1.89	2.08	2.25	2.42
	(3) −.46	(5) .00	.39	.72	1.01	1.26	1.49	1.69	1.88
		(6) −.84	−.39	.00	.34	.63	.90	1.12	1.32
			−1.16	−.72	−.34	.00	.31	.56	.79
				−1.44	−1.01	−.63	−.31	.00	.25
					−1.68	−1.26	−.90	−.56	−.25
						−1.89	−1.49	−1.12	−.79
							−2.08	−1.69	−1.32
								−2.25	−1.88
									−2.42

Table **10.3**   Standard Error of Measurement* for Tests with
Different Values of a_g and Different Lengths

NUMBER OF STAGES	NUMBER OF ITEMS	VALUE OF a_g					
		.30	.50	.70	1.00	1.50	2.00
		S.E.$_m$	S.E.$_m$	S.E.$_m$	S.E.$_m$	S.E.$_m$	S.E.$_m$
3	6	.926	.833	.742	.631	.508	.433
6	21	.866	.727	.611	.487	.364	.293
9	45	.816	.654	.530	.409	.295	.232
12	78	.774	.598	.474	.358	.254	.197
15	120	.737	.554	.432	.322	.226	.174
18	171	.706	.518	.399	.295	.205	.158
21	231	.678	.488	.373	.274	.189	.145

* Estimated by applying equations 8.1 and 8.2 successively, with the assumptions that $c_g = 0$ and that each item is at the appropriate difficulty level for the current estimate of the examinee's ability level.

what is possible may be obtained from Table 10.3. This table shows the relative standard errors of measurement (standard deviation = 1.00) that will result from tests of different lengths and different values of the discrimination parameter a_g, if it is possible at each stage to give the examinee an item that corresponds exactly to the prior estimate of the examinee's ability level just before the item was administered.

With a suitable pyramidal test, the degree of precision represented by the standard errors of Table 10.3 can be achieved for each individual through the range of ability extending from the easiest item in the final stage of the pyramid to the most difficult. A conventional test with the same number of items as the pyramidal has stages can be prepared that will provide as much precision as the pyramidal test *over a narrow range*. Such a test would be composed of items homogeneous in difficulty and targeted as some specific level, often the average ability level in the group. It is only as one is concerned with equal precision over a wide range of ability that the pyramidal test, or in fact any adaptive test, is an improvement over a test composed of items of uniform difficulty.

Table 10.3 makes it clear that a pyramidal test of manageable length—say, not more than 15 stages—will provide acceptable precision only when the values of the parameter a_g are relatively high. Thus, if one considers the minimum acceptable precision to be a standard error of measurement no greater than 4/10 of the standard deviation in the population, this can be achieved with an average a_g of .50 only with more than 21 stages, which implies a prohibitive number of items. With $a_g = .7$, an 18-stage test will achieve the desired precision; with

a_g = 1.0 a 10-stage test would prove satisfactory. It is also true that a 10-item test with a_g = 1.0 in which the items were of uniform difficulty, which would have a sharply peaked information function, could achieve this precision over a narrow range. When the items available for a test have only low to moderate correlations with the latent trait, the attempt to make a pyramidal test is relatively unprofitable. On the one hand, it requires a prohibitive number of items to achieve satisfactory precision; on the other, a conventional test made up of items of average difficulty functions with little loss of effectiveness over a fairly broad range of ability.

One cannot establish any fixed rules, but it does seem that the attempt to develop a pyramidal test is relatively fruitless unless the average a_g is at least .70 and hence the average biserial correlation for a group with the variability of those with whom the test is to be used is at least .57. When the average is that high or higher, a pyramidal test of 10 to 15 stages might be considered. With more than 15 stages, the required number of items would appear to make a test booklet unwieldy and, more important, the task of test development excessively burdensome.

Spacing of Items at Each Stage

The spacing of items at each stage of the pyramid depends on the range over which one wishes the test to differentiate and the relative importance of precision over different segments of that range. Because the principal virtue of an adaptive test is that it *can* measure with approximately equal precision over a wide range, it seems reasonable to assume that such equal precision will be desired in a pyramidal test that we are designing. If this is to be accomplished, the pyramid should spread out rapidly to near its maximum width, which must be as great as the range over which we wish equal precision, and then spread slowly or even be truncated. This pattern is shown in the pyramid on page 322, developed on the assumption that one wants to measure over a range of θ from +3.0 to −3.0, in standard deviation units and that one has a set of items for which $\overline{a}_g$ = 1.0. In this illustration, the information at θ = 3.0 for a person who has taken the items on the top border of the pyramid is 2.94, whereas the information at θ = 0.5 for a person whose record is P F P F P F is 2.95.

The specific design of the pyramid that will provide approximately equal information throughout the range of interest will vary with the value of $\overline{a}_g$ in the item pool. And the best solution to the problem depends on the number of stages. Furthermore, if the practical situation calls for greater precision in some segment of the range on the trait, consideration must be given to that requirement. However, if one knows the characteristics of the item pool and the desired outcome so far as relative precision is concerned, one can explore various models (estimating, by using the information function of the items, the information provided by selected routes through the pyramid) and choose the model that approximates the desired outcome.

			STAGE			
1	2	3	4	5	6	(7)
						3.0
					3.0	
				3.0		2.0
			3.0		1.8	
		2.5		1.5		1.0
	2.0		1.0		0.6	
0.0		0.0		0.0		0.0
	−2.0		−1.0		−0.6	
		−2.5		−1.5		−1.0
			−3.0		−1.8	
				−3.0		−2.0
					−3.0	
						−3.0

Assigning Scores on the Test

We require some system for assigning scores to the various possible combinations of passes and failures that may occur in a pyramidal test, on which different examinees may have responded to quite different sets of items. One general rationale that gives an approach to this problem is that of *maximum likelihood*. Consider persons standing at a specific level θ on the underlying trait. For these individuals one can specify the probability of passing a given item g in terms of the parameters of the item characteristic curve. In particular, the probability of passing g, given the value of θ, is given by

$$\frac{1}{1 + e^{-Da_g(\theta - b_g)}}$$

For a set of items, the probability of a particular combination of passes and fails is the product of the probabilities for the separate items. It may be written as

$$\Pi\left[P_g^{(1)}(1 - P_g)^{(0)}\right] \qquad g = 1 \text{ to } k$$

where the superscript (1) indicates those items that have been passed and the superscript (0) those that have been failed. This expression can be evaluated over a series of values of θ, incremented by small steps, and the mean or mode of the set of probability values determined. Either the mean or the mode (the difference between them will be small) serves to define the point of maximum likelihood and can become the score assigned to that combination of passes and failures. Thus, if a set of 6 items had been administered, all with parameters

$a_g = 1.00$, $b_g = \theta$, and $c_g = 0.00$, the probability that persons whose true positions on the latent trait is $\theta = 1.00$ will get any one of the items right is .8413. The probability that persons at this level on θ will get each possible number of right answers is as follows

6 right	.3546
5 right	.0669 × 6
4 right	.0126 × 15
3 right	.0024 × 20
2 right	.00045 × 15
1 right	.00008 × 6
0 right	.00002

However, the figure that we need is a measure of central tendency for this probability function over the whole range of values of θ. No such measure is possible when *all* items are gotten right, because the probability function is continually increasing with increase in the value of θ and does not have a maximum within finite range. There is also no definable maximum when all are gotten wrong. However, for the intermediate range of number right, the means of the probability distributions for our illustration are, respectively,

5 right	1.064
4 right	0.462
3 right	0.000
2 right	−0.462
1 right	−1.064

This is, of course, a much simplified model, and one will never find a set of items all of which have exactly the same parameters. The outcome from applying the maximum likelihood model varies somewhat depending on *which* items are gotten right as well as how many. Thus, if we have 6 items as above, but with values of $b_g - \theta$ of 0.6, 0.4, 0.2, −0.2, −0.4, and −0.6, the mean of the probability function for 5 right out of the 6 will have the following values, depending on which item was failed:

ITEM FAILED	MEAN
+ 0.6	1.22
+ 0.4	1.19
+ 0.2	1.16
− 0.2	1.07
− 0.4	1.03
− 0.6	0.99

These differences are appreciable, though they are small relative to the score differences associated with different numbers of correct answers. Furthermore, it is in general most likely that a person will fail in the more difficult of a set of items. In our model illustration, the relative probabilities of 5 successes with a failure on each one of the six items are as follows:

ITEM FAILED	RELATIVE PROBABILITY
+ 0.6	.152
+ 0.4	.109
+ 0.2	.077
− 0.2	.037
− 0.4	.025
− 0.6	.017

So, for a pyramidal test, it might be reasonable to assign, as a score for each possible number of correct responses, the value that would correspond to the maximum-likelihood value obtained on the assumption that failures occurred on the most difficult items attempted. It would then be possible to calculate this set of values in advance and prepare a score table for each possible number right. This would provide a very simple scoring procedure, but it would yield only as many score values as the number of stages plus one. And it would ignore the information provided by different patterns of failures.

A more complex procedure, but one that takes account of the pattern of successes and failures, would be to calculate the maximum-likelihood value for each possible route through the pyramid. Results for a selection of routes through the pyramid shown on page 325 have been calculated using the methods described immediately thereafter. In order to assign a score to a person who has passed all the items in his or her route through the pyramid, we assume that this person has moved on to a further stage, taken a still harder item (at $\theta = 4.0$), and failed it. The reverse is assumed for a person whose record through the pyramid is one of unrelieved failures. The results for a number of assumed routes through the pyramid appear on page 325. The samples are primarily routes with 3 or more successes. Mirror images of these routes could have been followed on the negative side, and would yield symmetrical negative scale results.

There are, unfortunately, a large number of routes through even a small pyramid, and each has its distinctive maximum-likelihood scale value. Furthermore, routes with the same *number* of failed items, and hence the same final outcome at the last stage, come out with quite different scale values, depending on where in the sequence the errors occurred. This is illustrated in the following table. Errors early in the sequence lead to the examinee's being exposed to an

NUMBER RIGHT	ROUTE FOLLOWED	MAXIMUM LIKELIHOOD SCALE VALUE	SIMPLIFIED SCORE
6	CCCCCC	4.08	21
5	CCCCCX	3.73	20
5	CCXCCC	2.89	17
5	XCCCCC	1.74	15
4	CCXCCX	2.10	16
4	CXCXCC	1.38	13
4	XCCXCC	0.61	12
4	XXCCCC	−0.23	10
3	CCCXXX	1.63	15
3	CCXCXX	1.27	14
3	CXCXCX	0.69	12
0	XXXXXX	−4.08	0

easier sequence of items, and then the same number of successes results in a lower scale value. A computer could certainly be programmed to calculate the maximum likelihood for any route when it occurred, but for other than computerized testing, this procedure seems impossibly laborious. A simpler scoring method is needed.

Some exploratory work has suggested a procedure that yields scores that appear to have a high and approximately linear relationship to the maximum-likelihood scale scores. The procedure is based on giving the individual credits for items passed that depend on the stage of the pyramid at which they are passed. If the pyramid has k stages, an individual gets k points for an item passed at the first stage, $k - 1$ at the second stage, $k - 2$ at the third stage, and so on down to 1 point for an item passed at the last stage. The scores resulting from this simple procedure are shown at the right in the foregoing table. They take integer values from 0 to $k(k + 1)/2$, where k is the number of stages. This simple technique seems likely to give a very serviceable score that takes into account both the number and the location of errors.

In Summary

The pyramidal model provides a testing pattern that can come close to the sequence of item difficulties that would be presented in a full Bayesian sequence. It can approximate equal precision over a wide ability range. The model could be adapted, with some difficulty, to noncomputerized testing. However, the large number of items required limits use of the model to pyramids with a fairly small number of stages—perhaps 10 to 15. Under these limitations, adequate precision of measurement is obtained only when the discrimination parameter,

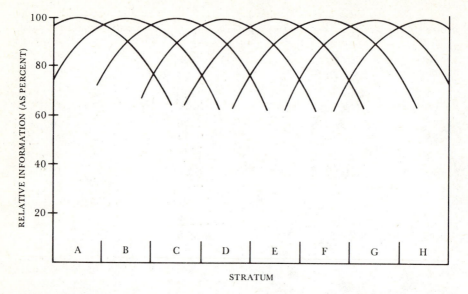

STRATUM

Figure 10.3   Information function for item at midpoint of each stratum.

a_g, is rather high. An average value of 1.00 would be satisfactory, but with average values below perhaps 0.7, the model has little to offer.

THE STRADAPTIVE TEST

In the stradaptive test, the range of difficulty to be covered by the test is sliced up into segments on the basis of difficulty level, and all the items falling within a segment (up to the required number) are grouped together in one stratum. The examinee is moved up or down from one stratum to another depending on whether an item is passed or failed. The stradaptive model differs from the pyramidal model in that no items in a stratum are ever by-passed. It differs from a full Bayesian solution in that no attempt is made to carry out finer discriminations than one full stratum. The relative simplicity of the decision on the next item to be administered, after a given item is either passed or failed, makes the model conceivably usable with a live examiner. With fairly sophisticated examinees, it might even be self-administering. The model uses items more efficiently than does a pyramid and is appealing to the test maker for this reason.

The developer of a stradaptive test faces seven questions. (1) Of how many strata should the test be composed? (2) How many items should there be in each stratum? (3) What principle should guide the order of presentation of the items *within* a stratum? (4) What decision rule should be used in moving an examinee from one stratum to another? (5) When should testing of an examinee be terminated? (6) How should a score be assigned to an individual? (7) What level of

Table 10.4 Width of Stratum in Standard
Deviation Units to Guarantee Two Strata
Will Meet the Efficiency Criterion

DISCRIMINATION PARAMETER a_g	CRITERION	
	90%	80%
2.00	0.27	0.39
1.50	0.36	0.52
1.00	0.54	0.78
0.75	0.72	1.04
0.50	1.08	1.56
0.25	2.16	3.12

precision attaches to the resulting score? We shall consider these questions in order.

Number of Strata

The decision about the breadth of a stratum should be based on evidence concerning the range over which test items provide nearly the maximum amount of information that they are capable of providing. This depends in turn on the typical size of the discrimination parameter a_g in groups of the sort with which the test is being used. The higher the typical a_g value, the narrower the range over which information provided by an item (and consequently a stratum composed of items closely similar in difficulty) approaches its maximum. One might set some such guideline as that there should be at least two strata that approach (say, within 90%) the maximum level of information for persons at any level of the latent attribute in which we are really interested. Graphically, the picture would be as portrayed in Figure 10.3. As illustrated here, an item at the lower edge of the difficulty range for stratum A and one at the upper edge of the difficulty range for stratum C would reach the 90% efficiency level at the middle of stratum B. Thus a person falling in the lower half of the ability range covered by stratum B would be effectively measured by items in strata A and B, whereas a person falling in the upper half would be effectively measured by items in strata B and C. The upshot is that the 90% efficiency range would need to cover a breadth of two strata.

Table 10.4 shows the breadth of the 90% and also the 80% efficiency range in units of θ for different values of a_g. Thus, if we wanted to specify a minimum of 90% efficiency for items in two adjoining strata, and if experience had indicated that, as applied to a group of the sort that we are concerned with, items of this type could be prepared having values of a_g around 1.00 (or biserial correlations with standing on the trait of about .70), each stratum could have a width somewhere between 0.5 and 0.6 standard deviation units. A test composed of 10 strata would then be adequate to provide uniform information and about 95% of maximum efficiency for a range of 5 standard deviation units—that is, from a θ of -2.5 to a θ of $+2.5$ in a group comparable to the one on which the scale units were established.

It is worth noting that, in this model, 90% is the *minimum* efficiency of an item in the two-strata spread, and that most of the items in at least one of the strata would have substantially higher efficiency than this. It is also interesting to note that, with $a_g = 1.00$, the difference in expected percentage of successes in adjacent strata would be no more than 20 if strata of a width of 0.5 σ were used (for example, 50% and 30% or 60% and 40%). With strata as narrow as this there would be some tendency for examinees to "wander"—that is, to pass items in one or two harder strata (where the probability of success might be 20% or 25%) and hence to spread their successes and failures over a total of four or five strata. In this way, a little of the precision that was built into the separate strata might be lost.

For this reason, it might be preferable to have somewhat fewer and broader strata. If we were to adopt 80% as a minimum for item efficiency, then with average a_g of 1.00 we come out with a stratum width of approximately 0.8 standard deviation units, and we could cover a range from -2.8 to $+2.8$ standard deviation units with seven strata. The shift in average percent correct from one stratum to the next would be about 30 percentile points. *Average* efficiency of all items in a pair of adjoining strata should remain above 90%, and there would certainly be less tendency to drift off into strata other than those of optimal difficulty.

If the items have a flatter item characteristic curve, with average a_g of about 0.50, for example, the strata could appropriately be a good deal broader. When average a_g equals .50, the standard of 90% efficiency would permit strata with a width of at least 1.0σ. The range from -2.5 to $+2.5\sigma$ could be covered by five strata and the range from -3.0 to $+3.0\sigma$ by six. It should be noted, however, that when one is dealing with items of such modest discrimination, much of the advantage of adjusting item difficulty to individual ability level is lost. Individual items function over a much broader range of the latent attribute but give less information at *any* level. Consequently, more items are needed in order to measure with precision, but they need not be matched so closely to the ability level of the individual.

Of course, the number of strata is critically related to the range of ages or grades over which the instrument is to be used. Thus, though a range of 6σ units might be fully adequate to provide equally precise measures of all of a group of 10-year-olds, data from the Cognitive Ability Tests, Verbal, suggest that for that test a range of 10 standard deviation units would be needed to cover a group ranging in age from 7 to 18. Thus the required number of strata would be nearly doubled. If still younger children were to be included, a further increase in the number of strata would be called for.

Table 10.5   Measurement Error Variance for Different Values of a_g and
Different Numbers of Items per Stratum*

NUMBER OF ITEMS PER STRATUM	a_g				
	.50	.70	1.00	1.20	1.50
2	.628	.476	.326	.262	.198
3	.528	.373	.237	.183	.133
4	.455	.306	.185	.141	.098
5	.394	.259	.152	.114	.078
6	.351	.224	.128	.097	.064
7	.318	.198	.111	.083	.055
8	.288	.177	.098	.072	.048
9	.265	.160	.087	.064	.042
10	.245	.146	.079	.058	.038

* Assumes examinee completes all items in two adjoining strata and does not drift over into adjoining strata. Cg assumed to equal zero, and all items assumed to match examinee ability.

These examples merely illustrate a rationale for attacking the problem of number of strata. Application of the rationale in any given case requires knowledge of the range over which equally effective discrimination is needed and of the typical level of discrimination in items of the type that will be used.

Number of Items per Stratum

Every time a person takes an item and either passes or fails it, she or he moves to a new stratum, so every examinee can be tested with at least twice as many items as the number appearing in each stratum. (The only exception to this is persons who consistently pass items in the most difficult stratum or consistently fail items in the easiest, and these persons lie outside the ability range for which we seek equally precise measurement.) Thus the number of items needed in a stratum is half the total number of items that we want to be able to give to any individual. This number, in turn, depends on the precision of measurement that we require and on the typical value of a_g, the items' discrimination parameter. Remembering that we will quite uniformly be administering items that will be functioning at near their maximum efficiency, we can prepare a table that displays the expected relative standard error of measurement as a function of the number of items and of a_g. These relationships are displayed in Table 10.5.

Table 10.5 displays the variance error of measurement, and this value subtracted from unity corresponds to the reliability coefficient in a group the variance of which is equal to 1.00 on the scale being used for the latent attribute. The table presents a somewhat unrealistically favorable picture, because it assumes that all the items are exactly at the ability level of the person being tested. Also, the table has been prepared for items that involve no guessing. With multiple-choice items, the ones that are passed provide somewhat less information, and for such a test the precision increases somewhat more slowly. However, the table does provide a rough guide to the precision that can be expected with items of different discriminating ability and tests of different lengths. If we wanted to specify precision equivalent to a reliability coefficient of .90, a working rule of thumb might specify:

a_g	ITEMS PER STRATUM
.50	too many to be practical
.70	15 or more
1.00	8 or 9
1.20	6 or 7
1.50	4 or 5

Order of Presentation of Items Within a Stratum

What guidance can be given about which item within a stratum should be presented first, which second, and so on? Weiss (1973) suggests that one arrange the items within a stratum in order, according to their discrimination parameter, and start with the most discriminating. This seems a reasonable guide, in that the most discriminating items will be used for the most examinees, and hence the precision of testing will be maximized. Often, the differences among items in their discrimination parameter will be fairly small and may be attributable largely to sampling fluctuations, and then order within the stratum would appear to make little difference. Perhaps then editorial judgments about the interest level, cultural appropriateness, or other nonstatistical properties of the items should determine which are the "best" items and should head the list.

Decision Rule for Moving from Stratum to Stratum

The simplest and most obvious decision rule for movement after each item is "up one on a pass, down one on a fail." However, this is not necessarily the best rule. We have seen that with multiple-choice items a correct answer provides somewhat less information than a wrong answer, because of the possibility of getting a right answer by guessing. Furthermore, Prestwood and Weiss (1977) report that examinees tend to pick, as appropriate for them, items somewhat easier than the ones that correspond to their finally estimated ability level. Both of these considerations suggest that one should be somewhat more ready to drop back after a failure than to move up after a success. It seems plausible that, with multiple-choice items, examinee morale might be improved, and efficiency of measurement hurt only a little if at all, by using the decision rule "up one on a pass, down two on a fail." This could be expected to raise the average proportion of passes from about 50% to more nearly 65%, should reduce guessing to some extent, and might make the test somewhat more palatable to examinees.

Rule for Terminating Testing

The length of test should be determined by balancing the desired degree of precision against the acceptable amount of testing time. A basic question is whether test length should be the same for all examinees, or whether the specified precision should be the same for all. These are not identical, because the amount of information achieved for a given examinee depends somewhat on that examinee's tendency to "wander" up and down the strata. *If* the test is computer-administered, so that the dispersion of posterior probabilities can be calculated after each item is administered, then setting a uniform standard of precision is a possible alternative. But if testing is conducted by a human examiner, continuously estimating precision is hardly possible. Under these circumstances, it seems one really has no choice but to tie the termination of testing in some uniform way to the number of items.

One strategy would be to continue testing until all the items in some one stratum had been used. With k items to a stratum, this would guarantee that every examinee had taken at least $2k - 1$ items. A larger number of items would be given to the "erratic" examinee who drifted up and down with strings of consecutive passes and failures, but one can argue that more items are needed for such an individual if one is to achieve equal precision of measurement.

If this procedure or some minor variant of it is adopted, the decisions on number of items to be administered and on number to be included in each stratum are closely tied together. The number of items per stratum would be half the specified minimum number of items to be administered and would have been chosen in the first place at a level that would yield the required level of precision.

Assigning a Score to an Individual

If the testing is completely computerized, the Bayesian formulas (p. 303) can be used to provide a mean for the posterior probability distribution as well as a measure of its dispersion. For a test that is examiner-administered and examiner-scored, some other procedure is required.

A relatively simple procedure is to determine the median stratum value of the items passed after the first change of direction. (If the original starting point was too low, there is likely to be a series of passes until the examinee reaches "his level." Conversely, if the starting point was too high, there is likely to be a string of failures.) After that change of direction, the proportion of passes will be nearly the same for all examinees, so the location of the passes on the ability scale can define the person's ability level. The diagram on pages 332–333 illustrates three response sequences to a seven-stratum design with six items per stratum, in which testing was continued until items in some stratum ran out. The score is interpolated to tenths of a stratum. The score value of a stratum is defined by the difficulty level of the items included in it, expressed in the scale of the latent attribute, so scores expressed as strata and fractions of a stratum can be converted to units of θ, the latent attribute. For example, if θ for stratum 3 is -0.60 and for stratum 4 is $+0.25$, then the score for case A would be

$$-0.60 + 0.8(0.25 + 0.60) = +0.08$$

Case A

```
1   2   3      4      5      6   7
                 ↓
            ( P  →  F )
                /
             P  →  F
                /
             P  →  F
                /
        P  ←  F
           \
             P  →  P  →  F
                      /
        P  ←  F  ←  F
_____ Med = 3.8
      2P      3P      P
```

Case B

```
1   2   3      4      5      6   7
                 ↓
            ( P  →  F )
                /
             P  →  P  →  F
                         /
             P  ←  F
                \
        P  ←  F  ←  F
           \
        P  ←  F
           \
             P  →  P  →  F
                   /
             P  →  F
_____ Med = 4.2
      2P      3P      3P
```

Case C

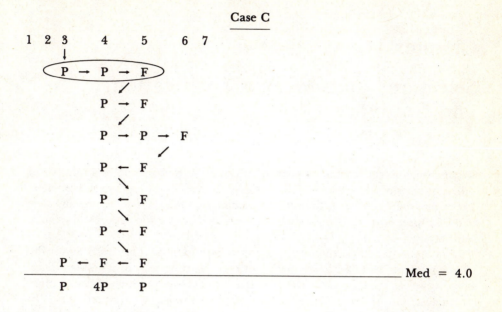

Med = 4.0

SUMMARY STATEMENT

Procedures for adaptive testing are largely in the early developmental stages. Most of the procedures discussed in this chapter have been tried only in an exploratory fashion. There are some computer-based programs in operation in the military establishment and in the Federal Civil Service. And multilevel modular tests are commercially available and are used to some extent to adapt test level to the ability level of individual students. But most testing is still uniform within age or grade groups. Most commercially distributed tests are still designed to function fairly well over a wide range of ability, the same test often being merchandised for use with the whole range of talent in several grades, with a correspondingly wide range of difficulty in the test exercises.

The increased efficiency of adaptive tests is easy to show in theory. Whether it will prove practical to attain that efficiency, in view of the increased complexity of test construction, test administration, and test interpretation, remains largely to be determined.

Chapter 11

Selection, Placement, Classification, and Guidance

Testing may be carried out to provide information for any one of a number of different types of decision. We shall consider four different types in this chapter. Let us first define the four, then set up a model that relates them to one another, and finally see what the implications of the model are for the design and use of a test battery.

In *selection* decisions, the tester's objective is to identify those individuals who will be most successful in a specific job or training program. In *placement* decisions, as we use the term here, the objective is to determine which of two or more treatments will carry each individual further toward a common goal. In *classification*, the problem is to determine in which of several different roles the individual is likely to make the largest contribution to an organization's functioning. In *guidance,* test results are designed to help an individual choose from among a range of educational or vocational alternatives the one that will be most satisfactory for her or him.

To permit a rational model that will make possible a unified discussion of these different types of decision, we must first develop the concept of *utility*. This is a somewhat elusive concept and one that is often very difficult to translate into numbers, but it provides an essential bond to hold different types of test uses together in a common logical model. Utility is roughly defined as the value of an individual in a given role. In a very simple production line job, utility might be approximately represented by the average number of widgets produced per hour. In a sales job, it might be approximated by the number of cars or insurance policies sold. Of course, even for these illustrations, this is a gross oversimplification. For the widget maker there is a matter of spoilage, of regularity of attendance at work, of ability to get on with fellow employees. For the salesperson there may be lost sales and clients antagonized, frequency of repeat sales or of lapses and returns, impact on other salespersons. To operationalize *utility* satisfactorily for even a single job is a forbidding task. But to ignore the fact that some such concept is central to rational decision making is to retreat from the reality of life.

Within a single job category, the indicators that we accept as partial criteria are accepted because we believe them to be related to utility, and we accept that relationship as being monotonic if not actually linear. Implicitly we assert that the salesperson who sells more is more valuable then the one who sells less, that the secretary who is rated higher by a supervisor is more valuable than the one who is rated lower, that the student who gets a 3.00 grade point average is more acceptable than the one who gets a 2.00. Whenever we combine partial criteria into a composite criterion score, the weighting scheme represents an implicit judgment about the contribution of each partial indicator to knowledge about the utility of the individual. We rarely try to express this utility function explicitly, and perhaps we should. But as long as we remain within a single job or a single training program, we seem to get on fairly well.

It is when we try to compare different jobs or different educational alternatives that the issue of utility becomes both more crucial and more frustrating. Should the Army assign recruit R to training as an electronics technician or as a clerk-typist? Should student S major in physics or in pharmacy? Should 10-year-old T be given intensive remedial teaching or placed in a class for the mentally retarded? In each case, we need to estimate the utility of the outcomes from qualitatively different "treatments" that lead to qualitatively different results. In what common terms can these outcomes be expressed?

There are certain possibilities that have a degree of plausibility, and it will pay us to consider these. First and simplest, there is the probability of successfully completing training. For a person to have entered a training program and then been "washed out" generates a certain amount of negative utility: cost with no compensating benefit for the organization—and probably for the individual. The graduate represents a certain amount of positive utility: potential for future contribution. One *could* consider the minus and the plus to be the same from one training program to another. But this is certainly an oversimplification and perhaps a gross distortion of reality. A military organization might consider a trained and competent electronics specialist many times more valuable than a similarly trained and competent clerk-typist. To student S, even modest success in physics may be valued more highly than outstanding achievement in pharmacy. Simple survival through training is at best a crude first approximation to a common measure of utility in different jobs or training programs.

Another approach has been to attempt to put a "dollar value" on success—or failure—in different training programs or job specialties. On the negative side, it is probably not too difficult to estimate the cost that has gone into recruiting and training a person who has then "washed out" and produced no useful result. Training programs differ in length, in physical facilities required, and in human resources committed to training and supervision. Thus the costs of training a fighter pilot are enormously greater than those of training a cook. So a dollar cost might be placed within reasonable limits on those who were admitted to training and failed. Estimating the dollar value of a graduate from training or of an employee in some capacity is a good bit more tricky. Of course, in some cases it is possible to estimate the cost to train, and in these cases this could serve as a first approximation to the utility of a trained person. Average income in different occupations might serve as a crude multiplying factor to estimate the "dollar value" of someone who had successfully trained for and entered into a certain occupation. However, the dollar criterion leaves one vaguely unsatisfied when it comes to comparing the utility to society of, for example, the competent high school teacher and the competent professional basketball player.

Another possible source for a multiplying factor for comparing utility of different occupations could be a pooling of judgments of persons in various walks of life. There have been a number of studies reported in which the prestige of different occupations has been assessed by pooling the ratings of a panel of judges. The same could be done, basing the judgments on some definition of utility. Like the other procedures, of course, this one tries to establish an index value to attach to each occupation as a total aggregation of persons. This estimated value would need to be modified to take account of the individual's predicted level of success within the occupation, a modification that would need to take into account not only the average utility of exemplars of the occupation but also of their variability in utility.

So far, we have spoken of utility primarily from the organization's point of view—the employer's or the larger society's. But in some contexts, at least, it is necessary to give heed to utility from the point of view of the individual. If student S must decide whether to enter a pre-med or a business administration program, that student and anyone who aspires to help that student must try to assess not only the probabilities of successfully completing the program but also the worth, in terms of that individual's hierarchy of values, of the rewards that may be expected to accrue from successful completion. One requires a calculus of values as well as a calculus of probabilities.

We may have presented a rather forbidding picture of the problem of establishing a common scale of utility, and the difficulties *are* formidable. But the attempt is crucial if a rational basis is to be established for personnel classification or for personal guidance. In order to set forth the model for these uses of test results, we will assume that the problem has been solved, at least to a workable approximation. At this point, we will lay out the general model, and then we will consider what guidance the model provides for the design of test batteries to serve different decision functions.

THE UTILITY MATRIX

Consider the total set of persons with whom we are concerned and the total set of "jobs" that constitute possible alternatives for these persons. We use the generic term *jobs* to include work placements, programs of education or training, alternative forms of therapy, or whatever set of alternatives represents the available options. *Treatments* might be a better term, though it tends to convey an unduly medical flavor. In any event, there is a range of possible alternatives, and we shall use the label "jobs" or sometimes "treatments."

We shall consider that an all-wise Providence might know what the utility of each individual i would be if he or she chose to enter, or were assigned to, job j.

(In a different context, utility might be the improvement that patient p would make if assigned to therapy t.) We designate this utility U_{ij}. Thus we conceive of a matrix of utilities with a row for each person and a column for each treatment, as shown below.

PERSONS	JOBS						
	1	2	3	$\cdots$	j	$\cdots$	n
1	U_{11}	U_{12}	U_{13}	$\cdots$	U_{1j}	$\cdots$	U_{1n}
2	U_{21}	U_{22}	U_{23}		U_{2j}		U_{2n}
$\vdots$							
i	U_{i1}	U_{i2}	U_{i3}		U_{ij}		U_{in}
$\vdots$							
N	U_{N1}	U_{N2}	U_{N3}		U_{Nj}		U_{Nn}

Not being an all-wise Providence, we have no access to this matrix of "true" utilities, so we approximate it as best we can in each case through one or more criterion indicators—training school grades, supervisory ratings, performance records, or proficiency tests—which we weight as wisely as we can to describe the "worth of an individual in a job." We try to select and weight the criterion indicators in such a way that, within a given job, the correlation over persons of estimated utility, $\hat{U}_{ij}$, and true utility, U_{ij}, will be a maximum and the mean estimated utility will equal the mean true utility. We try to apply weights to *different* jobs so that the ratio of the dispersions of their estimated utilities for any pair of jobs will equal the ratio of the dispersions of their true utilities—that is, so that

$$\frac{\sigma_{\hat{u}_j}}{\sigma_{u_j}} = \frac{\sigma_{\hat{u}_k}}{\sigma_{u_k}} \qquad \text{for any } j \text{ and } k$$

We carry out testing (and gather other sorts of data) in order to predict the estimated utilities and, through them, the true utilities. Thus the end product of our research is a regression equation, expectancy table, or similar synthesis of information that produces a predicted criterion score that can be converted into a predicted utilty, $\tilde{U}_{ij}$. In this way, the predicted utility is tied to the estimated utility, which is our best representation of true utility. Our goal will be to reduce to a minimum the discrepancies between certain of these predicted utilities and the actual utility that results if a person chooses or is placed in a certain job and to develop a decision strategy that will maximize the overall utility of the result. Selection, placement, classification, and guidance involve different segments of this total utility matrix, and an examination of the ways in which they involve these segments indicates the characteristics of an effective test battery, together with the strategies that are indicated for use of test results.

Note that at this point we are dealing with three concepts that are linked together in a serial fashion:

1. Predicted utility $\tilde{U}_{ij}$ is a prediction, based on tests or other variables, of where the individual will fall on a scale of

2. Estimated utility $\hat{U}_{ij}$, which is a weighted composite of performance indicators weighted so as to correspond as closely as possible to

3. True utility U_{ij}, the value of a given person's true level of performance in a specific job.

It is worth noting in passing that the link between estimated and true utility is at least as crucial as that between predictors and criterion indices. It is only as the correspondence between estimated and true utility is strong, and as the form (linear or other) of that relationship becomes clear to us, that we can proceed effectively and rationally in personnel decisions.

SELECTION

The objective of personnel selection is to maximize the utility of persons chosen for one specific job. Thus our interest is limited to one specific column of the matrix of utilities and of predicted utilities, the column j that corresponds to the specific job j for which we are choosing from among the available candidates. We must assume that estimated utility $\hat{U}_{ij}$ is monotonically, if not linearly, related to "true" utility—that, as we move up the scale of estimated utility, persons at any higher level will on the average have a higher "true" utility than those at any lower level. And we will expect a similar relationship between predicted utility $\tilde{U}_{ij}$ and estimated utility $\hat{U}_{ij}$. The existence of a monotonic and even linear relationship between the prediction that we arrive at from test scores and other data and the criterion variable or variables that are the basis of estimated utility can usually be tested empirically and guaranteed, if need be, by appropriate transformations of predictor variables. The existence of a monotonic relationship between estimated utility $\hat{U}_{ij}$, and "true" utility must generally be accepted on faith rather than being empirically testable. Thus it would be difficult to get empirical proof that a 3.50 freshman GPA is in the long run "worth more" than one of 2.50, or that physicians earning $75,000 a year have more social value than those earning $50,000 a year.

Accepting the assumption of a monotonic relationship between estimated and true utility, our goal in selection research is to develop procedures that maximize the relationship of predicted to estimated utility for the specific job category with which we are concerned. The decision strategy to maximize utility in the selection context is a very simple one: Within the constraint imposed by the number of vacancies to be filled, choose those individuals with the highest predicted utility—that is, the highest scores on the predictor composite.

Applying this decision strategy is perfectly straightforward *if* all applicants can be tested and evaluated before any decisions must be made and if one knows that all applicants will accept an invitation and enter the job. If some turn-downs are to be expected, as in college admissions where some candidates make multiple applications, then a strategy must be developed for handling the anticipated withdrawals. An estimate of the percentage of refusals to be expected may be made on the basis of prior experience, and an appropriate excess of applicants may be admitted. As another option, a group may be admitted as alternates, to be accepted if vacancies occur. Or some combination of the two strategies may be applied.

Testing often extends over a considerable period of time—it may even be continuous—and a decision with respect to each applicant may be required almost immediately after testing. This would be typical in an industrial employment office. In that case, a minimum qualifying score must be established that can be applied as soon as tests and other data have been gathered. From the organization's point of view, the cutting score should be set as high as possible while still qualifying enough applicants to meet hiring needs. To do this one needs estimates of (1) the distribution of predicted utility, $\tilde{U}$, for future applicants, (2) the flow of candidates and the proportion who will accept offered employment, and (3) the anticipated need for new placements in the job by the employing organization. The first of these can usually be based on test results and the resulting composite scores from prior groups of applicants and can be up-dated as testing continues. The second and third can be based on past employment rates and turn-down experience, modified by what is known about economic conditions and about future organizational plans. The estimates can be combined to determine a cutting score that will provide a "sustained yield" adequate to meet organizational needs.

To illustrate, suppose that past testing had produced a group of applicants with a mean predicted utility of 160, with a standard deviation of 65. Recruiting procedures have produced a flow of 80 applicants a month, and 80% of those applicants who were offered a job have accepted. It is anticipated that it will be necessary to hire 40 new employees a month, on the average. Assuming that these values are the ones that will operate in the future, we have

$$40/0.80 = 50 \text{ per month to be offered employment}$$
$$50/80 = 62.5\% \text{ of applicants}$$
$$= -0.32 \text{ on the normal curve}$$
$$\text{Cutting score} = 160 - (0.32)(65) = 139$$

If quota requirements must be met for certain subgroups, such as minority group members or women, it may be necessary to carry out separate calculations for each such subgroup, using estimates of number of applicants, rate of acceptance, and mean and standard deviation of scores for each subgroup. The implication is that a different qualifying score may have to be set for these groups.

The strategy for design of a testing battery is also relatively simple. Given a set of predictors, one starts with the one having the highest correlation with the criterion composite that represents the best available estimate of utility. One then adds on at each step that additional predictor that has the highest partial validity. The question of how far to proceed in adding further variables was discussed in Chapter 9. (Another procedure that is in some ways slightly preferable is to start with the regression equation for the complete set of predictor variables and then drop at each stage the one with the smallest regression weight.)

Substantial partial validity ordinarily requires relatively low correlations with variables already in the prediction equation, so in assembling a pool of tests for tryout one should try to identify the full range of competencies that facilitate criterion performance and to have them all represented in the research battery. However, an efficient selection variable may be psychologically complex, duplicating many aspects of job demands. High school grades, for example, give a relatively good prediction of college freshman grades just because both depend on many of the same personal and situational factors. By the same token, "general ability" tests that are a composite of verbal, quantitative, spatial, and reasoning abilities give a relatively good prediction of performance in many training situations. Their versatility makes them appealing in practice, and there is little evidence that prediction of success in training could be improved appreciably by dividing such a complex measure up into several more specialized and differentially weighted tests.

The limitation of using complex tests is that they *do* tend to correlate substantially with each other. Consequently, once having selected the best one or two tests, it is often difficult to find any others with large enough partial validities to add appreciably to the validity of the composite score. In selection, of course, the final payoff lies in the closeness of correspondence of the predicted utility with the criterion-estimated utility (and, by implication, the true utility). Whether the closest correspondence is achieved by a single complex test that attempts to match all aspects of the demands of the job or by a battery of tests of simple psychological functions that attempt collectively to cover the elements that go into job performance is hard to estimate in advance. Simple selection is the context in which the most plausible case can be made for a complex job-miniature type of test.

MULTIPLE SELECTION

In an industrial or military personnel program, it is often economical to develop a common test battery that can be used, in whole or in part, to select persons for many different jobs. Each applicant may be a candidate for only one specific job, but there are also other applicants who are candidates for other jobs. Expressed in our matrix model, the matrix can be partitioned, with the first n_1 rows representing candidates for job 1, the next n_2 rows representing candidates for job 2, and so forth. Within the first section of the matrix, we are concerned only with U_{i1}, $i = 1, 2, \ldots, n_1$, the utility of candidates 1 to n_1 in job 1. In the next section we are concerned only with U_{i2}, $i = (n_1 + 1), \ldots, (n_1 + n_2)$, the utility of the next n_2 candidates for job 2, and so on.

Within each section of the matrix, the strategy with regard to acceptance and rejection parallels that for simple selection. That is, if all applications are in hand before a decision must be made, the desired number will be selected by working down from the one with the highest predicted utility, $\bar{U}$. If decisions must be made applicant by applicant, as testing is completed, a cutting score will be established for each job on the basis of the concept of "predicted yield," as set forth for simple selection.

A battery that is to be used for multiple selection will usually have to be more comprehensive than one to be used only to select persons for a single job. It will have to cover abilities that are significant predictors of utility in *any* of the jobs for which selection is being carried out. It is also likely that the scales will tip in the direction of tests of purer psychological functions. A test that has been designed to parallel closely the demands of some one specific job is not likely to provide so close a match for others. However, simpler tests may be combined in different ways and with different weights for each of a variety of jobs. The advantage of a wide range of simple tests will increase as the set of jobs becomes more diverse. Thus separate tests of verbal, quantitative, and spatial functions permit their use in varying combinations, weighted in different ways and in combination with any other tests in the battery, in a way that would not be possible with a single "general ability" test.

The range of tests to be tried out in research to establish a multiple selection battery should be based on job analysis of all, or at least a varied sample, of the jobs for which selection is to take place. These analyses will suggest, often with repetition from one job to another, the types of functions for which tests should be developed. When a battery has been assembled, we assume that all of the tests will have been administered to applicants for all of the jobs and that validity estimates will have been obtained for each test for each job. (If a selection is already being made of those admitted to certain of the jobs, it will be necessary to apply the corrections for curtailment discussed in Chapter 7.) It will then be necessary to decide which tests to retain in the final selection battery. Because one usually has to hold the battery down to a manageable size, one wants to select the subset of tests that is, by some criterion, the best subset of a given length.

Horst (1955) offers one solution to the problem of the best subset that is an extension of the stepwise regression procedures described in Chapter 9. Horst's procedure assigns equal importance to each of the jobs and uses average covariance of test score with standardized criterion score as the function to be maximized. The procedure is illustrated below with an example involving a battery of four tests and a set of five jobs. (These data were drawn from a larger set involving the Air Force Airman Classification Battery and records of success in training school.)

The basic data consist of a matrix of test intercorrelations and vectors of validity coefficients. These are shown in Table A.

TEST	TABLE A			
	1	2	3	4
1. Word knowledge	—	.58	.47	.31
2. Dial and table reading	.58	—	.46	.32
3. Mechanical principles	.47	.46	—	.50
4. Tool functions	.31	.32	.50	—
JOB				
a. Intelligence operations	.65	.72	.40	.20
b. Aviation instrument mechanic	.48	.57	.54	.45
c. Machinist	.48	.68	.61	.63
d. Baker	.32	.29	.21	.27
e. Clerk-typist	.45	.64	.34	.07

The first step is to determine the sum of squared correlations for each test with the five criterion variables. The validity coefficients are squared and summed to give

WORD KNOWLEDGE	DIAL AND TABLE READING	MECHANICAL PRINCIPLES	TOOL FUNCTIONS
1.1882	1.7994	0.9834	0.7172

The largest sum (the largest amount of covariance of a test with the set of criterion variables) is for test 2, dial and table reading, so this test becomes the nucleus of our multiple selection test battery. We then partial this variable out of the matrix of test intercorrelations and the vectors of validity coefficients to get the residual relationships that hold when the effect of test 2 is eliminated. For each entry, we compute

$$r_{ij} - r_{2i}r_{2j}$$

The entries are shown in Table B.

TEST	TABLE B			
	1	2	3	4
1. Word knowledge	.6635	—	.2032	.1244
2. Dial and table reading	—	—	—	—
3. Mechanical principles	.2032	—	.7884	.3528
4. Tool functions	.1244	—	.3528	.8976
JOB				
a. Intelligence operations	.2324	—	.0688	− .0304
b. Aviation instrument mechanic	.1494	—	.2778	.2676
c. Machinist	.0856	—	.2972	.4124
d. Baker	.1518	—	.0766	.1772
e. Clerk-typist	.0788	—	.0456	− .1348

Note that variable 2 disappears in that all entries involving that variable are now zero.

Now, to decide which is the best test to add to our core test, we square and sum the test × criterion residuals in each column of Table B. This gives us the following result:

1 WORD KNOWLEDGE	2 DIAL AND TABLE READING	3 MECHANICAL PRINCIPLES	4 TOOL FUNCTIONS
.1129	—	.1782	.2922

These results indicate that test 4, tool functions, will predict the most additional criterion variance when added to test 2. The actual amount of additional variance is given by

$$\frac{\text{sum of squared residuals}}{\text{residual variance of the test}}$$

or .2922/.8976 = .3255. The total criterion variance predicted by tests 2 and 4 in combination is 1.7994 + .3255 = 2.1249.

We now need a vector for variable 4 in matrix B in which each element is multiplied by the reciprocal of $r_{44.2}$, the diagonal entry. (This is, in effect, multiplying each row entry by $1/(1 - r_{24}^2)$, and the resemblance of this term to a denominator term in the formula for partial correlation can be noted.) The row becomes

1	2	3	4
.1386	—	.3930	1.000

The effects of test 4 can now be partialed out, using these values as correlations of test 4 residuals with the other test residuals. Thus the entry in the cell 1,3 becomes

$$.2032 \; - \; (.1386)(.3930) \; = \; .1487$$

The residual matrix after the partialing out of test 4 is shown in Table C. Repeating the process of summing the squared residual correlations with training school criteria gives .0951 for test 1 and .0643 for test 3, so the third test to add would be test 1, word knowledge.

TEST	TABLE C			
	1	2	3	4
1. Word knowledge	.6443	—	.1487	—
2. Dial and table reading	—	—	—	—
3. Mechanical principles	.1487	—	.6339	—
4. Tool functions	—	—	—	—
JOB				
a. Intelligence operations	.2366	—	.0807	—
b. Aviation instrument mechanic	.1123	—	.1726	—
c. Machinist	.0284	—	.1351	—
d. Baker	.1272	—	.0070	—
e. Clerk–typist	.0975	—	.0986	—

The further contribution that test 1 makes to the test-criterion covariance is .0951/.6443 = .1476, giving a total of 1.7994 + .3255 + .1476 = 2.2725.

Repeating the cycle one more time, partialling out variable 1, leaves a diagonal entry of .5765 for test 3 and residual correlations of test 3 with each of the training criteria of .0260, .1466, .1285, − .0224, and .0760, respectively. The sum of these validities squared is equal to .0450, and the contribution to predicted criterion variance is .0780, which, added to the previous total, gives 2.3505. Because the total variance of 5 criterion variables is 5.0, the set of 4 tests is able to account for 2.3505/5 = .4701, or 47%, of the criterion variance. Of the predictable variance, the amount added by each test is as follows:

TEST	PERCENTAGE OF TOTAL
2	76.6
4	13.8
1	6.3
3	3.3

The sequence in which tests contribute provides a guide to the order in which they should presumably be added to a test battery.

We have determined the order in which tests should be added to the battery, but we have provided no guidance about how many it is worth keeping. One way of approaching this would be to apply the F-test described in Chapter 9 (page 252) to each job in turn for the test added last. If all the F-ratios are nonsignificant, or if only one or two are significant at the .05 level, it would seem that that test could certainly be discarded. The procedure could then be repeated for the next to last test and continued with other tests until a number of significant F-ratios were obtained. At that point, the basis for decision would shift to the feasible length for the battery, and dropping additional tests would be for the purpose of holding the battery to a manageable length.

This procedure treats all of the job categories as equal in importance for the design of the test battery. However, it is likely that certain jobs should receive more weight, either because degree of excellence in that job makes more difference (there is a greater dispersion of individual utility values), or because greater numbers are being assigned to the job. It would be possible to assign a weight to each job on the basis of some combination of these two factors. (There appears to be no a priori "right" way in which the two elements should be combined, but we are disposed to use some type of product of the two—perhaps the estimated dispersion of utility times the square root of the estimated numbers to be placed on the job.) Once the set of weights has been determined, all of the squared validity coefficient would be multiplied by the corresponding weight and summed. And at each stage, the variable chosen to be added to the battery would be the one with the largest weighted sum of residual covariances.

PLACEMENT

Placement and classification are similar in that alternative assignments are considered for each individual. They differ, as we use the terms here, in that placement is concerned with alternative routes to a common goal, whereas classification leads to quite different goals. Suppose that there are two ways of teaching the multiplication facts, one that emphasizes "discovery" and logical relationships and one that emphasizes relatively rote memorizing. Suppose, further, that there is reason to believe that children with certain characteristics can learn the facts better by one method and children with other characteristics by the other method. The goal for both groups of children is the same: effective mastery of the multiplication facts, as evidenced by a well-designed mastery test. Placement research attempts to develop measures that distinguish between those who will progress better via the discovery method and those who will progress better via the rote method, so that each child can be placed in the treatment in which he or she is likely to learn best. Here the treatments are different but the desired outcomes are the same.

Returning to our utility matrix, we can see that we are now interested in some two, three, or other small number of columns of the matrix, where each column represents a specific treatment. The treatments may vary in method, as in our illustration. They may differ in tempo, as when different class sections move through a field such as basic algebra at different rates. They may differ in focus, as when one section of an introductory psychology course is "student-centered" and another is "subject-centered." But if placement is to be useful, there must be some categories of persons who will make better progress under one treatment and some who will progress better under the other. The comparison of utilities under the different treatments is facilitated in that all have, at least in large measure, the same goals, so a common outcome measure and a common metric for utility are appropriate for all.

There are several patterns in which the outcomes from the different treatments may be related to a predictor measure. We illustrate these for a two-treatment model in Figure 11.1. In Chart A, a situation is displayed in which there are substantial but equal relationships of the predictor measure to achievement under *both* treatments. The regression lines are parallel and, as we have displayed it, at all levels of score on the predictor the predicted utility under treatment I is greater than that under treatment II. Under these circumstances, though the predictor might have been used quite effectively as a *selection* device if we had simply been interested in picking those likely to do well, it would be absolutely useless for *placement*. The only rational placement strategy would be to place all individuals, whatever their score level, in treatment I.

Chart B illustrates a situation in which the predictor is more closely related to utility under treatment I than under treatment II but in which treatment I still surpasses treatment II over the whole range represented in the graph. If facilities permitted it, all cases should be placed in treatment I. However, if for some reason there were a limit on the numbers that can be placed in treatment I, the greatest overall utility would accrue from placing in that treatment those persons high on the predictor variable.

Chart C illustrates a situation in which differential placement is clearly indicated. Though the predictor variable is positively related to utility under each treatment, the relationship is *much* stronger under treatment I. Furthermore,

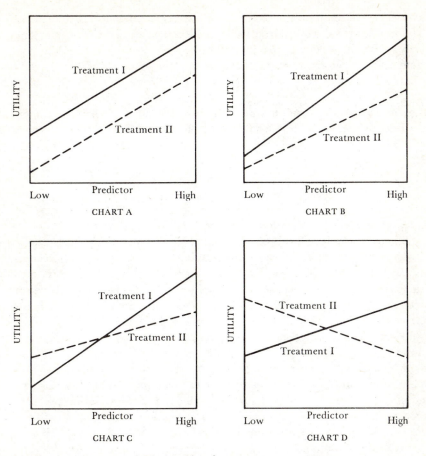

Figure 11.1 Patterns of relationship of test scores to treatments.

those low on the predictor variable (below the cross-over point of the two regression lines) can be expected to do better under treatment II and can advantageously be placed in that treatment.

Chart D illustrates the placement researcher's dream — a dream that rarely materializes in the world of reality. In this model, the slopes of the regressions are actually reversed. Those who are low on the predictor variable tend to do better under treatment II, whereas those who are high on the predictor tend to do better under treatment I. Here, under appropriate placement, persons at all levels can be expected to show an "average or better" performance.

The charts in Figure 11.1 make clear what is required in a test or testing composite that is to be used for placement decisions. A test that has an equal (even if strong) relationship to each treatment, as in chart A, is worthless. It provides absolutely no basis for differential placement. A test is useful in proportion as it has *different* degrees of relationship to different treatments. Of course, the ideal test would be one that was positively related to success under one treatment and negatively related to success under the other.

If there are just two treatments, the variable to be predicted is

$$\hat{U}_{i1} - \hat{U}_{i2}$$

the difference in estimated utility under the two treatments. When the dispersion of utility is equal for both, the correlation of a predictor with this difference is exactly the difference between the correlations with the individual outcomes. That is,

$$r_{t(1-2)} = r_{t1} - r_{t2}$$

The predictor variable for which we are searching is one that shows a substantial difference in correlation with outcome under the different treatments.

What kind of variable will this be? It is hard to tell, but it seems likely that it will be quite different from the type of variable that is effective in a selection context. To the extent that a selection test is a *general* measure of readiness to learn, it seems likely that it will be substantially related to progress under each treatment and hence that it will provide little basis for choice between them. "Job analysis" of treatments should try to clarify the respects in which they differ and to identify the characteristics of a person that seem likely to be related to those differences.

The model that we have described here under the rubric of "placement" also appears in the psychological literature under the heading "aptitude–treatment interaction." An extended discussion of the model and of research that provides evidence on differential relationships of measures of ability and of personality to different educational treatments is provided by Cronbach and Snow (1977). The literature is fairly voluminous but often contradictory. It must be admitted that the past history of successes when tests are used for placement decisions has not been impressive.

CLASSIFICATION

In classification we are also concerned with multiple alternatives for each individual. Here, however, the alternatives lead to qualitatively different goals. We are interested in knowing whether an individual's predicted utility is greater as a cook or a clerk or a mechanic, as a lawyer or a physician or an engineer. In the purest classification model, we are concerned with the complete matrix of utilities, because any individual might be assigned to any job. Thus each column of the matrix of utilities corresponds to a different job or training program—with possibly an additional column labeled "Reject. Do not admit to any program." Each row of the matrix corresponds to the set of utilities for a given individual. We require a predicted utility for each individual in each job, and we want those predicted utilities to correspond as closely as possible to the "true" utilities—or, at least, to the estimated utility as defined by some criterion measure or composite of measures. This pure model rarely if ever occurs in the civilian world. In the civilian world individuals apply for jobs; they are not assigned to them by some outside authority. The nearest approach to the pure classification model occurs in the military, and especially in time of war.

In classification we face in full all of the problems of measuring utility, because we require a common scale on which utility of persons in different jobs can be compared. How good a cook has utility equal to that of an average clerk-typist? How good a combat infantryman has utility equal to that of an average M.P.? These are sticky questions, but to arrive at any rational strategy for classification decisions, we must give some answer to them. But before discussing them further, let us inquire into what is needed in an effective predictor battery for use in classification.

In classification, we are concerned with choices. The person who is assigned to one job or training program is not available for assignment to some other. Conversely, if there is a single slot to be filled in job category A and we fill it with candidate X, we are foreclosed from assigning candidate Y to that job specialty. In view of this, we are concerned with *differences* in predicted utility. For each candidate, we would like the dispersion of predicted utilities to be as great as possible. As in placement, one source of dispersion lies in differing correlations of predictor variables with measured success in different jobs. If mechanical aptitude has high correlation with success as a machinist but low correlation with success as a cook, those with high mechanical aptitude are likely to have greater utility if assigned to training as machinists than if assigned to training as cooks. Predictor variables that we should seek, then, are those that show a wide dispersion in their validities against the criterion composites in different jobs. As we examine the matter further it will also become apparent that, in a test battery, it is desirable for the several tests (1) to show low correlations with each other and (2) to show quite different patterns of validity for the set of jobs among which assignment is being made.

However, there *is* a role for tests of functions common to a number of jobs if those jobs differ substantially in importance. Thus, in the set of data reported on page 342, the word knowledge test correlated .48 with success in Aviation Instrument Mechanic school and .45 with success in General Clerical school. Suppose now that the net utility (gross utility less cost to recruit and train) of the average recruit assigned to instrument mechanic training is 150 units (in some for now undefined metric) with a standard deviation of 100 units. Then the equation for predicted utility for a given standard score on the word knowledge test is

$$\tilde{U}_{AIM} = 150 + (.48)(100)z_{WK}$$

If, at the same time, the net utility of an average recruit assigned to clerical training is 100 units with a standard deviation of 50 units, we have, for predicted utility of assignment to clerical training,

$$\tilde{U}_{\text{CLER}} = 100 + (.45)(50)z_{\text{WK}}$$

We can prepare a table showing the predicted utility in the two assignments for individuals at different standard-score levels on the word knowledge test. The values for each assignment and for the difference between assignments are as follows:

STANDARD SCORE	$\tilde{U}_{\text{AIM}}$	$\tilde{U}_{\text{CLER}}$	Diff$_{(\text{AIM-CLER})}$
+2.0	246	145	101
+1.0	198	122.5	75.5
0.0	150	100	50
−1.0	102	77.5	24.5
−2.0	54	55	− 1
−3.0	06	32.5	−26.5

With the parameters as given, it is clearly advantageous that the recruits best on word knowledge be assigned to aircraft instrument training, rather than to clerical training, though the test is almost identical in its validity for both schools. This table brings out the point that, when there is sufficient difference in the *dispersion* of utilities, a test can serve a useful classification function even though it has the same correlation with the criterion indicator of utility in each of the jobs.

The greater dispersion of utility for one of two jobs would be quite plausible if (1) superior performance in the job made a more important contribution to the success of the organization, (2) mistakes made in the job were potentially more damaging to the organization, and/or (3) training costs for the job were substantially higher so that failures in training represented a substantially higher cost. It seems likely that all of these conditions could exist in the current illustration.

We have illustrated the point that predictors with nearly identical validities for different jobs can still be useful for the classification function if different jobs differ substantially in dispersion of utility values—as they often do. However, it is still true that effective classification is made possible primarily by tests that show markedly different relationships to criterion indicators of validity in different jobs. Thus, if we compare cryptographic operator with machinist, the word knowledge test is equally predictive of training school success in the two specialties, but three other measures showed strikingly different relationships. Correlations with training school success for these four variables are shown below.

	CRYPTOGRAPHIC OPERATOR	MACHINIST
Word knowledge	.49	.48
Tool functions	.07	.63
Biographical Inventory—Crafts	.09	.48
Biographical Inventory—Services	.28	— .10

Given the intercorrelations that were found for these variables, a composite of the last three of them, weighted as follows:

0.44 Tool Functions + 0.25 Biographical Inventory (Crafts) − .30 Biographical Inventory (Services)

yields a correlation of .68 with the difference between predicted utility as machinist and that for cryptographic operator, if the dispersion of utilities is the same for both assignments.

We must ask now what type of test is likely to show a large dispersion of validities. It seems likely that, for ability tests, this will be a relatively pure test of a relatively simple psychological function, because that specific function would probably be involved in certain jobs but not in others. Complex tests may show validity for many jobs, but with different aspects of the test providing the reason. However, it must be admitted that *solid* evidence to support the wider dispersion of validities for pure tests of a single factor is not really in hand, partly because the massive validity studies of tests of different levels of complexity that would be required in order to provide satisfactory empirical evidence have simply not been carried out.

Measures of interests and temperament present interesting possibilities as classification tests, because different jobs seem to match rather different interest and temperament patterns. However, interest and temperament patterns seem likely to be directly related to satisfaction with the activities and conditions of particular jobs. If there is a relationship to success, it may arise indirectly as a by-product of greater satisfaction.

When we start talking about a classification test *battery*, we are concerned not only with the dispersion of validities* of tests taken singly, but also with the dispersion of partial validity coefficients when the other predictor variables in the battery are held constant. The partial validities are very much dependent on the intercorrelations of predictor variables and are reduced in proportion as the correlations among the variables are high. The need to reduce the correlations

---

* In all of this discussion, we should really be concerned with contributions to predicted utility but, because of the unfamiliarity of the concept of utility in this context, we speak, for the present, of validity—that is, the correlation with *the criterion indicator*.

among predictors provides another argument in favor of factorially simple (and presumably minimally correlated) tests.

Once a research battery has been assembled and tried out and validity data have been assembled for all of the tests for each of the jobs among which assignment must be made, one faces the problems of which tests and how many to retain in the battery for the operational classification and assignment program. Horst (1954) has developed an approach, based on the dispersion of partial validities, that parallels the procedure described on pages 341–345 for choosing tests for a multiple selection battery. Here, the criterion by which an additional test is selected at each stage is that of maximizing the dispersion of validity coefficients, as represented by their variance. Referring to Table A on page 342, we calculate

	1	2	3	4
$\Sigma\, r_{ic}^2$	1.1882	1.7994	.9834	.7172
$(\Sigma\, r_{ic})^2/n$	1.1329	1.6820	.8820	.5249
$nS_{r_{ic}}^2$	.0553	.1177	.1014	.1923

The variable with the greatest dispersion of validities, and hence the initial one to be included in a *classification* battery would be test 4, tool functions.

The procedure of eliminating the influence of a variable so as to provide a matrix of residuals is the same as for multiple selection, though the variable eliminated in this case is different. Table B′ shows the residual matrix when test 4 is eliminated first.

			TABLE B′		
	1	2	3	4
1. Word knowledge	.9039	.4808	.3150	—
2. Dial and table reading	.4808	.8976	.3000	—
3. Mechanical principles	.3150	.3000	.7500	—
4. Tool functions	—	—	—	—
a. Intelligence operations	.5880	.6560	.3000	—
b. Aviation instrument mechanic	.3405	.4260	.3150	—
c. Machinist	.2847	.4784	.2950	—
d. Baker	.2363	.2036	.0750	—
e. Clerk–typist	.4283	.6176	.3050	—

The procedure of calculating the variance of the residual validities is carried out as for the initial variable, and we get

	1	2	3	4
$\Sigma\ r^2_{ic\,\cdot\,4}$	.7820	1.2636	.3749	—
$(\Sigma\ r_{ic\,\cdot\,4})^2/n$	.7052	1.1340	.3328	—
$nS^2_{r_{ic\,\cdot\,4}}$	.0768	.1292	.0421	—

Thus the second variable to be added is test 2.

The cycle is repeated as many times as there are variables (or until one decides to stop because the residual dispersions have become very small), and the operational battery consists of those tests with the largest dispersions.

Once the tests to be included in the battery have been decided on, whether for the case of multiple selection discussed earlier or for the case of classification discussed here, regression weights for each criterion variable can be calculated following the procedures set forth in Chapter 9.

This procedure has operated with validity coefficients rather than with predicted utilities. If, as is likely to be the case, jobs differ substantially in the spread of utility that is represented by having in the job a person who does it very well versus having a person who is minimally competent or less, then it may be quite desirable to take into account the dispersion of predicted utilities in the procedures for selecting tests. Then each job will be characterized by a weighting factor, W_j:

$$W_j\ =\ \sigma_{\hat{U}_j}/\sigma_{\hat{U}}$$

the ratio of dispersion of estimated utilities for that job to the average dispersion of estimated utilities over all jobs. In the matrix of validity coefficients, the entries in each row corresponding to a given job would be multiplied by the weight for that job to yield entries for each test that are proportional to the ability of that test to differentiate the predicted utility of candidates in that job. This matrix could be substituted for the matrix of validities in Horst's procedure and the rest of the procedure carried out as indicated in the illustration. The result would be, at each stage, the subset of tests that is most effective in differentiating individuals' levels of utility in different job assignments. Results from using the procedure with our previous illustration are shown below. It was assumed, for purposes of the illustration, that weights corresponding to the (judged) dispersion of utilities were as follows:

Intelligence Operations	1.5
Aviation Instrument Mechanic	2.0
Machinist	1.0
Baker	0.8
Clerk–Typist	0.6

We then get, for each job, a vector in which validity is weighted by relative dispersion of predicted utilities, as follows:

	WORD KNOWLEDGE	DIAL AND TABLE READING	MECHANICAL PRINCIPLE	TOOL FUNCTIONS
Intelligence Operations	.98	1.08	.60	.30
Aviation Instrument Mechanic	.96	1.14	1.08	.90
Machinist	.48	.68	.61	.63
Baker	.26	.23	.17	.22
Clerk–Typist	.27	.38	.20	.04

From this we calculate the dispersion of each test's ability to predict utilities:

$\Sigma(Wt \cdot r_{jc})^2$	2.253	3.126	1.967	1.347
$[\Sigma(Wt \cdot r_{jc})]^2/n$	1.740	2.464	1.415	0.874
$nS^2_{(Wt \cdot r_{jc})}$	.513	.662	.552	.473

With these rather sharply differentiated weights, the choice for the most effective classification test shifts back to test 2, dial and table reading. We can then calculate residuals as before, and determine the best test to add to this first one. The successive calculations proceed as shown beginning on page 352.

Some guides to the number of tests to be retained in a battery are needed. It seems unlikely at this time that any mathematical significance test could specify whether the improvement in differential validity (much less the improvement in differential utility) from adding one more test is greater than could be expected by chance. One might consider examining the partial validities or the regression weights at each stage to see whether they were significantly different from zero and using the shortest battery that reduced all partial validities to a chance level or for which the next test had nonsignificant regression weights. However, there is no particularly convincing rationale for this criterion. It may well be that factors of practical feasibility, supplemented with a "feel" for the data, will have to remain the guide for the present.

We turn now to the strategy for assigning persons to jobs. This becomes a good deal more complex enterprise than in the case of simple selection, because action with respect to one person influences the options that are available for the assignment of others. We can illustrate this with a very simple example of three candidates and three positions to be filled. Suppose that our tests had produced the following matrix of predicted utilities.

CANDIDATE	PREDICTED UTILITY		
	Job A	Job B	Job C
1	125	140	100
2	50	80	40
3	10	20	30

At first glance it appears that candiate 1 should be assigned to job B; it is the job for which this candidate has the highest predicted utility and candidate 1 is the candidate with the highest predicted utility for this job. But that would mean that candidate 2 would have to be assigned to job A, a job in which that candidate's predicted utility is quite low. It becomes clear on closer inspection that *overall* predicted utility is maximized when candidate 1 is assigned to job A, 2 to B, and 3 to C—this in spite of the fact that candidate 3 is the person of the three who is least likely to be effective in job C.

We assume that the basic goal of assignment is to maximize overall predicted utility, while filling the quotas to be met in the different jobs. Referring to our matrix of predicted utilities, in which a column represents a job and a row an individual, we must select one cell from each row and n_j cells from each column, where $j = 1, 2, \ldots, k$, and n_j represents the numbers in each of the different jobs. If

$$n_1 + n_2 + \cdots + n_k < N$$

that is, if we have a surplus of persons over the number required to fill the quotas in all the jobs, then we can introduce a column $k + 1$ labeled "reject," in which the utility of every person is zero, and assign the surplus to this column in such a way as to maximize the sum of the utilities of those assigned to the first k columns.

It is possible to develop a procedure (see Dwyer, 1954, 1957) that converges quite rapidly on the optimal assignments, given a group of individuals and a reasonably small number of job categories. The procedure is a generalization of the selection decision strategy of "pick 'em off the top" that adapts this simple strategy to the quota demands of the different jobs. We will illustrate the procedure with data from a set of 25 individuals and 5 job categories.

Our starting place is a matrix of predicted utilities providing a value for each person in each job category. This is shown as Matrix A. We start also with a quota, n_j, of persons to be assigned to each job. For this illustrative problem the quotas are given as 3, 8, 2, 7, and 5, respectively, and are shown at the top of Matrix A. The first step in the procedure is to scan each column of the matrix to identify the n_j highest scores in that column. These have been marked with asterisks in Matrix A, where all cases have been marked in the event of tied scores. The lowest value marked in each column represents an initial estimate of the minimal predicted utility that qualifies an individual for assignment to that job. These values, labeled v_j, are shown at the bottom of the matrix.

Of course, in the initial identification of possible assignments, there are some persons who come up to the threshold value for several jobs and some who do not make it for any. We must determine what appears to be the *best* assignment for each individual. To do this, we next scan each row of the matrix in terms of the minimum qualifying values, v_j, to find out how much each person surpasses or falls short of the threshold in each job and to identify that person's initially "best" assignment. Thus, for person 1, the values are $51 - 55 = -4$, $59 - 52 = 7$, $32 - 41 = -9$, $36 - 39 = -3$, and $37 - 48 = -11$, and the "best assignment" is to job 2, for which the persons falls 7 points above the threshold. The maximum value of $\tilde{U}_{ij} - v_j$ is shown in the column to the right of Matrix A. We will call this value u_i.

Combining the job thresholds and the person optimal values, we now compute a new matrix, Matrix B (p. 358), in which each entry is equal to

$$\tilde{U}_{ij} - u_i - v_j$$

The entries in this matrix are all zero or negative. A zero entry indicates an optimal assignment; a negative entry indicates how far an assignment to that job would fall short of being optimal. We now asterisk the zero entries and count the number in each column. In our count, we count separately the cases in which a zero entry appears *only* in a given column and the cases in which it appears jointly in that and in some other column. This count, designated q_j, is shown at the head of Matrix B, just below the row indicating the quota for each job. A column labeled J_i at the right of the matrix identifies the job or jobs to which each candidate would be assigned at this stage.

We note that the numbers available for assignment to the 5 jobs at this point do not match our quotas. Thus, we have 12 candidates for job 4, where we need only 7, and no candidates for job 3. There are other discrepancies as well. Clearly, we must adjust one or more of the "threshold" values and, because the largest discrepancy appears as an excess in job 4, we can appropriately raise the threshold in this job so that fewer will appear optimal in this assignment. Raising

Matrix A

Person	JOB 1	JOB 2	JOB 3	JOB 4	JOB 5	u_i
Quota (n_j)	3	8	2	7	5	
1	51	59*	32	36	37	7
2	47	47	35	36	41	− 3
3	51	48	29	39*	46	0
4	50	59*	41*	32	49*	7
5	32	22	21	17	33	− 15
6	36	52*	19	17	31	0
7	47	52*	27	27	40	0
8	48	54*	30	35	51*	3
9	48	44	33	20	41	− 7
10	49	35	31	38	37	− 1
11	46	42	28	41*	38	2
12	37	41	27	25	43	− 5
13	57*	55*	28	39*	39	3
14	55*	58*	33	42*	43	6
15	51	43	27	37	48*	0
16	45	31	30	22	40	− 8
17	39	37	20	24	30	− 15
18	43	42	19	33	39	− 6
19	46	37	37	39*	45	0
20	44	47	33	39*	37	0
21	36	30	20	22	22	− 17
22	41	28	26	29	32	− 10
23	52	55*	42*	39*	51*	3
24	49	35	29	36	42	− 3
25	57*	56*	40	46*	48*	7
v_j	55	52	41	39	48	

Matrix B

	JOB					
	1	2	3	4	5	
Quota (n_j)	3	8	2	7	5	
Assignment (q_j)	0 + 1	7 + 1	0	12	5 + 2	J_i
Person						
1	− 3	0*	− 16	− 10	− 18	2
2	− 5	− 2	− 3	0*	− 4	4
3	− 4	− 4	− 12	0*	− 2	4
4	− 12	0*	− 7	− 14	− 6	2
5	− 8	− 15	− 5	− 7	0*	5
6	− 19	0*	− 22	− 22	− 17	2
7	− 8	0*	− 14	− 12	− 8	2
8	− 10	− 1	− 8	− 7	0*	5
9	0*	− 1	− 1	− 12	0*	1,5
10	− 5	− 16	− 9	0*	− 10	4
11	− 11	− 12	− 15	0*	− 12	4
12	− 13	− 6	− 9	− 9	0*	5
13	− 1	0*	− 16	− 3	− 12	2
14	− 6	0*	− 14	− 3	− 11	2
15	− 4	− 9	− 14	− 2	0*	5
16	− 2	− 13	− 3	− 9	0*	5
17	− 1	0*	− 6	0*	− 3	2,4
18	− 6	− 4	− 16	0*	− 3	4
19	− 9	− 15	− 14	0*	− 3	4
20	− 11	− 5	− 8	0*	− 11	4
21	− 2	− 5	− 4	0*	− 9	4
22	− 4	− 14	− 5	0*	− 6	4
23	− 6	0*	− 2	− 3	0*	2,5
24	− 3	− 14	− 9	0*	− 3	4
25	− 5	− 3	− 8	0*	− 7	4

the threshold, v_j, by some amount is the equivalent of subtracting that amount from

$$\tilde{U}_{ij} - u_i - v_j$$

for each individual. We must make an adjustment that will shift the optimal assignment of some 5 individuals to one or another of the other jobs.

We want each person's optimal assignment to be represented by a zero, so there will be some individuals for whom a corresponding adjustment will have to be made in their u_i. Inspection of column 4 of Matrix B, in terms of the values in the other columns of the matrix, suggests that an adjustment of 3 points of v_4, and a corresponding adjustment in u_i for a number of persons (to produce at least one zero in their row), will accomplish about the number of shifts in optimal allocation that we need.

Application of these adjustments produces Matrix C. Once again we determine eligibility for assignment to different jobs in terms of the zero entries in the matrix, counting the number of unique zeroes and the number of shared zeroes in each column. The count is at the top of Matrix C, and the possible assignments are shown at the right. We have made some improvement in the match between assignments and quotas, but some further adjustments are still called for.

Adjustments of -1 on job 1, -2 on job 3 and $+1$ on job 5, applied to the entries of Matrix C with compensating shifts of the u_i values as required to keep zero as the indicator of the optimal assignment, eventually lead us to Matrix D, with assignments as indicated by the asterisks. By a judicious allocation of cases that are eligible for more than one assignment, we are now able to meet all of our quotas. Applying the adjustments that we have made to the original thresholds, we have as final thresholds, v_j,

$$
\begin{aligned}
55 - 1 &= 54 \\
52 + 0 &= 52 \\
41 - 2 &= 39 \\
39 + 3 &= 42 \\
48 + 1 &= 49
\end{aligned}
$$

The procedure for assignment of any individual is to calculate $\tilde{U}_{ij} - v_j$ for that person for each job category and to assign the person to the job category in which the person is furthest above the threshold, or, if he or she is above in none, to the job for which the negative value is least. The final assignments made for this group are shown by the underlined entries in Matrix A. The sum of these underlined entries, 1111, is the maximum total utility that can be achieved within the quota constraints.

If one can consider the present sample of cases to be representative of the levels and patterns of abilities that will be found in future samples, and if the quotas are expected to be stable over time, use of the differences $\tilde{U}_{ij} - v_j$ provides a reasonable decision rule for assignment of future cases.

Matrix C

	JOB						
	1	2	3	4	5	Change in u_i	J_i
Quota (n_j)	3	8	2	7	5		
Assignment (q_j)	1 + 2	8 + 2	0	4 + 4	6 + 5		
Person							
1	−3	0*	−16	−13	−18	0	2
2	−3	0*	−1	−1	−2	−2	2
3	−2	−2	−10	−1	0*	−2	5
4	−12	0*	−7	−17	−6	0	2
5	−8	−15	−5	−10	0*	0	5
6	−19	0*	−22	−25	−17	0	2
7	−8	0*	−14	−15	−8	0	2
8	−10	−1	−8	−10	0*	0	5
9	0*	−1	−1	−15	0*	0	1,5
10	−2	−13	−6	0*	−7	−3	4
11	−8	−9	−12	0*	−9	−3	4
12	−13	−6	−9	−12	0*	0	5
13	−1	0*	−16	−6	−12	0	2
14	−6	0*	−14	−6	−14	0	2
15	−4	−9	−17	−5	0*	0	5
16	−2	−13	−3	−12	0*	0	5
17	−1	0*	−6	−3	−3	0	2
18	−3	−1	−13	0*	0*	−3	4,5
19	−6	−12	−11	0*	0*	−3	4,5
20	−8	−2	−5	0*	−8	−3	4
21	0*	−3	−2	−1	−7	−2	1
22	−1	−11	−2	0*	−3	−3	4
23	−6	0*	−2	−6	0*	0	2,5
24	0*	−11	−6	0*	0*	−3	1,4,5
25	−2	0*	−5	0*	−4	−3	2,4
Change to v_j	0	0	0	3	0		

Matrix D

	JOB						
	1	2	3	4	5	Change in u_i	J_i
Quota (n_j)	3	8	2	7	5		
Assignment (q_j)	2 + 6	5 + 5	1 + 4	5 + 2	3 + 3		
Person							
1	−2	0*	−14	−13	−19	0	2
2	−3	−1	0*	−2	−4	+1	3
3	0*	−1	−7	−1	0*	0	1,5
4	−11	0*	−5	−17	−7	0	2
5	−6	−14	−2	−10	0*	0	5
6	−18	0*	−20	−25	−18	0	2
7	−7	0*	−12	−15	−9	0	2
8	−8	0*	−6	−10	0*	0	2,5
9	0*	−2	0*	−16	−2	+1	1,3
10	−1	−13	−4	0*	−8	0	4
11	−7	−9	−10	0*	−10	0	4
12	−11	−5	−6	−12	0*	0	5
13	0*	0*	−14	−6	−13	0	1,2
14	−5	0*	−12	−6	−15	0	2
15	−2	−8	−14	−5	0*	0	5
16	0*	−12	0*	−12	0*	0	1,3,5
17	0*	0*	−4	−3	−4	0	1,2
18	−2	−1	−11	0*	−1	0	4
19	−5	−12	−9	0*	−1	0	4
20	−7	−2	−3	0*	−9	0	4
21	0*	−4	−1	−2	−9	+1	1
22	0*	−11	0*	0*	−4	0	1,3,4
23	−5	0*	0*	−6	−1	0	2,3
24	0*	−12	−5	−1	−2	+1	1
25	−1	0*	−3	0*	−5	0	2,4
Change in v_j	−1	0	−2	0	+1		

GUIDANCE

The use of tests in guidance can also be modeled in terms of the jobs-by-persons matrix of utilities, but with several differences. In the first place, in guidance we are typically concerned with one specific person, without reference to others. Thus concern focuses on a single *row* of the utility matrix: the utilities of different jobs for that individual. In the second place, as implied earlier, utility is to be thought of as utility *for that person,* rather than for any outside organization. In guidance, test results are used to help a person make the choices that are best for her or him. (We will need to explore the implications of this point further.) In the third place, the number and variety of "jobs" among which choices are to be made is often ill defined and relatively unbounded. This also raises a number of problems.

When we start to think of utility from the point of view of the individual, rather than from that of an organization—employer, school or college, society at large—rather different issues come to the fore. The main point is that satisfaction in a job, in addition to success, becomes a major consideration. Satisfaction involves the goals and values of the individual and is a highly individual matter. We do not have any well-defined calculus of values or any procedure for combining values with probabilities of success, but this must be done in some way or other if we are to generate a prediction of the utility of some line of action for a person. We might be able to develop expectancy tables that would enable us to state that Jennifer, in the light of her test scores, has 1 chance in 5 of being admitted to medical school and 4 chances in 5 of being admitted to secretarial school. However, if medical school has 10 times as much appeal for Jennifer as secretarial training, one might conclude that the combination of probabilities with values gives medical school a greater *net* utility for Jennifer and makes it reasonable for Jennifer to take those steps that would make her eligible to apply for admission to medical school.

The discussion up to here points to three roles of testing and counseling in the guidance context. First, it is necessary to provide some estimates of the probability of survival and/or the probable degree of success following different choices. One would like to be able to make a statement like this: "In the light of your past record and your test scores, you have about 7 chances in 10 of being admitted to law school and about 9 chances in 10 of completing training if admitted. The average law school graduate currently is initially employed at an annual salary of X thousand dollars. After 10 years the average law school graduate earns Y thousand dollars a year."

Second, it is necessary to help the individual clarify, and possibly quantify, his or her values in relation to different choices. This is a function that interest inventories have attempted to discharge, at least in part. The function is also served by persons or documents that provide occupational information. The counseling process is directed toward helping the individual to make explicit the values that person seeks in a job and to evaluate the extent to which those values will be realized in different lines of work. The third role, synthesizing probabilities on the one hand and values on the other into a final estimate of the desirability or "utility" of the choice from the individual's point of view, has received little formal analysis.

We have noted that another distinctive feature of the guidance model is that the limits of the row representing jobs are ill defined. If one turns to the *Dictionary of Occupational Titles,* one finds that there are literally thousands of identified jobs in the United States economy. Sometimes a person who is seeking help has narrowed the choice down to two or three categories from among this enormous array. Sometimes, however, the counselee's plans are still relatively unstructured, and he or she must be helped to explore the complex terrain of job and/or training possibilities that stretches out in all directions almost without limit. At that point, it becomes necessary to impose some structure on the world of work, just as test research has tried to impose structure on the world of human abilities. The thousands of specific alternatives need to be grouped in some way into a manageably small number of categories in terms of which an individual's abilities and propensities can be assessed and their fit to job conditions and demands can be appraised.

From time to time there have been attempts (see, for example, Thorndike, 1953; Orr, 1956) to organize jobs into homogeneous families. The approach requires that one define a useful set of dimensions with respect to which jobs differ and obtain appraisals of the degree to which and the level at which each of an array of jobs requires possession of each dimension. A useful set of dimensions should have the properties of being (1) dimensions with respect to which jobs show significant differences, (2) collectively inclusive, (3) distinct and relatively independent, and (4) possible to evaluate. Appraisal of level of demand has usually been obtained by pooling judgments of the job's requirements, using job analyses of some type as raw data. However, some bodies of data do exist, such as validation studies of the GATB (Manpower Administration, 1970), and follow-up studies in Project Talent (Flanagan et al. 1973), that provide empirical descriptions of persons working in or training for certain categories of jobs.

Once each of a pool of jobs is characterized by its typical demand for each of a set of worker characteristics (either by ratings or by the actual properties of persons in the job), some procedure is needed to group the jobs into clusters or "families" in terms of which an individual might be counseled. A plausible procedure would be to try to find groupings of jobs that are most similar in terms of having the least "distance" between the characteristic demand level or test-score centroid of the jobs. The calculations for finding the distance measure are fairly straightforward, given the covariance matrix for the dimensions used to describe job demand. The most straightforward way to proceed would appear to be to carry out a multiple discriminant analysis (see Chapter 9) of the dimensions of job demand, extracting enough orthogonal dimensions to account for most of the reliable between-jobs variance. Discriminant scores could then be calculated for each job specialty, and from these a Cartesian distance,

$$D = (D_1^2 + D_2^2 + \cdots + D_k^2)^{1/2}$$

could be determined for each pair of jobs. The matrix of distances could be systematically scanned for either very small distances, which would define jobs that appeared to belong in the same family, or very large distances, which would identify jobs that would serve to define different clusters.

By way of illustration, we can take the ten job categories that were reported in Table 9.1 (page 274). The Cartesian distances between pairs of occupations were calculated and are shown in Table 11.1. The greatest distance is between occupations 4 (dentist) and 7 (inspector–packer), so these two occupations define the poles around which two job clusters can be assembled. Assigning each job to the cluster that makes the average within-cluster distance a minimum and the between-clusters distance a maximum, we arrive at the following two clusters:

CLUSTER 1	CLUSTER 2
Cabinetmaker	Candy packer
Dentist	Dental lab technician
Engineer	Food service worker
Teacher	Inspector–packer
	Service station attendant
	Welder

The average of the discriminant values for the occupations within each cluster are as follows:

	DISCRIMINANT 1	DISCRIMINANT 2
Cluster 1	127	48
2	93	44

Clearly, the separation of the two clusters is primarily on the first discriminant, which we identified in Chapter 9 (page 273) as general ability with an emphasis on the quantitative.

One can continue the analysis and identify three clusters, starting with three jobs for which none of the between-jobs distances is small. In these data, the best job to define a third cluster is occupation 1, cabinetmaker. Once again assigning

Table 11.1 Cartesian Distances Between Job Discriminant Values

					JOB					
	1	2	3	4	5	6	7	8	9	10
1. Cabinetmaker	—	30	11	27	15	25	32	9	14	24
2. Candy packer		—	20	57	44	8	5	22	41	9
3. Dental lab technician			—	38	24	14	22	2	24	14
4. Dentist				—	18	52	59	36	19	52
5. Engineer					—	37	46	22	18	36
6. Food service worker						—	12	16	37	2
7. Inspector-packer							—	14	41	14
8. Service station attendant								—	22	16
9. Teacher, elementary or secondary									—	37
10. Welder, production line										—

jobs so as to make average within-cluster distance a minimum, we come up with the following three clusters:

CLUSTER 1	CLUSTER 2	CLUSTER 3
Dentist	Candy packer	Cabinetmaker
Engineer	Food service worker	Dental lab technician
Teacher	Inspector-packer	Service station attendant
	Welder	

The average discriminant values for the three clusters are

	DISCRIMINANT 1	DISCRIMINANT 2
Cluster 1	131	48
2	87	45
3	108	47

The clusters identified here are still defined primarily by three levels of intellectual demand, and the second discriminant dimension seems to play no significant role. However, this need not be the case. Within levels of intellectual demand, it might be possible to identify clusters that were differentiated with respect to other aspects of ability. And certainly clusters could be found that were differentiated with respect to interests and preferences.

Conceptually, the procedure of defining job families is straightforward. However, its application is not. One has no good *a priori* basis for determining how many clusters or families one should accept or what guide lines should determine the identification of or the boundaries for a cluster. And though some jobs cling together in a tight, homogeneous cluster, many more float out in no-man's-land, about equally distant from two or more focal points. Jobs, unfortunately, tend to distribute themselves fairly uniformly in the job-demand space—like the stars in the summer sky—rather than grouping into a small number of dense clusters like a set of spiral nebulae. Any partitioning of this job-requirement space into regions, each defining a job cluster, seems likely to be rather arbitrary and to leave many specific jobs hovering near the boundary lines.

The attempt to describe jobs in terms of the typical person presently in that job, and to counsel individuals on the basis of the closeness of their resemblance to that typical individual, carries an implicit assumption that "what is represents what should be." There is probably a kernel of truth in this and some likelihood that a person who deviates markedly from those who have entered into and survived in a job will be either unsuccessful or unhappy with it. However, a healthy skepticism about how universally this is true should temper any use of "centours" or other similarity measures as a basis for counseling.

Turning now to the test battery needed for guidance, we can see that it must be related both to those characteristics that appear repeatedly in the specification of job demands and to those characteristics with respect to which jobs differ. Because the range of jobs among which choices may need to be made is literally unlimited, the battery of available measures must be broadly inclusive. And because many guidance decisions represent differential decisions of A *rather than* B, tests must show differential relationships (in mean score or in predictive validity) for different jobs. Thus, in many ways, the properties that make up a battery suitable for classification decisions are the same ones that are called for in a battery for use in guidance decisions—with added importance to dimensions that define satisfaction with, rather than success in, an occupation.

CONCLUDING STATEMENT

We have set forth in rather broad outlines what seems to us to be a rational and consistent model for viewing four types of decisions that may need to be made from tests or other prediction devices. The model is an oversimplified one;

though we develop the idea of "utility," we do not elaborate the balancing notion of "cost." And, though the model may be logically sound as far as it goes, its application in any practical situation obviously involves a host of difficulties. These difficulties have been pointed out in this chapter and in Chapters 6 and 7. The information that would permit the model to be effectively applied, especially to classification and guidance decisions, is poorly approximated at the present time, and we may even question to what extent it will ever become available. Especially as social and individual values (as distinct from facts about prediction) enter into the problem, the gaps in our knowledge and in our procedures for using that knowledge become painfully evident.

In our more somber moments, we may question whether our data will ever become sufficiently solid to justify using scores on predictor instruments as a basis for making personnel decisions. However, those decisions *will* be made — on some basis or other. Persons will be employed, educated, assigned to jobs counseled with respect to their futures. It is well that we recognize the complexity of the enterprise and the pitfalls along the way. A realistic, if discouraging, model probably serves us better than a simplistic and superficial one if we are to move ahead to a sounder use of evidence from tests, or from any other sources, in personnel decisions.

Bibliography

Abrahams, N. M., and E. F. Alf, Jr. 1978. Relative costs and statistical power in the extreme groups approach. *Psychometrika*, 43, 11–18.

Angoff, W. H. 1971. Scales, norms and equivalent scores. In *Educational Measurement*. Ed. R. L. Thorndike. 2nd ed. Washington, D.C.: American Council on Education.

Bloom, B. S., ed. 1954. *Taxonomy of Educational Objectives*. New York: Longmans.

Buhler, R. A. 1953. Flicker fusion threshold and anxiety level. Unpublished doctoral dissertation. New York: Columbia University.

Campbell, D. T., and D. W. Fiske. 1959. Convergent and discriminant validation by the multi-trait multi-method matrix. *Psychological Bulletin*, 56, 81–105.

Coffman, W. E. 1978. *An Exploratory Study of Differences in Performance of Pupils in Grades 6, 7, 8 and 9 on the Items in the Iowa Tests of Basic Skills*. Iowa City, Iowa: University of Iowa. (ERIC Document Reproduction Service No. ED156713)

Comber, L. C., and J. R. Keeves. 1973. *Science Education in Nineteen Countries*. New York: Wiley.

Comrey, A. L. 1973. *A First Course in Factor Analysis*. New York: Academic Press.

Cronbach, L. J. 1951. Coefficient alpha and the internal structure of tests. *Psychometrika*, 16, 297–334.

———. 1971. Test validation. In *Educational Measurement*. Ed. R. L. Thorndike. 2nd ed. Washington, D.C.: American Council on Education.

Cronbach, L. J., Goldine Gleser, Harinder Nanda, and Nageswari Rajaratnam. 1972. *The Dependability of Behavioral Measurements*. New York: Wiley.

Cronbach, L. J., and R. Snow. 1977. *Aptitude and Instructional Methods*. New York: Irvington.

Cronbach, L. J., and W. G. Warrington. 1951. Time-limit tests: Estimating their reliability and degree of speeding. *Psychometrika*, 16, 167–188.

Darlington, R. B. 1978. Reduced-variance regression. *Psychological Bulletin*, 85, 1238–1255.

Davidoff, M. D., and H. W. Goheen. 1953. A table for the rapid determination of the tetrachoric coefficient. *Psychometrika*, 18, 115–121.

Dwyer, P. S. 1957. The detailed method of optimal regions. *Psychometrika*, 22, 43–52.

———. 1954. Solution of the personnel classification problem with the method of optimal regions. *Psychometrika*, 19, 11–26.

Fitzpatrick, Robert, and Edward J. Morrison. 1971. "Performance and Product Evaluation." In *Educational Measurement*. Ed. Robert L. Thorndike. 2nd ed. Washington, D.C.: American Council on Education.

Flanagan, J. C. 1939. General considerations in the selection of test items and a short method of estimating the product-moment coefficient from the data at the tails of the distribution. *Journal of Educational Psychology*, 30, 674–680.

Flanagan, J. C., D. V. Tiedeman, Mary B. Willis, and D. H. McLaughlin. 1973. *The Career Data Book*. Palo Alto, Calif.: American Institute for Research.

French, J. W. 1951. The Description of Aptitude and Achievement Tests in Terms of Rotated Factors. *Psychometric Monographs* No. 5. Chicago: University of Chicago Press.

Guertin, W. H., and J. P. Bailey, Jr. 1970. *Introduction to Modern Factor Analysis*. Ann Arbor, Mich.: Edwards Brothers.

Guilford, J. P. 1967. *The Nature of Human Intelligence*. New York: McGraw-Hill.

Gulliksen, H. 1950. *Theory of Mental Tests*. New York: Wiley.

Harman, H. H. 1976. *Modern Factor Analysis*. 3rd ed. Chicago: University of Chicago Press.

Henrysson, S. 1963. Correction of item-total correlations in item analysis. *Psychometrika*, 28, 211–218.

Horst, A. P. 1933. The difficulty of a multiple-choice test item. *Journal of Educational Psychology*, 24, 229–232.

———. 1954. A technique for the development of a differential prediction battery. *Psychological Monographs*, 68, No. 9 (Whole Number 380).

———. 1955. A technique for the development of a multiple absolute prediction battery. *Psychological Monographs*, 69, No. 5 (Whole Number 390).

Ironson, Gail H. 1980. Chi square and latent trait approaches to the measurement of item bias. "Item bias: the state of the art." Paper presented at the Third Annual Johns Hopkins University NSER.

Kuder, G. F., and M. W. Richardson. 1937. The theory of estimation of test reliability. *Psychometrika*, 2, 151–160.

Lindquist, E. F. 1953. *Design and Analysis of Experiments in Psychology and Education*. Boston: Houghton Mifflin.

Loevinger, Jane, Goldine C. Gleser, and P. H. DuBois. 1953. Maximizing the discriminating power of a multi-score test. *Psychometrika*, 18, 309–317.

Lord, F. M. 1980. *Applications of Item Response Theory to Practical Testing Problems*. Hillsdale, N.J.: Lawrence Erlbaum Associates.

Lord, F. M., and M. R. Novick. 1968. *Statistical Theories of Mental Test Scores*. Menlo Park, Calif.: Addison-Wesley.

Lorge, I., and Lorraine Kruglov. 1952. A suggested technique for improvement of difficulty prediction of test items. *Educational and Psychological Measurement*, 12, 554–561.

–––. 1953. The improvement of estimates of test difficulty. *Educational and Psychological Measurement*, 13, 34–46.

Manpower Administration, U.S. Department of Labor. 1970. *Manual for the General Aptitude Battery, Section III: Development*. Washington, D.C.: U.S. Department of Labor, Manpower Administration.

Meehl, P. E. 1954. *Clinical vs. Statistical Prediction: A Theoretical Analysis and Review of the Evidence*. Minneapolis, Minn.: University of Minnesota Press.

Nie, N. H., C. H. Hill, Jean G. Jenkins, Karin Steinbrenner, and D. H. Dent. 1975. *SPSS Statistical Package for the Social Sciences*. 2nd ed. New York: McGraw-Hill.

Novick, M. R., and P. H. Jackson. 1974. *Statistical Methods for Educational Research*. New York: McGraw-Hill.

Orr, D. B. 1956. The Distance Measure as a Statistic for Clustering Jobs. Unpublished Ph.D. dissertation. New York: Teachers College, Columbia University.

Owen, R. J. 1975. A Bayesian sequential procedure for quantal response in the context of adaptive mental testing. *Journal of the American Statistical Association*, 70, 351–356.

Peters, C. C., and W. R. van Voorhees. 1940. *Statistical Procedures and their Mathematical Bases*. New York: McGraw-Hill.

Phillips, L. D. 1973. *Bayesian Statistics for Social Scientists*. New York: Crowell.

Prestwood, J. S., and D. J. Weiss. 1977. *Accuracy of Perceived Test-Item Difficulties*. Minneapolis, Minn.: University of Minnesota Psychometric Methods Program Research Report 77–3.

Rasch, G. 1960. *Probabilistic Models for Some Intelligence and Attainment Tests*. Cophenhagen, Denmark: Danmarks Paedagogiske Institut.

Rusinah, T. Joned. 1980. A comparison of performance of blacks and whites and of males and females on the items of the Cognitive Abilities Test, Form 3. M.A. Thesis for M.A. in Education. Iowa City, Iowa: University of Iowa.

Sawyer, J. 1966. Measurement and prediction, clinical and statistical. *Psychological Bulletin*, 66, 178–200.

Stein, C. 1960. Multiple regression. In *Contributions to Probability and Statistics*. Ed. Ingram Olkin et al. Stanford, Calif.: Stanford University Press.

Symonds, P. M. 1931. *Diagnosing Personality and Conduct*. New York: Century.

Thorndike, R. L. 1971. Concepts of culture-fairness. *Journal of Educational Measurement*, 8, 63–70.

———. 1953. Who belongs in the family? *Psychometrika*, 18, 267–276.

Thorndike, R. L., and Elizabeth P. Hagen. 1977. *Measurement and Evaluation in Psychology and Education*. 4th ed. New York: Wiley.

Tinkelman, S. N. 1971. Planning the objective test. In *Educational Measurement*. Ed. R. L. Thorndike. 2nd ed. Washington, D.C.: American Council on Education.

Tucker, J. A. 1950. *Relative Predictive Efficiency of Multiple Regression and Unique Pattern Techniques*. Unpublished Ph.D. dissertation. New York: Teachers College, Columbia University.

Walker, Helen M., and J. P. Lev. 1953. *Statistical Inference*. New York: Holt.

Weiss, D. J. 1973. *The Stratified Adaptive Computerized Ability Test*. Minneapolis, Minn.: University of Minnesota Psychometric Methods Program, Research Report 73-3.

Wesman, A. G. 1971. Writing the test item. In *Educational Measurement*. Ed. R. L. Thorndike. 2nd ed. Washington, D.C.: American Council on Education.

Winer, B. J. 1971. *Statistical Principles in Experimental Design*. New York: McGraw-Hill.

Wright, B. D. 1977. Solving measurement problems with the Rasch model. *Journal of Educational Measurement*, 14, 97–116.

Wright, B. D., and N. Panchapakesan. 1969. A procedure for sample-free item analysis. *Educational and Psychological Measurement*, 29, 23–48.

Wright, B. D., and M. H. Stone. 1979. *Best Test Design*. Chicago: Mesa Press.

Appendix A
Table of Flanagan r's

TABLE 3. A TABLE OF THE VALUES OF THE PRODUCT-MOMENT COEFFICIENT OF CORRELATION IN A NORMAL BIVARIATE POPULATION CORRESPONDING TO GIVEN PROPORTIONS OF SUCCESS

Proportion of successes in the 27 per cent scoring highest on the continuous variable

	01	02	04	06	08	10	12	14	16	18	20	22	24	26	28	30	32	34	36	38	40	42	44	46	48	50
01	0	11	23	30	35	40	43	46	49	51	53	55	57	59	61	62	63	65	66	67	68	69	70	71	72	72
02	−11	0	12	19	25	30	34	37	40	43	46	48	50	51	53	55	56	58	59	61	62	63	64	66	67	68
04	−23	−12	0	08	14	19	23	26	30	33	36	38	40	42	44	46	48	49	51	53	54	56	57	58	60	61
06	−30	−19	−08	0	06	11	15	19	23	26	29	31	33	36	38	40	42	44	45	47	48	50	52	53	55	56
08	−35	−25	−14	−06	0	05	09	13	17	20	23	25	28	30	32	35	37	38	40	42	44	45	47	49	51	52
10	−40	−30	−19	−11	−05	0	04	08	12	15	18	21	23	26	28	30	32	34	36	38	40	41	43	45	47	48
12	−43	−34	−23	−15	−09	−04	0	04	07	11	13	16	19	21	24	26	28	30	32	34	36	38	39	41	43	45
14	−46	−37	−26	−19	−13	−08	−04	0	03	07	10	12	15	18	20	22	25	27	29	31	33	34	36	38	40	42
16	−49	−40	−30	−23	−17	−12	−07	−03	0	03	06	09	12	14	17	19	21	24	26	28	30	31	33	35	37	39
18	−51	−43	−33	−26	−20	−15	−11	−07	−03	0	03	06	08	11	13	16	18	20	23	25	27	28	30	32	34	36
20	−53	−46	−36	−29	−23	−18	−13	−10	−06	−03	0	03	06	08	11	13	15	17	19	22	24	26	27	29	31	33
22	−55	−48	−38	−31	−25	−21	−16	−12	−09	−06	−03	0	03	06	08	10	12	15	17	19	21	23	25	27	29	31
24	−57	−50	−40	−33	−28	−23	−19	−15	−12	−08	−06	−03	0	03	05	08	10	12	14	16	18	20	22	24	26	28
26	−59	−51	−42	−36	−30	−26	−21	−18	−14	−11	−08	−06	−03	0	02	05	07	09	12	14	16	18	20	22	24	26
28	−61	−53	−44	−38	−32	−28	−24	−20	−17	−13	−11	−08	−05	−02	0	02	04	07	09	11	13	15	17	19	21	23
30	−62	−55	−46	−40	−35	−30	−26	−22	−19	−16	−13	−10	−08	−05	−02	0	02	04	07	09	11	13	15	17	19	21
32	−63	−56	−48	−42	−37	−32	−28	−25	−21	−18	−15	−12	−10	−07	−04	−02	0	02	04	07	09	11	13	15	17	19
34	−65	−58	−49	−44	−38	−34	−30	−27	−24	−20	−17	−15	−12	−09	−07	−04	−02	0	02	04	06	09	11	13	15	17
36	−66	−59	−51	−45	−40	−36	−32	−29	−26	−23	−19	−17	−14	−12	−09	−07	−04	−02	0	02	04	06	08	11	13	15
38	−67	−61	−53	−47	−42	−38	−34	−31	−28	−25	−22	−19	−16	−14	−11	−09	−07	−04	−02	0	02	04	06	08	11	13
40	−68	−62	−54	−48	−44	−40	−36	−33	−30	−27	−24	−21	−18	−16	−13	−11	−09	−06	−04	−02	0	02	04	06	08	10

Proportion of successes in the 27 per cent scoring lowest on the continuous variable

Reprinted by permission of John C. Flanagan.

	42	44	46	48	50	52	54	56	58	60	62	64	66	68	70	72	74	76	78	80	82	84	86	88	90	92	94	96	98	99
	08	06	04	02	0	-02	-04	-06	-08	-10	-13	-15	-17	-19	-21	-23	-26	-28	-31	-33	-36	-39	-42	-45	-48	-52	-56	-61	-68	-72
	06	04	02	0	-02	-04	-06	-08	-11	-13	-15	-17	-19	-21	-23	-26	-28	-30	-33	-35	-38	-40	-43	-46	-50	-53	-57	-62	-69	-73
	04	02	0	-02	-04	-06	-08	-11	-12	-14	-17	-19	-21	-23	-25	-27	-30	-32	-34	-37	-39	-42	-45	-48	-51	-55	-59	-63	-70	-74
	02	0	-02	-04	-06	-08	-10	-12	-14	-16	-18	-21	-23	-25	-27	-29	-32	-34	-36	-39	-41	-44	-47	-49	-53	-56	-60	-64	-71	-75
	0	-02	-04	-06	-08	-10	-12	-14	-16	-18	-20	-22	-25	-27	-29	-31	-33	-36	-38	-40	-43	-45	-48	-51	-54	-58	-61	-66	-72	-76
	-02	-04	-06	-08	-10	-12	-14	-16	-18	-21	-22	-25	-27	-29	-31	-33	-35	-37	-40	-42	-45	-47	-50	-52	-56	-59	-62	-67	-73	-77
	-04	-06	-08	-11	-13	-15	-16	-18	-20	-22	-25	-27	-29	-31	-33	-35	-37	-39	-42	-44	-47	-49	-51	-54	-57	-60	-64	-68	-73	-78
	-06	-08	-11	-13	-15	-17	-19	-21	-22	-25	-27	-29	-31	-33	-35	-37	-39	-41	-43	-46	-48	-50	-53	-57	-60	-61	-65	-69	-74	-78
	-09	-11	-13	-15	-17	-19	-21	-23	-25	-27	-29	-31	-33	-35	-37	-39	-41	-43	-45	-47	-49	-52	-54	-57	-60	-63	-66	-70	-75	-79
	-11	-13	-15	-17	-19	-21	-23	-25	-27	-29	-31	-33	-35	-37	-38	-40	-42	-45	-47	-49	-51	-53	-56	-58	-61	-64	-67	-71	-76	-80
	-13	-15	-17	-19	-21	-23	-25	-27	-29	-31	-33	-35	-37	-38	-40	-42	-44	-46	-49	-51	-53	-55	-57	-59	-61	-65	-68	-72	-77	-81
	-15	-17	-19	-21	-23	-26	-27	-29	-31	-33	-35	-37	-39	-40	-42	-44	-46	-48	-50	-52	-54	-57	-59	-61	-64	-66	-70	-73	-78	-82
	-18	-20	-22	-24	-26	-28	-30	-32	-33	-35	-37	-39	-41	-42	-44	-46	-48	-50	-52	-54	-56	-58	-60	-63	-65	-68	-71	-74	-79	-82
	-20	-22	-24	-26	-28	-30	-32	-34	-36	-37	-39	-41	-43	-45	-46	-48	-50	-52	-54	-56	-58	-60	-62	-63	-65	-69	-72	-75	-80	-83
	-23	-25	-27	-29	-31	-33	-34	-36	-38	-40	-42	-43	-45	-47	-49	-50	-52	-54	-56	-57	-60	-61	-63	-66	-68	-70	-73	-76	-80	-83
	-26	-27	-29	-31	-33	-35	-37	-39	-40	-42	-44	-46	-47	-49	-51	-52	-54	-56	-57	-60	-61	-63	-65	-67	-70	-72	-74	-77	-81	-84
	-28	-30	-32	-34	-36	-38	-39	-41	-43	-45	-47	-48	-50	-51	-53	-54	-56	-58	-60	-61	-63	-65	-67	-69	-71	-73	-77	-78	-82	-85
	-31	-33	-35	-37	-39	-40	-42	-44	-45	-47	-49	-50	-52	-53	-55	-57	-58	-60	-61	-63	-65	-67	-68	-70	-72	-75	-77	-80	-83	-86
	-34	-36	-38	-40	-42	-43	-45	-47	-48	-50	-51	-53	-54	-56	-57	-59	-60	-62	-63	-65	-67	-68	-70	-72	-74	-76	-78	-81	-84	-87
	-38	-39	-41	-43	-45	-46	-48	-49	-51	-52	-54	-55	-57	-58	-60	-61	-63	-64	-66	-67	-69	-70	-72	-73	-76	-77	-80	-82	-85	-87
	-41	-43	-45	-47	-48	-50	-51	-53	-54	-56	-57	-58	-60	-61	-63	-64	-65	-67	-68	-70	-71	-72	-74	-76	-77	-79	-81	-83	-86	-88
	-45	-47	-49	-51	-52	-53	-55	-56	-58	-59	-60	-61	-63	-64	-65	-66	-68	-69	-70	-72	-73	-75	-76	-77	-79	-81	-82	-84	-87	-89
	-50	-52	-53	-55	-56	-57	-59	-60	-61	-62	-64	-65	-66	-67	-68	-70	-71	-72	-73	-74	-76	-77	-80	-81	-82	-84	-86	-88	-89	
	-56	-57	-58	-60	-61	-62	-63	-64	-66	-67	-68	-69	-70	-71	-72	-73	-74	-75	-76	-77	-78	-80	-81	-82	-84	-86	-88	-90	-91	
	-63	-64	-66	-67	-68	-69	-70	-71	-72	-73	-73	-74	-75	-76	-77	-78	-79	-80	-80	-81	-82	-83	-85	-86	-87	-89	-90	-91	-92	
	-69	-70	-71	-72	-72	-73	-74	-75	-76	-77	-78	-78	-79	-80	-81	-82	-82	-83	-83	-84	-85	-86	-87	-87	-88	-89	-90	-91	-92	-93

Proportion of successes in the 27 per cent lowest scoring on the continuous variable

TABLE 3.   A TABLE OF THE VALUES OF THE PRODUCT-MOMENT COEFFICIENT OF CORRELATION IN A NORMAL BIVARIATE POPULATION CORRESPONDING TO GIVEN PROPORTIONS OF SUCCESS (*Continued*)

Proportion of successes in the 27 per cent scoring highest on the continuous variable

	52	54	56	58	60	62	64	66	68	70	72	74	76	78	80	82	84	86	88	90	92	94	96	98	99
01	73	74	75	76	77	78	78	79	80	81	82	82	83	83	84	85	86	87	87	88	89	90	91	92	93
02	69	70	71	72	73	73	74	75	76	77	78	79	80	80	81	82	83	84	85	86	87	88	90	91	92
04	62	63	64	66	67	68	69	70	71	72	73	74	75	76	77	78	80	81	82	83	84	86	88	90	91
06	57	59	60	61	62	64	65	66	67	68	70	71	72	73	74	76	77	78	80	81	82	84	86	88	90
08	53	55	56	58	59	60	61	63	64	65	66	68	69	70	72	73	75	76	77	79	81	82	84	87	89
10	50	51	53	54	56	57	58	60	61	63	64	65	67	68	70	71	72	74	76	77	79	81	83	86	88
12	46	48	49	51	52	54	55	57	58	60	61	63	64	66	67	69	70	72	73	76	77	80	82	85	87
14	43	45	47	48	50	51	53	54	56	57	59	60	62	63	65	67	68	70	72	74	76	78	81	84	87
16	40	42	44	45	47	49	50	52	53	55	57	58	60	61	63	65	67	68	70	72	75	77	80	83	86
18	38	39	41	43	45	47	48	49	51	53	54	56	58	60	61	63	65	67	69	71	73	76	78	82	85
20	35	37	39	40	42	44	46	47	49	51	52	54	56	57	60	61	63	65	67	70	72	74	77	81	84
22	33	34	36	38	40	42	43	45	47	49	50	52	54	56	57	60	61	63	66	68	70	73	76	80	83
24	30	32	34	36	37	39	41	43	45	46	48	50	52	54	56	58	60	62	64	67	69	72	75	80	83
26	28	30	32	33	35	37	39	41	42	44	46	48	50	52	54	56	58	60	63	65	68	71	74	79	82
28	26	27	29	31	33	35	37	39	40	42	44	46	48	50	52	54	57	59	61	64	66	70	73	78	82
30	23	25	27	29	31	33	35	37	38	40	42	44	46	49	51	53	55	57	60	63	65	68	72	77	81
32	21	23	25	27	29	31	33	35	37	38	40	42	45	47	49	51	53	56	58	61	64	67	71	76	80
34	19	21	23	25	27	29	31	33	35	37	39	41	43	45	47	49	52	54	57	60	63	66	70	75	79
36	17	19	21	22	25	27	29	31	33	35	37	39	41	43	46	48	50	53	55	58	61	65	69	74	78
38	15	16	18	20	22	25	27	29	31	33	35	37	39	42	44	47	49	51	54	57	60	64	68	73	78
40	12	14	16	18	21	22	25	27	29	31	33	35	37	40	42	45	47	50	52	56	59	62	67	73	77

Proportion of successes in the 27 per cent scoring lowest on the continuous variable

42	44	46	48	50	52	54	56	58	60	62	64	66	68	70	72	74	76	78	80	82	84	86	88	90	92	94	96	98	99
76	75	74	73	72	72	71	70	69	68	67	66	65	63	62	61	59	57	55	53	51	49	46	43	40	35	30	23	11	0
72	71	70	69	68	67	66	64	63	62	61	59	58	56	55	53	51	50	48	46	43	40	37	34	30	25	19	12	0	−11
66	64	63	62	61	60	58	57	56	54	53	51	49	48	46	44	42	40	38	36	33	30	26	23	19	14	08	0	−12	−23
61	60	59	57	56	55	53	52	50	48	47	45	44	42	40	38	36	33	31	29	26	23	19	15	11	06	0	−08	−19	−30
58	56	55	53	52	51	49	47	45	44	42	40	38	37	35	32	30	28	25	23	20	17	13	09	05	0	−06	−14	−25	−35
54	53	51	50	48	47	45	43	41	40	38	36	34	32	30	28	26	23	21	18	15	12	08	04	0	−05	−11	−19	−30	−40
51	49	48	46	45	43	41	39	38	36	34	32	30	28	26	24	21	19	16	13	11	07	04	0	−04	−09	−15	−23	−34	−43
48	47	45	43	42	40	38	36	34	33	31	29	27	25	22	20	18	15	12	10	07	03	0	−04	−08	−13	−19	−26	−37	−46
45	44	42	40	39	37	35	33	31	30	28	26	24	21	19	17	14	12	09	06	03	0	−03	−07	−12	−17	−23	−30	−40	−49
43	41	39	38	36	34	32	30	28	27	25	23	20	18	16	13	11	08	06	03	0	−03	−07	−11	−15	−20	−26	−33	−43	−51
40	39	37	35	33	31	29	27	26	24	22	19	17	15	13	11	08	06	03	0	−03	−06	−10	−13	−18	−23	−29	−36	−46	−53
38	36	34	33	31	29	27	25	23	21	19	17	15	12	10	08	06	03	0	−03	−06	−09	−12	−16	−21	−25	−31	−38	−48	−55
36	34	32	30	28	26	24	22	20	18	16	14	12	10	08	05	03	0	−03	−06	−08	−12	−15	−19	−23	−28	−33	−40	−50	−57
33	32	30	28	26	24	22	20	18	16	14	12	09	07	05	02	0	−03	−06	−08	−11	−14	−18	−21	−26	−30	−36	−42	−51	−59
31	29	27	26	23	21	19	17	15	13	11	09	07	04	02	0	−02	−05	−08	−11	−13	−17	−20	−24	−28	−32	−38	−44	−53	−61
29	27	25	23	21	19	17	15	13	11	09	07	04	02	0	−02	−05	−08	−10	−13	−16	−19	−22	−26	−30	−35	−40	−46	−55	−62
27	25	23	21	19	17	15	13	11	09	07	04	02	0	−02	−04	−07	−10	−12	−15	−18	−21	−25	−28	−32	−37	−42	−49	−56	−63
25	23	21	19	17	15	13	11	09	06	04	02	0	−02	−04	−07	−09	−12	−15	−17	−20	−24	−27	−30	−34	−38	−44	−51	−58	−65
22	21	19	17	15	13	11	08	06	04	02	0	−03	−06	−08	−10	−12	−14	−17	−19	−23	−26	−29	−32	−36	−40	−45	−53	−59	−66
20	18	16	15	13	11	08	06	04	02	0	−02	−05	−07	−10	−13	−15	−17	−20	−22	−25	−28	−31	−34	−38	−42	−47	−54	−61	−67
18	16	14	12	10	08	06	04	02	0	−02	−04	−06	−09	−11	−14	−16	−18	−21	−24	−27	−30	−33	−36	−40	−44	−48	−56	−62	−68
16	14	12	10	08	06	04	02	0	−02	−04	−06	−08	−11	−13	−16	−18	−20	−23	−26	−28	−31	−34	−38	−41	−45	−50	−56	−63	−69
14	12	10	08	06	04	02	0	−02	−04	−06	−08	−11	−13	−15	−17	−20	−22	−25	−27	−30	−33	−36	−39	−43	−47	−52	−57	−64	−70
12	10	08	06	04	02	0	−02	−04	−06	−08	−11	−13	−15	−17	−19	−22	−24	−27	−29	−32	−35	−38	−41	−45	−49	−53	−58	−66	−71
10	08	06	04	02	0	−02	−04	−06	−08	−11	−13	−15	−17	−19	−21	−24	−26	−29	−31	−34	−37	−40	−43	−47	−51	−55	−60	−67	−72

Proportion of successes in the 27 per cent lowest scoring on the continuous variable

Appendix B
Table for Estimating
Tetrachoric Correlation

TABLE 1

Pearson's Q_3 Estimates of r_{tet} for Various Values of ad/bc

r_{tet}	ad/bc	r_{tet}	ad/bc	r_{tet}	ad/bc
.00	0–1.00	.35	2.49–2.55	.70	8.50–8.90
.01	1.01–1.03	.36	2.56–2.63	.71	8.91–9.35
.02	1.04–1.06	.37	2.64–2.71	.72	9.36–9.82
.03	1.07–1.08	.38	2.72–2.79	.73	9.83–10.33
.04	1.09–1.11	.39	2.80–2.87	.74	10.34–10.90
.05	1.12–1.14	.40	2.88–2.96	.75	10.91–11.51
.06	1.15–1.17	.41	2.97–3.05	.76	11.52–12.16
.07	1.18–1.20	.42	3.06–3.14	.77	12.17–12.89
.08	1.21–1.23	.43	3.15–3.24	.78	12.90–13.70
.09	1.24–1.27	.44	3.25–3.34	.79	13.71–14.58
.10	1.28–1.30	.45	3.35–3.45	.80	14.59–15.57
.11	1.31–1.33	.46	3.46–3.56	.81	15.58–16.65
.12	1.34–1.37	.47	3.57–3.68	.82	16.66–17.88
.13	1.38–1.40	.48	3.69–3.80	.83	17.89–19.28
.14	1.41–1.44	.49	3.81–3.92	.84	19.29–20.85
.15	1.45–1.48	.50	3.93–4.06	.85	20.86–22.68
.16	1.49–1.52	.51	4.07–4.20	.86	22.69–24.76
.17	1.53–1.56	.52	4.21–4.34	.87	24.77–27.22
.18	1.57–1.60	.53	4.35–4.49	.88	27.23–30.09
.19	1.61–1.64	.54	4.50–4.66	.89	30.10–33.60
.20	1.65–1.69	.55	4.67–4.82	.90	33.61–37.79
.21	1.70–1.73	.56	4.83–4.99	.91	37.80–43.06
.22	1.74–1.78	.57	5.00–5.18	.92	43.07–49.83
.23	1.79–1.83	.58	5.19–5.38	.93	49.84–58.79
.24	1.84–1.88	.59	5.39–5.59	.94	58.80–70.95
.25	1.89–1.93	.60	5.60–5.80	.95	70.96–89.01
.26	1.94–1.98	.61	5.81–6.03	.96	89.02–117.54
.27	1.99–2.04	.62	6.04–6.28	.97	117.55–169.67
.28	2.05–2.10	.63	6.29–6.54	.98	169.68–293.12
.29	2.11–2.15	.64	6.55–6.81	.99	293.13–923.97
.30	2.16–2.22	.65	6.82–7.10	1.00	923.98 —
.31	2.23–2.28	.66	7.11–7.42		
.32	2.29–2.34	.67	7.43–7.75		
.33	2.35–2.41	.68	7.76–8.11		
.34	2.42–2.48	.69	8.12–8.49		

Reprinted from M. D. Davidoff and H. W. Goheen, "A table for the rapid determination of the tetrachoric coefficient." *Psychometrika*, 1957, 22, 43–52.

Appendix C
Iterative Procedure for
Estimating Regression Weights

METHOD 2—ITERATIVE SOLUTION

The basic relationship upon which the iterative method depends is the following

$$r_{ic} = \beta_1 r_{1i} + \beta_2 r_{2i} + \cdots + \beta_k r_{ki} \tag{1}$$

That is, the correlation of a test i with the criterion is equal to the sum of the products of each test's regression weight (β) and its correlation with test i.

The analysis starts with the square table of obtained correlations among tests in a battery and the column of empirically determined test validities. These are given on page 336, where the problem was stated. The first step is to *guess* what the beta weight will be for each predictor variable in this set of data. Some of the considerations which enter into making a shrewd initial guess are discussed later. To the set of guessed beta weights and to the given table of intercorrelations there corresponds some set of values for the validity coefficients which will satisfy equation (1). Thus, if we designate the guessed values of the betas $\tilde{\beta}$, we have

$$\tilde{\beta}_1 r_{1i} + \tilde{\beta}_2 r_{2i} + \cdots + \tilde{\beta}_k r_{ki} = \tilde{r}_{ic} \tag{2}$$

The estimated set of beta weights yields a set of values for the validity coefficients, i.e., that set of validity coefficients for which this would be the exact set of beta weights.

The calculation of the $\tilde{r}_{ic}$ values is simple and quite rapid if a calculating machine is available which will make an algebraic sum of products. The intercorrelations are set up in a square matrix with unity for the diagonal terms. A computing sheet is set up with rows spaced the same distance apart as the rows in the table of intercorrelations, and with variables numbered to correspond to the variables in the correlation table. Column I of the computing sheet contains the column of actually obtained validity coefficients. Column II contains the initial guessed beta weights. Column III contains the values of $\tilde{r}_{ic}$. The entries in this column are obtained by placing column II alongside each column of the correlation matrix in turn and getting the sum of products of the paired terms. The computing sheet for the illustrative example is shown in Table 2.

Reprinted with permission from R. L. Thorndike, PERSONNEL SELECTION. New York: John Wiley, 1949, pages 340-344.

Once an initial set of $\tilde{r}_c$ values has been obtained, the procedure becomes one of successive corrections to the beta weights one at a time until a set of $\tilde{r}_c$ values is obtained which corresponds to the empirical validities, r_c, within a specified limit of accuracy. In general, one starts with the variable for which the discrepancy between r_c and $\tilde{r}_c$ is greatest, adjusts the beta weight by an amount which will approximately eliminate the dis-

TABLE 2. COMPUTATION SHEET, ITERATIVE METHOD FOR DETERMINING REGRESSION WEIGHTS

	I	II	III	IV	V	VI	VII	VIII	IX	X	XI	XII
Variable	r_c	Wt_1	$\tilde{r}_{c(1)}$	$\tilde{r}_{c(2)}$	$\tilde{r}_{c(3)}$	$\tilde{r}_{c(4)}$	Wt_4	$\tilde{r}_c{'}_{(4)}$	$\tilde{r}_{c(5)}$	$\tilde{r}_{c(6)}$	Wt_6	$\tilde{r}_c{'}_{(6)}$
1	.62	.50	.672	.642	.626	.620	.47	.621	.615	.620	.47	.620
2	.50	.20	.544	.527	.513	.503	.19	.502	.497	.502	.19	.502
3	.44	.10	.484	.467	.450	.445	.10	.449	.439	.445	.09	.445
4	.36	.00	.410	.394	.364	.359	−.03	.360	.354	.364	−.02	.364
Adjustment			Var. 1 −.03	Var. 4 −.03	Var. 2 −.01			Var. 3 −.01	Var. 4 +.01			

$$R = \frac{0.4188}{\sqrt{0.4196}} = 0.646$$

crepancy, and then computes a new set of adjusted $\tilde{r}_c$ values. (Column IV in Table 2.) The procedure for making the adjustments is considered in the next paragraph. A second beta weight is then corrected and a new set of $\tilde{r}_c$ values obtained, and so forth. With practice, a certain knack is developed in selecting variables to adjust and deciding upon the amount of adjustment to make. Adjustments are continued until the $\tilde{r}_c$ and r_c values are in sufficiently close agreement. Two-place accuracy in regression weights is probably ample for any set of weights in personnel selection.

In making adjustments to the initial set of beta weights, the first principle is to adjust first the beta weight for which $|r_c - \tilde{r}_c|$ is greatest and to adjust it by approximately the amount

$r_c - \tilde{r}_c = d_j$. An adjustment of the weight for one variable will in general affect the values for all the $\tilde{r}_{ic}$'s. If we call the adjusted values $\tilde{r}_{ic(2)}$, we have

$$\tilde{r}_{ic(2)} = \tilde{r}_{ic} + d_j r_{ij} \tag{3}$$

This can easily be seen if we compare the terms of equation 2 for $\tilde{r}_{ic}$ and $\tilde{r}_{ic(2)}$. If the adjustment d_j is a fairly small amount or a round figure such as 0.10, each correlation in column j of the correlation matrix can be multiplied by d_j mentally, the product subtracted mentally from the corresponding entry of column III of the calculation sheet, and the difference entered in column IV. Column IV then becomes the column $\tilde{r}_{c(2)}$ of adjusted $\tilde{r}_c$ values. A second adjustment can be made on column IV in the same way, and so on. The beta weight to be adjusted next is always selected by comparing the column of $\tilde{r}_c$ values resulting from the immediately preceding adjustment with the r_c column (column I) on the computing sheet and noting the location of the greatest discrepancies. A check on the accuracy of all the arithmetical processes up to that point is possible at any point by repeating the operations of formula 2 with the most recent approximation to the beta weights. (See columns VII and VIII of Table 2.)

The correlation with the criterion of a weighted score based on any specific set of weights may be computed quite simply. It is given by the formula

$$R = \frac{\sum_{i=1}^{k} V_i r_{ic}}{\sqrt{\sum_{i=1}^{k} \sum_{j=1}^{k} V_i V_j r_{ij}}} \tag{4}$$

where V_i signifies the weight attached to variable i.. When the weights V_i correspond exactly to the regression weights, this formula simplifies to:

$$R = \sqrt{\Sigma \beta_i r_{ic}} \tag{5}$$

With formula 4, it is possible to determine the correlation between any set of weighted scores and an additional criterion variable. The formula can be used to find the validity of the

approximate weights at any particular stage in the approximation, as well as at the end, when the approximation has reached
the desired standard of accuracy. At this point, the validity
resulting from the weights will approximate very closely the
multiple correlation resulting from exact regression weights.
It is also possible to estimate the validity which will result from
any other set of weights, if some other consideration makes it
desirable to change the weighting system.

In actual computation, the numerator of formula 4 is the sum
of products of the column of the latest set of weights, each times
the corresponding validity coefficient in column I. The expression under the square-root sign is the sum of products of weights
times corresponding $\bar{r}_c$ values, i.e., times the validity coefficients
produced by that set of weights.

Although it would be possible, in this procedure, to start with
uniform weights for all tests or with any other set of weights, a
good deal of time can be saved if the initial choice is a fairly
close approximation to the final weights. Kelley and Salisbury
suggest starting by giving each test a weight one-half its validity
coefficient. However, a little practice with the method should
make possible considerably more efficient skills in that regard.
Certain hints can be given to the novice with the method, as
follows:

1. Initially, it often proves efficient to give a substantial
number of the variables, perhaps half, zero weights. This speeds
the work of preparing column III on the computation sheet.

2. If no calculating machine is available and the problem is
small, initial weights should be in round numbers, i.e., 0.10,
0.20, etc.

3. The size of the initial weights depends on the number of
variables. The more variables, the smaller the weights relative
to the validity coefficients. With five to ten variables, the weights
of those variables weighted might range from $\frac{1}{4}$ to $\frac{3}{4}$ of the
validity coefficient. With fifteen to twenty variables, the weights
might range from $\frac{1}{4}$ to $\frac{1}{2}$. The highest proportions would, of
course, apply to those variables with the highest validities.

4. Experience from previous work with the same criterion
and/or test variables can sometimes be used as a basis for an
initial set of weights.

There are also one or two tricks in applying corrections to the initial set of weights.

1. Where the bulk of the corrections required from the initial set of guessed weights are in the same direction, any given correction should be somewhat smaller than the amount $r_{ic} - \tilde{r}_{ic}$. This is due to the fact that when intercorrelations are largely positive the corrections on different variables tend to supplement one another.

2. Whenever corrections are being carried out by mental arithmetic, time is probably saved by making the initial large corrections in convenient amounts, such as 0.10 and 0.05.

One practical advantage of the present iterative method is that it is very simple to add any desired additional conditions to the set of weights one is deriving, and then determine the most valid set of weights which also satisfies these conditions. In much of the work in the AAF Aviation Psychology Program, the additional condition was imposed that no weights be negative. In this case, the weight for a variable would be corrected down as far as zero, but no further correction would be made. It is also a simple matter to drop out a test or group of tests (give them zero weights) and determine the weights which should then be used for the remainder of the tests. Any other desired conditions could be imposed in similar fashion.

There may be some concern that the procedures described in this section have an element of subjectivity, in that there is some choice as to which variables to adjust and how much to adjust them. However, it has been found repeatedly that different persons working with the same set of data come out with substantially the same set of weights, except for rounding errors of one point in the last place. As in the present example, the results have been found to agree, within the limits of accuracy to which the approximation is carried out, with results for the exact solution of the set of normal equations.

Index

Ability tests
  factors measured by, 36–37
  item formats for, 38–41
  item preparation, 38–44
  item review, 43–44
  misleads in, 42–43
Achievement tests, 44–47
Actuarial method, vs. Clinical Method, 268–269
Adaptive testing, 299–323
  alternation, 301, 316–317
  Bayesian, 302–307
  multilevel, 300, 307–311
  pyramidal, 301, 317–326
  self-selected, 300, 315–316
  stradaptive, 302, 326–333
  two-stage, 300, 311–315
Age equivalent score conversion, 108–113
Alpha, coefficient, 171, 176
Alternation testing, 301, 316–317
Area score conversion, 115–121
Assignment, personnel, 355–361
Attenuation, correction for, 153
Attribute, *see* Latent attributes
Attitude, interest measure, 49–52

Bayes' theorem, 289–290
  measurement applications, 294–299
Beta
  function, 291–292
  weight, 246
    iterative computation of, Appendix C
  significance test, 252
Bias, 228–245
  in complete test, 235–245
    group mean as indicator, 236–237
    relation to criterion as indicator, 238–242
    reliability as indicator, 237–238

  in test items, 230–235
    difficulty as index of, 232–235
    discrimination as index of, 231
Biserial correlation
  advantages and limitations, 72–73
  formula for, 71
Blueprint for test, 16–21

Centroid method, *see* Factor analysis
Classification
  assignment of personnel in, 355–361
  choice of tests for, 350–354
  model for, 348–350
Clinical vs. actuarial method, validity of, 268–269
Construct validity, 186–193
  correlational evidence, 187–190
  counterhypotheses, 192–193
  group differences as evidence, 190–191
  treatment effects as evidence, 191–192
Content validity, 184–186
Converted scores
  age equivalents, 108–113
  area conversion, 115–121
  grade equivalents, 108–113
  linear conversion, 113–115
  using Rasch model, 121–123
Correlation
  biserial, 71–73
  correction for spuriousness, 73–74
  Flanagan, 75, Appendix A
  multiple, 249
    significance test, 254
  point biserial, 71–73
  of sums, 150–151
  tetrachoric, 205, Appendix B
Correlation ratio, 216–217
Credible interval, 199
Criterion-referenced test, *see* Domain mastery test

Cross-validation, 254-255
Criterion indicator(s), 193-201
    group membership as, 220-222
    partial, 218-220
    shortcomings of, 194-198
    types of, 198-201
Curtailment, 208-215
    direct, 210-212
    indirect, 213-215
    multiple, 259-263
Cutoff, multiple, 263-265

Data collection, plan for, 26-28
Decisions, types of, 14
Dichotomous variables
    as criteria, 204-206
    item statistics, 71-73
Difficulty of test items
    adjustment for group differences,
        66-70
    as indicator of bias, 232-235
    statistics to estimate, 60-67
Directions for test, 32-36
Discriminant, multiple, 270-277
Discriminant analysis, 270-277
Discriminant function, 271
Discrimination
    as index of bias, 231
    and item analysis, 70-75
Distance measure, 247, 276-277
Domain mastery test
    concept of, 1-3
    item analysis of, 93-96
    reliability of, 181-183

Equating, standard error of, 136, 139,
    141
Equating test forms, 133-142
    linear vs. equipercentile, 136
Error
    definition of, 144-145
    problems in defining, 154-156
Estimating, of test item difficulty, 60-67
Eta (correlation ratio), 216-217
Extreme groups, use in validation,
    206-208

Factor analysis, 277-287
    by centroid method, 278-283
    issues encountered, 286-287
    reliability in, 285
    rotation in, 283-285

Factor score, 284-285
Flanagan correlation, 75, Appendix A

Generalizability, 143
Grade equivalent score conversions,
    108-113
Guessing
    correction formula, 61-64
    and item statistics, 60-64
    and test directions, 33-34
Guidance, 362-366

Heterogeneous item pool, analysis of,
    90-93

Information function
    of test, 82-87
    of test item, 80-82
Item
    bias in, 230-235
    constructed vs. selected response,
        34-36
    heterogeneous pool, analyses of,
        90-93
    information function, 80-82
    preparation of
        ability test, 38-44
        achievement test, 44-47
        attitude, interest measure, 49-52
    selection of, 79-87
        to maximize validity, 258-259
    tryout, plan for, 23-25
Item analysis
    difficulty estimation, 59-70
        by Rasch model, 96-104
    discrimination estimation, 70-75
    of domain mastery test, 93-96
    heterogeneous item pool, 90-93
    plan for, 23-26, 54-58
Item characteristic curve
    defined, 6
    illustrated, 7
    mathematical models of, 8-9
    parameters of, 8
        sample size and, 54-57

Kuder-Richardson reliability, 176-178
    estimated from item statistics, 78-79

Latent attributes
    classification of, 36-37
    definition of, 12-13

nature of, 4-5
relation of item to, 6-9
Latent trait, *see* Latent attributes
Lengthened test, estimate of
  intercorrelations, 152-153
  mean, 148
  reliability, 152
  standard deviation, 149-150
Linear score conversion, 113-115
Logistic function, 9

Mastery, *see* Domain mastery
Measurement
  of performance, 47-49
  of personality, 49-52
  standard error of, 147
Models of test
  domain mastery, 1-3
  latent trait, 4-9
Moderator variable, 269-270
Multilevel test, 300, 307-311
  scaling scores for, 117-121
Multiple correlation, 249, 254
Multiple cutoff, 263-265
Multiple discriminant, 270-277

Nonlinear combination of predictors,
  256-257
Nonlinear regression, 216-217
Normal ojive as model of test item, 8
Normalized standard scores, 115-121
Norms
  plan for data collection, 26-28
  preparing tables of, 130-133
  sampling procedures, 124-130

Parameters
  item
    asymptote, 8
    difficulty, 8
    discrimination, 8
    see also Item analysis
  test
    estimation from item statistics,
      76-79
    estimation without tryout, 87-90
Performance, measurement of, 47-49
Personality, measurement of, 49-52
Personnel
  assignment, 355-361
  classification, 348-361
  placement, 345-348
  selection, 338-340

Point biserial correlation
  formula for, 71
  limitations, 72-73
Predictive validity, 193-227
  clinical vs. actuarial, 268-269
  criterion indicators, 193-201
    partial, 218-220
    shortcomings of, 194-198
    types of, 198-201
  item selection to maximize, 258-259
  of multiple cutoffs, 263-265
  and multiple regression, 248-253
  practical problems in, 201-203
  reliability and interpretation of, 222
  statistics of, 203-227
    effects of curtailment, 208-215
    with dichotomous criterion,
      204-206
    multiple effects of curtailment,
      260-263
    nonlinear relation, 215-217
    from tails of distribution, 206-208
  of unique patterns, 265-268
  and utility of test, 223-227
Prior probability, 288
Pyramidal test, 301, 317-326

Rasch model
  goodness of fit, 103-104
  scaling test items and scores with,
    96-104
    by maximum likelihood, 101-102
    by PROX procedure, 98-100
  score conversion using, 121-123
Regression
  multiple, 248-251
    population estimates, 253-256
  nonlinear, 216-217
  stepwise, 252-253
    for multiple selection, 341-345
Reliability, 143-183
  by analysis of variance, 156-161
  classical model, 144-153
  of domain mastery test, 181-183
  from equivalent forms, 172-175
  in factor analysis, 285
  and interpretation of validity, 222
  Kuder-Richardson, 176-178
    estimated from item statistics,
      78-79
  of lengthened test, 152
  multifacet model of, 161-171
  retest, 172, 175

of speeded test, 178–181
split-half, 172, 175–176
variance components and, 156–171
Restriction of range, *see* Curtailment
Retest reliability, 172, 175
Rotation, in factor analysis, 283–285

Sampling
  in item tryout, 54–58
  for norming tests
    error in, 127–128
    multistage, 125–127
    practical difficulties, 128–130
    procedures, 124–130
Scales, 105–123
  age, grade
    preparation of, 108–111
    problems in, 111–113
  Rasch, 121–123
  standard score
    linear, 113–115
    normalized, 115–121
Score conversion, *see* Converted scores
Selection, 338–340
  multiple, 340–345
Self-selected test, 300, 315–316
Spearman-Brown prophecy formula,
    152
Split-half reliability, 172, 175–176
Standard error
  of equating, 136, 139, 141
  of measurement, 147
  of sampling, 127–128
  of sum, 149
Standard score
  linear, 113–115
  normalized, 115–121
Stradaptive test, 302, 326–333
Sum
  correlation of, 150–151
  standard error of, 149

Tailor-made testing, *see* Adaptive
    testing
Test
  ability, *see* Ability tests
  achievement, 44–47
  adaptive, *see* Adaptive testing
  bias, 235–245
  blueprint for, 16–21

constraints on, 15
decisions based on, 13–15
directions for, 32–36
domain mastery, 1–3, 93–96,
    181–183
format for items, 21–23
information function, 82–87
length, effect of, 148–153
levels of inference from, 228–230
manual for, 23
multilevel, 300, 307–311
parameters, estimation of
    from item statistics, 76–79
    without tryout, 87–90
performance, 47–49
personality, 49–52
pyramidal, 301, 317–326
relation to latent attribute, 5–6
schedule for development, 29–31
self-selected, 300, 315–316
stradaptive, 302, 326–333
two-stage, 300, 311–315
tryout of items, 23–25
Test item, *see* Item
Trait, *see* Latent trait
True score
  Bayesian estimaton, 294–295
  problems of defining, 154–156
Two-stage testing, 300, 311–315

Unique patterns, validity of, 265–268
Utility
  definition, 334–336
  estimated, 337
  matrix, 336–338
  predicted, 337

Validation
  cross-, 254–255
  extreme groups in, 206–208
Validity
  construct, 186–193
  content, 184–186
  predictive, 193–227
  and test item selection, 258–259
  of unique patterns, 265–268
Variance
  components, 161–171
  reliability by analysis of, 156–161
  of sum, 149–150